Second Edition

Consultation, Collaboration, and Teamwork for Students with Special Needs

Peggy A. Dettmer
Kansas State University

Norma T. Dyck
Kansas State University

Linda P. Thurston
Kansas State University

Allyn and Bacon
Boston • London • Toronto • Sydney • Tokyo • Singapore

Executive Editor: Ray Short
Executive Marketing Manager: Steve Dragin
Senior Production Administrator: Marjorie Payne
Editorial-Production Service: Chestnut Hill Enterprises, Inc.
Composition Buyer: Linda Cox
Manufacturing Buyer: Megan Cochran
Cover Administrator: Suzanne Harbison

Copyright © 1996 by Allyn & Bacon
A Simon & Schuster Company
Needham Heights, MA 02194

Library of Congress Cataloging-in-Publication Data
Dettmer, Peggy.
    Consultation, collaboration, and teamwork for students with
special needs / Peggy Dettmer, Norma Dyck, Linda P. Thurston. — 2nd ed.
        p.   cm.
    Includes bibliographical references and index.
    ISBN: 0–205–17445–0 (HC)
    1. Special education—United States.   2. Educational consultants—
United States.   3. Teaching teams—United States.   I. Dyck, Norma.
II. Thurston, Linda P.   III. Title.
LC4031.D47   1996
371.9'0973—dc20   95–36565
                                                                CIP

Printed in the United States of America
10   9   8   7   6   5   4   3   2   00   99   98   97   96

Contents

Preface

The time for consultation, collaboration, and teamwork in schools is now. Society's problems are immense and complex. Educated citizens are needed more than ever before in the history of civilization. The public demands that school graduates enter the work world as capable citizens, and it holds professional educators accountable for ensuring that capability.

To meet these demands, sweeping educational reforms have been proposed, attempted, discarded, rethought, and reinstated in the past several decades. These reform movements have generated complex goals. Innovative plans are ripped from administrative and legislative drawing boards to be put to use before the pages are dry, much less well researched. Meanwhile, as test scores decline and school structures crumble, teachers continue to cope hour by hour and day by day with their formidable assignment—that of preparing today's students to be competent citizens in tomorrow's world.

In the midst of all the criticism and directives flung at the educational system and the educational profession, the sage words of Henry David Thoreau to "Simplify, simplify" are appealing. As we close out one remarkable millennium in civilization's history and usher in the next, can it be that we have overlooked very basic concepts that could help improve the education of children and youth? The processes of consultation, collaboration, and teamwork, put into practice by professional educators with parents as their partners, will be essential for constructing an effective educational context for the twenty-first century.

These processes may appear simple and basic, but, on the contrary, they are quite difficult to carry out, and they do create changes that can be unsettling. But they do not require costly bureaucratic overlays, and they have enormous, ongoing potential for positive ripple effects.

This book is designed to serve as a bridge between theory and practice. It contains both background information and field-tested recommendations to help teachers, parents, administrators, and support personnel become more proficient in working together as collaborators within their existing school context. Each chapter contains applications and activities that encourage single readers or groups of readers to delve into the subtleties and intricacies of these powerful interactive processes.

The book is organized into three sections in order to focus in turn on context, processes, and content as they relate to school consultation, collaboration, and teamwork. Part One is the *Context* section. Chapter 1 presents school consultation and delineates both benefits and concerns that can result from consulting, collaborating, and teaming in educational settings. Chapter 2 describes key elements in planning, implementing, evaluating, and preparing for consultation and collaboration roles. Chapter 3 includes a brief history, theoretical bases, and research bases of school consultation. It summarizes systems, perspectives, approaches, prototypes, modes, and models for implementing school consultation and collaboration, and recommends synthesizing the components into workable methods for a variety of school contexts. Chapter 4 focuses upon the constructive use of individual differences among adults, which is one of the most powerful but too often neglected factors affecting school consultation, collaboration, and teamwork. Cultural, ethnic, and language differences are addressed that can have significant impact on the ability of people to work together. The need for differentiated consultation in the context of rural, urban, and other demographically specific settings is discussed.

In Part Two, the *Process* section, Chapters 5 through 9 introduce process skills and problem-solving tools needed for effective consultation and collaboration. Chapter 5 focuses on a ten-step problem-solving process. Chapter 6 addresses verbal and nonverbal communication and suggests techniques for dealing with resistance and resolving conflicts. In Chapter 7, conference and interview methods are discussed, along with time management, organizational and record-keeping practices, and components of ethical consultation. Chapter 8 features techniques for using technology to enhance consultation and collaboration. Several procedures and tools for the evaluation of consultation and collaboration outcomes are offered in Chapter 9.

Part Three, the *Content* section, includes Chapters 10 through 13. Chapter 10 describes models and strategies for structuring learning environments and facilitating student achievement through consultation, collaboration, and support from teams of educators. Chapter 11 focuses on family members as partners in their children's education. Chapter 12 promotes staff development as an integral part of consulting and collaborating. Finally, Chapter 13 emphasizes the importance of developing support systems and advocacy techniques to encourage collaboration and teamwork for a changing world's educational and social needs. This final "Looking Ahead" chapter predicts that the ideal outcome from school consultation, collaboration, and teamwork will be a transformation of school learning environments into settings in which education is special for all students and educators are successful in their complex, demanding profession.

Acknowledgments

The first edition of this book in 1993 was dedicated to our graduate students whose education roles required that they develop and use effective consultation and collaboration skills. As we explained at that time, our students both hindered and helped us with the writing. When we needed to write, they hindered because they were always there—taking classes, seeking information, requesting in-service, engaging in collaborative consultation with us for assistance with their own challenging and demanding roles. On the other hand, they helped us greatly with our writing by allowing us to "discover what we knew," and they verified that it was indeed important knowledge for bringing about better teaching and learning. Many times they contributed the seed of an idea, a key phrase, a caution, a necessary filter of skepticism, or, blessedly, a vote of confidence for our efforts. We began to sense then that we were on the right track.

Now, several years later, the concepts of collaboration and consultation are enriching many areas of contemporary life. School consultation is being promoted as a key component in the success of educational reform movements. The word *collaboration* appears frequently in the educational literature and has become a major element for progress in other professions, in business, and in government and international affairs. The concept of teamwork, employed so effectively in fields such as sports and music, is being applied productively to a wide variety of professional endeavors, including industry, medicine, and education.

The focus on consultation, collaboration, and teamwork in a variety of professional fields includes education and schools, and these processes are being accepted more and more as essential parts of preparation programs for educators. We are pleased that our personnel preparation grants, graduate degree programs, school district in-services, and the first edition of the book, have had a part in that development. We want now to dedicate this second edition to all educators—teachers, administrators, support personnel, and parents—who work hard each day to make education attainable and appropriate for every student.

When possible, we credit individuals for their contributions to our thinking and writing. However, within a collegial, collaborative process it is not easy to tell just where the contribution of one person occurs, another interfaces, and yet another takes over from there.

As we address this dilemma, we realize once again the complexity and the beauty of collaborative consultation. We know that our students' and educational colleagues' perceptions and suggestions were shared unselfishly without need for recognition or praise, in the spirit of professionalism and progress. This is what collaborative consultation is all about. Any oversights, omissions, or errors are ours, of course, but the essence of our philosophy comes from these colleagues and ultimately from the children and adolescents, schools and homes, they represent.

We trust that the material in this book will serve as a tangible example of the usefulness of consultation, collaboration, and teamwork in meeting the special needs of students and their educators. For all our former students who have been in our teacher preparation programs, and our current colleagues who encourage us with their purpose and perseverance as educators, we are very grateful. We applaud the dedication and commitment they bring to their demanding roles. Their energy, enthusiasm, and expertise are truly inspirational.

Chapter 1

The Foundation for School Consultation, Collaboration, and Teamwork

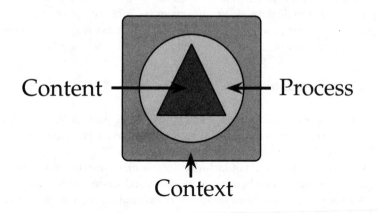

Content ← → Process

↑ Context

Introduction

What does the term *consultation* bring to mind? Is a consultant an expert? A specialist? Someone who assesses others' problems and makes recommendations for solving them? What does *collaboration* mean? Is it possible to collaborate within the school environment? What is *teamwork* in an educational setting? Can working in teams help educators meet the enormous challenges facing them in today's schools?

Life presents many situations in which people do not have all the information and expertise they would like, or the assistance that others could provide to help them work more effectively. In today's increasingly interdependent and specialized world it is unlikely that any one person has all the knowledge and skills needed for every situation. So it is reasonable to seek the services of consultants, to collaborate with other specialists, and to work with colleagues in teams.

The demand for *consultation* services is escalating in fields as varied as business, medicine, law, industry, fashion, construction, decorating, and finance. Sometimes consultants even have their own consultants! The appearance of the word *collaboration* in a wide range of literature has increased exponentially, just as the prevalence of the term *creativity* escalated in the 1950s and 1960s. *Teamwork* is now frequently used to discuss work philosophies and occupational formats. However, until recently these three concepts—consultation, collaboration, and teamwork—had been overlooked as key elements for structuring a strong educational system. Time and frameworks for collaborative, consultative, or teamed interactions among educators were virtually nonexistent. Furthermore, preparation for the complex processes of working together in the school environment was minimal in most teacher education programs. Now, however, the increasing complexity of school settings and intensified efforts toward school reform and restructuring have become catalysts for working collaboratively in schools.

Teaching is a multidimensional responsibility and teachers are involved more than ever with all facets of student development—cognitive, affective, physical, and social. Effective teaching and learning are not likely to occur without extensive interaction among educators, parents, and resource personnel in the home, in school, and in community settings.

Focusing Questions

1. What school conditions today call for greater emphasis upon working together?
2. How do educational reform and restructuring movements signal the need for consultation, collaboration, and teamwork in education?
3. What will be the effects of inclusion, or a unified educational system, on general education teachers, special education teachers, and support personnel?
4. What are definitions of consultation, collaboration, and teamwork that will be useful in the educational setting?
5. Who will serve as consultant, consultee, and client in school consultation?
6. What opportunities and benefits will become available for school personnel when educators consult, collaborate, and work together as professional teams?
7. What obstacles may hinder the practices of school consultation and collaboration?
8. What process skills and content skills are needed for consultation, collaboration, and teamwork within diverse school contexts?

Key Terms in the Chapter

Americans with Disabilities Act (ADA)
America 2000
autonomy

client
collaboration
communication

consultant
consultation
consultee
consulting teacher
content skills
cooperation
coordination
Goals 2000
iatrogenic effect
IDEA (see Public Law 101-476)
inclusion/full inclusion
Individual Transition Plan (ITP)
least-restrictive environment
mainstreaming
multiplier effects
normalization

positive ripple effects
preschooler with disabilities
process skills
Public Law 94-142 (1975)
Public Law 98-199 (1983)
Public Law 99-457 (1986)
Public Law 101-476 (1990–91)
Regular Education Initiative (REI)
school context
school reform
school restructuring
synergy
teamwork
transition from preschool to school
transition from school to the adult world
unified educational system

Scenario

The setting is the faculty room of a typical high school where two teachers are sharing school news and professional concerns.

ENGLISH TEACHER: I'm getting another special education student next week—severe learning disabilities, the cumulative folder says. I guess this is more fallout from Public Law 94–142, or the IDEA, or whatever it's called now—along with the behavior-disordered student I've been coping with all semester.

MATH TEACHER: (grinning) Must be because you're doing such a great job with that one. (serious tone) But I know what you mean. Our special education teachers aren't taking these kids out of our classes as much as they did when I started teaching.

ENGLISH TEACHER: They say a person designated as a consulting teacher is coming to our next departmental meeting to talk about helping the students with special needs. And we're going to be asked to collaborate—whatever that means—along with all the other things we do, of course.

MATH TEACHER: Say, don't those two words cancel each other out? "Consult" and "collaborate", that is. I believe you English teachers call that an oxymoron. For example, we might consult a tax accountant for some expert advice, but isn't collaboration where we all work together to accomplish our goals? As for teamwork, our coaches probably could predict what a difficult process that would be among a group of independent-thinking adults who are accustomed to doing things their own way.

ENGLISH TEACHER: Frankly, I'm not interested in word games or coaching strategies right now. I'm more concerned about finding out where the time is going to come from to do one more thing. And I want to know who will have bottom-line responsibility for which students.

MATH TEACHER: Right. I've had some concerns about mainstreaming all along, and now I think we really need some answers about inclusion. So, I hope we get them.

Educators' Responsibilities in Schools

> *Here is Edward Bear, coming downstairs now, bump, bump, bump, on the back of his head, behind Christopher Robin. It is, as far as he knows, the only way of coming downstairs, but sometimes he feels that there really is another way, if only he could stop bumping for a moment and think of it. (*Winnie-the-Pooh, *p. 3, by A. A. Milne)*

Teaching has never been easy, and it becomes more challenging every year. The public is demanding fiscal responsibility and competent school personnel. The media present diatribes against declining test scores and urge higher student achievement. Rising costs, public criticism, low teacher morale, and an avalanche of regulations and paperwork create pressures on schools that erode their ability to prepare students for a successful future. Some educators remain in the profession and juggle their daily routines within a burgeoning new agenda of reform and mandates. Others burn out and leave the profession. Still others simply "fizzle out," "rust out," or "coast out." The latter go through the motions of their profession in lackluster fashion, just getting by until retirement age arrives or a better opportunity comes along. These educators create situations that are particularly penalizing for students who have special needs and are the most vulnerable to the effects of uninspired teaching.

Autonomy in the Classroom

In the past, teachers tended to function autonomously in their classrooms (Goodlad, 1984). After the attendance forms, lunch counts, and other daily procedures were completed, they closed their doors and taught their specified content. They tried to handle each school situation with minimal assistance. After all, hadn't the teacher of eight grades in a one-room schoolhouse managed without special help? To ask for assistance would have been tantamount to proclaiming incompetency.

Goodlad (1984) has described teachers as autonomous within the context of isolation. Autonomy minimizes the impact of outside influences (Rosenfield, 1985). Because teachers seldom have the privilege of rich professional dialogue with colleagues, they are isolated from sources of ideas beyond their own backgrounds and experiences. The chunking of the typical school day is insulating. Teachers often go through an entire school day without speaking to an adult in a meaningful way (Eisner, 1988).

Even today, few structured arrangements exist to assist teachers in the performance of their complex roles. This is particularly problematic at the high school level where teachers might teach five classes, prepare two or more lessons, and face as many as 150 students during a school day that is divided into 50-minute periods (Cuban, 1986). Although schools are, in a certain sense, very social places and classrooms are multidimensional centers of activity, an individual teacher may feel stranded on a crowded island devoid of adult interaction and stimulation. In a poll of over 1,000 teachers conducted by *Learning* magazine and reported by the Education Commission of the United States, 78 percent of the respondents said that isolation from their colleagues is a major or moderate problem (Turner, 1987).

On one hand, teachers may desire more small-group meetings on mutual interests, regular grade level meetings, frequent chances to observe other teachers, and richer opportunities for in-service training. On the other hand, many teachers are not comfortable engaging in collaborative efforts with other teachers. Some state candidly that they did not choose a teaching career to work all that much with adults. Others think that calling on a colleague or requesting services from a school consultant will be perceived as a sign of professional weakness and incompetency.

Teachers have few incentives for getting together to collaborate or team-teach. They rarely have an opportunity to visit other school settings to obtain new ideas and revitalize their enthusiasm. When they do have the time and opportunity to interact with colleagues, it is likely to be during in-service or staff development sessions. Unfortunately, these activities often are too highly structured, inappropriately designed, or poorly managed to allow meaningful interaction. Many are scheduled at the end of a hectic day, when teachers are tired and want to turn their attention toward home or community responsibilities.

Teachers are visited now and then by supervisors, administrators, student teachers, and sometimes parents, in their classrooms. However, these occasions tend to create more feelings of anxiety and defensiveness than support and collegiality. Some schools encourage team teaching as a way of allowing teachers to support each other and broaden their teaching repertoires. But well-intentioned efforts to team-teach too often result in turn-teaching—"You teach this part of the lesson and then take a break while I handle the next part."

Wildman and Niles (1987) stress that professionals cannot be coerced into being collegial. Teachers who are accustomed to being in charge and making virtually all the day-to-day decisions in their classrooms cannot be ordered to just go out and consult and collaborate with each other to any meaningful degree. They need structure, training, practice, and feedback about their effectiveness in order to perform these sophisticated, demanding functions well. Unfortunately, the typical teacher preparation program provides little or no instruction and practice in collaborating with professional peers. Meanwhile, a growing body of school consultation literature and research forecasts wider use of consultation service and greater interest in collaboration and teamwork in the future. Current books, periodicals, conferences, staff development sessions, and media messages are convincing educators that by consulting, collaborating, and teaming, school personnel and parents can combine the best that they have to help students learn. Educational reform movements of the past three decades have strengthened these convictions.

Demands within School Reform Movements

During the 1970s and 1980s, educators witnessed an explosion of reports, proposals, and legislative mandates calling for educational reform. Reports such as *A Nation at Risk,* submitted by the National Commission on Excellence in Education in 1983, and as many as 30 other major reform reports in the 1980s, directed the nation's attention to the status and conditions of its schools. After these reports were publicized, public pressure to improve schools escalated.

The first wave of educational reform sought to strengthen the rigor of American public education (Michaels, 1988). The issues focused on accountability, lengthening of school days and years, and increased investments of time, money, and effort in education. The second wave of reform featured the individual school as the unit of decision-making. It promoted the development of collegial, participatory environments among students and staff, with particular emphasis on personalizing school environments and designing curriculum for deeper understanding (Michaels, 1988). One component of this second wave of reform was school restructuring. Many states initiated some form of school restructuring, however, few schools truly were restructured. Where restructuring efforts occurred, they tended to be idiosyncratic in that they were carried out by a small group of teachers, creating only marginal, easily eroded changes (Timar, 1989).

Effective restructuring calls for rethinking. In order to do that, educators must take their eyes off the rear-view mirror of first-wave reform and look carefully at the twenty-first century (Michaels, 1988). Futrell (1989) has charged that, in the 1980s, education was an arena of debate, not educational reform. When the redefinition of education was beginning, a primary outcome was just argument. But by the 1990s educators had learned the kinds of questions to ask. Many of these questions and the thinking they precipitated signaled the need for extensive consultation, collaboration, and teamwork by the entire school staff, and stressed the value of parents as partners. Futrell asserts that schools truly can be restructured only through cooperation, collaboration, and teamwork among many factions.

Friend and Cook (1990) reiterate that school reform efforts in the United States have been fueled by national concerns within four domains:

- Reestablishment of economic leadership, which will be determined by successful preparation of students to be effective workers and national leaders;
- Governance of schools, where teachers can participate more fully in decisions regarding their classrooms;
- Structure of schools, reorganizing traditional class groups and levels;
- Curricular reform, with collaborative staff activities and a climate of collegiality ensuring teacher participation in curriculum design and delivery methods.

Friend and Cook also point out that current reform efforts are regarded by many as a rehash of previous reform movements. However, the emerging interest in collaboration and teamwork adds a new dimension that could be the impetus for realizing major changes through school reform efforts.

The Regular Education Initiative (REI)

A significant ripple that helped create waves of educational reform was the Regular Education Initiative (REI), which called for a merger of general education and special education efforts. Demands for cost containment and growing concerns over labeling of students fueled interest in a merger of general education and special education. The primary impetus for the merger was the mainstreaming movement brought about by Public Law 94-142 in 1975. When Public Law 94-142 mandated placement for students with handicaps into a least-restrictive learning environment, classroom teachers were given the responsibility for the success of those students. However, in order to fulfill this new responsibility, they were promised help from special education personnel.

The least-restrictive environment mandate created changes in the way general education teachers and special education teachers were expected to interact in order to serve students with exceptional learning needs. Students with handicaps (now termed *disabilities*) are to be educated with nondisabled peers in regular school settings as much as possible. Special education teachers and general classroom teachers are to modify educational settings and teaching methods for exceptional students with handicaps. Such modifications facilitate the education of students with handicaps in a least-restrictive environment and minimize their social and educational isolation from age peers.

Thus the Regular Education Initiative, referred to by some educators as the General Education Initiative (GEI), precipitated major changes in the way education is delivered. All students, with the exception of the severely handicapped, are to be served primarily in a regular education setting. The rationale for the REI is that

the changes will serve many students not currently eligible for special education services;

the stigma of placement in special education programs separated from peers will be eliminated;

early intervention and prevention will be provided before more serious learning deficiencies occur; and

cooperative school/parent relationships will be enhanced (Will, 1986).

Many educators subsequently emphasized that the Regular Education Initiative was not an initiative of regular educators, but a change in both general and special education that was proposed by special educators and not general educators. This assumption has been the subject of considerable debate (Hallahan, Kauffman, Lloyd & McKinney, 1988). A number of special education personnel contend that regular educators are not interested in making the proposed changes required by the REI. So, without significant changes in educational programs, the children who were failed by a traditional educational system once again fail to be served in the merged system.

Public Law 98-199 was passed in 1983. It provided amendments that emphasized planning for transitional services for secondary students and authorized parent training and information centers (Shanker, 1994).

Public Law 94-142, which required states to develop procedures for educating every child in the least restrictive environment, was amended in 1990 by Public Law 101-476, the Individuals with Disabilities Education Act (IDEA). Key elements of that amendment are

all references to handicapped children were changed to children with disabilities;

new categories of autism and traumatic brain injury (TBI) were added, to be served with increased collaboration among all special education teachers, classroom teachers, and related services personnel;

more emphasis was placed on requirements to provide transition services for students 16 years old and older.

Also in 1990, the Americans with Disabilities Act (ADA) was passed, prohibiting discrimination against persons of all ages with disabilities in transportation, public access, local government, and telecommunications.

As the REI debate continues through the 1990s, resource teacher roles have become uniquely positioned for collaborating and teaming with general classroom teachers. As early as 1981, Lilly and Givens-Ogle stressed that teacher consultation practices are critical for cultivating the relationships between regular education and special education teachers that can facilitate student success within the least restrictive environment (Haight, 1984; Huefner, 1988). More and more practicing teachers and administrators are acknowledging that special education skills are needed by all classroom teachers. As things stand now, current patterns of funding, licensure requirements, job opportunities, and even professional identities are dependent on the existence of separate systems for special education and regular education. However, by sharing their responsibilities for students with special learning needs, all educators can contribute not only toward remediation of problems but also to prevention of problems.

Although the Regular Education Initiative has not proved to be a panacea, the philosophy on which it is grounded can avert the inappropriate practice of placing large numbers of children with relatively minor learning and behavior problems into special education pull-out programs. The long-term impact of the Regular Education Initiative on collaborative consultation will be negative if the two thrusts are perceived as synonymous, but positive if REI clarifies and refines the concepts and practices of consultation (Friend, 1988). Current research and practices indicate that the help for teachers that was promised as part of the mainstream movement can be delivered effectively and efficiently by consultants and consulting teachers.

Special educators must envision themselves as contributing members of the general education community and work toward integration of special education and general education (Lilly, 1987). Shared responsibility between regular educators and special educators can provide more coordinated and inclusive educational arrangements for all students.

In the meantime, however, people are not waiting for special educators to come and save them (Conoley, 1985). School doors open each morning, bells ring, students congregate, and classes begin. In those classes many students have special learning and behavior needs. Up to one-third of all school-age children can be described as experiencing difficulty in school, and, when the significant learning needs of gifted students are included, this figure increases substantially. As many as 10 percent of the students enrolled in public schools are eligible for special education services, while another 10 to 20 percent have mild to moderate learning problems that interfere with their school progress (Idol, West, & Lloyd, 1988; Will, 1986).

Although the public envisions "handicapped" children as crippled, deaf, blind, or retarded (Schenkat, 1988), up to 90 percent of the children served in special education programs have very mild disabilities (Shepard, 1987), being more accurately described as slow learners, second language students, misbehavers in school, often absent, moving frequently, or simply average learners in significantly above-average populations. Even so, educational programs for these students have taken up 50 to 70 percent of special education budgets. Paradoxically, 68 percent of students with disabilities in the 1980s received most of their education in regular classes (U. S. Department of Education, 1985; Friend & McNutt, 1984).

Inclusive or Unified School Systems

A more extreme position that has evolved in regard to the Regular Education Initiative is that special education and regular education should merge into a unified school system, or inclusive school system, structured to meet the needs of all students. Proponents of this position assert that all students are unique individuals with special needs requiring differentiated individual attention; therefore, practices that are effective for exceptional students should be used with all students (Stainback and Stainback, 1984). Inclusive schools will *include* students with special needs in the total school experience, rather than *exclude* them by placing them in special schools or classrooms.

While mainstreaming involves passing students out of general education classrooms, inclusive schools educate students with special needs in their home schools with grade peers. Special services are brought to the students instead of having students removed, or "pulled out," to go to the special services. "No students, including those with disabilities, are relegated to the fringes of the school by placement in segregated wings, trailers, or special classes" (Stainback and Stainback, 1992, p. 34).

The term *inclusion* is erroneously viewed by many professionals as a synonym for least-restrictive environment (LRE), which is mandated by federal legislation. However, the legislation does not define inclusion, or unified educational system as some prefer to designate the concept. It is more appropriate to speak of a continuum of services in which inclusion is just one of several alternatives within that continuum. Definitions that do exist will differ based on the interest group fostering the definition. The following definitions relating to inclusion appear in the literature:

- Inclusion: The commitment to educate each child to the maximum extent appropriate in the school and classroom he or she would otherwise attend (Rogers, 1993).
- Full (or Total) inclusion: The belief that instructional practices and technological supports are presently available to accommodate all students in the schools and classrooms they would otherwise attend if not disabled (Rogers, 1993).
- Inclusive schools: Schools in which all members accept their fair share of responsibility for all children, including those with disabilities. Aids and resources are utilized where needed regardless of official classifications of disability (Fuchs and Fuchs, 1994).

The concept of inclusion did not suddenly emerge out of a vacuum. Indeed, it appears to be the latest in a long line of special education program changes that have grown out of concern for more appropriate education. Early efforts to address special needs began in special schools or residential institutions where specialized therapy and care could be provided by a well-trained staff. When educators began to provide special services in schools, special classes were formed. A belief was prevalent that those with disabilities were not successful in the regular classroom because that setting could not provide for their needs. This assumption was not challenged until the 1960s when advocates for individuals with mental retardation argued for normalization. These advocates asserted that individuals with mental retardation should have opportunities for patterns and conditions of everyday life as close as possible to norms of mainstream society. This logic influenced the deinstitutionalization movement.

The courts upheld the right of individuals to refuse treatment and supported the civil rights belief that segregated education is inherently unequal and a violation of children's rights. The movement toward inclusion in the 1990s was built on this early foundation. (See Figure 1-1.)

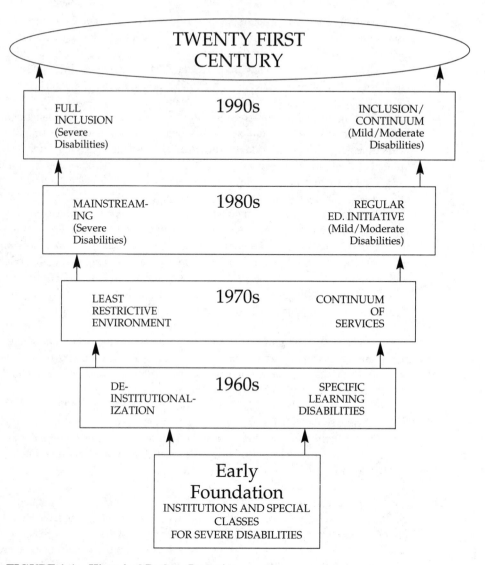

FIGURE 1-1   Historical Path to Inclusion

Identification and treatment of individuals with specific learning disabilities was a parallel movement of the 1960s. Advocates argued that some were erroneously labeled mentally retarded but had the potential to learn in a regular classroom environment if provisions were made for the specific learning disability. A few small programs for students disabilities began to spring up in public schools. Many of these programs provided resource rooms where attempts were made to remediate the learning disabilities. Resource teachers also provided support and consultation to the regular classroom teachers and were given a foundation for the consultation and collaboration models that were to emerge during the inclusion movement.

During the 1970s, the landmark legislation, P. L. 94-142, was passed by the U. S. Congress. Lawmakers were strongly influenced by the earlier normalization movement. At the heart of legislation was the least restrictive environment (LRE). This provision mandated that each individual should be evaluated individually to determine the most appropriate educational program in the least-restrictive environment. Educators could no longer arbitrarily place individuals with disabilities in a special school or self-contained classroom. A continuum of service options was to be available and the type of service or placement was to be as close to the normal environment as possible. Some advocates of inclusion have interpreted this LRE provision to mean that placement must be in a normalized environment, but most educators believe it meant the former interpretation. Later, the reauthorization of P. L. 94-142 would be challenged to clarify the matter (Shanker, 1994). At the time of this writing the issue is being debated by federal lawmakers.

A related movement of the 1980s was the Regular Education Initiative (REI), which was described earlier. A position paper by Madeline Will, former director of the U. S. Office of Special Education and Rehabilitative Services, stated that too many children were inappropriately identified and served in learning disabilities programs. She called for collaboration between special education personnel and general education personnel in providing services within the general classroom. Two distinct groups emerged to advocate for REI, the high-incidence group speaking for learning disabilities, behavioral disorders, and mild/moderate mental retardation, and the low-incidence group speaking for students with severe intellectual disabilities. A few in the latter group spoke out for the elimination of special education altogether (Fuchs and Fuchs, 1994). Both groups shared the following three goals:

- To merge special and general education into one inclusive system;
- To increase dramatically the service of children with disabilities in mainstream classrooms; and
- To strengthen the academic achievement of students with mild and moderate disabilities, as well as that of underachievers without disabilities.

To achieve these goals it was necessary to become involved in the total restructuring of schools. "Increasingly, special education reform is symbolized by the term 'inclusive schools'," (Fuchs and Fuchs, 1994, p. 299).

Clearly, restructured schools will demand teachers, administrators, support staff, and parents who can effectively work together to achieve common goals of appropriate education for all students. Consultation, collaboration, and teamwork are central elements to the success of both the REI and inclusion movements.

Essential Elements for Success of Inclusion

The National Center on Educational Restructuring and Inclusion (NCERI) conducted a study in 1994 to determine the current status of the inclusion movement. Although most students with disabilities continue to be educated in separate settings, inclusion programs are being implemented in many states across the country. The NCERI researchers determined that the following six factors are necessary for inclusion to succeed (Lipsky, 1994):

- Visionary leadership. School leaders must have a positive view about the value of education for students with disabilities and an optimistic view of teachers who can change and schools that can accommodate the needs of students with special needs. An overriding attitude that all children can benefit from inclusion is important.

- Collaboration. Successful inclusion presumes that "no one teacher can or ought to be expected to have all the expertise required to meet the educational needs of all students in the classroom" (Lipsky, 1994, p. 5). The processes of consultation, collaboration, and teamwork are recognized as essential for effective inclusion programs.
- Refocused use of assessment. Inclusive schools tend to use more authentic assessment measures such as those that will be discussed in Chapter 9. Assessment focuses on monitoring student progress.
- Supports for staff and students. Two essential support factors reported in the study are systematic staff development and flexible planning time for special education personnel and general educators to meet and work together. Another key support is involvement of parents in planning processes. Other useful supports include assignment of school aides, curriculum adaptation, therapy services integrated into the regular school program, peer supports, computer technology, and other assistive devices.
- Funding. Funding formulas in many states need to be changed in order for inclusion to be implemented successfully.
- Effective parental involvement. Inclusive programs place emphasis on substantive parent involvement through family support services and the development of educational programs that engage parents as co-learners with their children.

The survey also highlighted the following effective classroom practices that will be discussed more fully in Chapter 10:

- Co-teaching model
- Parallel teaching
- Co-teaching consultant model
- Team model
- Methods and resources teacher model

Early Childhood Education for Children with Disabilities

Concern for preschoolers from poverty-level environments and other conditions of disadvantage gained momentum in the 1960s. The passage of Public Law 99-457 in 1986 expanded attention to preschoolers from ages three and above. Public schools now are required to provide special services for children ages three and above who have disabilities. Public Law 99-457 has gone far beyond classroom concerns to include family, social workers, speech and language pathologists, medical personnel, and other professionals. The law authorizes funding for state grants and for experimental, demonstration, and outreach programs that are multidisciplinary in nature. An increase in services for preschool children with disabilities calls for increased collaboration among professionals, parents, and other care-givers. Collaboration, consultation, and teamwork are at the heart of these programs.

Early intervention programs for infants and toddlers with disabilities have proliferated following the early-childhood legislation. Family members and other care-givers outside the school now play an even more integral part in the education and well-being of these children. Because most disabilities of children in the early intervention programs are severe, services of specialists from several disciplines are essential. Moreover, parents play an integral part in the therapy through home-based programs. In these programs, therapists go into the homes to provide stimulation for the children and guidance and instruction for the parents. In order to meet the children's special needs, staff and parents must collaborate with all available resources, including health and medical personnel, social services personnel, public school personnel, and community resources such as preschool and day care centers. This need will be discussed further in Chapter 11 on parent partnerships and Chapter 13 on linking support agencies.

Transition from Preschool Settings to Kindergarten Programs

Although formal programs such as Head Start and Follow Through for young children have been successful in and of themselves, P L 99-457 reaches far beyond classroom interventions. Transition from the preschool settings to kindergarten school programs requires strong, continuous efforts toward collaboration and teamwork.

Preschool teachers will want to identify essential skills needed in the local kindergarten in order to prepare the children for that setting (Beckhoff & Bender, 1989; Salisbury & Vincent, 1990; McCormick & Kawate, 1982). Their contributions to elementary school programs are invaluable for getting new kindergarten students off to a successful start. Collaboration and teamwork among all parties involved with very young children are essential.

Transition from School to the Adult World

At the opposite end of the continuum from early childhood needs are the needs of students leaving school to enter the world of work and adult living. Heightened awareness of this important transition period for young people with disabilities grew in the 1980s. The transition movement of the 1980s was preceded by two similar movements in the 1960s and the 1970s (Halpern, 1992). During the 1960s, a work/study program emerged as an approach to preparing students with mild disabilities for adjustment into their communities. Two flaws of this movement were the funding mechanism that supported it and the requirement that rehabilitation agencies could not pay for services that were the responsibility of other agencies (Halpern, 1992). The 1970s' career education movement was an expansion of the work/study movement. However, it eventually was disowned as a federal initiative, leaving the door open for the emergence of the transition movement during the 1980s.

The goal of transition programs during the 1980s was to assist students with disabilities in obtaining educational services that will enable them to lead meaningful and productive lives. One of the realities was that no one parent, teacher, or counselor can adequately provide the necessary assistance. It requires a team effort provided by all parties involved in the interest of the students. The emphasis on college preparatory curriculum that grew out of school reform was appropriate for perhaps only 40% of the students (Daggett, 1989; Edgar, 1990; Goodlad, 1984; Pugach & Sapon-Shevin, 1987).

The decade of the 1990s is an important one for making transition approaches work in the local communities (Halpern, 1992). Educational and social reform movements have escalated attention to this age-group population of students who have special needs.

Schools now are responsible for generating Individual Transition Plans (ITPs) to assess students' career interests and help them focus on career possibilities. Community support is given through vocational transition liaisons, job coaching, work awareness classes, and school employment. Thorough assessment is vital for effective transition, and students with disabilities may need special comprehensive testing (Dragan, 1994).

Without concerted team effort, students with disabilities do not make successful transition to adult life. More than 50% remain unemployed or under-employed. Students, parents, teachers, guidance counselors, and other support personnel should contribute to the development of the ITP. In order for the transition process to be successful, all parties and agencies are required to work together systematically to plan for it (Clark & Knowlton, 1988; Rusch & Menchett, 1988). Collaborative consultation has been helpful in providing this support (Sileo, Rude, & Luckner, 1988). This topic will appear again in Chapter 13 on linking with external agencies.

Agenda of America 2000

In April of 1991, President Bush and Secretary of Education Lamar Alexander presented a four-part educational strategy called *America 2000*. The plan outlines several educational goals for the nation to achieve by the year 2000, including ideas and proposals for new national tests, new national standards, federal encouragement of choice, new federally appointed agencies for research, and a nationwide emphasis on English, mathematics, science, history, and geography (Howe II, 1991). The six goals (Bush, 1991; Halpern, 1992) are that

- By the year 2000, every child in the United States will begin school ready to learn.
- High-school graduation rates in the United States will increase to at least 90 percent by the year 2000.
- All students in grades 4, 8, and 12 will be tested for progress in key subjects.
- U. S. students will rank first in the world in science and mathematics achievement.
- Every adult will be a skilled, literate worker and citizen.
- Every school will be drug-free and will provide a climate in which learning can occur.

Some educators described the *America 2000* plan as vigorous, optimistic, and upbeat in its intent to mobilize public opinion and focus national energy on education without creating bureaucratic structures (Doyle, 1991; Sewall, 1991). Others criticized it as a call for cosmetic change that will not restructure schools from the ground up, as they need to be.

Howe (1991) contends that there were three major omissions of concern from *America 2000* target areas: school finance, growing poverty among children and youth, and cultural and racial diversity in American society. The plan purports to address all children, but overlooks the 10 percent of exceptional children who have special learning needs. Furthermore, considering the need for a diversity of schools and educational approaches and a wide range of alternatives to meet society's demands for practical education, the proposed instruction and testing may be educationally damaging for the 98 percent not destined to become academic scholars (Clinchy, 1991).

Some educators suggest that standardized testing may have already harmed low-achieving students and should be replaced by alternative forms of assessment based on projects, exhibits, and portfolios of student work, not accountability systems stipulated in *America 2000* (Lieberman, 1991). If these educators are correct in targeting diverse schools, approaches, and assessments as mandates for education by the year 2000, then consultation, collaboration, and teamwork are sure to be key components of meaningful school reform for the future.

Agenda of Goals 2000

The 1994 federal school reform package known as *Goals 2000* was signed into law by President Clinton in 1994. *Goals 2000* identifies eight goals to be met by the year 2000—the six described above that were outlined in *America 2000,* and two additional goals, which are

- The teaching force will have access to programs for continued self-improvement of professional skills; and
- Every school will promote partnerships that increase parent involvement and participation.

This package calls for voluntary national standards governing content and opportunity to learn and provides funds to help states implement the national goals for education in ways that those states choose. The legislation stipulates that any state applying for *Goals 2000* funds must establish statewide plans, including standards and assessments, for improving neighborhood schools. States will have flexibility to create statewide voluntary opportunity-to-learn content, performance, and occupational skills standards, along with assessments, that may be certified by the National Education Standards and Improvement Council (NESIC) if a state seeks certification. A National Education Goals Panel is to help NESIC develop national standards and will review the state standards and assessments for approval.

 Goals 2000 applies to all students, including those with exceptionalities. State agencies must make at least one subgrant to a rural local education agency and another to an urban one. Priority for grants is to be given to those agencies serving a greater number or percentage of disadvantaged students than the statewide average or ones that target preparation and continued professional development of those who teach students with disabilities (*"Public Policy,"* 1994).

Summary of School Reform Movements

Teachers, administrators, and support personnel are being bombarded with demands for significant changes in the ways they function. These changes are intended to be comprehensive and schoolwide. Cosmetic alteration of existing programs and policies simply will not be sufficient to address the complex issues and concerns.

 Key educational leaders are proposing that unless major structural changes are made in the field of special education, the field is destined to become more a problem and less a solution in providing for students' special needs (Reynolds, Wang, & Walberg, 1987). Urgent needs exist for coordinated educational services in regular school settings for all students, including those with special needs; time-limited waivers for school districts to experiment with the more coordinated programs; and alternatives to the current categorical systems of helping students who have special needs.

An integral element for ensuring school success in the wake of the reforms is the ability of the school staff to collaborate (Friend & Cook, 1990). Yet despite the increasing interest in collaborative formats, implementation of such formats has been sporadic. Phillips and Mc-Cullough (1990) cite the inconsistent use of the term *collaborative consultation,* the lack of overarching theoretical orientation, and myriad concepts of consultation as causes of the variable success. The literature on effective schools challenges educators to cultivate collegiality when planning and learning new skills (Lieberman, 1986). A collaboration ethic is needed, with general and special educators as co-consultants pooling interdisciplinary content, processes, and expertise (Phillips & McCullough, 1989). Until such an ethic is promoted widely, the necessary time and structure for collaborative consultation will not be forthcoming.

What Collaborative School Consultation Is

In recent years no education legislation has been passed by Congress, or, for that matter, has been considered that does not foster collaboration (Lewis, 1992). Now that reform movements have fueled the interest of educators and parents in the concepts of consultation, collaboration, and working together as teams, it is imperative that schools follow through to implement plans of action. Just what is *school* consultation? How can collaboration be a significant part of consultation? In what ways can school consultation and collaboration promote teamwork and meaningful partnerships among educators and parents for the special needs of students?

Defining Consultation, Collaboration, and Teamwork

Definitions of consultation and collaboration for school settings must be general enough to apply to a wide range of school structures and circumstances, yet flexible enough for useful adaptation to each context of local school needs. *Webster's Third New International Dictionary, unabridged* (1976) and *Webster's New Collegiate Dictionary, 8th edition* (1981) provide a wealth of synonyms for words related to these terms. There are also many useful related words, including *communication, cooperation, coordination,* and *teamwork* or *teaming.* When studied as a group, it is readily apparent that the words complement each other to form a foundation for understanding and using these concepts of complex human interaction. Examples are

> *consult:* Advise, confer, confab, huddle, parley, counsel, deliberate, consider, examine, refer to, group, communicate, review, apply for information, take counsel, discuss, seek the opinion of, and/or have prudent regard to.
>
> *consultation:* Advisement, care, counsel, conference, or formal deliberation.
>
> *consulting:* Deliberating together, asking advice or opinion of, or conferring.
>
> *consultant:* One who gives professional advice or services in a field of special knowledge and training or simply one who consults another.

consulting teacher: One with major teaching responsibilities who also works with other school personnel in order to serve special needs of students.

consultee: Described in social science literature as the mediator between consultant and client (Tharp, 1975).

client: Individual, group, agency, department, community, or sometimes even a nation, that benefits from the services of a consultant. A patron, end user, or buyer. (*Target* is sometimes used as a synonym.)

collaborate: Labor together or work jointly, especially in an intellectual endeavor, assist, associate, unite, pool.

communication: The act of transmitting, giving, or exchanging information, or the art of expressing ideas.

cooperation: The act of uniting, banding, combining, concurring, agreeing, consenting, or conjoining.

coordination: Bringing elements into a common action, movement, or condition, synchronizing, attuning, adjusting.

teamwork, teaming: Joining forces or efforts, with each individual contributing a clearly-defined portion of the effort, but also subordinating personal prominence to the efficiency of the whole.

Description of School Consultation, Collaboration, and Teamwork

The verbs *consult, collaborate, communicate, cooperate, coordinate,* and *team* are rich words for describing the types of interactive processes that can enhance student growth as well as increase teacher satisfaction with education. These words and the variants that were presented earlier appear in the educational literature in many different combinations.

In order to fit a variety of school contexts and educational needs, consultation and collaboration for schools will be defined and used in this book as follows:

Collaborative school consultation is interaction in which school personnel and families confer and collaborate as a team within the school context to identify learning and behavioral needs, and to plan, implement, and evaluate educational programs for serving those needs.

The collaborative consultant in schools is defined here as follows:

A collaborative school consultant is a facilitator of effective communication, cooperation, and coordination who confers and collaborates with other school personnel and families as one of a team to serve the special learning and behavioral needs of students.

In the scenario at the beginning of this chapter, the client (sometimes referred to as the target of services) is the new student who has a learning disability. The learning disabilities consultant will serve the student indirectly, for the most part, by collaborating with the classroom teacher, who will be the consultee and provider of direct service to the student. Some direct service might be provided by the learning disabilities consultant to the student, but for the most part the direct service will be the given by the classroom teacher.

Consultation involves the sharing of expertise. Those in the consultant role do not hold claim to all the expertise. Competent consultants often listen and learn. They sometimes help consultees discover what they already know. They help them recognize their own talents and trust their own skills.

To collaborate is to labor together. Collaborators do not compromise so much as they confer and contribute. While compromise implies giving up some part or conceding something, collaboration means adding to and making more. The very nature of the collaborative process requires diversity—diversity of experience, values, abilities, and interests. Individual differences of adults who consult and collaborate are rich ingredients for successful collaborations. The need to recognize and maximize adult differences and use them constructively will be the focus of Chapter 4.

Collaboration offers more immediate availability of other professionals to verify perceptions, to problem-solve collectively, and to apply several teaching and learning styles to the issue. Occasionally collaboration even serves by differentiating and separating rather than bringing closer together, so that the perspectives of dissimilar views are understood and appreciated. Then differentiated tasks can be allocated among individuals with different skills to contribute.

Antonyms for collaborating include *struggling* and *resisting*. Indeed, resistance from professional colleagues or parents is one of the major obstacles to effective collaborative interactions in the school setting. Communication, cooperation, and coordination are crucial aspects of effective collaboration. This discussion will be continued in Chapter 6.

The concept of teamwork in school settings is receiving increased attention among school professionals. Teamwork is working for the good of the whole—where individual preferences are subdued or set aside for the larger cause. As part of a team, each member contributes a clearly defined portion of the effort that comes together in creating a complete plan of action.

Many team-oriented schools are exemplary models of teacher empowerment and shared decision-making (*The Holmes Group Forum,* 1990). In the fall of 1990, two two-hour documentaries (PBS, hosted by Roger Mudd, and CBS, hosted by Charles Kuralt) showcased collegiality and teamwork among teachers. Parents were featured as partners with the schools in their children's learning. The premise was that schools with strong team activities are more successful than schools whose teachers and staff function autonomously. These two television documentaries that went out to millions of U. S. homes emphasized that successful teaching is built on partnerships and teamwork among professionals and parents for their students' needs.

Teamwork is not yet as efficient as it can and should be (Reynolds & Birch, 1988). Schools need precise guidelines for developing systems of consultation, cooperative teaching, teacher assistance teams, and pre-referral interventions (Phillips and McCullough, 1990). It is increasingly difficult for one educator to keep up with all the advancements in

---

APPLICATION 1.1   Ways to Collaborate as a Team

Think of many things you could do in team settings, using collaborative processes, that are virtually impossible to do in traditional, relatively autonomous roles in school or business settings. What positive effects might this teamwork have on all?

---

knowledge and processes. Teams of educators can energize and inform each other in dozens of ways.

An important question to ask is, "Would student needs, particularly those of students who have very serious, very special learning or behavior needs, be served more effectively and efficiently if educators regularly pooled their talents, energies, and resources to address these needs?" However, in order to be effective, teams must have a common planning time built into the work day and facilities that allow them to share resources and coordinate their curriculum and instruction.

How Consultation, Collaboration, and Teamwork Differ

All three processes—consultation, collaboration, and teamwork—as they occur in the school context involve interaction among professionals and parents working together to achieve common goals. However, subtle distinctions among the three do exist.

In school consultation, the consultant contributes specialized expertise toward an educational problem, and the consultee delivers direct service using that expertise. Consultants and consultees collaborate by assuming equal ownership of the problem and solutions.

Collaboration has been explained as a way of working in which both power struggles *and* inappropriate politeness are regarded as secondary to team goals. Friend and Cook (1992) distinguish between consultation and collaboration by describing collaborations as styles or approaches to interactions that occur during the consultation process. They propose that a collaborative approach can be used at some stages of consultation and not others, and with some consultees but not others. In their view, collaborative consultation must be voluntary, with one professional assisting another to address a problem concerning a third party. They emphasize that successful consultants use different styles of interaction under different circumstances and within different situations.

Teamwork typically creates leader and follower roles. An individual working with a team feels less alone and vulnerable. This is particularly helpful in circumstances involving change or innovation. Teamwork fuels team spirit, develops process skills that help teachers interact in more productive ways, and fosters a more intellectual atmosphere (Maeroff, 1993). One of the best examples of teamwork is in musical performance. Whether one is accompanying, performing in a small ensemble, or playing in an orchestra, band, or choir, it is the united effort that creates the musical experience.

Characteristics that consultation, collaboration, and teamwork have in common include

addressing problems within the school context;
engaging in interactive processes;

using specialized content for the purpose of achieving goals;
sharing resources; and
serving as catalyst for change or improvement.

Consultation, collaboration, and teamwork provide consultants and consultees the opportunity to engage in a "strengths" type of interaction, with each person using and building on the strengths of the others. Several examples from a school context will demonstrate similarities and differences among consultation, collaboration, and teamwork.

Problem-Solving with Consultation

A preschool teacher is concerned about a child in the group who is not fluent in speech. The teacher asks the speech pathologist to help determine whether this is a matter of concern, and, if so, what to do about it. The speech pathologist consults with the teacher, getting more information about the observed behavior, and makes additional observations. The consultant then uses expertise in speech pathology to address the teacher's questions.

In another instance, a speech pathologist provides individual therapy for a preschool child who has articulation errors or fluency disorders and dysfluent speech. The speech pathologist wants to know how these speech patterns are affecting the child's social development as well as performance in pre-academic skills such as letter naming and sound discrimination. The speech pathologist asks the teacher to serve as a consultant regarding this issue, and the preschool teacher provides the information requested.

Problem-Solving with Collaboration

The preschool teacher and the speech pathologist are both concerned about a child's generalization of speech skills learned in speech therapy sessions. The two teachers meet to discuss their mutual concern. They discuss their observations and engage in problem-solving activities to identify the problem clearly and select possible solutions. They agree to make some changes in their respective settings to solve the problem. If the solutions do not work, both are committed to try other possibilities.

In another situation, a teacher of students with behavioral disorders, along with the school counselor, three classroom teachers, and a student's parents, meet to discuss the behavior of that student. The individuals involved in the meeting engage in problem-solving to formulate a plan for addressing the problem. Each individual has a role to play in implementing the plan.

Problem-Solving with Teamwork

A team of professionals are providing services for severely and profoundly disabled infants and toddlers. Each professional has an area of expertise and responsibility, but the social worker has the leadership role. This is because the social worker is responsible for most parent contacts and often goes into homes to provide additional training and assistance for parents. The nurse takes responsibility for monitoring the physical well-being of each child and keeps in close contact with other medical personnel as well as parents. The speech pathologist works with the children to develop speech and language skills. The occupational therapist is responsible for teaching the children certain self-help skills. The physical therapist follows through with the medical doctor's prescribed physical therapy. Special education teachers provide language stimulation and modeling, coordinate schedules, and facilitate communication between team members. The team meets twice weekly to discuss individual cases.

In a middle school, seventh-grade teachers work as a team to plan curriculum goals, share instructional techniques and materials, and solve mutual problems. The language arts teachers take responsibility for monitoring the curriculum. The math teachers make suggestions that apply to their discipline. The learning disabilities teacher is a member of the team because so many learning-disabled students are mainstreamed. The team meets early every Friday morning. One of them has been selected by the team to serve as team leader.

When Educators Consult, Collaborate, and Work in Teams

Educators—including special education teachers, classroom teachers, school administrators, related services and support personnel, as well as parents—consult, collaborate and work as team members when they take part in one or more of these:

- Discuss students' needs;
- Listen to colleagues' concerns about the teaching situation;
- Help identify and define educational problems;
- Facilitate problem-solving in the school setting;
- Promote classroom alternatives as first interventions for students with special learning and behavior needs;
- Serve as a medium for student referrals;
- Demonstrate instructional techniques;
- Provide direct assistance to classroom teachers who have students with special learning and behavior needs;
- Lead or participate in staff development activities;
- Assist teachers in designing and implementing behavior change programs;
- Share resources, materials, and ideas with colleagues;
- Participate in team teaching or demonstration teaching;
- Engage in assessment and evaluation activities;
- Serve on curriculum committees, textbook committees and school advisory councils;
- Follow up on educational issues and concerns with colleagues;
- Ease colleagues' loads in matters involving students' special needs; and
- Network with other professionals and outside agencies.

What Collaborative School Consultation Is Not

School consultation is not therapy, nor is it counseling for the consultee (Brown, Wyne, Blackburn, & Powell, 1979). The focus must be upon educational issues relevant to the needs of the client, not the personal concerns of the consultee. West and Idol (1987) and Morsink, Thomas, and Correa (1991) differentiate counseling from consultation by describing counseling as focused on individuals and consultation as focused on issues.

Collaboration among professional colleagues is not talk or discussion for its own sake. It does not involve taking on the authority of school administrators, and it should not be a substitute for the individual teacher's accountability (Smith, 1987).

The consulting teacher is not the equivalent of a resource teacher who just spends more time with the regular classroom teacher (Huefner, 1988). Furthermore, the consultant role is not always the responsibility of the educational specialist. For example, while reading specialists, bilingual specialists, computer specialists, augmentative communication specialists, or low-vision specialists are often consultants, they become consultees when they seek expertise and information from a classroom teacher, school psychologist, administrator, parent, or resource person in the community. On some occasions a general classroom teacher is consultant for a special education teacher to contribute information about a student's problems within a social context not available to the special education teacher. In another instance, a parent might act as consultant for a situation in which the principal functions as consultee to help a teacher as client in a classroom situation.

A student could be consultant to a teacher consultee in a situation in which the parents are defined as clients because they are accentuating the student's school problems. The student might contribute to problem identification and interventions, with the teacher providing direct service to parents.

The client of a consultation is typically an individual; however, clients also can be a group or team of individuals, such as a family or a within-class group of students. On occasion the client might even be an entire staff, school system, or community. So consultant, consultee, and client roles are interchangeable according to student need and educational circumstance. (See Figure 1-2.)

Some authors stress that the term *collaborative consultation* creates possibilities for a new mix of consultation and collaboration practices, with each participant alternating among the consultant/expert role and the consultee/recipient role as differing knowledge and expertise warrant (Thousand, Villa, Paolucci-Whitcomb, and Nevin, 1992). Thus the solution-finding responsibility is jointly and equally shared.

Benefits of Collaborative School Consultation

School environments that promote collaborative consultation tend to involve all school personnel in the teaching and learning processes. Information is shared and knowledge levels about student characteristics and needs and strategies for meeting those needs are broadened. Importantly, many of the strategies are helpful with other students who have similar but less severe needs. A number of specific benefits of school consultation and collaboration can be anticipated. Several are suggested below.

Meeting the Intent of P.L. 94-142

As stated earlier, Public Law 94-142 stipulates that classroom teachers are responsible for the learning programs of students mainstreamed into their classes, but they are to receive assistance. Consulting teachers help classroom teachers develop repertoires of materials and instructional strategies. Many special education teachers find these practices more productive than racing from one student to another in the resource room as all work on

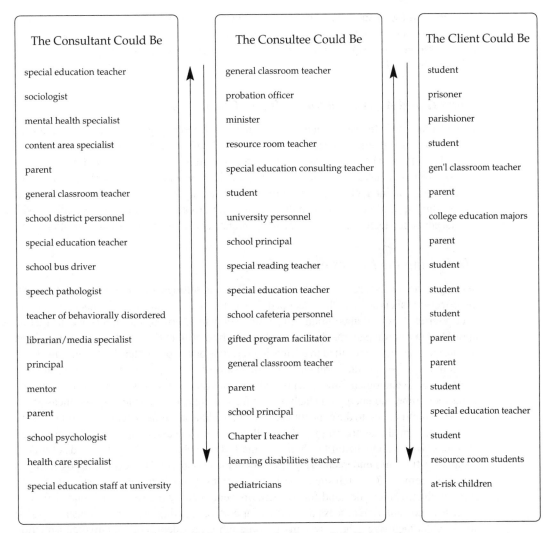

The Consultant Could Be	The Consultee Could Be	The Client Could Be
special education teacher	general classroom teacher	student
sociologist	probation officer	prisoner
mental health specialist	minister	parishioner
content area specialist	resource room teacher	student
parent	special education consulting teacher	gen'l classroom teacher
general classroom teacher	student	parent
school district personnel	university personnel	college education majors
special education teacher	school principal	parent
school bus driver	special reading teacher	student
speech pathologist	special education teacher	student
teacher of behaviorally disordered	school cafeteria personnel	student
librarian/media specialist	gifted program facilitator	parent
principal	general classroom teacher	parent
mentor	parent	student
parent	school principal	special education teacher
school psychologist	Chapter I teacher	student
health care specialist	learning disabilities teacher	resource room students
special education staff at university	pediatricians	at-risk children

FIGURE 1-2   Interchangeable Roles in Consultation and Collaboration

individual assignments. One learning disabilities teacher succinctly put it this way, "In my resource room, by the time I get to the last student, I find that the first student is stuck and has made no progress. So I frantically run through the whole cycle again. Tennis shoes are a must for my job!"

A consulting teacher who assumes an instructional role for a time in the general classroom frees the classroom teacher to study student progress, set up arrangements for special projects, or work intensively with a small group of students. The special education teacher might serve as team teacher, support facilitator, or consultant (Stainback & Stainback, 1989). Effective special education consultants find ways of helping teachers to be confident and successful with special needs students. When general classroom and special education teachers collaborate, each has ownership and involvement in serving special needs. This promotes a sense of responsibility among all teachers for appropriate service to all children (Lieberman, 1984).

Support and Assistance for Inclusive Classrooms

Consultation can help classroom teachers deal more effectively and efficiently with the wide range of individual student needs that they are likely to encounter in inclusive classrooms. As early as 1978, Miller and Sabatino reported that students who are served in consulting teacher programs make academic gains comparable with students in resource rooms, while the teacher-pupil interactions cultivate improved teaching behaviors. Some of the mystique surrounding special education is reduced when classroom teachers become familiar with special education techniques and come to appreciate and understand special education roles.

Minimizing the Effects of Labeling

Serving student needs resourcefully in heterogeneous settings will minimize the stigmatizing effects of labels such as "handicapped," "exceptional," or "disabled." It also can help reduce referrals to remedial programs. In an early study to determine the effects of consultation upon teacher referral patterns over a seven-year period, Ritter (1978) noted that the provision of consultation service resulted in decreasing referrals on the part of teachers over time. Fewer referrals for special education services will mean reduced expenditure for costly and time-consuming psychological assessments and special education interventions. Educators can focus more time and energy on teaching and facilitating and less on testing and measuring.

When introduced to the concept of school consultation, some special education personnel are concerned that after a time they will work themselves out of a job. They fear their positions will be abolished if teachers become fully capable of serving the needs of mildly disabled, gifted, and underachieving students in the classroom. However, this possibility is extremely remote. Research since 1980 demonstrates that, when consultation service is increased, there is more demand for the benefits generated by the service (Friend, 1988). A successful consultation process becomes a supportive tool that teachers increasingly value and use. As inclusive school systems become more prevalent, collaborative consultation will become even more critical for school program success.

Consultation services contribute to the total school program as a bridge between the parallel systems of special education and general education (Greenburg, 1987) and are an effective way of alleviating confusion over goals and relationships of general and special education (Will, 1984). When consultants and consultees collaborate in the educational setting, students are beneficiaries and schools are more nearly the kinds of places the public wants them to be.

Providing Assistance for Administrators

Administrators benefit from collaborative consultation when classroom teachers are efficient in working with a wide range of student needs. Consulting teachers can help ease the load that special education programs impose upon a building administrator and teaching staff. Principals find that it is stimulating to visit and observe in classrooms as team participants collaborate on ways of helping every student succeed in the school and reinforce teacher successes with all of their students. This is for many administrators a welcome change from the typical classroom visitations they make for purposes of teacher evaluation.

Managing the Cost of School Services

The consultation approach is a cost-effective use of school personnel when it enhances teacher skills for preventing learning problems that might otherwise escalate into more serious needs (Idol, 1986; Heron & Kimball, 1988). Students with borderline special needs can be served in classrooms with little or no additional expenditure of time and money. Special education resources also can become developmental capital for needed educational reforms. Through consultation and collaboration, single-case outcomes can be replicated with an entire class or throughout a school. Coordination of diversified school programs, funds, and services is a resource-saving effort that can be carried out by well-prepared school consultants.

Another important and frequently overlooked benefit is the maintenance of continuity in learning programs as students progress through their school experiences. This, too, is a savings in time, energy and resources of the educational staff and often the parents as well.

Providing Impetus for Staff Harmony and School Cohesion

A collaborative consultation approach is a natural system for nurturing harmonious staff interactions. More opportunities are available that allow special education and general education teachers to become part of the complete educational process. Teachers who have become isolated or autonomous in their styles and outlooks often discover that working with other adults for common goals is quite stimulating. Sharing ideas can add to creativity, openendedness, and flexibility in developing educational programs for students with special needs. In addition, more emphasis and coordination can be given to cross-school and long-range planning, with an increased use of outside resources for student needs. School consultation and collaboration also promote nonthreatening systems for evaluating teacher effectiveness.

Becoming a Catalyst for Staff Development

Consulting teachers are catalysts for in-service and staff development. Collaborative consultants can identify areas in which faculty need awareness and information sessions, and coordinate workshops to help all school personnel learn specific educational techniques (McKenzie, Egner, Knight, Perelman, Schneider, & Garvin, 1970).

Just as removal of the catalyst stops a chemical process, so can the absence of consulting teachers halt individualization of curriculum and differentiation of strategies for special needs (Bietau, 1994). Staff development leadership is such a promising aspect of the consulting teacher role that it will be addressed separately in Chapter 12.

Encouraging Parent Satisfaction and Involvement

Parents or guardians of the exceptional student often become extremely frustrated with the labeling, the fragmented curriculum, and the isolation from peers endured by their children. Therefore, they respond enthusiastically when they observe several educators functioning as a team for the student. Their attitudes toward school improve, and they become more involved in planning and carrying through with the interventions (Idol, 1988). They are more eager to share their ideas and help monitor their child's learning. They are particularly supportive when consulting services allow students in special education programs to remain in their neighborhood schools.

Activating Multiplier Effects of Special Services

Multiplier effects provide compelling arguments for the practice of school consultation. They create benefits beyond the immediate situation involving one student and that student's teachers. For example, by collaborating, school personnel are modeling this powerful social tool for their students, who are quite likely to experience collaborative climates in their future workplaces.

Direct services for consultees are one level of positive effects. (See Figure 1-3.) At this level the consultation and collaboration are most likely to have been initiated for one client's need. (Note that a client can be an entity such as a student group, school, family, or community, as well as a single student.) But consultation benefits often extend beyond level 1 of immediate need. At level 2, consultees use information and points of view generated during the collaboration to be more effective in similar but unrelated cases. Both consultant and consultee repertoires of knowledge and skills are enhanced so that they can function more effectively in the future (Brown et al., 1979). When consultation outcomes extend beyond single consultant/consultee situations of levels 1 and 2, the entire school system can be positively affected by level 3 outcomes. Organizational change and increased family involvement are potential results of level 3 outcomes.

Level 1 effects result from the following types of school situations:

> The consultant engages in problem-solving with a high-school teacher to determine ways of helping a severely learning-disabled student master minimum competencies required for graduation.

> The audiologist helps the classroom teacher arrange the classroom environment to enable a hearing-impaired student to function comfortably in the regular classroom setting.

Level 2 effects include these examples:

> The classroom teacher becomes more familiar with the concept of hyperactivity in children, subsequently regarding fewer children as attention-deficit disordered with hyperactivity and adjusting the classroom curriculum to more appropriately address very active children's needs in that classroom setting.

> The classroom teacher becomes comfortable with enrichment activities provided for gifted students through collaboration with the gifted program facilitator and makes enriching activities available to a larger group of very able children in the classroom.

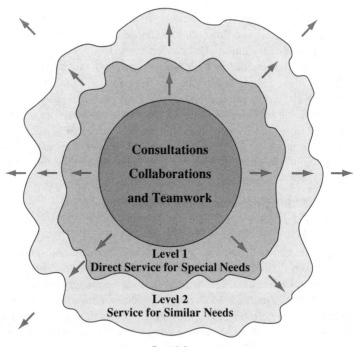

Consultations

Collaborations

and Teamwork

Level 1
Direct Service for Special Needs

Level 2
Service for Similar Needs

Level 3
Service Contributing to Institutional Changes
and Professional Development

FIGURE 1-3   Positive Ripple Effects of Consultation, Collaboration, and Teamwork

Level 3 effects involve these kinds of outcomes:

The efforts toward collaboration and teamwork result in a staff development plan called "Teachers Helping Teachers," during which teachers in a school system provide training for interested colleagues in their areas of expertise.

The school district's emphasis on consultation, collaboration, and teamwork pleases parents who find that their children are receiving more integrated, personalized instruction for their learning needs. The parents become more active and interested in the school's programs.

As discussed earlier, consulting teachers sometimes are concerned that if level 2 and 3 outcomes enable classroom teachers to handle some serious learning needs without their involvement, their positions may be eliminated if funds are reduced. It is important that the consulting role is not regarded as an add-on position to be dispensed with when money and personnel are in short supply but rather as an indispensable component of each school's present and future context.

The use of specialized intervention techniques for many more students than those identified, categorized, and remediated in special education programs is a major benefit of consultation. Multiple benefits (often described as positive ripple effects) that are created by collaborative consultation often can extend well beyond the immediate classroom, because consulting teachers are in a unique position to facilitate interaction among many target groups. These effects that ripple out from mutual planning and problem-solving across grade levels, subject areas, and schools are powerful instruments for initiating positive changes in the educational system. School personnel have increased opportunities for communication, multiple sources of information, broadened perspectives on teaching strategies for special needs, expanded availability of resources, diminished isolation in the classroom, and more involvement with service agencies beyond the school.

Obstacles that Hinder Consultation, Collaboration, and Teamwork

In spite of the anticipated benefits of school consultation, proponents of a collaborative school consultation approach face several major obstacles in initiating the concept within their school contexts. These problems must be recognized and addressed if consultation methods are to succeed. Most certainly, school consultation must not create an iatrogenic effect—a term borrowed from the medical profession to describe medical personnel action or prescription that turns out to be more debilitating to the patient than the illness it was designated to treat. An iatrogenic effect from a school service would cause clients to be in a worse state than they were prior to the service.

The literature for school consultation includes some material on theory and models, methodology, training and practice issues, guidelines and competencies (Heron and Kimball, 1988). However, little information is available on practical applications. Most of the material has been theoretical, focusing upon *why* consultation should occur rather than *how* it can be conducted. Huefner (1988) identifies risks as well as opportunities in a discussion of consultation practices. Johnson, Pugach, and Hammittee (1988) categorize obstacles into pragmatic barriers such as unclear definitions of the consultation process, and conceptual barriers, including a consultant's lack of credibility in the eyes of some classroom teachers.

During a national symposium on school consultation held in Austin, Texas, in 1987, participants focused on driving forces and restraining forces that affect school consultation. They summarized restraining forces as

- Lack of integration for consultation theories and models;
- Lack of consultation research, both basic and applied;
- Non-supportive attitudes toward consultation services;
- Inability to put consultation theory into practice;
- Scarcity of human and material resources to operationalize consultation models;
- Lack of preservice and inservice training in consultation;
- Organizational resistance to consultation; and
- Lack of interdisciplinary collaboration among educators.

Some of the obstacles to school consultation and collaboration loom as formidable barriers. These need to be dismantled before school consultation can take place. Examples of major barriers are issues of ownership, job security, role equality and respect, valuing of adult differences, and willingness to change. Other obstacles appear as hurdles to be vaulted or pushed aside. A hurdle might be teacher autonomy or prohibitive funding structures. Obstacles that are most amenable to adjustment will crop up as stumbling blocks to be noted and then corrected or avoided. In fact, it can be argued that some stumbling blocks are beneficial if they cause people to pause and reflect upon existing conditions and possible methods for improvement. In these cases, they serve as stepping stones to opportunity. Examples of stumbling blocks are the need for time, clarification of roles, and maintaining equitable caseloads.

Training programs in school consultation are needed to cultivate awareness of consultation as an educational tool and to develop effective attitudes and skills among those who will be consultants and consultees. Communication, cooperation, and coordination among administrative and teaching staffs for collaborative consultation must be achieved to establish role expectations and to provide the time and facilities necessary for success. Educators at all school levels, including institutions of higher education, must be involved in preparation for consultation, delineation of roles, implementation of a consultation framework, and assessment and support of consultation and collaboration.

The most significant obstacles to school consultation can be categorized into four groups (see Figure 1-4):

Lack of understanding about roles

Needed:
    Role clarification
    Role parity
    Appropriate role expectations

Lack of framework for consultation and collaboration

Needed:
    Methods for consultation and collaboration
    Resources (time, facilities, supplies)
    Management (organization, record keeping)

Lack of assessment and support of consultation

Needed:
    Evaluation
    Involvement
    Acceptance

Lack of preparation for the roles

Needed:
    Preservice awareness
    Certification and degree programs
    In-service and staff development

FIGURE 1-4   Obstacles to School Consultation and Collaboration

Lack of role definition;

Absence of a framework within which to consult;

Failure to document and evaluate both formal and informal consultations and collaborations; and

Little or no training in consultation skills.

Effective school consultation calls for distinct and equal roles for all participants, and clear expectations regarding those roles. Suitable frameworks, including time, facilities, and structure for the consultation, must be arranged. Training in consultation and collaboration roles is needed at the preservice, inservice, and advanced degree levels. In addition, documentation and evaluation of the consultation and collaboration efforts is a critical component in establishing role clarity and parity.

Consultation Process and Content in the School Context

School consultation combines process skills and content knowledge within the school context of each educational setting. (See Figure 1-5.) Schools have characteristics of hierarchy, subsystems, and rules (Hansen, Himes, & Meier, 1990). The school context is composed of many ecological factors that greatly affect consultation practices, such as community and political structures, cultural and ethnic diversity, the financial climate, personality structures of personnel, and student characteristics. These systems continuously exert pressures on the schools (Gallessich, 1973) and are not always within the control of school personnel, particularly teachers. Lack of organizational sensitivity to school contexts can be disastrous.

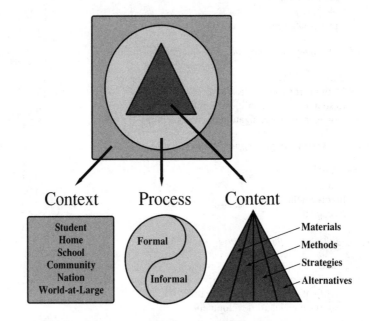

FIGURE 1-5   Components of School Consultation

CONTEXT

Student	Needs, styles, accomplishments, handicaps, interests, achievement levels, social skills, talents, peer status, gender, age, physical development, ability level...
Home	Family constellations, siblings, socio-economic status, cultural identity, family stability, parent involvement, cooperation, support...
School	School philosophy, climate, setting, staff, morale, instructional leadership, staff development, follow-up, modeling and coaching, facilities, support...
Community	Economic level, stability, resources, media, awareness levels partnerships, law and order, neighborhood unity, educational level...
Nation	Public support, citizenship, democracy, educational standards...
World	Peace, diversity, self-sufficiency, models, political conditions, equity, resources...

PROCESS

Formal	Meetings, structured problem-solving sessions, training activities, scheduled communications, planned innovations...
Informal	Conversations, shared responsibilities, compensations for personality differences, idea swapping, spontaneous innovation...

CONTENT

Materials	Books, worksheets, programmed instruction, kits, study aids, computer-based applications, tests, media, learning machines, laboratory equipment, instruments, artifacts...
Methods	Cooperative learning, peer tutoring, grouping arrangements, direct instruction, independent study, computer-assisted instruction, self-directed learning...
Strategies	Test taking practice, behavior managements, sensory augmentation, reinforcement schedules, flexible pacing, curriculum compacting...
Alternatives	Course options, testing alternatives, test-out and dual credit or half credit, revisions of requirements, modification of materials

FIGURE 1-6   Examples of School Consultation Components

The context of the school setting can be categorized into several descriptive areas: student, home, school, community, nation, and world at large. (See Figure 1-6.) Each of these areas affects the ease and efficiency with which consultation can occur. Everyone involved in consultation brings unique experiences and understanding to each collaborative situation (Henning-Stout, 1994). Critical contexts of the educational system in regard to consultation and collaboration include public attitudes, geographic features of the school environment, staff support, financial structure, parent involvement, political action, and legal issues. Characteristics of each school's context must be assessed objectively, understood, and appreciated by the school consultant.

Process skills include but are not limited to communication, coordination, and cooperation. They can occur in formal or informal settings. (Refer again to Figure 1-6.) With these skills, the consultant and consultee listen to each other and interact, seek to identify the problem, share information and ideas, resolve conflicts, conduct observations, develop courses of action, coordinate activities, follow through on results, and assess the outcomes for further planning and implementation. Process skills are described by Idol (1990) as the artful base of consultation.

Content skills include selection of materials and resources, proficiency with a variety of teaching methods and strategies, and awareness of learning options and alternatives. (Refer again to Figure 1-6.) It is too often the unfortunate case that consultees jump ahead to content, "buying" a quick remedy for the immediate situation rather than identifying the problem and collaborating on viable plans to resolve the problem. The content or knowledge base a consultant brings to the consulting process is described by Idol (1990) as the scientific base of consultation. Scientific bases and artful bases must be merged to produce school consultants and consulting teachers who can practice the scientific art of classroom consultation (Idol, 1990).

Consultation, Collaboration, and Teamwork as a Synergy of Context, Process, and Content

Effective school consultation results from the interaction of process skills and content methodology within the immediate school context. Contexts of a school setting are a given in the assessment of the educational scene, and schools without content would be unnecessary. Can there be content-free processes for consultation? No, because process is composed of content (Tharp, 1975). This is one of the greatest strengths of consultation. Process can serve content to provide services for students in each school context.

Collaboration that occurs in conjunction with consultation requires harmonious, efficient teamwork. Consultants and consultees meet to assess the student's situation, develop courses of action to help the student, to carry out the actions, and to follow through on the results. Each party contributes points of view, information, and suggestions for resolution of the situation.

Thus, consultation with collaboration is not an oxymoron, but *synergy*—"a behavior of whole systems unpredicted by the behavior of their parts taken separately" (Fuller, 1975, p. 3). When teamwork is effective, there is synergy. Each member contributes expertise both directly and indirectly, without superior-inferior connotations to develop educational plans within a climate of equality.

Process skills and content methodology are ineffectual and useless unless grounded in the specifics of each particular school context. For example, a process-based educational approach that is exclusively process specific will be perceived as "talk, talk, talk—never mind about what" (Britt, 1985) without firm roots in the consultees' content skills. Content-based consultation alone will rarely move beyond level l effects. But a synergistic combination of process skills, content methodology, and school context considerations can set the stage for effective consultation, collaboration, and teamwork to help students with special needs succeed in school.

Tips for Consulting and Collaborating

1. Be knowledgeable about the history and outcomes of school reform movements.
2. Keep up to date on educational issues and concerns.
3. Be aware of education legislation and litigation.
4. Survey the school context for ways to consult.
5. Attend to attitudes and norms within the school context.
6. Refrain from criticizing the school system. Instead, work within the system to bring about needed changes.
7. Do not wait to be approached for consultation and collaboration.
8. Try not to press for your own solutions to school needs, educators' needs, or student needs. Strive instead for collaborative efforts to problem-solve together.
9. Do not carry tales from one setting to another.
10. Refrain from assuming that colleagues are waiting around to be "saved."

Chapter Review

1. Educators have not developed positive attitudes toward consultation and collaboration. Teachers tend to function autonomously in their classrooms without requesting help from outside resources, and administrators provide few incentives for consultation and collaboration among their school personnel. Teacher preparation programs have not featured consultation and collaboration skills.
2. School reform movements that highlight the need for consultation and collaboration include the Regular Education Initiative and restructuring efforts, curriculum modifications for students with special needs, transition from preschool into school, and transition from school into the adult world.
3. An increasing number of professional educators and parents contend that students with disabilities should not be excluded from their neighborhood school programs and student peer groups. This movement, called *inclusion,* is another effort to define and operationalize the concept of least restrictive environment. It is tied to broader school reform movements that have evolved over the last two decades.
4. School consultation can be described as interaction in which school personnel and parents confer and collaborate as a team within the school context to identify learning and behavioral needs, and to plan, implement, and evaluate educational programs for serving those needs. The school consultant is a facilitator of effective communication, cooperation, and coordination who confers and collaborates with other school personnel and parents as a team to serve the special learning and behavioral needs of students.
5. A consultant, consultee (or mediator), and client (or target) in one school-related situation may function in any of the other capacities under different circumstances. For example, a special education teacher might be a consultant for one situation, yet in another situation function as the consultee. The student is usually but not always the client, or target, for the direct and indirect services provided by consultee and consultant.
6. Many opportunities are available for schools, parents, and students as a result of school consultation and collaboration, including service for a wider range of the student population who are at risk or have special learning needs; development of teacher competency for solving varied learning problems in different situations; increased ownership and involvement of teachers in helping all students succeed; reduced labeling and stigmatizing of students; and increased parent involvement in children's learning activities.

7. Although collaborative school consultation produces many benefits for schools, educators, and students, there are obstacles to be overcome in using this educational tool. These obstacles include lack of understanding about the consultant role; lack of a framework for consultations to occur; absence of documentation and evaluation of consultations, collaborations, and team efforts; and the need for training in process and context skills of consultation.

8. Consultation is a synergy of school context, process skills, and skills in content methodology.

To Do and Think About

1. Using material in this chapter, a dictionary, interviews, recollections from teaching experiences, discussion with colleagues or classmates, and any other pertinent references, formulate a description and philosophy about school consultation that reflects your viewpoint at this time.

2. Make a list of the positive aspects, and another list of the negative aspects, about the concept of inclusion. You may want to specify whether your list is indicative of inclusion for those with mild disabilities only, or full (total) inclusion for all special-needs students in regular classrooms.

3. Brainstorm with a group to list current issues and major problems in education. (See Chapter 5 for a discussion of brainstorming if you are not familiar with the technique.) After generating as many ideas as possible, mark those that seem most amenable to solutions afforded by consultation, collaboration, and teamwork. You might want to * those that in the past have "belonged" to special education, and discuss what part general education plays in dealing with those issues now.

4. List all the responsibilities you can think of that a teacher typically performs during the course of a school year. Use your recollections of student days, college coursework, student teaching, and any teaching experience that you have had. You will probably develop a long list of a wide range of duties and activities, and it most likely will include opportunities with potential for using consultation and collaboration tools.

   If you team up with other teachers in various grade levels, content areas and specialized roles to do this exercise, the combined lists could become be a colorful and impressive mosaic of teaching responsibilities. The process itself will be an example of teamwork, with each person adding information from his or her own perspectives and experiences. And so—collaborative consultation!

5. Using your list generated in activity 4, look for areas of teacher responsibility in which consultation and collaboration efforts might take place appropriately and helpfully for students with special needs. For example, under the managerial responsibility of ordering books and supplies, teams of teachers might collaborate to pool library money and plan orders of materials that address special needs of students for remediation and enrichment. In this way, shared decision-making in selecting resources could lead to shared planning and implementation of programs that use the resources collaboratively.

6. If you could "start all over" and make schools the way you want them, what would it take to make your ideal school a reality?

7. What questions or concerns about consultation and collaboration are uppermost in your mind at the end of this chapter?

For Further Reading

Educational leadership. (December 1994/January 1995). *52*(4). Topical issue on the inclusive school.

Hansen, J. C., Himes, B. S., & Meier, S. (1990). *Consultation: Concepts and practices.* Englewood Cliffs, NJ: Prentice-Hall.

Henning-Stout, M. (1994). Consultation and connected knowing: What we know is determined by the questions we ask. *Journal of Educational and Psychological Consultation, 5,*(1), 5–21.

Hoy, W. K. (1990). Organizational climate and culture: A conceptual analysis of the school work place. *Journal of Educational and Psychological Consultation, 1*(2), 149–168.

Idol, L., Paolucci-Whitcomb, P., & Nevin, A. (1986). *Collaborative consultation.* Austin, TX: PRO-ED.

Maeroff, G. I. (1993). Building teams to rebuild schools. *Phi Delta Kappan, 74* (7), 512–519.

Morsink, C. V., Thomas, C. C., & Correa, V. I. (1991). *Interactive teaming: Consultation and collaboration in special programs.* New York: Macmillan.

Reynolds, M. C., & Birch, J. W. (1988). *Adaptive mainstreaming: A primer for teachers and principals.* (3rd ed.). New York: Longman.

Stainback, S., Stainback, W., & Forest, M. (1989). *Educating all students in the mainstream of regular education.* Baltimore, MD: Brookes.

Chapter 2

Roles and Responsibilities in Consultation, Collaboration, and Teamwork

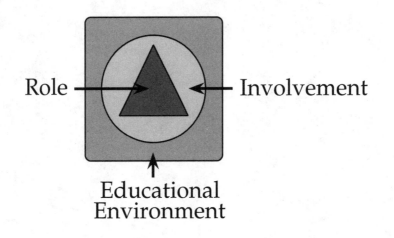

Role ——→ ▲ ←—— Involvement

Educational
Environment

Introduction

Major concerns of educators about consultation, collaboration, and teamwork in schools center around the roles, framework, evaluation, and preparation of personnel who will be engaging in these interactions. Their concerns are reflected in questions such as

> Who am I in this role?
> How do I carry out responsibilities of the role?
> How do I know whether I am succeeding?
> How do I prepare for the role?

A collaborative consultant role creates concomitant roles—the consultee who confers with the consultant, support personnel who become part of the consultation service, and the client who benefits from the process. These participatory roles must be understood and managed if school consultation is to be a useful tool. More educators would be inclined to support school consultation if they knew the parameters of the roles and could develop basic profiles of their responsibilities.

In order for collaborative consultation to succeed, central administrators and policymakers must first authenticate the need for consultant and consultee roles. Then building level administrators must stress the significance of the consultant role and ensure consultant parity within their staff. Teachers will need to support consulting teachers with their cooperation and not impede consultation and collaboration through apathy or resistance. Related services personnel and support personnel should be integrated into a school consultation context. Parents must receive information about the service and assurance that this type of service is appropriate for their child's needs. Ultimately, community members must be aware of the long-range purposes and probable benefits of indirect special services before they can be expected to support and pay for them.

Focusing Questions

1. What are the major concerns of school personnel about their roles in consultation and collaboration?
2. How does a collaborative consultant clarify the role and cultivate appropriate expectations of others toward that role? What other roles are created by school consultation, collaboration, and teamwork?
3. How do educators go about implementing and carrying out consultation services? How will they know that the consultation service is meeting student needs and creating positive ripple effects within the school context?
4. How can they prepare for their roles in consultation?
5. What competencies characterize effective consultants and consultees, collaborators, and team members?

Key Terms in the Chapter

caseload	role clarification
competencies	role delineation
evaluation	role parity
onedownsmanship	time
preservice teachers	

Initiating School Consultation, Collaboration, and Teamwork

Educational reforms, social concerns, and economic issues may have convinced educators that consultation, collaboration, and teamwork are promising practices for helping students with special needs, but conversion of paper plans and philosophies to real-world roles and

Scenario

The following scene takes place in a school district conference room, where three special education teachers are talking before their special education director arrives for a planning meeting.

LEARNING DISABILITIES TEACHER: I understand we're here to decide how we're going to inform staff and parents about the consultation and collaboration practices that we'll be implementing soon. But I think we'd better figure out first just what it is we *will* be doing.

BEHAVIORAL DISORDERS TEACHER: Definitely. I have a really basic question. What do I do the first day, and the first week, as a consulting teacher? I know you had some training in collaboration and consulting for your former job in another state, but this is new to the rest of us.

GIFTED EDUCATION TEACHER: Good question. And I've been thinking about all those personalities and teaching styles and subject areas we will be interacting with. They won't all like or want the same things.

LEARNING DISABILITIES TEACHER: I doubt this is something we can pick up and put into place overnight or by next week. From what I did learn about collaborative consultation in my former job, the secret for success lies in using good process skills.

GIFTED EDUCATION TEACHER: Yes, but at the same time we have to consider the content that each student needs to learn. So I'm a bit apprehensive about this new role, but I'm looking forward to having it available, too.

BEHAVIORAL DISORDERS TEACHER: Yes, I've suspected for some time now that our present methods of dealing with learning and behavior problems are not as effective and efficient as they should be. I agree that we must be optimistic about the benefits students *and* their teachers could receive from this.

responsibilities is not simple. The questions put forth in the scenario's school district conference room reflect real-world concerns that must be addressed thoughtfully:

> Where do I begin as a school consultant?
>
> What do I do the first day on the job?
>
> Let me see a sample schedule for the first week.
>
> Where am I to be headed by the end of the year?

Other questions and concerns that are likely to surface include

> Will I have the opportunity to work with students at all? That is why I chose teaching as a career.
>
> Where's my room? Will I get office space and supplies?

Can I fit at least a small group of students into that space for some group work?

I need training for consultation, but where do I get it?

How will I be evaluated in this position, and by whom?

If consulting prepares consultees for direct delivery of services for special needs, will I be working myself out of a job?

Participants in consultation and collaboration must be able to voice their concerns, confusions, and feelings of inadequacy as they sort out the requirements of new roles. School administrators have a responsibility to initiate and encourage intensive discussion of questions and issues among school personnel who are asked to embark upon significantly different service delivery approaches.

School consultation *per se* is not a new concept. The literature includes material on theory and models, methodology, training and practice issues, guidelines and competencies (Heron & Kimball, 1988). However, most of it is theoretical, focusing upon *why* consultation should occur, rather than upon *how* it can be conducted. Too little information is available on practical applications. Professional dialogues and practical materials are needed in order to cultivate positive attitudes and effective skills among consultants and consultees. Communication, cooperation, and coordination of administrative and teaching responsibilities will help establish role expectations and create a framework for implementing and carrying out effective school consultation.

Identifying Consultation, Collaboration, and Team Roles

As discussed in Chapter 1, individuals who serve as consultant (specialist), consultee (mediator), and client (target) in one consultative situation may exchange roles under different circumstances. For example, a special education teacher might be a consultant for one situation and consultee in another. The student is typically the client, or target, for the direct and indirect services of consultee and consultant, but in some cases the student could be a consultee or consultant. Consultation may be initiated by a special education teacher, school administrator, supervisor, or support service professional who has determined that a student's learning or behavior need requires attention from a collaborative team. It also might be initiated by a teacher, parent, or student acting in a consultee role. In either case, both parties—consultant and consultee—share responsibility for working out a plan to help the client (Heron & Harris, 1982.)

Roles and responsibilities may vary among individuals from situation to situation, but with appropriate role delineation, a collaborative spirit can prevail. Collaboration to achieve a common goal generally produces more beneficial results than isolated efforts by an individual. The whole of the combined efforts then is greater than the sum of its parts (Slavin, 1988). It is the basic idea that two heads are better than one, and several heads are better yet. The consultation process channels each individual's strengths and talents toward serving the client's needs.

Practitioners who have had experience as consultants reveal several problems that have surfaced during their work. They include

Losing touch with the students;

Uncertainty about what and how to communicate with resistant consultees;

Being perceived as a teacher's aide, "go-fer," quick-fix expert, or jack-of-all-trades;

Seeing consultation regarded as a tutorial for students;

Territoriality of professional colleagues;

Rigid curriculum and assessment procedures;

Unrealistic expectations;

Not having enough information and materials to share;

Being considered a show-off, or a bossy expert;

Professional politeness, but not acceptance;

Difficulty managing time and resources;

Lack of training;

Being assigned an overload caseload;

Too many "hats" to wear in the role;

Indecision about designing and setting up consultation methods;

And, most of all, a reluctance to change.

Key Elements in Consulting and Collaborating

Four major categories of roles and responsibilities for collaborative school consultation are displayed in Figure 2-1:

- Role delineation;
- Framework for the consultation and collaboration;
- Evaluation of consultation and collaboration; and
- Preparation for the roles.

Within the four categories, twelve key elements must be addressed in order to build workable strategies. Sequence of these twelve elements is critical. In many school contexts, educators begin "too late in the day," metaphorically speaking, to implement consultation, collaboration, and teamwork. Involvement and acceptance—the "four P.M. and five P.M." positions in the clock-like Figure 2-1—cannot be starting points. If they are, failure of school consultation is all but assured. Instead, educators in all educational contexts—administrators, university instructors, teachers, and support staff—must begin "very early in the morning" (see approximately the "six A.M." position in Figure 2-1) to prepare for the collaborative school consultation roles. This preparation should take place at preservice, graduate, and in-service levels.

Role Delineation in Collaborative School Consultation

The starting point for school personnel in school consultation, collaboration, and teamwork is careful *preparation* for those roles. However, in this book, role delineation will be discussed first to emphasize the purpose of this critical preparation. A specific school role such as counselor, general classroom teacher, specialist in learning disabilities, speech pathologist, or facilitator for the gifted program does not designate a consultation role. The consultation role is created by the circumstance that targets the need. The consultant, consultee, or client

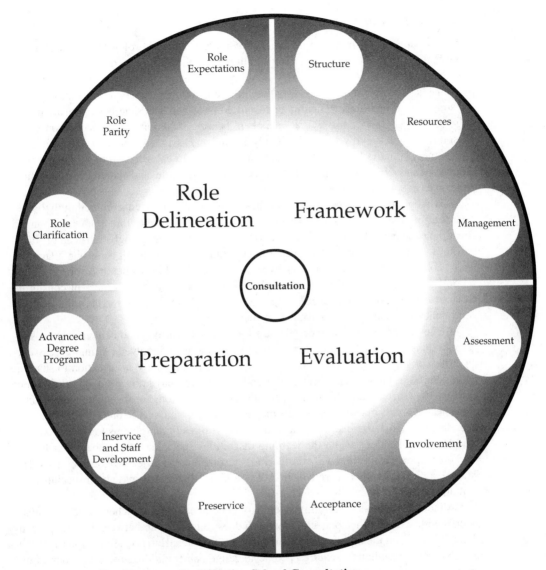

FIGURE 2-1   Key Elements for Effective School Consultation

role might be taken by a parent who provides information to a school administrator, or a learning disabilities teacher who helps a coach assess a student athlete's learning problem, or a mentor who provides gifted program facilitator material for class use by a gifted student.

A consultee teams up with and collaborates with the consultant to provide direct service for helping students succeed in school. The client role is delineated by the identified need or problem. As the need or problem is identified, the client role is designated. This concept reflects the contemporary approach to special services, where student needs, not student labels, determine the service and delivery method, and services are made available to address every need.

Role Clarification

The most important element in role delineation is clarification of roles. Until educators become familiar with the concepts of consultation and collaboration and ways they can participate as partners and team members, doubt and confusion about roles may exist. School personnel sometimes are not sure why they have consulting teachers or what these people are supposed to be doing. A facilitator for gifted programs who had been consultant in a large urban high school for several years kept hearing variations on the same concern— "Just how do you spend your day with only 30 students assigned to you? After all they *are* fast learners." So the facilitator developed a job matrix to categorize the planning, implementation, and evaluation aspects and expectations of the role, and shared it with teaching colleagues and administrators (Hay, 1984).

Classroom teachers may blame their heavy caseloads of students on seemingly lighter caseloads of consulting teachers. One high school English teacher told a newly appointed consulting teacher, "If you were back in your classroom teaching English instead of 'facilitating' for a few high-ability students, my own student load wouldn't be so big." Paradoxically, consulting teachers often have excessively high caseloads when travel time among schools is taken into account. If the caseload is too great, the effectiveness of consulting service will be diminished severely, for there will be little time for the coordination and communication so critical to consultation success.

Achieving coherent instructional plans for students' learning and behavioral needs requires extensive knowledge of role responsibilities among all involved (Allington & Broikou, 1988). A classroom teacher and a reading specialist may have information to share in addressing a struggling reader's strengths and deficits, yet may know relatively little about each other's curriculum, educational priorities, or expectations for the student. They must coordinate their efforts, or those efforts may be counterproductive. In one unfortunate case, a reading specialist was instructing a fifth grader with reading problems to slow down and read more deliberately, while the learning disabilities specialist was encouraging him to read much more rapidly and was considering referring him for gifted program services. The student, a pleasant and cooperative child, was trying valiantly to please both specialists simultaneously.

Although there has been minimal study of general education teachers' roles as collaborators with special educators, some research does suggest a gap between teacher perceptions of actual and ideal performance in collaborative roles. Harris (1993) emphasizes that collaborative consultation requires people to relinquish traditional roles in order to exchange skills and rotate assignments in ways that expand educational experiences for both students and the adults involved.

Consultees may question a consultant's ability to address their unique classroom situation, especially if the consultant is young and inexperienced. As one classroom teacher put it when asked about involving the special education consulting teacher, "I'd never ask for *her* help. What does she know about a full classroom of students? She's never had more than five or six at a time, and she never has taught in a regular classroom." Keller (1981) describes with irony some of the more common perceptions of resource teacher roles: the "invisible woman" who seldom ventures out of her room; the "fifth wheel" who is not taken seriously; the "new fellow on the block" who is perceived as an expensive extra providing no visible help to others; the "sweet young thing" just out of graduate school with limited classroom experience; and "Mr. or Ms. Wizard" who is supposed to work magic and fix children. While not all resource or consulting teachers suffer from such characterizations, the possibilities are there.

APPLICATION 2.1   Role Clarification

How to Begin

1. Read, study, think, interview others, and complete coursework if possible, to gain information and skills for the role.
2. Formulate a personal philosophy of and commitment to school consultation, collaboration, and teamwork.
3. Meet with central administrators of your school(s) to listen to their perceptions of this role.
4. If an advisory council is available, engage the members in discussion about consultation and collaboration roles. This council should include general and special education teachers, support personnel, administrators, parents, and other community leaders.
5. Meet with each building administrator to whom you are assigned, to practice responsive listening (see Chapter 6 for techniques) and learn their viewpoints. This is a *very important* step.
6. After meeting with all principals, reorganize your own thoughts and ideas, and gather more information if necessary.
7. Develop a tentative role description and goals based on administrators' views as well as your own perspective.
8. Return to central administration, trying out your role description and goals with them, and revise if necessary.
9. Return to building administrators to share the revised package and obtain their approval and support. Again, this is *very* important.
10. After honing your document to a concise format, put it up for discussion, explaining it to teaching staff and nonteaching staff and refining it even further, based on their comments.
11. Meet with parent groups to inform them about school consultation service and solicit their opinions.
12. Keep stressing the opportunities and benefits inherent in collaboration and teamwork enterprises.
13. Work out a master schedule for your role, and distribute it to administrators whose attendance centers will be affected.
14. Have an open house in your work area, with refreshments if possible, and distribute handouts that tell your goals and schedule.
15. Post your schedule for access by teachers, support staff, and especially secretaries.
16. Conduct needs sensing and needs assessment surveys to find out what school personnel and parents want to have happen. If appropriate, ask students, too. (See Chapter 12 for techniques.)
17. Ask for time during in-service or staff development meetings to discuss the program.
18. Begin to work first with receptive, enthusiastic teachers as consultees.
19. Begin right away to log consultations and related activities, for accountability and evaluation.
20. Solicit and welcome input from all, continually refining and reclarifying the role.

Role Parity

Along with role ambiguity and misunderstanding, school consultants may feel an absence of role parity. They may feel as if they do not belong to any one school or faculty. They may feel minimally important to students and the educational system. They also may complain of isolation from general classroom teachers because of differing responsibilities and from their specialty colleagues because of distance and schedules.

Substitutes may not be provided for consulting teachers when they are absent. In fact, these teachers may be pulled out of their own roles on occasion to substitute for absent classroom teachers or to perform other tasks that come up suddenly. Consulting teachers have been asked to guide visitors on a school tour, to drive the school bus, and to perform secretarial tasks. Meanwhile, classroom teachers are not going to wait with open arms for consulting personnel to come and save them. Inevitably, school bells ring, classroom doors open, and the school day commences. Life, and school, will go on every day for students and their teachers with or without support from others. All of this conveys a message of diminished parity for the consulting role and a subtle or not-so-subtle impression of non-importance.

Stress and burnout can result from an absence of role clarity and role parity. Teachers who feel as if they are second-class colleagues, not accepted or appreciated as a vital part of the staff, may develop defenses that erode their effectiveness. Some who travel extensively among schools in their cars have been dubbed "wind-shield" personnel. These problems are accentuated by the misconception that consultants have no ownership in student welfare and development. Students served indirectly by the consultant are not viewed as "belonging" to the consultant. Therefore, ongoing recognition and reinforcement of consulting teacher contributions toward student success are important for credibility of the role and morale of the educator.

Role Expectations

Sometimes colleagues have unreasonable expectations for the consultant role, rather like the Mr./Ms. Wizard situation mentioned earlier, and expect instant success and miraculous student progress in a very short while. When results with students are slower than the consultees have hoped, or do not happen at all, their attitudes may range from guarded skepticism to open disapproval of the consultation approach. A school consultant cannot be a panacea for every student's difficulties. Acknowledging this reality helps avoid another barrier—the ill-conceived notion that consulting teachers are going to threaten job security by replacing resource room staff and other support and ancillary personnel.

Educators may expect too much, or too little, from the consulting role. They may wish to see results too soon, or neglect to monitor results and then let ineffective service drag on too long. Consultees may exploit consulting service by expecting the consultant to "fix" the student, and, if this does not happen, then downplay consultation as a failure and collaboration as a flop. Consulting teachers may expect to work, and want to work, with students only and not with adults. "I was trained to work with kids, and that's what I enjoy," confided one consultant whose assigned role was providing indirect service only. Unrealistic and unreasonable expectations must be set aside in the early planning stages of school consultation methods. Consultants must set reasonable goals for themselves and not try to do too much.

APPLICATION 2.2   Building Role Parity

Becoming Part of the School Team

1. Get involved in each building where scheduled. Accept responsibility for lunch, bus, playground duty. Offer to help during book fairs, school carnivals, ball games, as much as time and energy will allow.
2. Don't be seen around the building doing nothing, or *seeming* to be doing nothing. Spending time in the library to locate resources for a consultee or student may be misperceived by others as recreational reading. This is not intended to discourage the activity, but to urge that the purpose of the activity be made clear to those who might like to minify or challenge the role.
3. Invite colleagues and parents to your room. Have student work displayed, and occasionally serve refreshments. One resource room teacher for behavioral disorders was disappointed that no teachers ever came to her room. So she began a 4:00 exercise class there for 15 minutes daily. As her room soon became the hub of after-school activity, colleagues also became much more knowledgeable about her students' progress in the resource room and their special needs in the classroom.
4. Avoid hierarchical relationships by practicing the communicative art of "onedownsmanship" (Conoley & Conoley, 1982). This is the opposite of the oneupmanship demeanor of being an expert and having a superior role.
5. If you have any choice in the matter, locate your work space in the mainstream of the school. Of course, consultee and client rights to privacy and confidentiality must be protected, but when consulting teachers are located at the far ends of hallways they are easily isolated and ignored. One consulting teacher expressed his frustration in feeling cut off from the life of the school. His room was in a most out-of-the-way location. "I am viewed as that teacher over there they occasionally send kids to," he said, "so I have tried to make myself visible and available before and after school."
6. Promote the value of consultation in education just as it is valued in the medical and legal professions. The "second opinion" is sought widely in these other important areas of life, but a teacher often is expected to handle problems by relying solely on his or her own resources.
7. Eat lunch with other staff members, and interact just enough, but not too much, in the teacher workroom. (See Chapter 12 for more about the "teachers' lounge.")
8. Ask teachers for their advice on educational issues and encourage them to demonstrate for you some of their favorite techniques. However, do not share their favorites with others unless you receive permission to do so.
9. Dress for the school and the occasion. Variables such as high/low status, titles, and clothes have a significant impact on consultation effectiveness (Kratochwill & Van Someren, 1985). One consulting teacher confided that she was having trouble being accepted by one particular school's staff. She approached the problem straight-on and asked what she was doing wrong. The reply surprised her. "You don't come here to *work* like the rest of us. You come in a suit and heels, all dressed up, to advise, observe, and supervise." She quickly altered her style of dress and was rewarded with changed attitudes at that school. In sharing her story with another consultant, the second replied, "Yes, I learned to do that. I have two schools, and, luckily for me, the colleagues who like to dress up are in my morning school. At noon I whip off the earrings and accessories, and slip on tennis shoes. Then I fit in at both places. It paid off for me."

Continued

APPLICATION 2.2   *Continued*

10. The golden question to ask of any colleague is this: "What can I do for you and your students *that you don't have the time and materials to do?*" Compare that question with any comment that might imply, "What can I do that you don't have the expertise to do?" After asking what you can do to help the busy, overworked, classroom-bound teacher, then suggest that you both talk about the need and how you can help. This is the starting point for the collaborative ethic and team effort.

The team approach may be awkward for an educator at first, not only for a consultant, but for the consultee as well. Sometimes the most difficult part of a support role is backing out once the consultee experiences success in meeting the client's needs (Stainback & Stainback, 1988). When the consultee no longer needs intensive support and assistance, the consultant should reiterate this point to herself or himself, "It *would* be wonderful to solve all the problems so that I eventually work myself out of a job." Although as discussed earlier, this is extremely unlikely to happen; the more successful the consultation services become, the more the teachers and administrators seem to value them for their immediate contribution and long-range positive ripple effects.

Consultation may not be the immediate choice of service delivery for students with extreme learning and behavioral problems. Many believe that students with severe emotional or behavioral disorders will continue to need more supportive environments than any regular classrooms can possibly provide (O'Neil, 1994). Data fail to support the premise that special education service for behavioral disorders can be reduced by interventions such as cooperative learning, peer tutoring, and involvement of consulting teachers in general educational settings. Braaten, Kauffman, Braaten, Polsgrove, & Nelson (1988) emphasize the need of teachers of behavior-disordered students for additional instructional resources, including staff, to handle dangerously disruptive behavior. They also emphasize the rights of other students for a safe and supportive learning environment. Severely disruptive behavior can result in rejection by peers and intolerance from teachers. This realization fuels one of the most controversial aspects of the inclusion concept. The public concern that this issue generated was accelerated by the 1993 award-winning movie "Educating Peter" shown on commercial television throughout the United States.

On the other hand, special education teachers who adopt a consulting teacher approach often find that colleagues become more understanding and accepting of their students and more willing to include them in the school mainstream. Some teachers have practiced informal consultation for many years as part of their special education roles. One teacher of students with behavior disorders implemented a consulting model in which she structured her responsibilities into three categories: students who spend the day in the mainstream, students who spend part of each day in the resource room, and students with less troublesome behaviors who are not staffed into the behavioral disorders program. She outlined her goals as follows (Pelletier, 1982, personal correspondence):

For students in the mainstream

- Daily contact with their teachers to provide support and handle problems immediately;
- Maintenance of behavior management systems for the student until the teacher feels they are no longer necessary;
- Parent contact to complement the teacher's contact;
- Coordination of planning with principal, social worker, special subject teachers, parents, community agencies;
- Direct service to student as needed, to help with assignments and interpersonal relationships; and
- Observation to monitor progress.

For students who attend the resource room

- Daily contact with classroom teacher;
- Monitoring system for behavior, designed with the classroom teacher in order to be responsive to the classroom management style and to the needs of the student;
- Planned direct service in the resource room;
- Crisis intervention;
- Parent contact, along with that by classroom teacher;
- Observations.

For students with less problematic behaviors

- Demonstration of intervention measures such as charting for classroom teachers;
- Sharing materials for specific academic needs;
- Information on school and community resources;
- Observations; and
- Participation in staffings.

This teacher commented that it was surprising to see on paper just how many aspects of consultation can apply to the special education teacher, especially one who serves behaviorally disordered children. In today's world of immense risk for children—fetal alcohol syndrome, prenatal effects of drugs, violence in society, fragmentation of the family, poverty, and much more, the need for the kinds of interventions this teacher has set up is profound. As stressed earlier, it would be foolhardy and myopic to suggest that consultants and consulting teachers will work themselves out of their jobs any time in the foreseeable future.

The involvement of as many school personnel as possible, through needs assessments, interviews, staff development, and both formal and informal communications, will minimize unwarranted expectations for consulting roles. Building in success through collaborations with more receptive and cooperative colleagues at first will generate confidence in the consultant and respect for the program.

Educators sometimes avoid collaborating because they feel the need to remain separate and to be independently visible. In too many instances jobs and professional identities depend on separate systems (Shepard, 1987). This entrenches role separatism. Unless school personnel are prepared for consultation and are involved in implementation of the plan, they may maximize the concern about potential problems and underestimate the power this educational service can generate when conducted appropriately.

Framework for School Consultation, Collaboration, and Teamwork

The framework element for school consultation, collaboration, and teamwork calls for structures to engage in consultation, time and facilities in which to meet, and management of the details, so consultation is as convenient and nonintrusive as possible.

Structure

Consultants need a structure within which to carry out their roles and responsibilities. Chapter 3 will set the stage for developing structures (note the plural) in which to conduct consultation, collaboration, and teamwork. However, for now, it is one thing to design a hypothetical method of consultation, quite another to design multiple methods for different situations, and an even greater challenge to select and put into motion the right method for each situation. This intricate task is easier if preceded by role clarification and assurance of role parity and appropriate role expectations.

The consultant will want to formulate several methods for consultation and collaboration in a variety of grade levels, subject areas, special needs categories, and school, community, and family contexts. The consultation structure should attend to the context of the system (such as school, neighborhood, family, athletic, or business arena). It also should include perspectives such as models, which will be discussed in Chapter 3. Consultants need not hesitate to design their own consultation method through trial and error in order to fit that model to school needs. Polling teachers to find out how they would use a consultant for their students is a good way to begin. Studying and observing structures from other school systems also is helpful.

Resources

One of the most overwhelming obstacles to school consultation is lack of time for consultation to occur. The scarcity of time is a major deterrent to success of the collaborative consultation process (Johnson, Pugach & Hammittee, 1988; Idol-Maestas & Ritter, 1985; Speece & Mandell, 1980; McLoughlin & Kelly, 1982). Idol (1986) recommends that resource teachers have at least one-third of their school time available for consultations. In an earlier study by Neel (1981), 48 percent of the special education teachers queried reported that they have no time scheduled for consultation and are expected to provide consultation services beyond regularly scheduled teaching hours. Most often they must use their own planning time for consultation, which is not an ideal way to enhance attitudes toward the consultation approach.

Many special education teachers and classroom teachers report that their school day is simply not designed to accommodate collaboration (Stainback & Stainback, 1988; Idol-Maestas, 1983). Even if the consultant can arrange and coordinate a schedule for meeting with consultees and following up on outcomes, it can be next-to-impossible to arrange

APPLICATION 2.3   Fulfilling Role Expectations

Living Up to Expectations

1. Provide colleagues with information that helps them see the fallacy of the "quick fix" for complex learning and behavior problems. Practical information written in realistic terms for practitioners will be most effective.
2. Promote an exchange-of-roles day in which consultants teach the class, and teachers observe, plan modifications, and consult with others.
3. Review goals with consultees, revise the objectives, and document successes, no matter how small they might seem.
4. Discourage any tendency of colleagues to regard the consultants as supervisors, evaluators, or therapists. Pugach and Johnson (1989) identify a major problem in achieving parity within collaborative models as the tendency among specialists to take on the expert role and disregard experienced classroom teachers as resources for students' special needs. They report that one candid specialist said in reference to classroom teachers, "Why doesn't anyone ask about all the things I have learned from *them?*"
5. Refrain from making any recommendations that conflict with administrative policy or teacher values.
6. When a consultee wishes only to have a student removed from the classroom, *right now,* just pretend not to hear, and instead suggest something that the consultee, or you and the consultee together, might try.
7. Know content areas well for the students about whom you consult. Also, be knowledgeable about regulations and recommendations governing special education, education for students at risk of failure, and school reform movements.
8. Develop a newsletter for school personnel and parents to inform readers, without breach of privacy or confidentiality, about program activities, educational issues, materials, and home/school partnerships, taking care not to identify individuals.
9. Seek out and provide resources for teachers and parents.
10. Continue to read, study, attend conferences, and take courses in consultation and related professional development.
11. Teach students in or out of classrooms where feasible.
12. Demonstration-teach for teachers who request. (Make the offer if no requests are forthcoming.)
13. Observe in classrooms, always following up with the teacher very soon. (See Chapter 7 for observation techniques.)
14. Maintain contact with parents.
15. Observe students outside the classroom (playground, lunch, extracurricular events) to get a different perspective.
16. Make attractive bulletin boards that complement the goals of consultation and collaboration, stressing teamwork and partnerships.
17. With a colleague or two or three, brainstorm periodically for ways to improve services and enhance collaborative efforts among educators.
18. Reach out to more reluctant colleagues, asking for their views, and offering materials, information, and assistance as it fits into their plans.
19. Encourage collaborative staff development activities and partnerships such as "Teachers Helping Teachers."

Continued

APPLICATION 2.3   *Continued*

20. Find texts and basals that work best in collaborative efforts.
21. Design curriculum materials and modifications to meet collaborator and student needs.
22. Seek grant money and seed money that benefit many teachers and students.
23. Evaluate the program regularly and thoroughly.
24. Reassess your plans, time allocation, resources, and program results, and revise them if necessary.
25. Share results of successful programs at regional, state, and national conferences.
26. Engage in research efforts for new knowledge about consultation and collaboration practices.
27. Carry out advocacy and public relations efforts for excellent education.

significant blocks of consultee time to participate in the collaboration. Working out such a plan is one of the most formidable tasks facing a consultant, particularly one who also has direct teaching responsibilities at specific times.

In spite of the difficulties involving allocation of time, and the significance of providing scheduled time for successful consultation, time has not been addressed first in this chapter. Just as the factor of cost should not be addressed first in designing a new product or procedure, neither should time constraints be allowed to impede planning for consultation and collaboration. The problem must be dealt with, of course. But if allowed to take precedence over other considerations, time can dictate thought patterns and restrict the free flow of innovative ideas.

Administrators must assume responsibility for allocating time needed by consultants and consultees to collaborate and work in teams. If they lend their authority to this endeavor, school personnel will be more willing to brainstorm ways of getting together. Schenkat (1988) points out that, if working conditions in schools were restructured to allow greater flexibility in scheduling, teachers could find the time to collaborate with colleagues and create solutions for learning and behavior problems of students with mild disabilities. This would help build bridges between special education and general education, while expanding services to all students who are at risk of failing in the school environment.

When consulting teachers first initiate consultation and collaboration, it is very likely that these activities will have to come out of their own time—before school, after school, during lunch hours, perhaps even on weekends. Even so, they must move as soon as possible to more appropriate times during the school work day. This is not only for their well-being, but to emphasize that consultation and collaboration are not add-on services that will be supplied as an extreme role overload by a zealous, dedicated few.

When time *is* arranged for a consultation, facilities must be available in which to conduct the consultation. The area should be pleasant, quiet, and relatively private for free exchange of confidences. Such a place is at a premium in a bustling school community.

Management

School consultation is a cost-efficient way to serve students with special needs (Heron & Kimball, 1988). But there is a danger of letting fiscal issues, rather than student needs, dictate the service delivery method. Assigning large caseloads to consulting teachers may save money in the short run, but could cost more eventually if student performance does not improve or if teachers burn out as a result (Huefner, 1988). Therefore, the caseload issue must be addressed with extreme caution.

Problems related to caseload are complex. For example, the average time needed to complete one Individual Education Program (IEP) has been assessed as 6.5 hours (Heron & Kimball, 1988; Price & Goodman, 1980). A consulting teacher with an overwhelming caseload of students and time-consuming responsibilities such as development of IEPs, will have no time to consult and collaborate. Although direct service can be a strategy for easing into indirect service, the load must be manageable. If a consulting teacher's caseload is too great, direct service is inadequate, possibilities for indirect services are minimal, and the program is self-defeating.

In the Resource/Consulting Teacher model (to be discussed more fully in Chapter 3), Idol-Maestas (1983) recommends that teachers spend 20 to 40 percent of their school day in consultation-related activities, such as discussing educational problems, presenting ideas for use in regular classrooms, in-service, observation, performing curriculum-based assessment, demonstrating instructional techniques (Wiederholt, Hammill, & Brown, 1983), and coordinating the program.

A consultant must be very organized and efficient. Greenburg (1987) notes a number of studies indicating that, although resource teachers may be committed to direct contact as their major activity, considerable portions of their time are required for record-keeping, paperwork, and teacher consultant responsibilities (McGlothlin, 1981; Miller & Sabatino, 1978; Evans, 1980). Consulting teachers manage and monitor consultee use of materials as varied as books, tests, kits, tapes, films, and media equipment. They help teachers develop systems of observation, monitoring, and assessment, along with performing these activities themselves. Their paperwork, scheduling, and communication systems must be efficient and effective. Techniques for managing these activities will be presented in Chapter 7.

Recommended caseload numbers vary depending on school context, travel time required, grade level, exceptionalities and special needs served, and structure of the consulting method. The numbers must be kept manageable to fulfill the intent and promise of consultation and collaboration. The key lies in documenting carefully all consultation activities *and* making note also of those that should have happened but were precluded by time constraints. Consultants can negotiate with their administrators for reasonable caseload assignments and blocks of time in which to consult, collaborate, and work in teams.

Evaluation and Support of Consultation and Collaboration

The third of four key elements in school consultation features evaluation and support. Educators will need to document the effectiveness of consultation and collaboration in order to ensure continuing support for this kind of educational service. School personnel are understandably skeptical of indirect service if it does not demonstrate its usefulness. They may be involved initially because they are told to, or because they have been talked into giving it a try, but their interest will wane if positive results are not forthcoming. There will be out-and-out resistance if they sense that it is detrimental to children specifically and to the educational process in general.

APPLICATION 2.4   Constructing a Framework

Finding Time, Facilities, and Resources

1. Rotate school visits and vary schedules for preparation periods.
2. Rearrange commitments so you are not always in the same building at the same time on the same days.
3. Arrange peer tutoring so you and the classroom teacher can have time to collaborate.
4. Invite colleagues to your work area and have aides or para-educators take over as you monitor.
5. Encourage administrators to fill in for consultants and consultees by teaching a lesson, managing a study period, or reading stories to students. This also has a positive ripple effect of allowing them to interact with students and experience the classroom from the teacher's perspective.
6. Team teaching among classroom teachers lends itself to collaborative arrangements.
8. A permanent "floating substitute" can travel among grades to free up consultees as well as consultants (West & Idol, 1990).
9. Volunteers, including parents and grandparents, and retired teachers (West & Idol, 1990) can provide enriching activities to students as well as released time for collaboration among teachers.
10. Record all consultative and collaborative activities, and encourage other collaborators to do so as well. Careful documentation of consultations and results can be used to underscore the benefits of this activity and to negotiate for consistent, significant consultation time.
11. Arrange for the physical and psychological comfort of all. Place furniture in arrangements that convey equality, not hierarchy.
12. Brainstorm with colleagues to find innovative ways of accessing time for collaboration—for example, early release days, team planning time for some teachers during assemblies and other events, or a roster of substitute teachers funded by community supporters who want to encourage more collaboration in schools.
13. Provide room to spread out materials, and equipment for viewing film or hearing tapes if necessary.
14. Refreshments, especially at the end of the day, are energizing and help establish camaraderie. (Note the change in atmosphere during an airplane flight after refreshments are served.)
15. Space for stashing coats, briefcases, and books is appreciated.
16. If collaborators are new to the building, provide maps of the neighborhood, building arrangement, and room location, with parking areas visibly marked.

Assessment of the Consultation

Assessment of consultation is a requisite for continuing to obtain consultation time and facilities. Involvement and acceptance by school personnel will increase when effectiveness of consulting as a professional practice in education is assessed. In keeping with the philosophy of collaboration, evaluation of the consultation should be designed cooperatively by personnel from varying roles.

McGaghie (1991) expresses strong dissatisfaction with most professional evaluations because:

They typically cover a narrow range of practice situations.
They are biased toward assessment of acquired knowledge.
They devote little attention to direct assessment of practical skills.
Little attention is given to assessment of professional or personal qualities.
Measurement problems exist.

All of these points are cogent criticisms with which to study the evaluation of school consultation and collaboration. McGaghie stresses that the key to professional assessment lies in ascertaining the nature of the professional role, not just mastery of information that experts think beginners should acquire. True job proficiency appraisal cannot be relegated to paper-pencil exams. The necessary competencies are not easily quantified, and there is no single answer for all professional problems and needs.

McGaghie (1991) cites the assessment system for becoming a chartered accountant in Canada as an exemplary one. A major part of that exam is a set of short and long business accounting problems or cases. The candidate is expected to "frame" each problem, identify its elements, figure out which parts require immediate *versus* delayed attention, formulate a problem solution, exercise judgment in developing alternatives, propose practical solutions, communicate effectively with users, and respond to users' needs. These exercises target the kinds of expertise school consultants should demonstrate. Persons responsible for assessing consultation and collaboration competency would do well to pattern their evaluation procedures upon this kind of exam. Desirable attributes of the professional are determined by many forces, with the key to assessment being the nature of the role a professional will fill, not just the information that "experts" think beginners should master.

Only two kinds of evaluation measures are readily available in the published research on education-based consultation (Tindal and Taylor-Pendergast, 1989): rating scales of judgments that represent a variety of skills and activities, and estimates of engaged time that note the activities required or demanded. Administrators, advisory council members, and policy-makers will need to study carefully the few procedures that are available for assessment, and beyond that, use their skills to design more helpful and practical assessment techniques that fit their school context and consultant role responsibilities.

The context of the school setting must be assessed as well. For example, a consultant may have excellent communication skills and a wealth of content with which to consult and collaborate, but if no time is provided for interaction, there will be few positive results. Chapter 9 focuses upon assessment and evaluation for consultation and collaboration practices.

Consultants will want to evaluate every stage of the process to keep heading in the right direction. (See Chapter 9 on formative evaluation.) Evaluation should include a variety of data-collection methods to provide the kinds of information needed by target groups. When assessment is completed, consultation and collaboration practices must not be judged inadequate for the wrong reasons or under erroneous assumptions. If time has not been allocated for the interactions, if staff have not had preparation and encouragement, and if administrative support is lacking, those elements should be targeted for improvement before consultation is disparaged or discouraged.

APPLICATION 2.5 Evaluation of Consultation

Finding Out How It Is Going

1. Teacher involvement in consultation and collaboration must not be perceived as a sign of weakness or inadequacy. Instead, consultees should be commended for taking advantage of services provided to help both educators and students succeed.
2. Involvement in consultation and collaboration should be valued as a strength on the performance evaluations of school personnel by administrators and supervisors.
3. Involve school personnel in developing and implementing consultation practices and assessing their outcomes. Figures 2–2 and 2–3 are forms that can be used by the consultee to determine benefits of the service and share that information with the consultant. The instrument should include space for open-ended response and may allow for anonymity if the consultee chooses.
4. Conduct self-assessment of consultation and collaboration. Self-assessment is a painful but necessary practice for the consultant. The Consultation Log provided in Chapter 7 includes a brief self-assessment.
5. Videotaping, having a colleague observe and report, and often just reflecting upon one's habits are all potentially helpful ways of growing professionally. Reflection leads to insights about oneself, prompting changes in self-concept, changes in perception of an event or person, or plans for changing some behavior (Canning, 1991). One speech/language pathologist analyzed her emerging consultation skills this way:

> *In my early perception of consulting I viewed myself as the expert. Experience has taught me I am not. Expert language usually is understood by very few. Knowing how to frame good questions is an invaluable tool. I used to think I knew what was best for the child. Experience again has shown me this is not so—we must all get our respective "what's bests" on the table and mediate. I felt that I needed to have all the workable solutions to the problem at hand, but this was assuming too much. I thought everyone likes and respects the "expert" and wants his or her help. I now perceive my task as one of earning the right to become part of the planning for any child. This means I must be as knowledgeable as possible, not only in my own field, but about the total environment (physical and mental) of each child. I am still learning that effective intervention takes time and careful planning. (name withheld)*

6. Other self-assessment questions the consultant can ask include:

   - What solutions have I offered for discussion?
   - What documentation have I gathered to support my opinions?
   - Can I list the questions I want to ask the consultee?
   - Can I listen and work cooperatively on the problem?
   - Can I be honest about my feelings toward the child, the problem, and the personnel involved?
   - Will I follow through on the plan?
   - Will I document the efficacy of the plan?
   - Will I try new methods and strategies?
   - Will I persist in the plan?
   - Will I give feedback to the consultee about the situation?
   - Am I willing to ask for help or advice?

Please evaluate your use of the consulting teacher service provided in the _____ program by providing the following information.
Respond with:

1 = Not at all   2 = A little   3 = Somewhat   4 = Considerably   5 = Much

1. The consulting teacher provides useful information. _____
2. The consulting teacher understands my school environment and teaching situation. _____
3. The consulting teacher listens to my ideas. _____
4. The consulting teacher helps me identify useful resources that help my students' special needs. _____
5. The consulting teacher explains ideas clearly. _____
6. The consulting teacher fits easily into the school setting. _____
7. The consulting teacher increases my confidence in the special programs. _____
8. I value consulting and collaborating with the consulting teacher. _____
9. I have requested collaboration time with the consulting teacher. _____
10. I plan to continue seeking opportunities to consult and collaborate with the consulting teacher. _____

Other comments: _____

FIGURE 2-2   Consultee Assessment of Consultation and Collaboration

Involvement in Consultation and Collaboration

Friend and Cook (1990) emphasize that collaborative programs must address "voluntariness" before detailed planning can occur. Others have stressed that participation in collaboration must be voluntary on the part of the consultee. However, for some school personnel, that desirable condition may never appear. In these instances administrator influence and appealing tactics by the consultant may help. Sometimes a bandwagon effect can exert power in getting everyone on for the ride. Broadcasting the successes and promoting the benefits of consultations and collaborations that have occurred may get the bandwagon rolling and the reluctants on board.

Most important, however, is involving people right from the start, in needs assessments, planning efforts, evaluations, staff development presentations, and personal contacts to instill ownership and even arouse a little curiosity. Techniques and incentives for promotion of consultation, collaboration, and teamwork through staff development will be discussed in Chapter 12.

Acceptance of School Consultation

Consultation signals change. Collaboration requires practice. Teamwork means giving up part of the ownership. These realities make acceptance of school consultation more difficult

Dear _____,

Please take a couple of minutes to help me improve my consulting skills by completing this checklist. Any additional comments you wish to make would be greatly appreciated. Thank you!

_____

Marty Schneider

	A Strength	O.K.	Needs Improving
1. Helped me to be comfortable working together.	_____	_____	_____
2. Communicated clearly.	_____	_____	_____
3. Worked to make our time productive.	_____	_____	_____
4. Listened.	_____	_____	_____
5. Asked facilitating questions.	_____	_____	_____
6. Showed trust and dependability.	_____	_____	_____
7. Demonstrated flexibility.	_____	_____	_____
8. Presence/time spent not disruptive.	_____	_____	_____
9. Left me wanting to work together again.	_____	_____	_____
10. Other Comments:			

FIGURE 2-3   Checklist for Evaluating Collaborative Consultation

and enthusiastic involvement by all school personnel more challenging for its advocates. Consultation in the minds of many general educators is associated with special education. If teachers resent having more responsibility for special education students, they may blame school consultation and consultants for this condition. Consultees and support personnel need a precedence for accepting and adapting to this model. Most of all, they need administrator support and encouragement. Consultants must seize every opportunity to cultivate these conditions.

Preparation for School Consultation Roles

Preparation programs for mastering the skills of school consultation and collaboration are a necessity. Opportunities and incentives must be provided for three populations:

- Preservice students should prepare to be consultees and potential consultants.
- Degree-program graduate students in consultation should prepare to be consultants and to train consultants and consultees.
- Inservice teachers should prepare for roles as consultees and advocates for integrating consultation and collaboration into their school contexts.

Skills of the consultant and consultee are enhanced through training activities, coaching, and feedback in process and content skill areas.

Preservice Preparation

Teacher preparation programs do not often include consulting process skills such as communication and conflict resolution in teaching methods. Not so many years ago, studies revealed that consultation training in college and university programs was very much the exception rather than the rule (Lilly & Givens-Ogle, 1981). Some progress has been made since that time in teacher preparation programs, but much more is needed (West and Brown, 1987).

Phillips, Allred, Brulle, and Shank (1990) suggest that collaboration and consultation skills can be cultivated by teacher educators at the preservice level. They recommend that teacher preparation programs provide introductory education courses in which general and special education preservice teachers participate jointly in practicum experiences that serve

---

APPLICATION 2.6   Gaining Acceptance

Being Accepted as One of the School Team

1. As a consultant, portray oneself as assistant to the teacher.
2. Become more visible, visiting each classroom and making positive comments about what is going on there.
3. Always have an ear open to opportunities to help out, and spin off helping situations to become more established as a consulting teacher.
4. Be realistic and understanding about the demands that are placed upon classroom teachers, administrators, and parents in fulfilling *their* roles.
5. Be realistic about what consultants can do.
6. Keep school personnel wanting more consultation services, making them so valuable that if they were taken away from the schools, the role and its services would be missed.
7. "Advertise" consultation successes.
8. Keep providing benefits for them. "What can I do for you and your students that you do not have time or resources to do?" is the operative question.
9. Identify ways for parents, as consultees, to contribute and have ownership in programs for their children.
10. Create and nurture many opportunities for special education programs and related services to interface with general education programs.
11. Institute communication networks among staff, parents, advocacy groups.
12. Demonstrate strategies, methods, and materials to any who will listen.
13. Identify successful, exemplary consultation and collaboration practices, *especially* when they occur in your school district!
14. Share newest trends and techniques in a nonpatronizing way.
15. Work with a group of collaborating colleagues to write a guide on the use of consultation and collaboration. Present it to new faculty members, and periodically conduct refresher sessions for all staff development activities.
16. Send notes of appreciation to consultees regularly.
17. Do not expect a uniformly high level of acceptance and involvement from all but keep aiming for it.

a diverse range of children's needs. However, this approach requires concerted effort by college and university personnel, for many of them have not been trained to perform collaboration and consultation functions themselves, let alone facilitate development of these behaviors in their students.

Some veteran educators will be nervous about having "novice teachers" address consultation practices before they have experienced student teaching and real-world teaching. Nevertheless, the seeds of awareness can and should be planted early that may bear fruit later in important ways for students with special needs. After all, for most new teachers, there is not much time or experience gained between that last day of teacher training and the first day they are all alone in classrooms with real students of their own.

Graduate Certification and Degree Programs

Formal training in consultation lags behind the increasing demands for service (Curtis & Zins, 1988). White and Pryzwansky (1982) assert that resource teachers in schools are not prepared to deliver consultation and are keenly aware of their insufficiencies in that regard. If teachers are not trained in consultation, they will tend to shy away from pertinent feedback and provide only broad generalizations or retreat into paperwork associated with the role (Gersten, Darch, Davis, and George, 1991). Kauffman (1994) contends that training of special educators is often so superficial and general that they have no real expertise as instructional specialists and no in-depth understanding of disabling conditions and their instructional demands. He stresses that special education teachers who are being prepared to consult and collaborate with general educators must have special instructional and behavior management expertise or their input will have little meaning beyond that of the general educators.

The number of preparation programs is increasing (Dickens & Jones, 1990; Gersten, Darch, Davis, and George, 1991; Thurston & Kimsey, 1989), but universities have far to go to meet the training needs. Some states require training in consultation skills for teacher

---

APPLICATION 2.7   Preservice Preparation

Getting Ready for Consultation and Collaboration

1. At several points in every teacher preparation program of study, textual and class information should feature examples of teachers working together, problem-solving together, team-teaching, and learning together in staff development activities. University instructors must model these kinds of educational structures as well.
2. Student teachers need to observe experienced teachers teaming and collaborating and sit in on consultations.
3. Videotapes and simulations of consultation episodes can be used at the undergraduate level.
4. Interactive video, with opportunities to select actions and observe the outcomes of those actions, are promising tools for providing undergraduate training in a safe and correctable professional environment.

certification. Inclusion of this training in standards for accreditation of teacher education programs would be one way to encourage more emphasis on collaborative school consultation and collaboration at the graduate and preservice levels. School administrators should recruit prospective consultants who welcome the opportunity for working with adults as well as students in school settings.

Training programs need to center around elements featured in this book so aspiring consultants will develop the communication and problem-solving tools they need to succeed in their school context. While each training program will be unique, a basic program must prepare future school consultants for effectiveness in four areas:

- Delineating their roles;
- Creating a framework that allows them to fulfill their roles;
- Evaluating their effectiveness; and
- Helping prepare colleagues for collaborative consultation even as they expand their own proficiencies.

Preparation programs must provide experiences well beyond the "mentioning" mode of professional training that offers only superficial exposure to a large amount of information and minimal or no practice with complex ideas and behaviors. Course syllabi should include not only the conventional learning strategies of lecture, reading, and discussion, but a strong focus on experiential content. Small-group activities, simulations and role-plays, interviewing, videotaped consultation practice, reaction and reflection papers, resource searches, and practice with the tools and strategies of technology will help practicing educators be more comfortable and capable in interactive school roles.

Inservice and Staff Development for Consultation

Training institutions may eventually include consultation in special education programs, but White and Pryzwansky (1982) note that school personnel now teaching are largely unprepared to deliver consultation service. In 1987, West and Idol reported that staff development for school collaboration had received little attention (Bradley, 1994, West and Idol, 1987). Friend and Cook (1990) assert that teachers are being set up to fail when they enter the profession with content expertise and method but without skills for working effectively with colleagues.

The lack of preparation for consultation is compounded by a dearth of empirical studies that might provide evidence for or against various components of consultation training. However, movements such as school reform, restructuring, and mainstreaming have stimulated some efforts such as those reported by Rule, Fodor-Davis, Morgan, Salzberg, and Chen (1990). In their study, Rule and colleagues identified the need for administrative support, technical assistance, and follow-up assistance, as well as the in-service training.

At the in-service and staff development level, consultation and collaboration programs can be tailored to each school context. Staff development should be looked upon by consultants as a golden opportunity for promoting consultation, collaboration, and teamwork. It can help teachers become more successful in their very complex roles. This important topic is the focus of Chapter 12.

APPLICATION 2.8   Graduate Programs

Developing Competencies for Consulting and Collaborating

Graduate programs for special educators, general educators, and school administrators should include course content and assignments designed to help them attain the following goals:

1. Understand school consultation theory and its application in serving special needs of students.
2. Recognize barriers that inhibit effective use of collaborative consultation.
3. Develop skills of facilitating team effort in preassessment, diagnosis, and prescriptions for students' special learning and behavioral needs.
4. Develop verbal and nonverbal communication skills of listening, avoiding communication roadblocks, dealing with resistance, being appropriately assertive, and resolving conflicts.
5. Improve ability to problem-solve collaboratively with school colleagues, students, and parents.
6. Increase skills in locating and directing use of instructional materials and resources that will serve students' special needs.
7. Expand self-understanding and ability to use constructively the individual differences, including multicultural diversity, that exist among adults.
8. Develop self-assessment techniques that enable one to continually improve skills of consultation and collaboration.
9. Formulate personal strategies for professional management of time, records, resources, and ethics in school-based consultation.
10. Develop a personal plan for implementing collaborative consultation and teamwork in one's own professional role.

Consultant Competencies

A consultant wears many hats. Consultants are context systems analysts, process specialists, and content information banks, as well as role models and educational leaders. Consulting and collaborating require flexibility, adaptability, resilience, and the tolerance for delayed reinforcement or none at all. A person in this role is called on to diagnose, problem-identify, problem-solve, prescribe, evaluate, and follow-up, but all as part of a team whose members do not always understand or even want to understand each other. Therefore, effective school consultants are knowledgeable about special education and general education curriculum and methods. They recognize and value adult differences among colleagues. They understand how schools function and have a panoramic view of the educational scene. They are diplomatic at the same time that they are innovators.

Successful school consultants relate well to teacher colleagues and staff members, administrators, students, and parents. They have good communication skills, a patient and understanding demeanor, and assertiveness when it is needed. The consultant links people with resources, refers people to other sources when necessary, and teaches when that is the most appropriate way to serve student needs. A consultant is self-confident, but, if running low on resources and ideas, the consultant may even find a consultant for himself or herself!

Perhaps most of all, the consultant is a change agent. As one very experienced consulting teacher put it, "You have to be abrasive enough to create change, but pleasant enough to be asked back so you will do it some more" (Bradley, 1987). The ideal consultant encourages other educators, including parents, to help students with special needs succeed in school. Most encouraging of all, consultation, collaboration, and teamwork among educators in schools and at home can nurture the potential and productivity of all students. See Figure 2-4 for a composite of characteristics demonstrated by effective school consultants and collaborators.

Facilitative	Personal	Knowledgeable	Coordinative
Reflective listener	Considerate	Skilled in content area(s)	Prioritizes
Assertive	Thoughtful	Up-to-date with information	Efficient
Visible	Communicative	Resourceful	Manages time
Non-judgmental	Self-assured	Skilled in process area(s)	Can say no
Properly persistent	Reliable	Can develop networks	Documents
Open to ideas	Goes extra mile	Knows procedures	Ethical
Flexible	Perceptive	Knows legislation	Schedules
Patient	Sensible	Creative	Decisions
Confidential	Self-reliant	Innovative	Available
Unbiased	Positive thinker	Knows regulations	Shares material
Diplomatic	Caring	Skilled in leadership	Punctual
Objective	Sensitive	Applies research	Strives for best
Avoids roadblocks	Empathic	Conducts staff development	
Puts forth effort	Determined	Desires to learn	
Admits mistakes	Hard-working	Knowledge-linker	
Gives compliments	Kind		
Brief when need be	Personable		
Professional	Sincere		
Advocating	Friendly		
Guides	Approachable		
Participates	Calm		
Dependable	Respectful		
Recognizes feelings	Has sense of humor		
Responsive	Tactful		
Spokesperson	High energy level		
Cooperative	Courageous		
Open-minded			

FIGURE 2-4   Characteristics of Effective School Consultants and Collaborators

Tips for Consulting, Collaborating, and Teaming

1. Value consultation and collaboration as tools for improving long-range planning and coordination among educators.
2. Attend extra-curricular functions of assigned schools as much as possible, and offer to help if feasible.
3. Carry your share of the load in contributing to social funds, work schedules, and other professional obligations and courtesies.
4. Do not share problems or concerns with classroom teachers unless they can have significant input or you have a suggestion for them that might help.
5. Stop by and see building administrators when in the building, leaving brief notes if they are unavailable.
6. Log all visits and consultations.
7. Have lunch, workroom breaks, and informal visits with building staff often.
8. Have a visible, accessible work space.
9. Attend monthly grade level/departmental meetings to interact with colleagues and to learn of their needs and concerns.
10. Ask for help when you have a problem, because it has a humanizing, rapport-building effect.
11. Find ways to inform, support, and interact with principals, promoting the idea that each is a "prince-and-a-pal" or "princess-and-a-pal."
12. Leave the door open, both figuratively and literally, for future partnerships and collaborations.
13. Know when to stay in the consultation and when it is time to get out.
14. Have a specific way, time, and place consultees can interact with consultants.
15. Be sure the consulting teacher's work plan for the student does not overlap or contradict the consultee's plan.
16. Initiate a suggestion-box approach to demonstrate your interest in colleagues' input and ideas.
17. Be knowledgeable about related services and support that are available both in school and in the community.
18. Use resource personnel to a greater extent.
19. Provide adequate privacy when talking with consultees.
20. "Dress for success" in each setting, matching your level of dress with the context in order to establish parity.
21. If serving two or more schools or districts, refrain from carrying stories (either good or bad) from one setting to another.
22. Visit every teacher in the building regularly.
23. Don't be seen around your building(s) doing nothing.
24. Be available—and available—and available.

Chapter Review

1. Several questions reflect the immediate concerns of consultants and consulting teachers: What do I do? How do I begin? What is my schedule for a week? How do I know I am succeeding? How do I prepare for this kind of role?
2. The consultant role creates concomitant roles of consultee and client. These roles are interchangeable.
3. Key elements in the success of school consultation and collaboration are role delineation, a framework for these activities, evaluation and support of the efforts, and preparation for consultation and collaboration.

4. Teachers should begin preparation for consulting, collaborating, and teamwork roles at the pre-service level in their teacher preparation program. This preparation should continue after they are in service, with staff development for practicing teachers who have not had such training.
5. Consultant competencies include skills of communication, organization, diplomacy, knowledge-ability, self-confidence, and a genuine interest in working with adults as well as with children and youth.

To Do and Think About

1. Interview three school professionals (elementary, middle school, and high school levels if possible) and two parents to find out their views of school consultation and collaboration, and the consulting-teacher role. You can approach this in one of two ways—by giving interviewees definitions if they ask "What do you mean?" by the terms, or you can encourage them to share their own perceptions of the terms by defining them in their own way. Compare the interview results, and make inferences. Note any indication of willingness to collaborate or glimmer of awakening interest in consultation and determine how these positive signs might be followed up productively. For example, one interviewer was rewarded with this experience:

   > *This secondary school teacher saw a special education consultant as a "prescriptive and purchase" person to a great extent. After talking a little longer, however, he was making statements like, "Maybe they could show me how to make adjustments with my homework or class assignments so the students could be successful." I see a possibility here for long-term effects and transfer.*

   > *(Elvera B.)*

2. Begin an "obstacle remover" chart for each of the four key element areas depicted in Figure 2–1 (role delineation, framework, evaluation and support, and preparation) by referring to Chapter 1 for examples and discussion of the more obvious obstacles.
3. If you were to pick up a newspaper and see a want-ad for a consulting teacher to assist students with learning and behavioral problems in any of the following school contexts, what would you expect that job description to include?

   - elementary school in a suburban area
   - large consolidated middle school in a rural area
   - high school in an inner-city area

4. A person's design for his or her work day puts a certain framework around the day and gives meaning to the rhythms of activity that help define the role. Using one of the settings in Activity 3 above, visualize an ideal day in a consulting teacher's life. Think of the context, the role, the schedule, the goals and activities for that day, and how the impact of that day's events might be appraised.
5. What characteristics and competencies should each of the consultants in Activity 3 above possess? Write a job description for a collaborative consultant at the grade level(s) and curricular area(s) in which you are most interested. The examples of characteristics given in Figure 2–4 may help you get started. How would you publicize and promote your job description to attract the most suitable applicants for the position?

6. Develop a file of humor and satire about consultation that would be helpful in developing rapport with colleagues. As a start, consider this one which has been around for awhile:

   The consultant is one who drives over from the central office and borrows your watch to tell you what time it is.

   How can humor and satire be used to the consultant's advantage in interactions with consultees? If you have a humorous bent, or the creative urge, make up a joke, cartoon, or comic strip about consulting or collaboration that could be used to defuse resistance and build rapport toward school consultation.

For Further Reading

Brown, D., Pryzwansky, W.B., & Schulte, A. C. (1991). *Psychological consultation: Introduction to theory and practice.* Needham Heights, MA: Allyn & Bacon. Chapters 6 and 7, on roles of consultants and consultees.

Conoley, J.C., & Conoley, C.W. (1982). *School consultation: A guide to practice and training.* New York: Pergamon Press.

Hansen, J.C., Himes, B.S., & Meier, S. (1990). *Consultation: Concepts and practices.* Englewood Cliffs, NJ: Prentice-Hall. Chapter 3 on consulting with educational institutions.

Hay, C. (1984). One more time: What do I do all day? *Gifted Child Quarterly, 28*(1), 17–20.

Heron, T.E., & Harris, K.C. (1987). *The educational consultant: Helping professionals, parents, and mainstreamed students.* Austin, TX: PRO-ED. Chapter 2 on the consultant role.

Morsink, C.V., Thomas, C.C., & Correa, V.I. (1991). *Interactive teaming: Consultation and collaboration in school programs.* New York: Macmillan. Chapter 4 on understanding roles and perspectives of team members.

C h a p t e r $\mathcal{3}$

Background, Theory, and Structural Elements of School Consultation

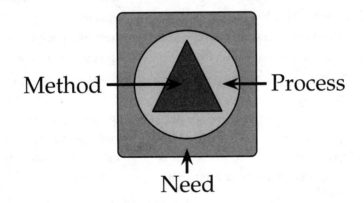

Introduction

Consultation, collaboration, and teamwork probably began around cave fires ages ago. As men and women listened to the ideas of others in the group and voiced their own opinions, they honed skills of communication and collaboration. These skills have become more and more essential for survival and progress in an increasingly complex, interconnected world.

All members of every society must interact effectively and work together cooperatively if the world is to survive. In this age of global interdependence, educators play a major role by helping young people learn to communicate, cooperate, and collaborate effectively. Schools must provide the structure that will serve students' needs and help them develop the interpersonal competencies required for survival in the world they will inherit.

Focusing Questions

1. What is the historical background of school consultation, collaboration, and teamwork?
2. Is there a theoretical base for school consultation?
3. What research is needed to determine the best practices in school consultation?
4. What structural elements are components for developing appropriate consultation methods to fit school contexts and student needs?
5. What models of consultation, collaboration, and teamwork have evolved in education and related fields?
6. How should educators incorporate existing models and other structural elements into useful school consultation methods?

Key Terms in the Chapter

Adaptive Learning Environments Model (ALEM)	School Consultation Committee model
approach	Schoolwide Enrichment Model (SEM)
Class-Within-A-Class Model (CWC)	semantics
collaborative consultation model	Stephens/systems model
Mainstream Training Project (MTP)	Success-For-All (SFA)
method	synthesis
mode	system
model	thought experiment
perspective	triadic model
prototype	Vermont Consulting Teacher Program model
Resource/Consulting Teacher Program model	

A Brief History of School Consultation

School consultation probably originated in mental health and management fields (Reynolds and Birch, 1988). Friend (1988) cites the work of Caplan (1970) in training staff members to counsel troubled adolescents in Israel at the close of World War II. Building on Caplan's work, mental health services escalated and moved into school settings, where consultation services of school psychologists generated promising results. Gallessich (1974) and Pryzwansky (1974) discuss the role of consultation in school psychology as it was broadened to encourage collaborative relationships. Such relationships were nurtured to help teachers, administrators, and parents deal with future problems as well as immediate situations.

Scenario

The setting is a school administration office where the superintendent, the principal, and the special education director are having an early-morning conference.

SPECIAL EDUCATION DIRECTOR: I've assigned five people on our special education staff to begin serving as consulting teachers in the schools we targeted at our last meeting.

PRINCIPAL: I understand the high school is to be one of those schools. I'm all for trying a new approach, but at this point I'm not sure my staff understands how this method of service is going to affect them.

SUPERINTENDENT: Are you saying we need to spend a little more time at the drawing board and get the kinks out of our plan before flinging it at the teachers?

PRINCIPAL: Yes, and I think the parents also will want to know what will be happening.

SPECIAL EDUCATION DIRECTOR: I've been compiling a file of theoretical background, research studies, program descriptions, even cartoons and satire, involving consultation and collaboration approaches. Let me get copies of the most helpful material to you and the principals of the other targeted schools. Perhaps we should plan in-service sessions for teachers and awareness sessions for parents before we proceed.

SUPERINTENDENT: That sounds good. Draft an outline and we'll discuss it at next week's meeting. I'll get the word out to the other principals to be here.

School Consultation before 1970

Gallessich (1973) notes a professional dialogue emerged during the 1950s that stimulated the development of strategies for implementing consultative services in schools. By the mid-1960s, the term *school consultation* was listed in *Psychological Abstracts* (Friend, 1988). School counselors began to promote the concept of proactive service, so that by the early 1970s, consultation was being recommended as an integral part of contemporary counseling service. This interest in collaborative relationships on the part of counselors and psychologists reflected a desire to influence those individuals, groups, and systems that most profoundly affect students (Brown et al., 1979).

Since the late 1950s, the consulting teacher plan for delivery of special services has received frequent attention in the special education literature. There are early examples of consulting in the areas of speech and language therapy, and programs for the hearing impaired and visually impaired. Emphasis on teacher consultation for learning-disabled and behavior-disordered students surfaces in the literature as early as the mid-1960s. At that time, for the most part, consultants were not special educators, but clinical psychologists and psychiatric social workers.

The behavioral movement, which was gaining momentum in the late 1960s and early 1970s, fueled interest in alternative models for intervention and efficient use of time and other resources. This interest sparked development of a text by Tharp and Wetzel (1969) in which they presented a triadic consultation model using behavioral principles in school settings. This triadic model is the basic pattern on which many subsequent models and methods for consultation were constructed.

By 1970 the special education literature contained references to a method of training consulting teachers to serve handicapped students at the elementary level (McKenzie et al., 1970). The Vermont Consulting Teacher Program model, using a consulting teacher to serve students with mental handicaps, was put into place in 1970 (Haight, 1984).

School Consultation after 1970

The decade of the 1970s was a very busy time in the field of special education. Intensive special education advocacy, federal policy making for exceptional students, and technological advancements affected special education practices for handicapped students (Nazzaro, 1977). By the mid-1970s, consultation was being regarded as a significant factor in serving students with special needs. Special education became a major catalyst for promoting consultation and collaboration in schools (Friend, 1988).

Haight (1984) cites several sources for learning more about special-education teacher consultation as it has occurred since 1970: Chandler (1980); Coleman et al. (1975); Evans (1980); Knight et al. (1981); McKenzie et al. (1970); McLoughlin and Kass (1978); Miller and Sabatino (1978); Neel (1981); and Nelson and Stevens (1981). Much of this literature on consultation focuses on indirect service to students by consultants who worked with consultees, direct service by resource consulting teachers, and various combinations of direct and indirect service.

By the mid-1980s, consultation was becoming one of the most significant educational trends for serving students with special needs. To investigate this trend, a questionnaire was sent by West and Brown (1987) to directors of special education in the fifty states. Thirty-five state directors responded. Twenty-six of the respondents stated that service delivery models in their states include consultation as an expected role of the special educator. The twenty-six states reported a total of ten different professional titles for consultation as a job responsibility of special educators. About three-fourths of the respondents acknowledged the need for service delivery models that include consultation. However, only seven stated that specific consultation competency requirements are included in their policies.

As interest in school consultation escalated in the 1980s, the National Task Force on Collaborative School Consultation, sponsored by the Teacher Education Division of the Council for Exceptional Children, sent a publication to state departments of education with recommendations for teacher consultation services in a special-education services continuum (Heron and Kimball, 1988). Guidelines were presented for: development of consultative assistance options; definition of a consulting teacher role with pupil-teacher ratio recommended; and requirements for preservice, in-service, and certification preparation programs for personnel development. The report included a list of education professionals skilled in school consultation and a list of publications featuring school consultation.

In 1987, personnel from the Research and Training Project on School Consultation at the University of Texas sponsored the Austin Symposium on School Consultation. The theme for the symposium was "Interdisciplinary Perspectives on Theory, Research, Training, and Practice of School Consultation." Major presenters, panel members, and participants met under the leadership of Frederick West and Lorna Idol for three days of discussion and planning. One outcome of the symposium was a paper developed by the group on *Driving and Restraining Forces and Issues Impacting the Future of School Consultation.*

By 1990 a new journal focusing on school consultation, the *Journal of Educational and Psychological Consultation,* appeared in the literature. A preconvention workshop on school consultation and collaboration programs and practices, sponsored by the Teacher Education Division (TED) of the Council for Exceptional Children (CEC), was a featured event at the 1990 annual CEC conference in Toronto. Blueprints and contexts for collaborative program planning and practices were presented by Marilyn Friend and Lynne Cook.

Implementation of consultation practices in the field of education for gifted students has become one of the most viable fields for extensive use of collaborative consultation. Dettmer (1989), Dettmer and Lane (1989) and Idol-Maestas and Celentano (1986) recommend consultation practices to assist with learning needs of gifted and talented students. Dyck and Dettmer (1989) suggest methods for facilitating learning programs for gifted learning-disabled students within a consulting teacher plan.

All in all, social movements and school reforms of the 1980s and early 1990s fueled the interest in school consultation, collaboration, and teamwork that had begun in the 1960s and 1970s. The result has been an increasing number of journals, periodicals, studies, pilot programs, federal and state grants, and training projects, as well as a number of teacher preparation programs, for the application of consultation and collaboration practices in schools.

Theoretical Bases of School Consultation

Is school consultation a theory-based practice or an atheoretical practice related to a problem-solving knowledge base? Differing points of view exist in regard to this issue. Studies of consultation center around the analysis of existing structures, or models, as some educators refer to them. Bergan (1977) addresses consultation through operant learning theory, while Brown and Schulte (1987) present a model based on social learning theory.

West and Idol (1987) propose that school consultation can be regarded as theory-based if it is identified across more than one literature source focusing on the relationship between consultant and consultee. On the other hand, if the topic is identified by problem-solving methods, it should be regarded as knowledge-based in the area of problem solving. They suggest that ten models of consultation can be delineated, of which six have clearly identifiable theory or theories. These six include mental health, behavioral, process, advocacy, and two types of organizational consultation. West and Idol further note that a seventh model, the collaborative consultation model, has the essential elements for building theory because it contains a set of generic principles required for collaborative relationships between consultants and consultees.

Initial work by West, Idol, and Cannon (1987) examined principles of collaborative relationships empirically for the purpose of building sound theories of successful communication and collaboration practices. Brown, Pryzwansky, and Schulte (1991) assert that consultation is not a conceptual wasteland, but stress that there is work to be done in strengthening the theoretical base.

Research Bases of School Consultation

As school consultation theory building continues and the concepts of consultation, collaboration, and teamwork within school partnerships capture the attention of education policymakers and practitioners, researchers seek new information to guide planning and programming efforts in these areas. West and Idol (1987) stress the importance of defining clearly the constructs and principles for consultation and collaboration, in order to expedite basic research for testing a match between model and theory. In this way there is a clear line of progression from theory development to model building to basic research to field-based application.

Heron and Kimball (1988) note that the emerging research base in school consultation addresses several areas:

- theory and models (West and Idol, 1987);
- methodology (Gresham and Kendell, 1987);
- training and practice (Friend, 1984; Idol and West, 1987);
- professional preferences for the consultation service (Babcock and Pryzwansky, 1983; Medway and Forman, 1980);
- guidelines (Salend and Salend, 1984); and
- competencies for consultants (West and Cannon, 1988).

Categories of School Consultation Research

Gresham and Kendell (1987) organize research in school consultation around three areas of investigation: (1) outcome research, (2) process research, and (3) practitioner use. They suggest that training should be a possible fourth area. Outcome research focuses on changes in consultee classroom behavior, knowledge, and attitudes, as well as changes in client classroom behavior and frequency of consultation use (Bergan, 1977; Gutkin and Curtis, 1982; Pryzwansky, 1986). Outcomes also involve growth in student achievement after consultation with parents (Jackson, Cleveland, and Merenda, 1975) and comparisons of problem severity in schools with and without consultants (Gutkin, Singer, and Brown, 1980). Process research examines the amount of teacher time required for consultation (Witt and Elliott, 1985), the ability to identify the relevant problem (Bergan and Tombari, 1976), and use of communication skills (Gutkin, 1986), as well as the need for "common-sense" language, not jargon (Witt et al., 1984). Research in practitioner use of consultation includes studies of preferences for job functions (Gutkin and Curtis, 1982) and perceived importance of consultation to school psychologist services (Curtis and Zins, 1981).

Gresham and Kendall (1987) have argued that research methodology in school consultation is elementary at best. They describe most consultation research as descriptive, which may be useful for identifying key variables in consultation processes and outcomes but not for determining interactions between variables or directions of influence upon the outcomes of consultation. They stress that consultation research must assess the integrity of consultation plans, since many plans are not being implemented by consultees as designed (Witt & Elliott, 1985).

Fuchs, Fuchs, Dulan, Roberts, and Fernstrom (1992) share the views of Pryzwansky (1986) that many studies on consultation are poorly conceptualized and executed. Conducting the research well requires careful planning, attention to detail, interpersonal skills, flexibility, positive relationships with school personnel, and research skills (Fuchs et al.).

Gresham and Kendell (1987) find little empirical evidence to show that what people are calling consultation actually *is* consultation. They urge researchers to define the research variables more explicitly, control them more carefully, and measure them more accurately. Pryzwansky and Noblit (1990) recommend qualitative research using a case study approach to maximize the observations and experiences of the consultant. Witt (1990) purports that research on collaboration is a dead end unless it can be shown that collaboration is related to important outcomes.

One promising format for effective research studies is collaborative action research (Calhoun, 1993). Participants build collegiality and learn to manage the group process. The process has the potential to improve the organization as a problem-solving entity. Not only teachers and students, but parents and the general community become involved in collecting and interpreting data and selecting options for action (*School Team Innovator,* April 1994). Clearly, collaborative school consultation will be more widely utilized when solid research substantiates its benefits to students and its positive ripple effects for education.

Structures for School Consultation

Overlapping philosophies of consultation have evolved from a blending of consultation knowledge and practices from several fields. This overlap creates a tangle of philosophy and terminology that is problematic for educators endeavoring to develop viable school consultation structures and explain them to the public.

The practice of school consultation is by definition situation-specific, and to make matters more problematic, the concepts of consultation, collaboration, and teaming are still so ambiguous that busy teachers and administrators tend to become frustrated by a perceived lack of consensus and direction. It is time to sort out and refine the myriad consultation terms, theories, research findings, and practices into structures that are useful and well received in the school setting. After considering all existing structures that have been proposed, discussed, and on occasion researched, educators will need to select and refine the methods that work best for their school context.

Semantics of Consultation

When focusing on complex educational issues and school concepts, it is tempting for educators to slip into "educationese" (convoluted and redundant phrases), "jargon" (in-house expressions that approximate educational slang), and "alphabet soup" (acronyms that seem like uncracked codes to lay people).

In order for theories and applications for school consultation to become an accepted, integral part of school programs, it is advantageous to draw on semantics, the study of meanings, as a way of crystallizing concepts. Semantics is a helpful tool with which to begin simplifying and sorting out the tangle of concepts. Meanings of words vary from user to user and from context to context. This semantic principle is obvious in regard to abstract words such as *education, democracy,* and *society,* but more elusive when deciding on the meaning of a word so simple as *chair* (Sondel, 1958). For example, to a dentist, chair might mean an appliance that is used at work. To a college professor, it might mean a coveted position, while to a convicted murder it might portend death (Sondel, 1958).

> *Words make the trip through the nervous system of a human being before they can be referred outward to the real thing—chair, or whatever it is. Don't assume that everyone responds to your words in precisely the same way you do. Make the context in which you use the words clear, and do this through the use of words that refer to specific things. (Sondel, 1958, p. 55)*

The tool of semantics can be used to organize the existing maze of philosophy and terminology about consultation in a number of fields into six basic elements for structuring viable methods of school consultation.

Structural Elements for School Consultation

Consultation terms and procedures involve components of six elements—system, perspective, approach, prototype, mode, and model (see Figure 3–1). These six elements are defined in this book as:

- system—the unity of many parts serving a common purpose;
- perspective—a particular viewpoint;
- approach—a preliminary step toward a purpose;
- prototype—a pattern;
- mode—a form or manner of doing; and
- model—an example.

Characteristics of these six elements can be combined to create a workable school consultation method for each local context and learning situation.

For brevity and graphic clarity, the six elements are designated in this book by the upper-case form of their first letter—for example, system = S. (When two elements begin with identical letters, another prominent letter in the word is used.) Thus the six categories are designated as S (system), P (perspective), A (approach), R (prototype), E (mode), and M (model). A good method of school consultation attends to elements from each of the six categories but is designed to be appropriate for the school context in which it will be implemented.

Systems for School Consultation

The first structural element to be discussed is system. The word *system* (S) is a powerhouse of semantic utility. For this study of consultation, *system* means a complex unity composed of many diverse parts that serve a common purpose. The most natural system within which to conduct school consultation and collaboration is, obviously, the school. However, as pointed out in Chapter 1, and to be elaborated on in later chapters, educators are involved not only in the academic or cognitive part of student development, but also in physical, emotional, social, and life-orientation aspects. Educators include not only teachers, but parents, related services and support personnel, other caregivers, and the community in general.

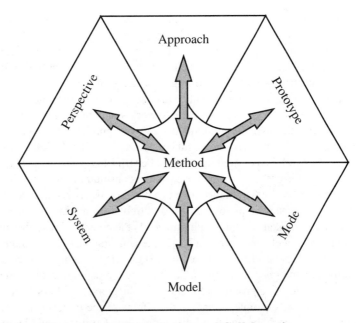

FIGURE 3-1   A Structure for Consultation and Collaboration

Systems (S) in which educators function to serve special needs of students include: home and family, community, medical and dental professions, mental health, social work, counseling, extracurricular, and advocacy and support groups. Other systems with which consultants and collaborators might be involved from time to time in addressing very specialized needs are: therapy, industry, technology, mass communications, cultural enrichment, and special interest areas such as talent development.

Perspectives on Consultation

A *perspective* (P) is an aspect or object of thought from a particular viewpoint. Consultation perspectives that have evolved in education and related fields include:

- purchase;
- doctor-patient; and
- process.

These categories have sometimes been referred to as approaches, and at other times as models. However, in order to organize the terminology, they will be differentiated here as perspectives.

A purchase perspective is one in which the consumer shops for a needed or wanted item. The consumer, in this case the consultee, "buys" services that will help that consultee serve the client's need. For example, the teacher of a developmentally delayed student might ask personnel at the instructional media center for a list of low-vocabulary, high-interest reading material with which to help the student have immediate success in reading. The purchase perspective makes several assumptions (Neel, 1981): (1) that the consultee describes the need precisely; (2) the consultee is in the right "store" to get something for that need; (3) the consultant has enough "inventory" (strategies and resources) to fill the request; and (4) the consultee can assume the costs of time, energy, or modification of classroom procedures.

As a consumer, the consultee is free to accept or reject the strategy or resource, using it enthusiastically, putting off trying it, or ignoring it as a "bad buy." Even if the strategy is effective for that case, the consultee may need to go again to the consultant for similar needs of other clients. For this perspective to work, many things have to go right, so the consultee must think through the consequences of the purchase technique (Schein, 1969). Little change can be expected in consultee skill as a result of such consumer-type interaction. Thus the overall costs are high and the benefits are limited to specific situations.

A doctor-patient perspective casts the consultant in the role of diagnostician and pre-scriber. The consultee knows there is a problem but is not in a position to correct it. Con-sultees are responsible for revealing helpful information to the consultant. Again, this perspective makes several assumptions: (1) the consultee describes the problem to the con-sultant accurately and completely; (2) the consultant can explain the diagnosis clearly and convince the consultee of its worth; (3) the diagnosis is not premature; and (4) the pre-scribed remedy is not *iatrogenic* in outcome—meaning, as discussed in Chapter 1, that it would create more problems for student, educators, or school context than the initial con-dition did. For example, an iatrogenic effect created by teachers who have gifted students that leave classrooms to attend gifted program activities could be resentment and antago-nism toward them by their peers and perhaps even by adults.

A classroom teacher might use a doctor-patient perspective by calling on a special edu-cation teacher and describing the student's learning or behavior problem. The consultant's role would be to observe, review existing data, perhaps talk to other specialists, and make di-agnostic and prescriptive decisions. With the doctor-patient perspective, as in the medical field, there is generally little follow-up activity on the consultant's part, and the consultee does not always follow through with conscientious attention to the consultant's recommendations.

In a process perspective, the consultant helps the client perceive, understand, and act on the problem (Neel, 1981; Schein, 1969). Consultant service does not replace the consul-tee's direct service to the client. In contrast to the purchase and doctor-patient perspectives, the consultant neither diagnoses nor prescribes a solution. As Neel puts it, the consultee be-comes the consultant's client for that particular problem.

Schein (1978) sorts process consultation into two types—a catalyst type in which the consultant does not know a solution but is skilled toward helping the consultee figure one out, and the facilitator type where the consultant contributes ideas toward the solution. In both catalyst and facilitator types of process consultation, the consultant helps the consultee clarify the problem and develop solutions. Skills and resources used to solve the immediate problem might be used later for other problems. Assumptions are: (1) the consultee can di-agnose the problem; (2) the consultant is able to develop a helping relationship; (3) the con-sultant can provide new and challenging alternatives for the consultee (who is the consultant's immediate client) to consider; and (4) decision making about the alternatives will remain the responsibility and privilege of the consultee.

In the process perspective for consultation, the consultee who needs help with a student or school situation collaborates with a consultant to identify the problem, explore possible alternatives, and develop a plan of action. The consultee then implements the plan.

All three perspectives have strengths; therefore, each is likely to be employed at one time or another in schools (Vasa, 1982). One factor influencing the adoption of a particular perspective is the nature of the problem (West, 1985). For example, in a noncrisis situation, the consultee may value the process perspective. However, all three have drawbacks as well. In crisis situations the consultee may need a quick solution, even if temporary, for the problem. In such cases the purchase or doctor-patient perspectives would be preferred. Situations that immediately affect the physical and psychological well-being of students and school personnel require immediate attention and cannot wait for process consultation. However, when process consultation is employed regularly, many of the skills and resources that are developed for solving a particular problem can be used again and again in situations involving similar problems. This makes process consultation both time efficient and cost effective for schools.

Approaches to School Consultation
An *approach* (A) is a preliminary step toward a purpose. School consultation approaches may be formal or informal. Formal consultations occur in planned meetings such as staffings, conferences for developing Individual Education Plans (IEPs), arranged meetings between school personnel, and organized staff development activities. They also include scheduled conferences with parents, related services personnel, and community resource personnel.

In contrast, informal consultations often occur "on the run." These interactions have been called "vertical consultations" because people tend to engage in them while standing on playgrounds, in parking lots, at ball games, even in grocery stores. They are dubbed "one-legged consultations" when they occur in hallways with a leg propped against the wall (McDonald, 1989; Hall and Hord, 1987). Conversations also take place frequently in the teacher workroom. This aspect will be addressed more fully in Chapter 12 as a form of informal staff development.

It is very important to designate these informal interactions as consultations because they do require expenditures of time and energy on the part of both consultant(s) and consultee(s). Highlighting them as consultations will help establish the concept of school consultation and promote efforts toward constructing a suitable framework for the support of consultation and collaboration. Informal consultations should be encouraged because they can initiate more planful, productive consultation and collaboration. They often become catalysts for meaningful in-service and staff development activities. In some cases they may cultivate team efforts that would have been overlooked or neglected in the daily hustle and bustle of school life.

Prototypes for School Consultation
A *prototype* (R) is a pattern. Categorical descriptions include mental health consultation, behavioral consultation, advocacy consultation, and process consultation. In the continuing effort in this book to sort out and organize consultation terminology, these categories are termed prototypes.

Mental health consultation is a prototype with a long history (Conoley and Conoley, 1988). The concept originated in the 1960s with the work of psychiatrist Gerald Caplan. Caplan conceived of consultation as a relationship between two professional people in which responsibility for the client rests on the consultee (Hansen, Himes, and Meier, 1990). Caplan (1970) proposed that consultee difficulties in dealing with a client's problems usually are caused by any one, or all, of four "lack-ofs":

- Lack of knowledge about the problem and its conditions;
- Lack of skill to address the problem in appropriate ways;
- Lack of self-confidence in dealing with the problem;
- Lack of professional objectivity in approaching the problem.

In mental health consultation the consultant not only helps resolve the problem at hand, but enhances the consultee's ability to handle future situations more effectively. Caplan's most important intervention goal is to reduce the consultee's loss of professional objectivity whereby the consultee identifies subjectively with the client, or tries to fit the client into a category and assume an inevitable outcome (Conoley and Conoley, 1982). When the mental health prototype is used for consultation, consultee change may very well precede client change. Therefore, assessment of success should focus on consultee attitudes and behaviors more than on client changes (Conoley and Conoley, 1988). This is an important, desirable effect for school consultants and collaborators to consider.

Another prototype frequently used is behavioral consultation. This problem solving procedure is also intended to improve the performance of both consultee and client. Since behavioral consultation is based on social learning theory, skills and knowledge contribute more to consultee success than unconscious themes such as objectivity or self-confidence (Bergan, 1977). Behavioral consultation probably is more familiar to educators and thus is more easily introduced into the school context than is mental health consultation. The consultant is required to define the problem, isolate environmental variables that support that problem, and plan interventions to reduce the problem. Conoley and Conoley (1988) regard behavioral consultation as the easiest prototype to evaluate, since problem delineation and specific goal setting occur within the process. Evaluation results can be used to modify plans and to promote consultation services among other potential consultees.

A third kind of consultation prototype is advocacy consultation. The client is the community, not the established organization (Gallessich, 1974), with the consultant serving the "client" directly as trainer and catalyst, and indirectly as advocate (Raymond, McIntosh, and Moore, 1986). This concept is considered by some as highly political, with one group trying to overcome another for a greater share of the finite resources. Advocacy consultants stress that power, influence, and politics are the motivating influences behind human behavior (Conoley and Conoley, 1982). At some place in the consulting relationship, these consultants face the realization that facilitation of school context goals is contrary to their values. Advocacy consultants need specific consulting skills for organizing people and publicizing events to serve special needs appropriately.

Process consultation is sometimes included as a fourth prototype, along with mental health, behavioral, and advocacy consultation. However, in this book it is treated as a perspective, not a prototype.

Modes of School Consultation
A *mode* (E) is a particular form or manner of doing something. Modes for school consultation can be regarded as direct delivery of service to clients or indirect delivery of service to

consultees. A direct service delivery mode allows a consultant to work directly with a special needs student. For example, a learning disabilities consulting teacher or a speech pathologist might use a technique with the student, while a parent or classroom teacher consultee observes and assists with the technique.

As early as 1962, Reynolds described a hierarchical configuration for special education services that differentiated indirect service in least restrictive settings from direct service in more restrictive settings. The hierarchy (Reynolds, 1962) began at Level 1, the least restrictive level for students, in which special needs were handled in the regular classroom. Then attention to more severe needs was given at Level 2 in the regular classroom with consultation. Level 3, the regular classroom with supplementary teaching or treatment, was more restrictive, followed by Level 4, the regular classroom with resource room service, Level 5 for a part-time special class, and so on to Level 10, or placement in a hospital or treatment center. Within this hierarchical configuration, the intensity of special needs at any given time for an individual student determines the level of service needed to offer an appropriate program. The less severe the need, the closer that placement can be made to the general classroom setting.

Direct service to students usually is carried out subsequent to a referral (Bergan, 1977). The consultant may conduct observations and discuss the learning or behavioral need directly with the student (Bergan, 1977; Heron and Harris, 1987). The consultant becomes an advocate and the student has an opportunity to participate in decisions made pertinent to that need. Another example of direct service is teaching coping skills to students for their use at home or at school (Graubard, Rosenberg, and Miller, 1971; Heron and Harris, 1982).

Some states have limited consulting teachers to spending a specific portion of their time in direct service to special education students. Other stipulations require that the direct service teaching time must occur in the presence of the classroom teacher, and that general classroom students should participate in the activities if at all appropriate. This service is not to be equated with team teaching, a concept that is discussed in Chapter 10.

In contrast to direct service, the indirect service delivery mode calls for "backstage" involvement among consultants and consultees to serve client needs. The consultant and consultee interact and problem solve together. In doing so, the consultant provides direct service to the consultee, who then provides related direct service to the client.

While school consultation typically is regarded as indirect service to students through direct work with their teachers or parents (Lilly and Givensogle, 1981), variants of service delivery are possible in particular circumstances. It is in this arena that some of the most significant changes have occurred since the enactment of Public Law 94-142 and, more recently, the movement toward inclusive schools and unified educational systems. Attention continues to be focused on appropriate use of both indirect and direct service delivery modes in the wake of both the Regular Education Initiative and other efforts to restructure school programs. Indirect service has conceptual merits and pragmatic potential for multiplying the impact of professional services (Pryzwansky, 1986). This is an important consideration in times of shrinking fiscal and staff resources.

Models for School Consultation

Models (M) are patterns, examples for imitation, representations in miniature, descriptions, analogies, or displays. A model is not the real thing, but an approximation of it. It functions as an example through which to study, mimic, replicate, approximate, or manipulate intricate things. Models are most useful for examining objects or ideas when they are too big (such as a model of the solar system) or too small (a DNA molecule) to copy. They also help to understand things that cannot be replicated because they are too costly (a supersonic jet plane), too complex (the United Nations system), or too time intensive (travel to outer space). These qualities make the model a useful structure on which to pattern complex human processes such as school consultation and collaborative interactions.

Six of the more familiar models that have been adopted or modified for school consultation over the past twenty-five years are:

- the triadic model;
- the Stephens/systems model;
- the Vermont Consulting Teacher Program model;
- the School Consultation Committee model;
- the Resource/Consulting Teacher Program model; and
- the collaborative consultation model.

The Triadic Model.   The triadic model, developed by Tharp and Wetzel (1969), is a classic consultation model from which many school consultation models have evolved. It includes three roles—consultant, consultee (or mediator), and client (or target). In this most basic of the existing consultation models, services are not offered directly, but through an intermediary (Tharp, 1975). The service flows from the consultant to the target through the mediator. The consultant role is typically, although not always, performed by an educational specialist such as a learning disabilities teacher or a school psychologist. The consultee is typically, but not always, the classroom teacher. The client or target is usually the student with the learning or behavioral need. An educational need may be a disability or a talent requiring special services in order for the student to approach his or her learning potential.

When studying the triadic model, or any other consultation model, it is important to recall the discussion in Chapter 1 about school consultation roles. Roles are interchangeable among individuals, depending on the school context and the educational need. For example, on occasion a learning disabilities consulting teacher might be a consultee who seeks information and expertise from a general classroom teacher-consultant. At another time, a student might be the consultant for a resource room teacher, the consultee, with the parents as the clients, or targets, for intervention intended to help their child. Tharp gives the following example:

> *Ms. Jones the second-grade teacher may serve as mediator between Brown, the psychologist, and John, the problem child. At the same time, she may be the target of her principal's training program and the consultant to her aide-mediator in the service of Susie's reading problem. The triadic model, then, describes relative position in the chain of social influence. (Tharp, 1975, p. 138)*

In later years, Tharp elaborated on the linear aspect of the triadic model to include influences of others on consultant, mediator, and target, and the interactions that those influences facilitate (Tharp, 1975).

Tharp identifies several advantages of the triadic model (Tharp, 1975), including the clarity it provides in delineating social roles and responsibilities, and the availability of evaluation data from two sources—mediator behavior and target behavior. However, it may not be the most effective model for every school context and each content area with the process skills and resources that are available. Advantages and concerns in using a triadic type of model of school consultation are included in Figure 3-2.

Triadic Types of Models

Advantages	*Possible Concerns*
A way to get started with consultee	Little/no carry-over to other situations and problems
Quick and direct	
Informal and simple, keeps problems in perspective	Needed again for same or similar situations
	Only one other point of view expressed
Objectivity on the part of the consultant	Expert consultation skills needed by consultant
Student anonymity if needed	May not have necessary data available
Appropriate in crisis situations	Little or no follow-up
Time-efficient	Tendency to blame lack of progress on consultant
May be all that is needed	
Can lead to more intensive consultation/ collaboration	

Stephens/Systems Types of Models

Advantages	*Possible Concerns*
Each step in concrete terms	Extensive paperwork
Follows familiar IEP development system	Assumes spirit of cooperation exists
Collaborative	Time-consuming
Changes easily made	Might become process-for-process sake
Formative and developmental	May seem "much ado about little"
Strong record-keeping	Assumes training in data-keeping and observation
Avoids the "expert" role	Multiple steps overwhelming to busy teachers
Has an evaluation component	Delayed results
Much accountability	
Provides whole picture of need, plan, and results	

Resource/Consulting Teaching Types of Models

Advantages	*Possible Concerns*
Provides direct and indirect service	Energy-draining
Parent involvement	Time often not available
"In-House" approach to problems	Scheduling difficult
Opportunity for student involvement	High caseloads for consulting teacher
Compatible with non-categorical/interrelated methods	Indirect service not weighted as heavily as direct
	Training needed in effective interaction
Ownership by many roles in problem-solving	Delayed, or no, reinforcement for consultant
More closely approximates classroom setting	Administrator support and cooperation essential
Spreads the responsibility around	
Opportunity to belong as a teacher/consultant	
Opportunity for regular contact between consultant/consultee	

FIGURE 3-2

(Continued)

FIGURE 3-2 *(Continued)*

School Consultation Committee Types of Models

Advantages	*Possible Concerns*
Administrator involved	Only one day of training for special assignment
Multiple sources of input	Time-consuming
Skill gains from other teachers	Possible resentment toward specialized expertise
Familiar to those using preassessment/building team	Potential for too much power from some committee members
Time provided for professional interaction	Solution might be postponed
Many points of view	Confidentiality harder to ensure
Good for major problem-solving	Indirect, not direct service to student
Focuses on situations of the school context	Could diffuse responsibility so no one feels responsible
Involves a number of general education staff	
Can minimize problems before they get too serious	

Vermont Consulting Teacher Types of Models

Advantages	*Possible Concerns*
Active participation by parents and teachers	Time, travel, scheduling
Teachers learning from the training	Possible chain-of-command problems
New, even experimental, procedures possible	Teachers may resent "imported expert"
Student performance, not label, determining placement	Job security dependent on number of students identified
Supports mainstreaming and parent involvement requirements	Time needed for task analysis for participating role
Collaborative efforts with major institutions	Time required for personnel to reach general consensus
Different professional perspectives	Perhaps not feasible in larger states
Ongoing program evaluation	Requires specification of minimum achievement levels in certain time frame

Collaborative Types of Models

Advantages	*Possible Concerns*
Fits current reform movements	Little or no training in collaboration
Professional growth for all through shared expertise	Lack of time to interact
Many ideas generated	Working with adults not preference of some educators
Maximizes opportunity for constructive use of individual differences among adults	Requires solid administrator support
Allows administrator to assume facilitative role	Takes time to see results
Parent satisfaction	

Stephens/Systems Model.   The systems model constructed by Stephens (1977) is an extension of his directive teaching approach (Heron and Harris, 1982). It includes five phases:

- assessment, observation, data collection;
- specification of objectives, problem identification;
- planning, finding ways of resolving the problem;
- implementation of the plan, measurement of progress; and
- evaluation, data analysis.

Baseline data are collected on target behaviors. Then interventions are planned, and additional data are collected to compare intervention effects. If the plan of treatment is not effective, further assessment is conducted. The consultant helps the consultee devise criterion-referenced assessments or coding devices (Heron and Harris, 1987). This helps consultees become an integral part of the program and acquire skills to use after the consultant leaves. Advantages of using the systems model, as well as possible concerns to be considered, are included in Figure 3-2.

Resource/Consulting Teacher Program Model.   The Resource/Consulting Teacher Program model (R/CT) has been implemented at the University of Illinois and in both rural and large urban areas (Idol, Paolucci-Whitcomb, and Nevin, 1986). It is based on the triadic model, with numerous opportunities for interaction among teachers, students, and parents. The resource/consulting teacher offers direct service to students through tutorials or small-group instruction and indirect service to students through consultation with classroom teachers for a portion of the school day. Students who are not staffed into special education programs can be served along with exceptional students mainstreamed into general classrooms. Parents are sometimes included in the consultation.

In the R/CT model, emphasis is placed on training students in the curricula used within each mainstreamed student's general classroom (Idol-Maestas, 1983). Close cooperation and collaboration between the R/CT and the classroom teacher are required so that teacher expectations and reinforcement are the same for both the resource room and regular class setting (Idol-Maestas, 1981). Advantages and concerns regarding the R/CT model are included in Figure 3-2.

School Consultation Committee Model.   McGlothlin (1981) provides an alternative approach for school consultation in the form of a School Consultation Committee model. The committee typically includes a special education teacher, a primary classroom teacher, an upper-grade classroom teacher, the building principal, and persons involved in ancillary and consultant roles. After a one-day training session conducted by an outside consultant, the committee meets as frequently as needed to screen referrals, assess problems and develop plans, and evaluate the results of those plans. The consultant remains available to help the committee as needed (McGlothlin, 1981).

The School Consultation Committee is a familiar approach for school personnel who have had experience on preassessment teams and other referral groups. Advantages and concerns in using this model are given in Figure 3-2.

Vermont Consulting Teacher Program Model.   The Vermont Consulting Teacher Program model is a collaborative effort of local school districts, the Vermont State Department of Education, and University of Vermont personnel for providing consultative services statewide to teachers who have children with disabilities in their classrooms (Heron and Harris, 1987). This model, another adaptation of the triadic model, includes four phases after student referral:

- entry-level data collection and diagnosis;
- specification of instructional objectives;
- development and implementation of a plan; and
- evaluation and follow-through.

There are three forms of instruction within the model: (1) university coursework for teachers, (2) specialized workshops as an alternative to the coursework format, and

(3) consultation through working partnerships between consulting teacher and classroom teacher (Knight et al., 1981). Through the coursework, teachers learn principles of measurement, behavior analysis, and instructional design. These principles are then applied to the teaching and learning processes in the classroom. A key feature is that the consulting teacher must individualize the program to meet the specific needs of the classroom teacher (Heron and Harris, 1987). Parent involvement is an integral component of the model. Advantages and concerns related to the model are listed in Figure 3-2.

Collaborative Consultation Model.   The collaborative consultation concept is a model in which the consultant and consultee are equal partners in consultation—identifying problems, planning intervention strategies, and implementing recommendations through collaboration (Idol, Paolucci-Whitcomb, and Nevin, 1986; Raymond, McIntosh, and Moore, 1986). Pryzwansky (1974) provided the basic structure of the collaborative approach by emphasizing the need for mutual consent on the part of both consultant and consultee, mutual commitment to the objectives, and shared responsibility for implementation and evaluation of the plan. The consultant, mediator, and target have reciprocally reinforcing effects on one another, which encourages more collaborative consultation later (Idol-Maestas, 1983).

Inclusion of students with special learning and behavioral needs into the total school environment will require school personnel and parents to engage in collaborative consultation at a much more intensive level than they have in the past two or three decades. Special education teachers, general education teachers, parents, administrators, work-study supervisors, and other support personnel must become teaching teams. Several new models have evolved in the past two decades that incorporate extensive collaboration and consultation into the school context. Five of those models are described briefly to illustrate the accelerating trend to involve all school personnel in the progress of every student. They are

- The Adaptive Learning Environments Model (ALEM);
- Class-Within-A-Class (CWC);
- Success-For-All (SFA);
- Mainstream Training Project (MTP); and
- Schoolwide Enrichment Model (SEM).

Adaptive Learning Environments Model (ALEM).   The Adaptive Learning Environments Model (ALEM) (Wang & Birch, 1984) uses the concept of team teaching. It is one of the earliest of the more recent attempts to change general classroom environments in order to accommodate the needs of all children, including those with disabilities. According to its developers, the ALEM concept depicts schools as social systems that must respond effectively to individual differences. Schools are accountable for ensuring that students acquire basic academic skills, a positive self-perception of academic and social competence, practical competence in coping with the social and academic demands of schooling, and responsibility to the broader social community. All students are taught in the regular classroom as adapted to include

- A multi-age and team-teaching organization that increases flexibility in the classroom where individual differences are viewed as the norm rather than the exception;

- Highly structured diagnostic-prescriptive academic instruction, with each student expected to make steady progress when provided with learning experiences based on individual needs;
- Student planning and monitoring of own learning;
- An open-ended, exploratory learning element promoting social and personal development and often involving cooperative learning methods;
- Built-in support systems that include consultation and collaboration by school administrators, health professionals, and special education teachers;
- A family-involvement program that attempts to reinforce the integration of school and home experiences.

ALEM has been researched in a variety of settings, including rural, suburban, and middle-class areas, with a wide range of students, including disadvantaged, handicapped, and gifted. The developers maintain that it is one of the most multi-faceted and visible efforts to integrate exceptional children into general classrooms. Wang (1986) reports consistently positive trends on student achievement in basic skills and social behavior. Improved attitudes toward differences among students occur in classes where exceptional students are integrated. The research base also supports the thesis that a high degree of implementation of ALEM can be attained in classroom settings that differ in terms of aims, needs, and contextual characteristics. Major strengths of ALEM are the data-based approach to improving the degree of program implementation and an individualized staff development program (Wang & Walberg, 1988).

Other researchers (Fuchs & Fuchs, 1988) question such positive results. They contend that the research on the effectiveness of ALEM is equivocal at best. Therefore, they call for more research before educators embark on a large-scale, full-time mainstreaming program such as ALEM.

Class-Within-a-Class (CWC).   The Class-Within-a-Class (CWC) program was developed to be an alternative service delivery model as part of the Park Hill Secondary Learning Disability Project funded by the Missouri Department of Elementary and Secondary Education, Section Special Education (Reynaud, Pfannenstiel, & Hudson, 1987). The underlying philosophy of the program is that all children have the innate potential to learn, and it is the role and responsibility of the public school system to provide opportunities for all learners to be successful. The total program includes collaborative curriculum planning between teams of learning disabilities (LD) teachers and content area teachers and use of a learning strategies curriculum (Deshler & Schumaker, 1986). The LD teachers are in the content classrooms during instruction and provide a variety of support services in classrooms to students who have special needs.

These are the essential elements of the Class-Within-a-Class approach:

1. Teachers who are compatible and willing to work in a team effort are selected by the administrators.
2. The teaching team meets regularly to plan classroom activities.
3. Teacher roles are defined with the general classroom teacher being responsible for maintaining the integrity of the class and the special education teacher collaborating to support the classroom teacher and to serve as a resource to students.

4. High-school-aged learning disabled students with achievement below fourth grade and elementary aged students more than two years below grade level are excluded.

5. When possible, all students of a certain grade level are in the same classroom so the LD teacher can "go with them" to class.

The CWC approach is rapidly gaining widespread acceptance (Hudson, 1992). Although extensive research documenting the effectiveness of CWC has not been published at this time, preliminary results indicate that the approach is very effective if teachers are adequately prepared for collaboration and the guidelines are carefully followed (Hudson, 1992). Before embarking on the use of this model, however, schools should consider carefully the work of Slavin and Madden (1989) that suggests that in-class models are no more effective than pull-out programs.

Success-for-All (SFA).   The Success for All program was developed and implemented in an inner-city elementary school in Baltimore, Maryland (Madden, Slavin, Karweit, & Livermon, 1989). The developers wanted to see what would happen if they decided (1) to ensure that each child in every school would reach the third grade on time with adequate basic skills; (2) no child would be assigned to special education for a learning problem unless he or she had serious disabilities; and (3) no child should need to be retained in a grade or relegated to long-term remedial services. The program includes these elements:

1. Certified teachers with experience in Chapter 1 programs, special education programs, or primary reading programs are employed to work one-on-one with students who are having difficulty keeping up with their reading groups in the classroom.

2. Students in grades 1–3 are in age-grouped classes of about 25 students for most of the school day but are regrouped for a 90-minute reading period into classes of about 15 students at the same performance level.

3. Curriculum-based assessments are made every eight weeks to determine each student's progress. Information from the assessments is used to make program modifications for each student and identify students who need other types of assistance.

4. Half-day preschool for four-year-olds and full-day kindergarten for five-year-olds is provided. The curriculum in these programs places heavy emphasis on development and use of language and provides a balance of academic readiness and nonacademic activities.

5. Two social workers and one parent liaison work full- time at the school as a family support team.

6. A program facilitator, along with the building principal, takes responsibility to oversee operation of the program.

7. Teachers are given detailed manuals developed for the program, supplemented by two days of in-service at the beginning of the school year, and followed by several brief inservice sessions throughout the year.

8. When a student's learning problems cannot be dealt with in the regular classroom and with the help of tutors, special education resource services are provided.

The first year Success-for-All program evaluations indicated that preschool and kindergarten children in the experimental school scored higher than the control group children in language development and reading word attack. Children from first grade through third grade in the experimental school out-scored the control children on every reading measure. More recent research shows substantial reading gains in seven districts around the United States (Slavin, Madden, Dolan, and Wasik; 1994). In contrast, Semmel and Gerber (1990) point out that the Success-for-All program is the most expensive and most ambitious approach for responding to the "problems of learner heterogeneity."

Mainstream Training Project (MTP).   Some school districts have responded to concerns about meeting the diverse needs of students with projects that combine consultation, collaboration, and in-service. The Mainstream Training Project (MTP) is an example at the secondary school level (Tindal, Shinn, Waltz, & Germann, 1987; Waltz, 1990). Within this model, the special education cooperative provides a five-phase training program designed to assist classroom teachers in accommodating for all types of learners. During the first phase, all school staff are given inservice dealing with general information about learners with disabilities, description of services provided through special education, and due process procedures. The second and third phases involve summer workshops for classroom and special education resource teacher teams from each school district. The topics included are

1. Literature review of effective teaching practices;
2. Classroom management strategies;
3. Cooperative learning methods;
4. Individual mastery learning techniques;
5. Use of learning centers;
6. Direct instruction teaching techniques;
7. Reading in the content areas;
8. Writing as a tool for learning;
9. Teaching study skills and actively engaged learning;
10. Evaluation, grading options, and test-writing.

After the teachers have begun to master this content, phase four begins and consultation support is provided in applying the knowledge in the teachers' classroom practices. Typical responsibilities for the consultant, consultee, and students are

1. The regular education teacher assumes daily management of the program, including completion of student observations, evaluative checklists, or tests, and implements any curricular modifications established at the outset.
2. The special education teacher assumes responsibility for helping the teacher collect data, for consulting with the teacher about programs, and for coordinating modification if the student's performance is below the performance levels that are expected.
3. The student follows the agreement and completes all tasks and activities required at the appropriate times. Students are directed to seek assistance if they are having difficulty completing the tasks/requirements (Tindal et al., pp. 100–101).

Once teachers demonstrate competent application of the knowledge in their classrooms, they move into phase five, which involves assisting in training other teachers in phases one through four.

The Mainstream Training Project explicitly uses consultation and collaboration as an integral part of the success of the program. Data collected initially to determine the effectiveness of the program lacked sufficient research design control to draw strong conclusions. However, it is noteworthy that students receiving the consultation services earned grade point averages no different from students who did not have consultation agreements. Since the consultation group students were predicted most likely to fail, data tend to support the effectiveness of the program.

Cancelli and Lange (1990) caution that, within the in-service approach, the consultant owns the problem. By contrast, in most consultation, the teacher owns the problem and the consultant assists with problem clarification in problem-solving. These concerns should be kept in mind when planning the goals of inservice and staff development and will be addressed further in Chapter 12.

Schoolwide Enrichment Model.   Gifted program personnel often serve as consultants or consulting teachers to plan and coordinate appropriate learning opportunities for gifted and talented students. Most students identified as gifted or very talented in one or more areas spend the major portion of the school day in the general classroom. In order to provide more productive learning time for gifted students and to redeem them from years and years of curriculum redundancy, gifted program consultants should work closely with classroom teachers and resource people in the community to challenge students in their areas of special interests and strengths.

Meaningful school experiences for very able students usually differ in pace, breadth, and depth from experiences offered by the regular school program. Differentiated curriculum can be provided by methods such as flexible pacing of subject matter, group activities for interaction with mental peers, personalized learning options, and relevant enrichment of the course content.

One of the most widely used systems for differentiating the curriculum of gifted and talented students is the Schoolwide Enrichment Model, a comprehensive plan developed by Joseph S. Renzulli (1985) and associates. This model serves gifted and talented students in both general classrooms and special resource rooms. In the Schoolwide Enrichment Model, the gifted education facilitator's role is similar to that of a varsity coach who is responsible for the general physical fitness of all students in the school but also facilitates the development of gifted athletes. A Schoolwide Enrichment Team of faculty members, parents, and students gives teachers and administrators the direction they need to expand the scope of school-based experiences directed toward special interests and talents.

Staff development, parent involvement, extensive use of resource personnel, long-range planning, and intensive evaluation are integral components of the Schoolwide Enrichment Model. The coordinator of the enrichment program, who may or may not have other school responsibilities depending on the size and scope of the program, consults and collaborates with classroom teachers, administrators, resource persons, and parents, as well as with the students, to facilitate learning at the pace and level that very capable students need in order to develop their potential. The coordinator also provides direct service to identified gifted students, co-teaches process skills in the general classroom, and manages special projects carried out by students in their interest areas. The coordinator assists classroom teachers to eliminate unnecessary assignments. This gives students the opportunity to progress through the regular curriculum in an efficient, often accelerated, manner (Reis & Renzulli, 1986).

The roles and responsibilities carried out by the Schoolwide Enrichment Model coordinator point out the value of collaboration and consultation activities for serving the special needs of a particular student population. In addition, they underscore the contribution of consultation services toward an atmosphere of excellence as these services affect the total school program in positive ways.

Many research studies have been conducted on various components of the Schoolwide Enrichment Model. Several of the studies examine long-term effects of participation in the model across a period of more than ten years. Studies from the first part of that period are summarized in a two-volume technical report (Renzulli, 1984). Since publication of the technical report, numerous research articles have appeared in professional journals substantiating the success of the Schoolwide Enrichment Model for students identified as gifted, talented, and creative (Renzulli, 1986).

Other widely used gifted program models that encourage consultation and collaboration among teachers, support personnel, parents, and students include the Autonomous Learner Model (Betts, 1986), Talents Unlimited (Schlichter, 1986), the Individualized Programming Planning Model (Treffinger, 1986), the Integrative Model (Clark, 1988), the Purdue Three Stage Enrichment Model for Elementary Level (Feldhusen & Kolloff, 1986), and the Purdue Secondary Model (Feldhusen & Robinson, 1986). Each of these models supports the philosophy that gifted students must receive differentiated services regularly for their special needs, not just a few minutes once or twice a week in brief, isolated programs having little or no continuity with general classroom curriculum.

Research studies support the value of cooperative ventures such as those created by collaborative consultation (Idol, Paolucci-Whitcomb, and Nevin, 1986). Johnson and Johnson (1980) note that cooperative interaction among faculty and administrators can be as powerful a tool for adults as cooperative learning can be for children. However, Morsink, Thomas, and Correa (1991) warn that while collaborative consultation can result in shared expertise among professionals, implementation to date has focused primarily on a triadic relationship between general and special educators. Advantages, as well as potential concerns, for the collaborative model are given in Figure 3-2.

Synthesizing Structural Elements into Methods of Consultation

Any plan for school consultation should take into account the school's needs with regard to consultation by including facets of all the components that have been introduced:

S. System (school systems, other social systems);
P. Perspective (purchase, doctor-patient, process);
A. Approach (formal, informal);
R. pRototype (mental health, behavioral, advocacy);
E. modE (direct, indirect); and
M. Model (triadic, Stephens/systems, Resource/Consulting Teacher Program, School Consultation Committee, Vermont Consulting Teacher Program, collaborative consultation and models that feature it—Adaptive Learning Environments, Class-Within-A-Class, Mainstream Training Project, Schoolwide Enrichment, and Success-for-All).

The most relevant factors of these six key components can be synthesized into an appropriate method for serving a student or educator's special needs as they occur. Once again, refer to Figure 3-1. Note that the Method area in the middle draws from each of the six descriptive elements to provide components for developing consultations for special needs.

Educators will recognize the need for having all six elements—systems, perspectives, approaches, prototypes, modes, and models—understood and available for potential combination into appropriate methods for serving special needs of students within every school context. *Locally developed methods* for addressing *special learning needs* are the most effective school consultation practices educators can employ.

APPLICATION 3.1   Reflecting on Structures for School Consultation, Collaboration, and Teamwork

A helpful activity for thinking about complex functions is the thought problem. Thought problems, practiced by eminent scientists such as Einstein, take place in the mind, not in the laboratory or classroom. The idea is to manipulate variables and concepts mentally, "seeing" them from all angles and deferring judgment until all conceivable avenues have been explored. A thought problem is an opportunity to reflect on something intently before presenting it for discussion and critique by others. Much of the time this type of activity precedes intricate processes such as consultation.

The following thought problem has several parts, one for each of the models described earlier. This exercise encourages you to be *very* "Einsteinian" as you reflect on school consultation, and manipulate and embellish your images of the models.

First, study again the brief descriptions of consultation models. Then select one of the models, perhaps one of the more recently developed ones. Manipulate its components mentally to create a graphic way of illustrating a consultation method that could be useful in your school context. Einstein used trains, clocks, kites, rushing streams, and even swirling tea leaves to reflect on phenomena and conceptualize his ideas. You may find it helpful to use building blocks, toy people, pictures, or other special effects as you manipulate the elements of your ideas. Here are some examples for starters:

1. How might you have depicted the interactions intended for the triadic model? One thinker/illustrator created a restaurant scene, with the consultant as behind-the-scenes cook, the consultee as the counter cook and server, and the client as the diner. Another person devised the heads graphic in Figure 3.3. How do you visualize an interactive graphic for a triadic type of consultation?
2. How would you picture the Stephens/systems model? One person made the ball field form in Figure 3.4 which resembles the original circular graphic which was introduced with this model. Consultation is effectively depicted through this around-the-bases approach.
3. Try visualizing the Resource/Consulting Teacher Program model. What benefits can this itinerant version of the interaction have for students with special needs? (See Figure 3.5.)
4. An illustrator might select a more linear design for illustrating components of the School Consultation Committee model. One possible interpretation is a mobile design (see Figure 3.6), and another would be a computer–type flow chart.
5. An interpretation of the Vermont Consulting Teacher Program model could include a backdrop or foundation that represents a state agency or university.
6. Note the development of a triadic school consultation interpretation (see Figure 3.7) into a more collaborative method for consultation (see Figure 3.8). How might it look to you in your educational context?

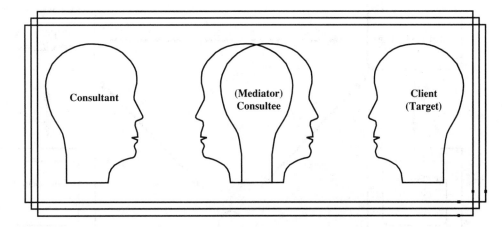

FIGURE 3-3   Example of Basic Triadic Consultation (By Arlene Haack)

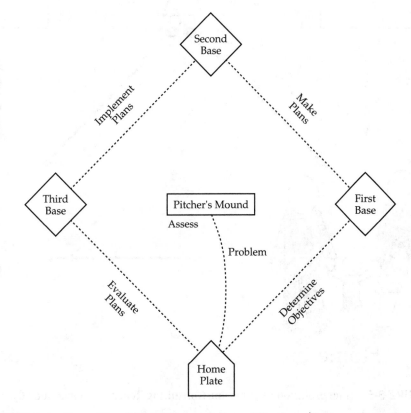

FIGURE 3-4   Consulting Field: Interpretation of Stephens/Systems Consultation (By Patti Pfeifley)

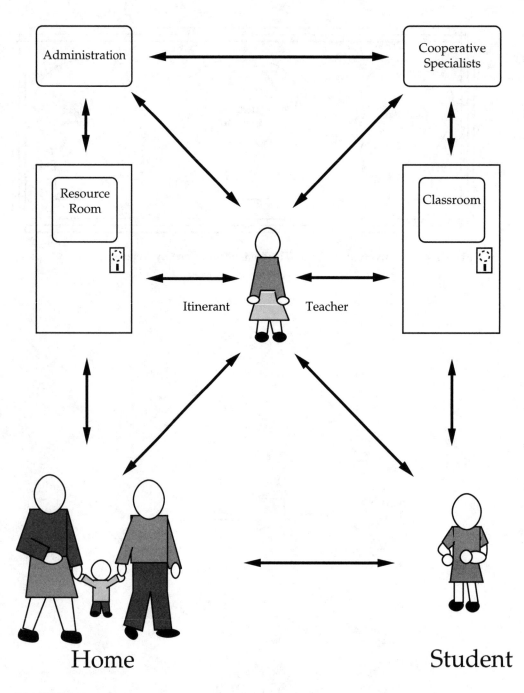

FIGURE 3-5   Interpretation of Itinerant/Consulting Teacher Interaction (By Eric Ross)

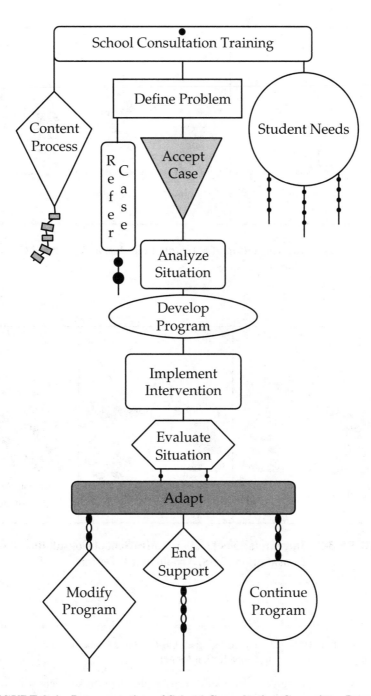

FIGURE 3-6   Interpretation of School Consultation Committee Interaction

FIGURE 3-7   Interpretation of a Triadic Foundation for School Consultation (By Sharon Arnold)

FIGURE 3-8   Interpretation of Collaborative School Consultation Based on Triadic Consultation (By S. Arnold and P. Dettmer)

APPLICATION 3.2   Formulating an Outline for a Collaborative Consultation Model

Now, after creating your mental models, try explaining their key steps with words, either in outline or paragraph form. Then reread the advantages and concerns for each model in Figure 3.2 and test your graphics for benefits and avoidance of concerns.

APPLICATION 3.3   Selecting an Appropriate Method for Specific Situations

Seven potential situations for school consultation, collaboration, and/or teamwork are presented below. There are no right or wrong configurations for structuring methods to address the needs presented within these seven situations. Each should be approached by considering several points:

1. Is this a situation in which consultation and collaboration will be beneficial for the person(s) in need? (If the answer is yes, proceed to next points.)
2. Who best fits the consultant, consultee, and client roles in each?
3. How might interaction among roles be structured? What should happen first? Who will do what? When will the interaction conclude? (Do not dwell on the specific consultation process at this time. That will be addressed in Chapter 5.)
4. Consider the structural elements that will be included in the method you develop for addressing each of the situations:

    4.1 In what *system* (school, home, medical) will the consultation be conducted?
    4.2 Will the most helpful *perspective* be a purchase, a doctor-patient, or a process relationship?
    4.3 Should the *approach* be formal or informal?
    4.4 Is the most descriptive *prototype* the mental health, behavioral, or advocacy pattern?
    4.5 Will the consultation be provided in a direct or an indirect service delivery *mode?*
    4.6 Which *model* seems to fit the need and the other five consultation components best?

One person doing this exercise may decide the best way to address the identified problem is with the triadic model, using indirect service from the consultant to the client, in an informal behavioral interaction within the school system. Another person's problem may have been served most appropriately within a Vermont Consulting Teacher Program model, using direct service to administrators in an advocacy-type interaction, and a formal approach calling for the doctor-patient perspective in a communitywide system. To carry out this task, recall that *methods* of consultation should be designed by using facets of the six structural elements that will best meet each student's special needs.

5. What may be major obstacles in carrying out the consultation and collaboration process? Major benefits? (Remember the all-important multiplier effects—those positive ripple effects that allow educators to serve a wider area of need than the immediate client.)

Situations to Use For This Application

Situation 1: A fourth-grade boy has been in the educable mentally handicapped (EMH) program since first grade. He was first diagnosed as learning disabled, but later staffed into the EMH program. The mother presented a birth history that supported the decision and seems to have accepted it. However, two older brothers living away from home insist that there is nothing wrong with their little brother. Each time the mother visits with them she becomes confused, intimidated, and frustrated. The child is becoming more resistant and passive, and is gaining weight rapidly. How should the EMH teacher address the problem?

Continued

APPLICATION 3.3 *Continued*

Situation 2: The speech pathologist has been asked by the gifted program facilitator to consult with her regarding a highly gifted child who has minor speech problems but is being pressured by the parents and kindergarten teacher to "stop the baby talk." The child is becoming very nervous and at times withdraws from conversation and play. How can the speech pathologist structure consultation and collaboration?

Situation 3: A school psychologist is conferring with a teacher about a high school student she has just evaluated. The student is often a behavior problem, and the psychologist is discussing methods for setting up behavior limits with appropriate contingencies and rewards. The teacher makes numerous references to the principal as a person who likes teachers to be self-sufficient and not "make waves." How should the school psychologist handle this?

Situation 4: A fifth-grade student with learning disabilities (LD) is not having success in social studies. The student has a serious reading problem but is a good listener and stays on task. The LD resource teacher suspects that the classroom teacher is not willing to modify materials and expectations for the child. The teacher has not discussed this situation with the LD teacher, but the student has. Parent-teacher conferences are next week. What should happen here, and who will make it happen?

Situation 5: In a third-grade class a student is an average learner but is often seen in the halls walking near the wall with one hand touching the wall. He appears sad, lonely, and unsure of himself. The special education teacher of a self-contained classroom for students with behavioral disorders has heard of this child getting into fights on the bus and the playground. Today the third-grade teacher stops the special education teacher during the lunch break and says the student was crying at recess and resisting communication. He is not doing any work, but just sitting and eyeing his classmates with a look of frustration and anger. What should the special education teacher do?

Situation 6: A high school learning–disabilities consultant is visiting with a principal at the principal's request. The principal expresses concern about the quality of teaching of two faculty members and asks the consultant to observe them and then provide feedback. How should the consultant handle this situation?

Situation 7: A local pediatrician contacts the director of special education and asks her to meet with local doctors to discuss characteristics and needs of children with disabilities. How should this opportunity be structured for maximum benefit to all?

Tips for Collaborating and Consulting

1. Locate articles focusing on consultation, collaboration, and teamwork, summarize highlights, and prepare a "fact sheet" for other school staff, including administrators.
2. Have articles shared in Tip 1 available for any who might ask to read the entire work.
3. Make a bulletin board for the teacher workroom depicting models you created with the material in this chapter.
4. Prepare a brief description of a consultation and collaboration method and add it to the model display in Tip 3.

5. Be on the alert for new methods or revisions of existing methods, through which consultation and collaboration can occur in your school context.

Chapter Review

1. School consultation evolved from practices in the mental health and medical services fields. The earliest uses of school consultation were in areas of speech and language therapy, and services for visually-impaired and hearing-impaired students.

2. There are differing points of view concerning the existence of a theoretical base of school consultation. Some researchers consider school consultation theory-based if the relationship between consultant and consultee can be identified across more than one literature source.

3. Research in school consultation and collaboration has been organized around investigations of outcomes, processes, and practitioner use. There is a need for more reliable and valid instrumentation, more specific definition of variables and more careful control of variables during research.

4. Structural elements to develop effective methods of school consultation can be categorized as: systems (institutions and contexts); perspectives (purchase, doctor-patient, process); approaches (formal, informal); prototypes (mental health, behavioral, advocacy); modes (direct, indirect); and models (triadic, Stephens/systems, Resource/Consulting Teacher Program, School Consultation Committee, Vermont Consulting Teacher Program, and the collaborative consultation model).

   Several variants on the collaborative consultation model have evolved to address school restructuring and inclusion movements. The Adaptive Learning Environments Model (ALEM) is one of the earliest of the more recent models. The goal of ALEM is to eliminate the need for pull-out programs by providing classroom alternatives that will address the learning needs of all students. Extensive collaboration between parents, teachers, administrators and other professionals is critical for the success of ALEM.

   Class-Within-A-Class (CWC) is an innovative delivery model that strives to reduce pull-out programs by serving learning disabled students full-time in general classes. Special education teachers go into the classrooms during instruction to collaborate and consult with the teacher and provide additional support to learning disabled students in the class.

   Success-for-All (SFA) is a comprehensive program aimed at preschool and primary levels. Its main purpose is to prevent failure by assuring reading success during the early school years. Individual tutoring, cross-age grouping, and extensive collaboration are important features of this program.

   The Mainstream Training Project (MTP) uses in-service training for preparing classroom teachers at the secondary level to serve students who have learning difficulties. When classroom teachers have been trained in using effective teaching methods for students with learning and behavior problems, special education consultants work closely with them to monitor student progress and assist in implementation of newly learned teaching techniques.

   The Schoolwide Enrichment Model is designed to provide more challenging learning experiences for gifted and talented students in the regular classroom. Classroom teachers are supported by consultation services from facilitators for gifted programs. Teachers and facilitators collaborate in providing gifted and talented students with curriculum options and alternatives such as flexible pacing, enrichment, personalized instruction, and challenging group experiences.

5. Major models currently used in school consultation have unique features that make them useful in particular situations and for special needs of consultees and clients. Each of the models also has some areas that may make the model more difficult to implement or less effective within particular contexts and for certain student needs.

6. The most effective strategy for school consultation and collaboration will be a synthesis of appropriate features from the six elements, which are blended to create a situation-specific method for serving a student's special learning needs within that student's school context.

To Do and Think About

1. Pinpoint several changes that have occurred in special education during the past twenty years, and suggest implications for school consultation methods.
2. Using other references and sources, make a time line of key educational policies and reform that helped initiate interest in school consultation, collaboration, and teamwork. (An old window shade is a good material on which to make and display this kind of project.)
3. Make sketches or three-dimensional representations of the models you visualized in the applications exercise above. Does your graphic capture the intent of the model? Does it permit analysis of the model to determine its advantages and cautions in a variety of school settings?
4. Visit schools where consultation and collaboration play an integral role in serving students' special needs. Using the information related to Figure 3-1, analyze the consultation systems, perspectives, approaches, prototypes, modes, and models that seem to be in use in those schools. Then summarize the results into brief, innovative descriptions of the methods that seem to have evolved from the synthesis of these components.

For Further Reading

(Note: The reader is advised to focus on the key points of these recommended readings without getting tangled in the maze of philosophies and terms which, as explained in this chapter, often are not consistent across authors and consultation structures.)

Brown, D., Pryzwansky, W. B., and Schulte, A. C. (1991). *Psychological Consultation: Introduction to Theory and Practice.* Needham Heights, MA: Allyn and Bacon. Chapters 1, 2, and 3 in particular.

Conoley, J. C., and Conoley, C. W. (1982). School consultation: *A Guide to Practice and Training.* New York: Pergamon Press.

Journal of Educational and Psychological Consultation. All issues, and Vol. 1, No. 4, 1990 and Vol. 3, No. 2, 1993 in particular.

Morsink, C. V., Thomas, C. C., and Correa, V. I. (1991). *Interactive Teaming: Consultation and Collaboration in Special Programs.* New York: Merrill. Chapter 2 in particular.

Remedial and Special Education Journal. Issues focusing on school consultation and collaboration.

Salend, S. J. (1994). *Effective Mainstreaming: Creating Inclusive Classrooms (2nd ed.).* New York: Macmillan.

Schlax, K. (1994). Eight Tips for Effective Integration of Therapists. *Inclusive Education Programs 1*(2):11.

Schrag, J. and Burnette, J. (1994). Inclusive schools. *Teaching Exceptional Children,* Spring, 64–68.

Ysseldyke, J., Thurlow, M., Wotruba, J. & Nania, P. (1990). Instructional arrangements: Perceptions from general education. *Teaching Exceptional Children, 22*(4): 4–8.

C h a p t e r **4**

Individual Differences and Effects on School Consultation, Collaboration, and Teamwork

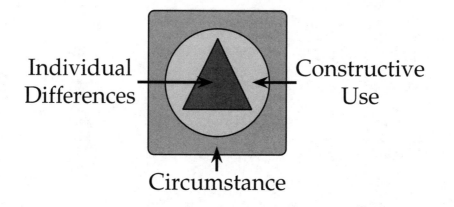

Introduction

Awareness of individual differences and constructive use of those differences are two extremely important educational concerns. Although educators "talk a good game" about individual differences of students, they rarely focus on individual differences among the *adults* with whom they teach and interact. Even teachers who are attentive to individual interests and preferred learning styles of their students may overlook the impact of differing values, styles, and interests upon professional collaboration and teamwork.

Educators are challenged to treat each student as a unique learner. Individualization for student needs is an important aspect of teacher planning. However, individual traits of adult colleagues that cause them to think and act in unique ways are too often overlooked. Tolerance for diverse perspectives of adults toward problems and issues is one of an educator's most important assets when consulting, collaborating, and working in teams to facilitate student learning.

However, the study of adult differences is, for the most part, ignored in teacher preparation programs. Responding effectively to individual differences among adults is vital preparation for engaging in the professional interactions that help identify and serve student needs. It should be the launch pad for the implementation of professional interactions.

Focusing Questions

1. How do individual differences among adults affect interactions in the school context?
2. What are examples of adult differences that occur during consultation, collaboration, and teamwork?
3. How will educators benefit from self-study of their own preferred functions and styles?
4. How can adult differences be used constructively within the school context?
5. How does cultural diversity affect school consultation and collaboration practices?
6. How can consultation create needed links among various agencies that provide services for students with special needs?

Key Terms in the Chapter

cultural diversity
ethnic group
kinesics
learning styles
macroculture
microculture
military dependent students
multiculturalism

nonverbal behaviors
paralanguage
personality
preferences
proxemics
"psychopest"
rural

Valuing Individual Differences Within the School Context

The patchwork quilt appeals to the artistic sense because it has so many varieties of color, texture, and design. If each piece of fabric in the patchwork were identical, the fabric would probably seem dull and drab. The most interesting patchworks are those in which each piece contributes brightness and uniqueness to the overall collage of colors and textures. Even if some of the colors or textures might clash elsewhere, when aggregated into a patchwork design the result is a vibrant, colorful fabric that enlivens the setting.

In much the same way, schools are a patchwork of attitudes, personalities, values, and interests. Each individual in the school setting is different, contributing her or his uniqueness to brighten the whole. Sometimes individual characteristics may clash, but if individualities of students *or* adults are repressed, the school climate becomes drab and dull.

Scenario

(Comments overheard at various times of the day in a typical teachers' workroom of a typical school):

"I was hoping to try that model. Why don't other people on our faculty want to give it a shot? It's been working so well in the other school across town . . ."

"Here we go again. Another newfangled idea to spin us around for our latest ride on the school reform merry-go-round . . ."

"Why are some people so negative toward new ideas before they even try them or give them a chance? . . ."

"We never see eye-to-eye on anything in our department . . ."

"Seems like we do the same old thing, with people falling in line like sheep who stay together and never try new ground . . ."

"I just can't figure out where that parent is coming from."

"*Another* meeting? They drag on and on, with nothing accomplished and nothing to show for all that wasted time . . ."

"What a hurry-up mess that meeting was! Not enough time even to figure out the problem, much less work on solutions. So, nothing accomplished and nothing to show for it . . ."

Recognizing Adult Differences Within the School Context

Much of the seemingly random variation in human behavior is actually quite orderly and consistent, because it is based on the way people prefer to use their perception and judgment (Lawrence, 1982; Keirsey & Bates, 1978). If one person views the world and reacts to it in ways unlike another, it is because that person processes information differently. Different viewpoints contribute diverse insights that help broaden understanding of problems and generate promising alternatives for solutions to those problems.

It is easy and convenient, but myopic, to endorse only one way of doing something—one's own—while wondering why everyone else is not clever enough, and agreeable enough, to concur and fall into step. However, a situation perceived one way by one educator might be looked upon quite differently by another who has completely different values, interests, and attitudes.

In order to serve students best, educators do not need to think alike—they need to think together. Thinking together divergently can be very productive. Understanding and valuing uniquenesses of adults in their orientation toward the world and their styles and preferences for processing information are key factors in the success of collegial relationships.

Conscientious educators who respect the individualism and independence of their students need to respect and protect these rights for their colleagues and for the parents of their students as well. Educator Madeline Hunter advised teachers to move toward dialectical thinking, which does not mean to abandon one's own position but to build correction into their viewpoints by taking an opposing view momentarily. She urged that all should "come out of armed camps . . . where we're not collaborating, so that 'I understand why you think it's right for your students to line up while I think it's better for them to come in casually'" (Hunter, 1985, p. 3). She stressed that, when educators show respect for other points of view, they model the cooperation that is so necessary for the future of communities, cities, nations, and the world.

Today's students are the future leaders of a shrinking global community. It is vital that educators prepare them to function successfully in diverse, multicultural societies. Teachers can promote the cooperation and collaboration skills that their students will need to survive in this increasingly complex, intertwined world. The most effective way of convincing and preparing students is to model the skills every day in the school setting with their colleagues. By doing so they demonstrate that they value diversity, respect differing philosophies, and accommodate individuality in teaching and learning styles. The consultant role is a natural and appropriate vehicle for teaching the constructive use of individual differences among people of all ages.

As educators take the time to reflect upon the thoughts and feelings that drive their actions, they must realize that each person in the work team, classroom, family, or organization also has sets of thoughts and feelings that govern their individual behaviors as well. One of the most overlooked but crucial factors in teacher preparation is the ability to relate constructively to others, including colleagues, by responding to them and their preferences and needs with emotional maturity (Jersild, 1955).

Assessing Individual Preferences

During the 1970s and 1980s a plethora of methodologies and instruments materialized to help understand human behavior and improve human relationships. A number of the instruments

---

APPLICATION 4.1   Putting the Pieces Together

The leader prepares several "puzzles" ahead of time. Pictures of adults interacting, schoolroom pictures, or pictures of children working or playing are effective. There should be one puzzle for each 5 or 6 people, and the size should be 8 ½ × 11 or larger. A 1-inch "frame" around each picture should be left intact, and the rest cut into enough large pieces so that every participant can have 2 or 3. After dividing into groups of 5 or 6 people, one person in each group takes the frame. Every participant (including the frame-holder) takes 2 or 3 pieces of the disassembled puzzle. (The puzzle pieces should be large enough so that several words can be written on them.) The group then discusses their similar and different characteristics and preferences. The person with the frame writes around that frame several characteristics *everyone* in that group shares—for example, "We are all female," or "We all *don't* have a cat." Next, each person writes on each of his or her pieces a personal characteristic that belongs to no one else in the group—for example, "I was born in a taxicab en route to the hospital," or "Brussels sprouts is my favorite vegetable." Then the group assembles the puzzle and shares the information with all groups. When displayed with an interaction-focused title, the assembled and glued puzzles make effective bulletin board displays featuring individual differences. (Occasionally puzzles may be provided that are missing a piece or two. This metaphorically illustrates the "missing element" that might decrease the effectiveness of a group with a task to complete.)

A variation of the activity is to distribute a background page with a flower's center to each group for recording the things in common, and 2 or 3 cutout "petals" to each person for listing unique characteristics, with a flower garden of differences and similarities being the result.

have been used in such diverse social service areas as education, counseling (for marriage and family, personal, and career needs), religion, business and industry, and other social institutions. Personality theory, cognitive style theory, and aptitude-treatment interaction (ATI) were precursors to a mushrooming interest in learning styles paradigms (Keefe and Ferrell, 1990). Learning styles became an everyday word in the educational vocabulary of the 1970s and 1980s.

In a synthesis of learning style research, Lawrence (1984) suggests that, although the term "learning styles" is loosely and variously defined, it generally includes

- Cognitive style, in the sense of preferred or habitual patterns of mental functioning, information-processing, and formation of ideas and judgment;
- Patterns of attitudes and interests that influence what a person attends to in potential learning situations;
- Disposition to seek out learning environments that are compatible with one's cognitive style, attitude and interest, and to avoid those that are not;
- Disposition to use certain learning tools and to avoid others.

Assessment of individual differences can take place with one or more instruments among a wide range of existing tools and techniques, including Gregorc's instrument for profiling learning style (Gregorc & Ward, 1977), aptitude-treatment interaction theories relating individual differences to instructional method, the Kolb cognitive style concepts (Kolb, 1976), the McCarthy (1990) 4MAT system, the Dunn and Dunn learning style assessment (Dunn and Dunn, 1978), and the Myers Briggs Type Indicator (Myers, 1962), to name only a few of the more prominent examples.

Each of these systems has been used in a variety of contexts to increase awareness and understanding of human preferences that influence behavior. To balance the zeal of those who support each system, there are those who caution against overgeneralizing and oversimplifying complex human attributes with techniques such as self-report assessment and dichotomous interpretations—for example, concrete/abstract, morning/evening, extrovert/introvert, or impulsive/reflective comparisons. Nevertheless, Carl Jung, the eminent Swiss psychologist, professed that people differ in fundamental ways even though all have the same instincts driving them from within (Jung, 1923).

Personality is the complex of characteristics that distinguishes an individual and characterizes him or her in relationships with others. It results from inner forces acting upon and being acted upon by outer forces (Hall and Lindzey, 1978). Any one of a person's individual instincts is not more important than that of another person's instincts. What *is* important is the person's own *preferences* for personal functioning. These individual preferences provide the "patchwork quilt" of human interaction that can be so constructive and facilitative for teamwork and group problem-solving. For example, a person who looks for action and variety, shares experiences readily, prefers to work with others, and tends to get impatient with slow, tedious jobs, is indicating preferences that are quite different from one who prefers working alone, laboring long and hard on one thing, and seeking abundant quiet time for reflection. An individual who is interested in facts, works steadily and patiently, and enjoys being realistic and practical contrasts with one who prefers to generate multiple possibilities, attends to the whole aspect of a situation, and anticipates what will be said or done.

A person who needs logical reasons, holds firmly to convictions, and contributes intellectually while trying to be fair and impartial has different type preferences from one who relates freely to most people, likes to agree with others, and cultivates enthusiasm among others. An individual who likes to have things decided and settled, functions purposefully, and seeks to make conditions as they "should be," does not have the same preferred style as one who has a more live-and-let-live attitude, leaving things open and flexible with attitudes of adaptability and tolerance.

Every person is equipped with all the attributes and can use them as needed but typically *prefers* to focus intensively upon one or the other at a time. Murphy (1987) explains this point by using the example of color. Just as red cannot be blue, one cannot *prefer* both polarities simultaneously. If a person prefers to apply experiences to problems, that person cannot also prefer to apply imagination to those problems. But he or she can use imagination if need be and may benefit from practicing such skills in order to use that approach more productively.

Jung (1923) proposed that each individual has everything needed to function completely. The least-preferred functions as well as the most-preferred functions can contribute to productivity and self-satisfaction. The less-preferred functions provide balance and completeness. They are also the wellsprings of enthusiasm and energy. As an individual's most childlike and primitive functions, they can be quite useful by creating a certain awkwardness and unrest that cultivates innovation. But preferred functions are generally called upon when ease, comfort, and efficiency are most important.

Self-Study of Preferred Styles and Functions

Schools contain in miniature most of the factors people face in their lives, and each person within the school is an experiment in life—an attempt at a new solution and adaptation (Jung, 1954). However, until individuals engage in self-study, they are likely to see others through the biases and distortion of their own unrecognized needs, fears, desires, anxieties, and sometimes hostile impulses (Jersild, 1955). School consultants would do well to analyze their own philosophies, values, and inclinations before attempting to work intensively with others and *their* preferences and values (Brown, Wyne, Blackburn, & Powell, 1979). As educators reflect upon their own characteristics and preferences, they often make comments such as these:

"I have lots of skills, but I don't seem to get them put together to do what I want."

APPLICATION 4.2   An Important Concern to Me Now

Think of something that concerns you very much at this time. With what is it interrelated? What values are at stake? How do your individual preferences and styles of thinking and working highlight this concern? What outcomes will be important for you in connection with the concern? Do you think that other adults (friends, colleagues, family) might address your concern differently if it were theirs? What might be the outcome(s) of the way in which you think they would approach your concern? What does the comparison of your approach and the one(s) others might use say about individual differences among adults in the work environment?

"I am fed up with these reports that have to be done on such short notice. If data are turned in hastily and carelessly, what is their value?"

"I worked really hard on that project, and then everybody else seemed to forget that the ideas were mine when it came time to give out recognition."

"Should I state my views, or wait and see what everyone else thinks and then fall in line?"

"It seems as if all I do with this faculty is put out fires."

"If I didn't show up tomorrow, I'm not sure any of my colleagues would notice or care, so long as there is a substitute teacher here to corral the kids."

Self-study can be undertaken through a variety of methods and settings, including group work, role playing, reading, conferences, and workshops. Personality, temperament, and learning style tools named earlier in this chapter are useful when discussed in in-service and staff development sessions or in department meetings with small-group activities to highlight the rich variety inherent in human nature. Of course, no single journal article, book, conference, or training package will provide sufficient material to fully understand the sophistication and complexity of individual differences. As stated earlier, oversimplification and overgeneralization of complex constructs such as personality must be avoided. Conclusions should not become labels. Rigid interpretations must give way to open mindedness and respect. With these cautions, teachers *can* begin to interact with their colleagues more effectively and serve their students more successfully if they work at understanding the variations of personality types and the effects on learning styles and teaching styles (Dettmer, 1981). As an additional incentive, it usually is lots of fun!

It is not necessary to use a formal personality assessment to explore the constructive use of individual differences. A warm-up list of descriptors can be enough to activate meaningful discussions about human variability and to allow some very general subgrouping for getting a perspective of the value of human variability in problem-solving situations.

The importance of self-understanding is substantiated by these comments from an educator during coursework to prepare her for the consulting teacher role in special education:

Having now taken the [personality instrument] two times, I have a better understanding of myself. More important, however, is that I have an increased understanding of type theory. Being a bit wary of type-casting, I was surprised to find that my type profile did not change from one administration to the next. Of course, caution must be exercised in using any instrument. With little or no understanding of the theories behind it, one easily could dismiss the instrument or misinterpret it. Even more detrimental would be using results to stereotype or place blame or make excuses.

Without further study, I doubt I could determine anyone else's type. Yet being aware of different preferences is enough to foster my long-held belief that a teacher must approach the curriculum in a myriad of ways. By being sure there is "something for everyone," a teacher can make the best attempt at reaching all the students.

Self-study helps educators become more aware of their own attributes and weave their own best qualities into new combinations for helping students with diverse interests and learning needs (Dettmer, 1981). Too few teacher preparation programs provide opportunities for this important self-exploration. Conoley (1987) was an early advocate in promoting the awareness that individual differences of collaborating adults was the key to a theory and practice of school consultation. Safran (1991) criticizes the shortsightedness of researchers who omit factors such as personality, interpersonal affect, and "domineeringness" from their research designs that focus on consultation and collaboration.

Constructive Use of Adult Differences for School Consultation

Understanding differing preferences and types is particularly helpful when one person communicates with another, or lives with another, or makes decisions that affect another's life (Myers, 1980a). Problems in human relationships are minimized when the basis of the misunderstanding is realized. In his material on "The 7 Habits of Highly Effective People," Covey (1989) stresses that individuals must seek first to understand—*to understand and then be understood*. He advocates building skills of empathic listening that will inspire openness and trust.

Six graduate students in a university class for developing collaborative consultation skills wrote about their experiences with a personality preference indicator:

Lori: *When we split into groups in class, it was really interesting to discuss things because with the way in which we were grouped everybody was on the same wavelength. It would be nice if, when we collaborate, we could work with people in the same type category; however, that would make work and life dull and uninteresting. As I was skimming through descriptions of other types than mine, I noticed that there are some types I would tend to go head-to-head with—the people who have to have everything organized, or those who think their opinion is the only opinion . . .*

Donna: *In reviewing descriptions provided by the personality instrument, I can visualize people I know and work with. This information can be valuable to my planning consultant groups. I usually gravitate toward those most like me. I've always thought we worked more quickly and efficiently together. I see now the importance of a diverse group of professionals in preparing the most suitable guidelines and educational plans for exceptional children.*

Tonya: *A fact I found interesting is that the most effective groups are those that have a span of different preferences. The responses and outcomes of a widely spanned group are more diverse, global in perspective, and possibly even more open-minded. . . . A teacher must be a facilitator to all students and therefore has an obligation to be flexible and ingenious with teaching methods.*

Janet: *Since I have taken the personality assessment I have been more aware of different types, especially at meetings I have attended. I like to observe and study human behavior, and the information I obtained is helping me to have a better insight as to why people react the way they do in different situations. It has also helped me to understand that I need to have patience and understanding for those who do not think the same way I do.*

May (a graduate student from Taiwan): The most valuable benefit I earned from this self-report inventory is that I became more understanding of myself and more aware of the difference among people. I have been thinking what kind of person I really am for a long time. Now, I discover the answers. Because of its results, I know my work habits, communication types, preferred teaching situation and interaction.... More important, however, is that I have become more respectful of the differences among other people. Each person's individual preferences and values are indispensable for effective teamwork. For being a consulting teacher, to understand the team members' different preferences has become more important.

Elizabeth: I can easily state what I gained most from the activity. It was an opening of my mind. Being human, I have had a tendency to think my personality type is the "best" or most conducive for teaching. I have learned [in] this session that there is not a "best" type for teaching. Rather, opposite types each have strengths which need to be recognized even though they are different from mine.... I have always preferred to work with others whom I felt comfortable with, probably because they had a similar personality type to mine. This, I have discovered, is not necessarily the best scenario for being productive. As a whole, then, I would say what I learned was to openly accept and work with opposite types without criticism and with a realization that much success can be garnered from opposing types working together.

Data from a variety of occupational and academic groups have been used to study vocational preferences, aesthetic preferences, aptitudes, work habits, family and marriage relationships, creativity, and values. Isabel Briggs Myers (1975) liked to help married couples reconcile their different points of view by pointing out three alternatives:

You can consider that it is wrong of your partner to be different from you, and you can be indignant. That diminishes your partner and gets you nowhere. Or your can consider that it is wrong of you to be different from your partner and be depressed. That diminishes you and gets you nowhere. The proper solution is to consider that the two of you are justifiably and interestingly different, and be amused (Myers, keynote address October 16, 1975).

Differences among people in interaction techniques, preferred outcomes, work habits, and communication styles are important for school consultants to acknowledge when they are facilitating consultations and collaborations. Teachers often differ dramatically in their preferences. A consultant may work with one teacher who pays close attention to detail, examining every test score and asking questions about particular assignments, and another who scarcely looks at the test scores, preferring instead to solicit verbal, generalized assessment of the student's capabilities from other professionals.

A study by Lawrence and DeNovellis (1974) revealed that teachers with different preferences tend to behave differently in the classroom. Carlyn (1977) studied the relationship between personality characteristics and teaching preferences of prospective teachers. Some are more interested in administrative functions and others have a strong need for independence and creativity. Some prefer planning school programs, while others enjoy working with small groups of students. Some people like action and variety more than quiet and reflection. Some like to work with others in groups, whereas others prefer to work alone or with one person. Some people get impatient with slow jobs and complicated procedures. Others can work on one thing for a long time, and they resent interruptions. Carlyn concluded in her study that teachers of different personality type preferences also preferred different kinds of teaching situations. These kinds of preferences and values help explain why some teachers will experiment with modifications and materials a consultant suggests, while others resist or just never seem to get around to doing it.

When a group of educators with different types of preferences collaborate, they have the opportunity to contribute a variety of strengths within the interaction. Those who like to bring up new possibilities and suggest ingenious ways of approaching problems will benefit from having other people supply pertinent facts and keep track of essential details. When some are finding flaws and holding to an existing policy, others contribute by selling the idea, conciliating, and arousing enthusiasm (Myers, 1980b).

Opposite types may or may not attract but they definitely need to be available for greatest team productivity. Such differences can be useful but managing them elegantly is a tremendous challenge for a consultant or consulting teacher. As stated earlier, the primary goal in consulting, collaborating, and working as a team is not to think alike, but to think together. Each person's individual preferences and values are important to the effectiveness of interaction. Differences in schools and classrooms are not just disagreements between adult and child, or teacher and student, or administrator and teacher or para-educator and consulting teacher. They reflect differing orientations to the world, individual learning styles, personal values, and individual work habits. These differences, when understood and appreciated, can be constructive for serving student needs.

Using Adult Differences to Facilitate Productive Team Interaction

Good teamwork calls for the recognition and use of certain valuable differences among all members of the team (Myers, 1974; Kummerow & McAllister, 1988). The most effective teams do not agree all the time, but they use individual differences constructively (Kummerow & McAllister, 1988; Truesdell, 1983). Individuals have far more potential than they use at any one time, and the power of this potential in team settings is exponential. Team

---

APPLICATION 4.3　Sharing a Professional Experience

In a small group of 5 or 6 people who share your general type preferences, describe an experience from your teaching or schooling in which you put forth significant effort but ended up feeling unappreciated, unreinforced, and perhaps a bit of a failure in that instance. After all in the group have shared a personal example (with each having the privilege of passing up the opportunity if they prefer not to share), discuss ways in which members of the group reacted to each other's experience.

APPLICATION 4.4   Using Individual Differences Constructively

Choose a favorite lesson or subject area and imagine that you and a consultee will be team teaching this material. How would you go about this? Although it would be important to know something about your co-teacher's style and preferences, you should ask yourself whether there are things you should study about *yourself* before embarking on this collaborative endeavor? How can you share that information with your colleague and learn comparable information about that person in order to team more effectively?

success comes from division of labor and efforts toward mutual respect among members, openness to the contributions of others, and facilitative communication. Educators can learn a great deal from talking with colleagues with whom they differ both theoretically and methodologically (Gallesich, 1973). With a common vocabulary and a framework of respect for individuality, teamwork can be much more productive.

Influence of Adult Differences on Communication

Many communication problems among team members are due to individual differences. A statement that seems clear and reasonable to one person may sound meaningless or preposterous to another (Myers, 1974). One may want an explicit statement of the problem before considering possible solutions. Another member of the team might want at least the prospect of an interesting possibility before buckling down to facts. Yet another may demand a beginning, a logically arranged sequence of points, and an end (*especially* an end, Myers cautions). Another will really listen only if the discussion starts with a concern for people and the direct effects of the issue on people.

Myers stresses, "It is human nature not to listen attentively if one has the impression that what is being said is going to be irrelevant or unimportant" (Myers, 1974, p. 4). Communication is such a critical part of successful consultation and collaboration that it will be the focus of concern in Chapter 6.

Influence of Adult Differences on Problem-Solving

Individual differences play a significant role in the efficiency of problem-solving (Campbell & Kain, 1990). Some individuals are more accurate in problem identification, while others need less time to come up with possible solutions. One person may focus more on the problem and the facts, while another focuses on process and the meaning behind the facts. If an individual needs to solve a problem alone, he or she must manage multiple perspectives, but problem-solving by a well-mixed team of individuals enables most perspectives to be represented efficiently. Many heads are better than one. With pooled experiences, interests, and abilities, synergy results.

No specific preference is predictive of success in communication or problem-solving within the group, and research shows that teams with a complete representation of types outperform virtually any single-type or similar-type team (Blaylock, 1983). The likelihood of having team *versatility* is better than might be expected, for a single group of several individuals will contain many, if not most, of the preferences. (See Figure 4-1.)

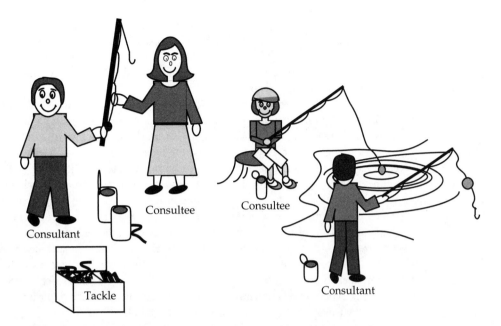

FIGURE 4-1 Individual Differences (By E. Vega and N. Dyck)

Using Knowledge of Adult Differences Wisely

The phrase, "A little knowledge is a dangerous thing," should be heeded when addressing the issue of knowledge about individual differences. Just as teachers have learned to be discriminating in applying learning styles methodology to the classroom, so should consultants apply principles of type theory judiciously.

The following points summarize cautions along with possibilities for using knowledge about adult *or* student differences constructively.

1. Consultants can work from a knowledge of personality assessment or learning style concepts without knowing the formal profiles of individuals in that group; in fact, they probably *should* do so. This premise will be more fully developed by the next several points.

APPLICATION 4.5   Preferred Recognition and Reward

In Application 4-4 you shared an experience with colleagues who have similar styles and preferences. This time, form groups of 5 or 6 who have differing styles. Discuss ways in which you would like to be recognized, and perhaps rewarded, reinforced, or even praised, for something you did that required effort and skill. Then talk over with the group the variations in outcomes that different individuals prefer. How might this affect a work context such as the school and the teaching profession? How could you provide reinforcement to people who have different preferences from yours?

2. It is not always possible, necessary, or even desirable to ascertain people's preferences with a standardized instrument. The most important need is to develop the attitude that human differences are not behaviors intended to irritate and alienate each other. Rather, they are systematic, orderly, consistent, often unavoidable differences in the ways people prefer to use their perception and judgment.

3. Each set of preferences is valuable, and at times indispensable, in every field.

4. Well-researched personality or temperament theory does not promulgate labeling of individuals. Learning styles theory and right-left brain function research have fallen victim on occasion to unwarranted use of labels—"He's so right-brained, that he can't..." and "She's a concrete sequential, so she won't...". The world probably does not need any more labels for individuals, and this is particularly cogent in the field of special education. Such labels often contain hierarchical connotations (IQ tests, entrance exams), negative connotations ("stuck up" or "flaky"), derogatory overtones ("operates in the fast lane"), and trendy associations ("horoscope reader") (*The Type Reporter, No. 37*, pp. 1–2). Consultants must take care to avoid such connotations, as well as phrases containing absolutes ("always...never...") and stereotyping through humor, anecdotes, excuses, and job division based on type (Lawrence, 1988).

5. Problems in human relationships caused by the conflict between opposite types can be lessened when the basis of the conflict is understood.

6. As the saying goes, "The map is not the territory." Type preferences never tell all there is to know about the rich and abundant variety of individuals that make up the human population of the world.

7. Any individual can reserve the right to change, experiment, or surprise another by being "out of character." Some of the most adamant resistance to type theory has come from those who regard type descriptions as stereotyping. Most people do not want to be regarded as completely predictable and unoriginal (*The Type Reporter No. 37*, p. 2.) People resent the "psychopest" who professes to know all about them and gives unsolicited interpretations (Luft, 1984).

8. Even among people with the same type preference, no two will function the same. It is like a garment—no two people look the same in it (*The Type Reporter No. 37*). It is inappropriate and unjust to assume too much from analysis of individual differences. No generalization should be applied to a single case, for any case could be an anomaly. As an example, Hammer (1985) stresses that a book (*Moby Dick,* for example) can be read in different ways by different people. One reader may have an eye toward the narrative as a thrilling sea adventure, while another may appreciate the symbolism of the whale's whiteness. The danger is in *assuming* what pleases others and how it pleases, to the point of denying opportunities for other experiences. Teachers who assume that "Her type does not like to read," may stop offering her books. If a teacher believes that a student will not enjoy a particular kind of learning experience, he may be denying the student necessary opportunities to develop (Hammer, 1985). These lessons were learned the hard way in uses and misuses of learning styles theory and should not have to be relearned.

9. Preferences should not be used to make decisions during hiring, voting, or similar selection processes. The appropriate use is to explain a job or a role requirement to an applicant in terms of what it entails, and allow the applicant to determine whether he or she perceives a goodness-of-fit (*The Type Reporter, No. 37*).

10. All good teaching methods have value for some students at certain times and in particular places. By the same token, each method will be received differently by each student (Murphy, 1987a). (Recall the analogy of the garment mentioned above.)

11. Valuing individual differences will require more than merely tolerating them. It means accepting the fact that people *are* different and the world is the better for the diversity (Murphy, 1987a).

12. Teacher preparation programs must be more enterprising and effective in preparing graduates to have a superlative ability for understanding individual differences among educator-colleagues as well as students.

13. Much more research is needed on the constructive use of individual differences, especially in the area of school consultation, collaboration, and working in professional teams.

Effects of Cultural Diversity On School Consultation and Collaboration

After generations of being hailed as a cultural melting pot, the United States began to be regarded more descriptively as a "salad bowl." Each component of a salad bowl has its own flavor and piquancy but contributes significantly to the composition of the whole. An even more illustrative metaphor than salad bowl for describing the cultural composition of the United States in the 1990s is *mosaic*. Each cultural, racial, ethnic, and religious group contributes to the value and beauty of the whole society.

The melting pot, the salad bowl, and more recently the mosaic metaphor underscore ideas that have enhanced multicultural sensitivity in this country over the past two hundred years or so. As Hallahan and Kauffman propose (1991):

- Cultural diversity is to be valued.
- Common cultural values hold our society together.

What is culture? A quote by an unknown source cautions us: "Culture, like religion, is a mighty big word ... Handle with care" (Tyler, p. 84, 1979). With that caveat in mind, one finds that Webster's Dictionary contains this description:

Culture is the body of customary beliefs, social forms, and material traits constituting a distinct complex of tradition of a racial, religious, or social group.

It is helpful to think of culture as including six major elements (Banks, 1988; Hallahan & Kauffman, 1991):

1. Values and behavioral styles;
2. Languages and dialects;
3. Nonverbal communication;
4. Awareness of one's cultural distinctiveness;
5. Frames of reference, or normative world views and perspectives;
6. Identification, or feeling a part of the cultural group.

These six elements comprise a nation's culture (the macroculture), while smaller cultures (the microcultures) contain unique variations of them (Banks & Banks, 1989; Hallahan & Kauffman, 1991). It is constructive to define culture broadly, because demographic variables (age, gender, residence), status variables (social, educational, economic), and affiliations (formal, informal) all contribute.

Different regions of the country are becoming more unlike in very important ways. A policy or practice that benefits one region may be questionable or objectionable in another (Hodgkinson, 1985). Demographers have projected that by the year 2000 the United States will be a nation in which one of every three persons is a person of color. The educational system will be called upon more and more during the next several decades to serve new pluralities. Old concepts about cultural affiliations will no longer suffice.

Assessing Multicultural Awareness of Educators

Multiculturalism in the 1990s is not a separate field of study but a continuous theme resonating throughout all fields. In education the mandates of multiculturalism are to

- Increase knowledge about cultural diversity;
- Foster positive attitudes toward cultural pluralism; and
- Promote skills in arranging multiple learning environments that enable individuals from every culture to develop their potential.

Hallahan and Kauffman (1991) stress that educators must become comfortable with their own microcultural identification. Only after they have assessed their own attitudes and values toward cultural diversity will they be able to promote understanding and appreciation of diverse cultural groups. They must examine their spoken and unspoken attitudes about cultures different from their own, taking care to ferret out any narrow viewpoints or shallow thinking. As just one example of a teacher's shrunken perspective, one student who was of Native American heritage brought a program home from school with an illustration of "The Pilgrims' First Thanksgiving." The child's father wryly noted the caption under the illustration "informing" readers that the Pilgrims had served pumpkin, turkey, corn, and squash to the Indians, and the Indians had never seen such a feast before (Dorris, 1979).

Sample items for assessing one's multicultural awareness are provided in Figure 4-2. The items can be used for personal reflection and self-study. Discussion of the items and expansion of the list with other items would provide a powerful staff development experience. This list also could be administered as part of a study module for a teacher preparation course on consultation and collaboration. (Refer to Application 2.8, Graduate Programs, Developing Competencies for Consultation and Collaboration, in Chapter 2.) As a subtopic under course goal number 7, several appropriate objectives would be:

1. Acquire a knowledge of the philosophy, theory, and application of multicultural education.
2. Increase awareness of the value of cultural diversity.
3. Expand knowledge of current issues in multicultural education.
4. Acquire information about contemporary and historical cultural experiences of various ethnic groups, including their contributions to American society.

A = Always;   U = Usually;   S = Sometimes;   R = Rarely;   N = Never

Personal Efforts

_____ 1. I realize that any individual in a group may not have the same values as others in the group.

_____ 2. I avoid words, statements, expressions, and actions that members of other culture groups could find offensive.

_____ 3. I read books and articles to increase my understanding and sensitivity about the hopes, strengths, and concerns of people from other cultures.

_____ 4. I counteract prejudicial, stereotypical thinking and talking whenever and wherever I can.

School Context

_____ 5. I include contributions of minority populations as an integral part of the school curriculum.

_____ 6. I strive to nurture skills and develop values in students and colleagues that will help members of minority groups thrive in the dominant culture.

_____ 7. I know where to obtain bias-free, multicultural materials for use in my school.

_____ 8. I have evaluated the school resource materials to determine whether they contain fair and appropriate presentation of minority groups.

Parent/Community Relations

_____ 9. I invite parents and community members from various cultural backgrounds to be classroom resources, speakers, visiting experts, or assistants.

_____ 10. I value having a school staff composed of people from different cultural backgrounds.

_____ 11. I exhibit displays showing culturally diverse people working and socializing together.

_____ 12. I advocate for schools in which all classes, including special education classes, reflect and respect diversity.

FIGURE 4-2   Examples of Multicultural Assessment Items

5. Recognize potential cultural biases in school functions such as student assessment, parental involvement, staff development, and consultation.
6. Increase ability to interact successfully in cross-cultural settings.
7. Accept differences in patterns of child development within and between cultures in order to form realistic student goals and objectives.
8. Demonstrate familiarity with appropriate multicultural resources, which will include people, places, and things.

Efforts in the last several years to raise cultural awareness and improve the skills of educators for working with minority students and families have not caught up with the large cultural gap in many schools and communities (Preston, Greenwood, Hughes, Yuen,

Thibadeau, Critchlow, & Harris, 1984). Furthermore, problems in assuring truly multicultural education are compounded by the lack of minority group personnel in special education.

Distinguishing Ethnicity from Exceptionality

Hallahan and Kauffman (1991) emphasize the need to distinguish between ethnicity and exceptionality in serving students with special needs. In focusing upon this need they draw upon Banks' definition of an ethnic group as one that shares a common ancestry, culture, history, tradition, and sense of peoplehood in becoming a political and economic interest group (Banks, 1988). Multicultural education as it relates to students with special needs must ensure that ethnicity is not mistaken for exceptionality (Hallahan & Kauffman, 1991). As one important example, the word *disadvantaged* should not be paired with *cultural*. A person is not disadvantaged by having an affiliation with any culture. The appropriate term is *cultural diversity*. Ethnic standards for a particular group should never be held up as measuring sticks for standards of another group. To do so could result in inappropriate labels of exceptionality rather than recognition of cultural diversity.

Multicultural awareness means that people can disagree without the need to regard one side as right and the other as wrong. Tyler (1979) stresses that "right ways" of conducting particular social activities can be diametrically opposed.

Cross-cultural variations have important effects on collaborative problem-solving. Examples of ethnically based values and behaviors that may affect group interaction are preferences regarding (Sue & Sue, 1990):

- Proxemics (personal space), such as physical distance between communicants and arrangement of furniture for seating;
- Kinesics (or body movement) such as posture, facial expression, and eye contact;
- Time orientation;
- Paralanguage (vocal cues beyond words) such as loudness, hesitations, inflections, and speed; and both verbal and nonverbal messages.

In some cultures the way to respond to a question that shows finesse is to skirt the subject and arrive at it indirectly, while in another culture being direct and forthright is admirable. As another example, in certain cultures public congratulation is offensive because group accomplishment is valued more than individual achievement, while in others public congratulation would be an incentive to continue excelling. Variations of actions involving handshakes, head nods, eye-brow raising, and finger-pointing have widely different meanings in diverse groups. Awareness of these differences, and respect for different customs within diverse cultures, can become major factors in interaction within school settings and in collaborative efforts by school personnel.

Consulting teachers and collaborators must model respect for diversity and assist other school personnel in cultivating ethnic identities of students through classroom activities that range from traditional through nontraditional styles. This will reduce stereotyping and accommodate diversity, much to the advantage of multicultural students with special needs (Heron & Harris, 1987). One powerful and constructive way educators can model respect is to convey intentions of learning *from* another culture and not just learning *about* it.

A Chinese student studying special education in the United States was enrolled in a university course on school consultation and collaboration. This student wrote:

Since I came to the United States, I have been involved in a totally different circumstance I have never confronted before.... I really observe and analyze a life with different implications and features. I was puzzled at the scene in which American students rushed in and out of classroom each day, while in China we may have more leisure time chatting or discussing among students. Classmates in China usually stand for [sic] close friends, who take years to study, work, play, and live together. Here in America, only a few faces are familiar to me as one semester passed... I sometimes feel myself retiring, quietly friendly, sensitive, modest about my abilities. This in fact reflects some aspect of culture in our society. I was nurtured to become a "good boy"—courteous and modest. Thus I, like many other Chinese students, shun disagreements, do not force my opinions or values on others.

Professional educators will want to encourage parents of students from culturally diverse groups to become involved in their children's education to the greatest extent possible. However, Heron and Harris (1987) caution that parent-training programs must convey respect for parents' language, culture, knowledge, and environmental constraints when such exist.

Barriers to active parent participation include work responsibilities, time conflicts, transportation problems, and child care needs. These findings (Lynch & Stein, 1990) have been supported across all ethnic and income groups. Educators must refrain from applying

---

APPLICATION 4.6 A Multicultural Autograph Session

Find a person who fits each item below and have that person autograph your paper. Try to use a different person for each item. You may enter your own autograph once if you qualify for that item.

1. Someone who speaks Spanish. _____
2. Someone who has been in more countries than you have. _____
3. A person who owns a world atlas. _____
4. Someone who has eaten sushi. _____
5. A person who has driven on the left side of the road. _____
6. A person who has seen a movie in a foreign language _____
7. Someone who has eaten couscous. _____
8. A person who has studied French. _____
9. Someone who has a penpal in another country. _____
10. Someone with a friend or a relative from another culture. _____

When you have completed your autograph page, sit down and interact with those around you, sharing descriptions of multicultural experiences you have had and discussing places you would like to travel and cultures about which you would like to learn more.

stereotypical characteristics to all individuals from a given cultural group (Heron & Harris, 1987, Sue & Sue, 1990). Students are individuals, and different generations of families have different perspectives. Consulting teachers should seek information about culturally diverse populations from primary and contemporary sources. This includes direct information from people as well as recent publications about community values that differentiate those that are traditional from those that are more integrated with the context in which they occur.

Language Needs of Students from Culturally Diverse Groups

Linguistics plays a major role in the ways parents and school personnel communicate about students (Lynch & Stein, 1990). Non-English speaking students in the schools present major new challenges in education. Consultants should consider language and culture as means to appropriate programs and not as ends (Baca & Cervantes, 1984; Heron & Harris, 1987). The cultural background of many minorities dictates different patterns of communication (Sue & Sue, 1990). School personnel will need to articulate student needs carefully so that suitable programs are designed for students from culturally diverse populations who have special needs.

There has been much emphasis in recent years on programs for bilingual education and English as a second, or perhaps even a third, language. Bilingual education is an unresolved issue, with educators not in agreement about the most effective processes. However, it does seem that bilingual programs using both English and non-English languages for instruction are more beneficial than those emphasizing only one language (Heron & Harris, 1987). English as a second language (ESL) is a program that can be offered independently or incorporated into bilingual programs.

Needs of Rural and Isolated Populations

What is rural? Perhaps more than anything else, it is a state of mind—an "I can do it" attitude growing out of the necessity of functioning independently without the built-in support system that is more available in urban settings (Teagarden, 1988). Rural schools in remote areas are characterized by geographic isolation, cultural isolation, too few students for some kinds of grouping, too few staff members covering too many curricular and special program areas, resistance of students to being singled out, limited resources, and most of all, distance that necessitates great amounts of personnel time spent in travel. Some special education resource personnel spend up to half of their workday on the road (Meyen & Skrtic, 1988). The consulting teacher has become a mainstay of school districts in which miles and more miles separate students who have special learning and behavior needs.

Communication is more likely to be person-to-person in rural areas whereas it may be written or phoned in urban settings. In the rural setting teachers are highly visible, therefore more vulnerable to community pressure and criticism. Rural educators are left much to themselves to solve problems and acquire skills for their roles (Thurston & Kimsey, 1989). These qualities of rural school life create advantages for consulting teacher approaches but certain disadvantages for the indirect service delivery. Few rural schools are fully prepared and able to meet the needs of special needs students without consulting and other indirect services. Therefore, it is necessary for consultants and consulting teachers to become intensively involved in providing learning options and alternatives for students. The consulting teacher can coordinate collaborative effort among teachers, administrators, parents, and other community members so that few resources seem like more.

In a comparative study of consultant roles and responsibilities in rural and urban areas, Thurston and Kimsey (1989) found that rural and urban teachers conduct similar consulting activities, but rural teachers have less formal recognition of their consulting roles. They seemed less confident in their consulting skills than their urban counterparts. Major obstacles include too many other responsibilities, lack of time, lack of administrative support, travel hardships, and too much paperwork. In contrast, obstacles reported by consulting teachers in urban areas include too many other responsibilities, too much paperwork, and disinterested parents.

In no other setting is the positive ripple effect, or multiplier effect, more useful than in rural areas with limited access and resources. These multiplier benefits can be maximized by playing upon the strengths of the rural community, including smaller class sizes, more frequent interaction between students and staff, greater involvement of parents in the school and its activities, and active students who participate in most phases of school life. Rural-area students tend to be resourceful, open to a wide range of experiences, somewhat independent, and capable of self-direction. These pluses can be used to advantage by consultants in designing collaborative arrangements for special needs. Since students in rural areas often dislike being singled out, it is important to involve them in planning learning programs in which they are comfortable and interested.

Needs of Military Dependent Students

Military dependent children and youth and others who move frequently are largely overlooked as a population having special needs who can benefit significantly from consultation services. When families move from site to site, they frequently become frustrated with the tangled web of records, referrals, screenings, and conferences. They need accurate, clear records to ease their transitions from school to school. Consultants and consulting teachers can become a lifeline for military dependent and other transitory students by assisting busy classroom teachers with coordination and synchronization of student records, and coordination of orientation activities and conferences.

Consultants also can facilitate the integration of students into activities with their new peers. Much more could be done in the way of making military dependent and transitory students feel welcome in new environments. Curricular units and learning centers that highlight their travels and former experiences will be constructive for other students even as they make the military dependent child feel more welcome. Their strengths can be used to remediate gaps they may have incurred from dissimilar educational programs and frequent adjustments to new situations. Furthermore, students who have traveled widely can be valuable resources for their classmates and teachers.

Practices for Promoting Multicultural Education

Educators will want to design activities that not only reduce prejudice and stereotypes but promote the contributions from culturally diverse groups representing minority populations in particular. Multicultural education is not an activity for the last 30 minutes of school on

Friday. The principles of multicultural awareness and acceptance should be infused throughout the entire school program. Consultant roles can be particularly facilitative and supportive in this endeavor. The consultant can assist in assessing the instructional environment and designing effective instruction for culturally diverse groups.

The hidden curriculum is a critical area for multicultural awareness and acceptance. Informal discussions, bulletin board displays, selections read to the class, speakers brought into the classroom, all are helpful if planned carefully. Selected teaching activities can promote an acceptance and even a fascination for differences, as well as allowance for different opinions and points of view, and increased understanding of how people sometimes are limited by their cultural assumptions. Consultants must work to ensure that the hidden curriculum builds, and does not destroy, positive attitudes and understanding.

Consultants also are in a position to encourage fuller use of the resources within the entire community. They might bring in successful citizens who represent culturally diverse groups to tell about their heritage, their interests, and their roles in society. They might pair these resource people with students having special needs, particularly if they have the same cultural background as the student. Since studies show that parents from some culturally diverse populations tend to be less knowledgeable about and involved in their children's education than other parents (Ramirez, 1990; Lynch & Stein, 1990), consultants will be challenged to find ways of collaborating with them to inform and involve them. Awareness, appreciation, and sensitivity toward individual differences and cultural diversity are vital attributes for consultants as they communicate, cooperate, and coordinate with a wide range of resource and support personnel, teachers, parents, and the students themselves.

Consultants as Links among Diverse Social Agencies

A vast array of social service agencies exists for serving students with special needs; however, their services often overlap and many are large, unwieldy bureaucracies with a maze of bewildering requirements (Guthrie & Guthrie, 1991; Hodgkinson, 1989). The situation calls for extensive collaboration among agencies for productive integration of services.

Educators may be the most feasible linkage in developing cooperation and coordination among organizations and agencies which serve children with special needs. As budget constraints restrict the continuation or growth of many educational and social programs, special education consultants can play pivotal roles in the future for serving children with special needs. They are in good positions to become effective, cost-efficient links between education and other social agencies.

It will be a challenge for educators to form new paradigms that decompartmentalize services for students with special needs. Guthrie and Guthrie (1991) state that service providers must step outside the boundaries of their job descriptions on occasion to do what needs to be done for students. They suggest going to community centers, schools,and homes, devoting more time than usual to families and outside resources. These functions are compatible with the processes and content familiar to those in school consultation roles. Guthrie and Guthrie warn against the "all-talk, no action" posture, excessive jargon, and failure to follow up. These points are readily recognizable to school consultants who have developed skill in avoiding such pitfalls.

Collaboration and team effort can begin in any agency. These strategies become powerful forces for education when they create positive ripple effects for students in schools, social services, business partnerships, and most of all, neighborhoods and homes. They will be discussed further in Chapter 13.

Tips for Consulting and Collaborating

1. Listen to the other person's point of view. Seek to understand the content of the person's ideas and the meaning it has for that person.
2. Encourage each member of a collaborative group to share knowledge and perceptions about an issue, in order to establish a solid framework in which to discuss the issue.
3. Take the time to assess preferences of consultees before deciding upon a consultation method.
4. Encourage input from as many sources as possible when deliberating upon a difficult problem, in order to take advantage of many styles, preferences, and cultural perspectives.
5. Appreciate perceptions and preferences different from one's own by engaging in a dialectical conversation. Do not feel that it is necessary to change your position or to convert the other person to your position.
6. When students with special needs are mainstreamed, share with their receiving teachers any helpful information about the students' learning styles and preferences; however, take care not to stereotype students or alter teacher expectations inappropriately.
7. Everyone is not an expert at everything. Find ways to acknowledge and use suggestions from others.
8. Respect the rights of others to hold different beliefs. While one may not agree with others, one must assume they are acting in ways they believe appropriate.
9. Really care about another person's feelings and ideas and show it through actions.
10. Reasons exist for things that people do or say, so try to discover them.

Chapter Review

1. Most educators are attuned to the need for responding to individual differences of their students; however, little attention has been given to individual differences among school personnel and the ways in which those differences affect the school context and professional interactions.
2. Adult differences affect professional interactions in communicating, identifying problems, generating solutions to problems, and evaluating performance.
3. Before educators attempt to understand the uniqueness and individuality of their colleagues, they should analyze their own preferences and individuality.
4. Problems caused by disharmony between opposite types can be lessened when the basics of the disagreement become understood. Adult differences can be used to advantage in teamwork and problem-solving. When all preferences are available through contribution of varying preferences among team members, all facets of a problem can be studied and a wide range of options generated.
5. School consultants and consulting teachers are in ideal positions to infuse multicultural education into the school context. They can facilitate greater parent involvement from culturally diverse populations, coordinate bilingual and English-as-second-language programs, and develop awareness and sensitivity toward needs of culturally diverse groups. Their services are particularly valuable in rural areas, as well as with military dependent children and others who move frequently.

6. School personnel recognize the strength as well as the needs of children and youth; therefore, they can serve an important role in promoting integrated programming among all agencies that are involved with a child's development. They are in excellent positions to link the personnel and the services of school, social agencies, business partnerships, homes, and other community organizations into collaborative efforts that will help students who have special needs.

To Do and Think About

1. Discuss ways in which provocative issues related to individual preferences and styles might be explored without endangering professional collegiality and school morale.
2. Design a bulletin board that celebrates individual differences among adults. Where might you display it?
3. Interview teachers from schools having multicultural populations, asking them to suggest ways in which consultation and collaboration might help meet students' special needs. What steps should be taken to carry out these ideas?
4. Visit with colleagues or classmates about openended topics such as

- What is good and what is not good about being a teacher?
- What changes do I hope will take place in education in the next ten years, and how will I need to change if they do happen?
- What are my best attributes as a teacher?
- What teaching strengths do I value in others?
- (If group members know each other well enough)—What teaching strengths do I value within this group?

For Further Reading

Brownwood, A. W. (1987). *It takes all types!* San Anselmo, CA: Baytree.

Bruner, J. S. (1960). *The process of education.* Cambridge, MA: Harvard University Press.

Corey, M. S., and Corey, G. (1992). Group processes and practice. Pacific Grove, CA: Brooks/Cole.

Covey, S. R. (1989). The 7 habits of highly effective people. New York: Simon & Schuster, Inc. (Book or tape format)

Jersild, A. T. (1955). *When teachers face themselves.* New York: Teachers College Press, Columbia University.

Journal of Psychological Type (formerly named *Research in Psychological Type*). All issues.

Jung, C. G. (1923). *Psychological types.* New York: Harcourt Brace.

Keirsey, D., & Bates, M. (1978). *Please understand me.* Del Mar: CA: Prometheus Nemesis.

Kummerow, J. M., & McAllister, L. W. (1988). Team-building with the Myers-Briggs type indicator: Case studies. *Journal of Psychological Type, 15,* 26–32.

Lawrence, G. (1982). *People types and tiger stripes: A practical guide to learning styles,* (2nd ed.). Gainesville, FL: Center for Applications of Psychological Type, Inc.

Morsink, C. V., Thomas, C. C., & Correa, V. I. (1991). *Interactive teaming: Consultation and collaboration in special programs.* Columbus, OH: Merrill. Chapter 6 on considering cultural diversity in the interactive process, and Chapter 10 on implementation with culturally diverse students.

Myers, I. B. (1980). *Gifts differing*. Palo Alto, CA: Consulting Psychologists Press.

Schmuck, R. A., and Schmuck, P. A. (1979). (3rd ed.) Group processes in the classroom. Dubuque, IA: Wm. C. Brown.

Sue, D. W., & Sue, D. (1990). *Counseling the culturally different: Theory and practice* (2nd ed.). New York: John Wiley.

Tyler, V. L. (1979). Intercultural interacting. Provo, UT: BYU, David M. Kennedy Center.

C h a p t e r **5**

Problem-Solving Strategies for Consultation, Collaboration, and Teamwork

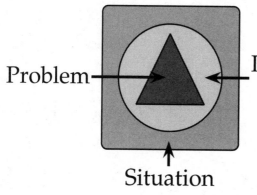

Problem → ← Problem Solving Strategy

↑ Situation

Introduction

The development of a structured format for consultation is integral to collaboration and teamwork among educators. Using a consulting process within a structured format is like preparing food according to a recipe. After fundamental processes have been mastered, proficient cooks can adapt their procedures to just about any setting, individual need, preference, or creative impulse. In similar fashion, a basic "recipe" for consultation, once mastered, can be adapted to any school context, grade level, content area, or special learning need.

Consultation and collaboration increase the flexibility and expand the teachers' repertoire for identifying student needs and developing plans to address the needs resourcefully.

122

When consulting teachers, classroom teachers, support personnel, and parents complement and reinforce each other by using effective problem-solving methods and strategies, schools become better places for learning.

Focusing Questions

1. What are fundamental components in a problem-solving process?
2. In what ways are communication, cooperation, and coordination needed in the consultation process?
3. Why is problem identification so important in consultation and collaboration?
4. What basic steps should be included in the consultation process?
5. What kinds of things should consultants and consultees say and do during their professional interaction?
6. What group problem-solving tools and techniques are particularly helpful for consultants and collaborators?

Key Terms in the Chapter

brainstorming	interfering themes
buzz groups	lateral thinking
circle response	POCS (problem, options, consequences, solution)
concept mapping	problem identification
follow-up	problem-solving process
huddle groups	process for consultation
idea checklist	reciprocal teaching
jigsaw	

The Problem-Solving Process

Educators must focus on a multitude of student needs and educational goals. This requires astute judgment, in order to select the most effective and efficient means of maximizing gains for all students' educational goals (Lanier, 1982). It also necessitates gathering information from a variety of sources, in order to be knowledgeable about methods and materials that will serve diverse needs of students in a wide range of school contexts. Educators must focus on identifying learning and behavior problems and making appropriate decisions about educational programs. In order to do so, they need excellent problem-solving skills. Problem-solving ability comes more naturally and easily to some than to others. It is not likely that most problem-solving activity is carried out by any specific formula or "recipe." But skills for solving problems efficiently and effectively, particularly in groups, can be improved with training and practice.

Pugach and Johnson (1995) suggest two general categories for problem-solving in the context of teacher collaboration: (1) schoolwide problems, and (2) specific student problems. Within the realm of educational reform of the 1980s and 1990s, school personnel are

Scenario

The setting is the office area of an elementary school, where a special-education staff member has just checked into the building and meets a fourth-grade teacher.

CLASSROOM TEACHER: I understand you are going to be a consulting teacher in our building to work with learning and behavioral disorders.

CONSULTING TEACHER: That's right. I hope to meet with all staff very soon to determine your needs and work together on plans for addressing those needs.

CLASSROOM TEACHER: Well I, for one, am glad you're here. I have a student who is driving me and my other twenty-four students up the wall.

CONSULTING TEACHER: In what way?

CLASSROOM TEACHER: Since she moved here a few weeks ago, she has managed to upset completely the classroom system that I've used successfully for years.

CONSULTING TEACHER: Is your new student having trouble with the material you teach?

CLASSROOM TEACHER: No, she is a bright child who finishes everything in good time, and usually correctly, I might add. But she is extremely active, almost frenetic as she busy-bodies around the room making a nuisance of herself.

CONSULTING TEACHER: What specific behaviors concern you?

CLASSROOM TEACHER: Well, for one thing, she tries to help everyone else when they should be doing their own work. I've worked a lot on developing independent learning skills in my students, and they've made good progress. They don't need to have her tell them what to do.

CONSULTING TEACHER: So her behavior keeps her classmates from being the self-directed learners they can be?

CLASSROOM TEACHER: Right. I have to monitor her activities constantly, so my attention is diverted time after time from students I'm working with. She bosses her classmates in the learning centers and even when they play organized games outside. At this rate she will have serious difficulties with peer relationships.

CONSULTING TEACHER: Which of those behaviors would you like to see changed first?

CLASSROOM TEACHER: Well, I need to get her settled into some additional activities by herself rather than bothering other students.

CONSULTING TEACHER: What have you tried until now to keep her involved with her own work?

CLASSROOM TEACHER: We use assertive discipline in this school, so when she disrupts, I put her name on the board. By the way, the parents don't like this at all.

CONSULTING TEACHER: We could make a list of specific changes in behavior you would like to see and work out a program to accomplish them . . . There's the bell. Shall we meet tomorrow to do that?

Scenario *Continued*

CLASSROOM TEACHER: Sounds good. I'd like to get her on track so the class is more settled. The other children will like her better and she will be able to learn other things, too. And the parents will be happier as well. I'll see you here tomorrow. This consulting process may be just what we need!

finding it necessary and expedient to work collaboratively on schoolwide issues. Full inclusion is an example of schoolwide problem-solving undertaken in a collaborative way by all school staff. Specific student needs are the more common type of issue that teachers deal with in a problem-solving mode. However, both categories of problems provide an opportunity to broaden the educational climate for students with special needs.

Pugach and Johnson (1995) also suggest that another important outcome of collaborative problem-solving on a system-wide basis is development of a support structure for teachers to improve classroom instruction. For this kind of professional development, it is helpful to begin with a fundamental problem-solving process. Gordon (1977) outlines six general components that are important for solving problems effectively.

1. identification and definition of the problem,
2. generation of alternative solutions,
3. evaluation of alternative solutions,
4. decision-making,
5. implementing the decisions, and
6. following up to evaluate the solution.

These components include the basic elements of the problem-solving processes that are most frequently employed in a wide variety of business and professional areas. It can be helpful to use the thought problem concept introduced in an earlier chapter to picture the problem-solving process. A graphic illustration of the problem-solving process could be pictured by someone as a stepwise procedure (see Figure 5-1). Graphic representations and metaphors are useful when discussing collaboration and teamwork with consultees and with administrators who assist with consultation structures.

Communication, Cooperation, and Coordination in Problem-Solving

Communication, cooperation, and coordination are basic ingredients of good consultation. A problem-solving process that reflects high levels of each of these will allow educators to share expertise bearing on the problem. Learning and behavior problems are not always outcomes of student disabilities. Many students are simply "curriculum disabled" (Conoley, 1985), needing a modified or expanded approach to existing curriculum so they can function successfully in school (Pugach and Johnson, 1990). In order to modify the learning

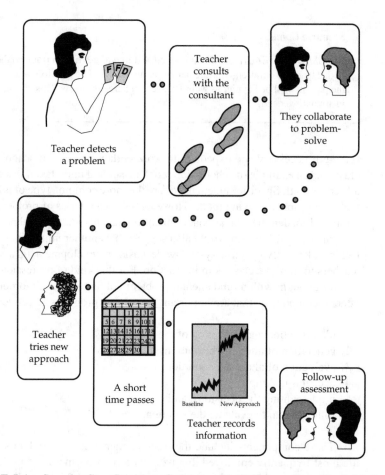

FIGURE 5-1   Step-by Step Problem-Solving with Collaboration (By J. M. Loeb)

environment both in school and at home, educators must identify those aspects of students' curriculum that are interfering with their development.

Interfering Themes
Consultation provides an arena in which to address four interfering themes that can restrict an educator's ability to facilitate student development. These interfering themes, identified by Caplan (1970), include:

    lack of knowledge about students' needs;
    lack of skills in dealing with the needs;
    lack of confidence in using appropriate strategies; and
    lack of objectivity in assessing the situation.

During collaboration, consultants should use every opportunity to reinforce the efforts and successes of classroom teachers and also convey a desire to learn from them and their experiences. Too often, classroom teachers, who occupy the lowest position in a hierarchy of specialists (Pugach, 1988), and parents, who can be somewhat removed from the school setting, are overlooked as possibilities for solutions when learning and behavior problems are explored.

When communicating and cooperating with consultees to identify the learning or behavior need, it is important that consultants avoid sending messages intimating that classroom teachers and parents are deficient in skills that only special education teachers can provide (Friend and Cook, 1990; Huefner, 1988; Idol, Paolucci-Whitcomb, and Nevin, 1986). Nurturance of communication skills and cooperative attitudes will encourage feelings of parity and voluntariness among all school personnel and parents during the problem-solving process. Students who are assigned to resource settings in other schools for part of the week or school day may have teachers in each setting who never communicate about those students and their programs. This is a serious drawback of some cluster group arrangements in which students travel from one school to another, and no planned interaction among school personnel takes place.

Coordination of collaborative effort is a necessity. Special education teachers who cannot identify basal reading curriculum used in various levels, and classroom teachers who cannot identify the nature of instruction taking place in the resource room, make problem identification more difficult (Idol, West, and Lloyd, 1988). They may even intensify the problem. All parties must think about their own roles in the problem situation and endeavor to learn from each other by interacting, deferring judgment, and coordinating their services.

A team approach is a productive way to assess the context, conditions, interfering themes, and circumstances surrounding the student's needs and the school programs designed to meet those needs. A noted politician who had been endeavoring to get his colleagues to cooperate and collaborate reminded them that astronomers from all parts of the world collaborate because there is no one place from which every part of the sky can be observed. This message is cogent to educators as well, who need to observe each student and consider all needs in the cognitive, affective, physical, and social domains while problem solving for student programs. The perceptions and perspectives of each educator, including parents, are invaluable in identifying learning or behavior problems of students and developing goals to remediate the problems.

A goal motivates action and provides direction for that action. Douglass and Douglass (1993) suggest that goal-setters think SMART: Specific, Measurable, Achievable, Realistic, and Timed. Establishing goals, and constantly reviewing existing goals, are crucial processes in defining problems to be solved and decisions to be made. When groups lose sight of the goal, priorities cannot be established, work plans cannot be defined, and expected outcomes cannot be realized.

The POCS Method of Problem-Solving

The value of communication, cooperation, and coordination in collaborative problem solving can be accentuated by using the POCS method of problem solving (Thurston, 1987):

problem identification (P),
generating *options* (0),
determining the *consequences* (C), and
planning the *solution* (S).

A worksheet of POCS (problem, options, consequences, and solution) for taking notes on ideas generated is helpful for consultants as a problem-solving guide (see Figure 5-2).

The Problem
The first and most critical step in the POCS method of problem solving is to identify the problem (Schein, 1969; Bolton, 1986). The most sophisticated teaching methods and the most expensive instructional materials are worthless if the student need is misidentified or overlooked.

Problem: _____

Expected Outcome: _____

		Options		*Consequences*

1. _____   _____

2. _____   _____

3. _____   _____

4. _____   _____

5. _____   _____

6. _____   _____

Chosen Solution: _____

Responsibilites and Commitments: _____

Follow-up Date and Time: _____

FIGURE 5-2   The POCS Method of Problem Solving (by L. P. Thurston)

It can even be argued that inaccurate definition of the problem situation has potential for iatrogenic results. These hurt more than help, just as identifying an illness incorrectly can delay help or prescribing inappropriate medication might be seriously counterproductive.

Problem identification requires special emphasis, if the consultation process is to produce results. In problem identification, consultation variables such as interview skills, flexibility, and efficiency have greatest impact on problem solving (Bergan and Tombari, 1976). Consultants who are skilled in problem analysis are most able to identify appropriate target behaviors and develop workable interventions (Bergan and Tombari, 1976). Information on the student's behaviors, discrepancies between current and desired performance, and baseline data are needed to determine the level of potential target behaviors (Polsgrove and McNeil, 1989).

When information about student needs is multisourced, it can give a more accurate perspective on learning and behavior problems, the settings in which they are demonstrated, severity and frequency of the problems, and persons who are affected by those behaviors (Polsgrove and McNeil, 1989). The need for multiple sources of information to help solve problems will be discussed in the section on the ten-step consultation process.

Obtaining information from multiple sources requires effective communication skills by all who can contribute information. Communication is such an important aspect of successful school consultation that it is addressed separately in Chapter 6. Expressing thoughts and feelings with clarity and accuracy entails effective listening and appropriate assertiveness. The problem will never be solved if all parties think they are working on different issues. Problems are like artichokes—they come in layers. Only after the outside layers are stripped away can problem solvers get to the heart of the matter. Good listening facilitates movement to the heart of the problem.

Options

Problem solving also involves generating options to solve the problem. Brainstorming, or thinking of many solutions without judging or criticizing, is important in order not to get stuck in routines and answers. Some consultants find it helpful to encourage the person who "owns" the problem to make the most suggestions. For example, if the problem is making a decision about post-secondary education for a student with learning disabilities, the student and the parents should be encouraged to generate the most options. This is important for several reasons. When people participate in decision making, they feel more ownership toward the results than when the decision is forced on them. Also, as explained by Johnson and Johnson (1987), people are more apt to support decisions they helped create than those imposed on them, regardless of the merit of the ideas.

An important second reason for prompting the owner of the problem to give initial suggestions is that a consultant should avoid giving advice and being presented or perceived as the expert. Several researchers have shown that the nonexpert model of educational consulting is more effective in special education (Margolis and McGettigan, 1988; Idol-Maestes, Lloyd, and Lilly, 1981). The suggestions and opinions of others need to be listened to with respect and fully understood before additional suggestions are offered.

Finally, teachers and others are more likely to be resistant if the problem-solving process is perceived as advice giving by the consultant. Problems that come up in school consultation often reveal the need for changed classroom practices. This can engender resistance that will not yield to an "I'm the expert and you're not" model. Advice giving and hierarchical structure may be unintentionally communicated if consultants promote the options generated as being their ideas.

If a consultant is regarded as *the* expert, there is pressure on that consultant, and false expectations are created. It is hard to win in this kind of situation. The best practice for the consultant is to communicate equality, flexibility, and a sharing attitude. Three questions assess the equality that is or is not present in a professional consulting relationship:

- Does the consultant recognize the consultee's expertise and opinion?
- Does the consultant encourage the consultee to generate ideas and make decisions?
- Do consultees feel free to *not* do as the consultant might recommend?

Eager, competent consultants who are ready to solve problems and produce quick results, instant cures, and dramatic increases, too often jump in and try to solve problems alone. Consultees may react with resistance, negativism, or hostility by hiding their feelings, withdrawing, or blaming others if things do not work out.

It is difficult for consultants to avoid the "quick fix." But the quick fix is inappropriate (DeBoer, 1986). It is demeaning to the one who has been struggling with the problem. Others need to feel that the consultant fully understands their unique situation and the source of their frustrations before they are ready to participate in problem solving and listen to the suggestions of colleagues. Consultants must listen before they can expect to be listened to, treated with parity, or approached again voluntarily by consultees.

All learning situations and all students are unique. In response to a question about classroom management, a high school teacher replied, "I don't know all the answers, because I haven't seen all the kids." While students and situations may appear similar in some ways, the combinations of student, teacher, parents, and school and home contexts are unique for each problem.

Furthermore, in many cases, people with problems already have their answers. They just need help to clarify issues or an empathic ear to face the emotional aspects of the concern. If people keep talking, they often can solve their own problems. Joint problem identification and idea generating assure that professional relationships are preserved, professional communication is enhanced, and professionals maintain a greater feeling of control and self-esteem.

Good consultants do not solve problems—they see that problems get solved. So they facilitate problem solving, and "nix the quick fix." As Gordon (1977) asks, whose problem is it? Who really owns the problem? Busy consultants do not need to take on the problems of others, and such action would inhibit consultees from learning and practicing problem-solving skills. Everyone who owns a part of the problem should participate in solving it. That may involve collaboration among several people—teachers, administrators, vocational counselors, students, parents, and others. When problem ownership is a question, consultants and consultees should focus on the problem rather than on establishing ownership for the problem. All individuals will need to attend carefully to minimizing roadblocks and maximizing assertion and listening skills.

Consequences

Effective consultants facilitate problem solving in such a way that all members of the group feel their needs are being satisfied and an "equitable" social and professional relationship is being maintained (Gordon, 1977). Members of the problem-solving team work together to evaluate all the suggestions made, with each discussing the disadvantages and merits of the suggestion from his or her own perspective. Agreement is not necessary at this point, because the barriers and merits important to each person are taken into account. Honest and open communication, good listening skills, and the appropriate level of assertiveness are vital at this step.

Solutions

Better decisions are made with a cool head and a warm heart (Johnson, 1992). Johnson suggests asking oneself if the decision helps meet the *real* need. Real needs are based on reality, not illusion or wishful thinking, and on personal and professional goals. Next, one should ask, What information do I need? Do I have enough information to create options I didn't realize I had? Have I thought of the consequences of each option? Have I *really* thought through the options? Taking time to ask all the necessary questions is a key to Johnson's (1992) decision-making process. "Better decisions often depend on seeing, at the time, what becomes obvious to you later" (Johnson, p. 50, 1992). Asking many questions helps make options and choices obvious.

The problem-solving group selects a workable solution all are willing to adopt, at least on a trial or experimental basis. The consultant promotes mutual participation in the decision. Group members more readily accept new ideas and new work methods when they are given opportunity to participate in decision making (Gordon, 1977). Many times a complex problem can be solved as each person in the group discovers what the others really want or, perhaps, fear. Then solutions can be formulated to meet the goals and protect the concerns of all involved.

In collaborative problem solving, whether using the POCS method or another effective method, the role of the consultant is to facilitate interaction and teamwork. This involves good listening, assertive responses, and successful resolution of conflicts, which will be discussed in greater detail in Chapter 6.

Consultants, consultees, support staff and others involved in collaborative interaction will assume one or more of a variety of functions during the process. These can include, but are not limited to, interaction role functions such as *initiator* of the process, *convener* of the meeting, *information gatherer, questioner, timekeeper, energizer, elaborator, innovator, integrator, humor dispenser, alternative opinion seeker, red-flag waver, standards/regulations adherent, gatekeeper, implementation designer* for the plan, *harmonizer, summarizer, evaluator* of the activity. Consultation encourages collective thinking for creative and imaginative alternatives and allows all involved to have their feelings and ideas heard and their goals met. The ultimate goal for effective problem solving is to provide the best education possible for students with special needs.

The Ten-Step Process for Consultation

Now that problem identification, options, consequences, and solution finding have been discussed, it is appropriate to coordinate these activities into a structured consultation process. The ten-step process outlined in Figure 5-3 can help consultants and consultees communicate, cooperate, and coordinate their efforts in identifying educational problems and planning for student needs.

1. Prepare for the consultation.
   1.1 Focus upon major topic or area of concern.
   1.2 Prepare and organize materials.
   1.3 Prepare several possible actions or strategies.
   1.4 Arrange for a comfortable, convenient meeting place.

2. Initiate the consultation.
   2.1 Establish rapport.
   2.2 Identify the agenda.
   2.3 Focus on the tentatively defined concern.
   2.4 Express interest in the needs of all.

3. Collect information.
   3.1 Make notes of data, soliciting it from all.
   3.2 Combine and summarize the data.
   3.3 Assess data to focus on areas needing more information.
   3.4 Summarize the information.

4. Isolate the problem.
   4.1 Focus on need.
   4.2 State what the problem is.
   4.3 State what it is not.
   4.4 Propose desirable circumstances.

5. Identify the problem.
   5.1 Encourage all to listen to each concern.
   5.2 Identify issues, avoiding jargon.
   5.3 Encourage expressions of frustrations and concerns.
   5.4 Keep focusing on the pertinent issues and needs.
   5.5 Check for agreement.

6. Generate solutions.
   6.1 Engage in collaborative problem-solving.
   6.2 Generate several possible options and alternatives.
   6.3 Suggest examples of appropriate classroom modifications.
   6.4 Review options, discussing consequences of each.
   6.5 Select the most reasonable alternatives.

7. Formulate a plan.
   7.1 Designate those who will be involved, and how.
   7.2 Set goals.
   7.3 Establish responsibilities.
   7.4 Generate evaluation criteria and methods.
   7.5 Agree on a date for reviewing progress.

8. Evaluate progress and process.
   8.1 Conduct a review session at a specified time.
   8.2 Review data and analyze the results.
   8.3 Keep products as evidence of progress.
   8.4 Make positive, supportive comments.
   8.5 Assess contribution of the collaboration.

9. Follow up on the situation.
   9.1 Reassess periodically to assure maintenance.
   9.2 Provide positive reinforcement.
   9.3 Plan further action or continue the plan.
   9.4 Adjust the plan if there are problems.
   9.5 Initiate further consultation if needed.
   9.6 Bring closure if goals have been met.
   9.7 Support effort and reinforce results.
   9.8 Share information where it is wanted.
   9.9 Enjoy the communication.

10. Repeat consultation as appropriate.

FIGURE 5-3   The Ten-Step Process for Consultation (by P. Dettmer, N. Dyck, and K. Woods)

Step 1: Preparing for the Consultation

As consultants plan and prepare for consultation and collaboration, they focus on the major areas of concern. They prepare helpful materials and organize them in order to use collaborative time efficiently. It is useful to distribute information beforehand so that valuable interaction time is not consumed reading new material. But consultants must take care to present the material as tentative and open to discussion. Of course, it is not always expedient to plan in depth prior to consultations. Sometimes they happen informally and without notice—between classes, during lunch periods, or on playgrounds. While consultants will want to accommodate these occasions for interacting with colleagues, they also need to look beyond them for opportunities to engage in more in-depth sessions.

They will want to provide convenient and comfortable settings for the interaction, arranging seating so there is a collegial atmosphere with no phone or drop-by interruptions. Serving coffee or tea can help set congenial climates for meetings.

Step 2: Initiating the Consultation

Consultants need to exert much effort in this phase. When resistance to consulting is high, or the teaching staff has been particularly reluctant to collaborate, it will be difficult to establish first contacts. This is the time to begin with the most receptive staff members in order to build in success for the consulting program. Rapport is cultivated by addressing every consultee as special and expressing interest in what each one is doing and feeling. Teachers should be encouraged to talk about their successes. The consultant needs to display sensitivity to teachers' needs and make each one feel important. The key is to *listen*.

The consultant will want to identify the agenda and keep focusing on the concern. It is helpful to have participants write down their concerns before the meeting and bring them along. Then the consultant can check quickly for congruence and major disagreements.

Step 3: Collecting Information

The data should be relevant to the issue of focus. However, data which seem irrelevant to one person may be the very information needed to identify the real problem. So the consultant must be astute in selecting appropriate data that include many possibilities but do not waste time or resources. This becomes easier with experience, but for new consultants, having too much information is probably better than having too little.

Since problem identification seems to be the most significant factor in planning for special needs, it is wise to gather sufficient data from multiple sources. A case-study method of determining data sources and soliciting information is particularly effective in planning for students who have special learning and behavior needs. See Figure 5-4 for a case-study framework that includes up to sixteen data sources to provide information for problem solving. When a number of these sixteen are tapped, the central problem becomes much more clear and more easily addressed.

Step 4: Isolating the Problem

As discussed earlier, the most critical aspect of problem solving is identifying and defining the problem at hand. Bolton (1986) emphasizes that consultants and consultees must define the problem by focusing on the need, not the solution. Without problem identification, problem solving cannot occur (Bergan and Tombari, 1976). Consultants can help isolate what the problem is, and what it is not. After the problem has been identified and stated, collaborators should propose desired circumstances related to that problem.

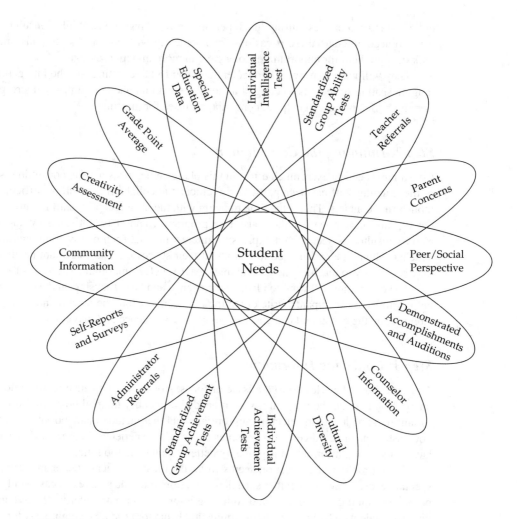

FIGURE 5-4   Case Study Information

Step 5: Identifying Concerns Relevant to the Problem

All concerns and viewpoints relevant to the problem should be aired and shared. A different viewpoint is not better or worse, just different. An effective consultant keeps participants focusing on the student need by listening and encouraging everyone to respond. However, a certain amount of venting and frustration is to be expected and accepted. Teachers and parents will demonstrate less resistance when they know they are free to express their feelings without retaliation or judgment. Consultants should remain nonjudgmental and assure confidentiality, always talking and listening in the consultees' language.

As information is shared, the consultant will want to make notes. It is good to have everyone look over the recorded information from time to time during the consultation as a demonstration of trust and equality, as well as a check on accuracy. (A log format for recording information and documenting the consultation is provided in Chapter 7.)

Step 6: Generating Solutions

Now is the time for creative problem solving. If ideas do not come freely, or if participants are blocking productive thinking, the consultant might suggest trying one or more of the techniques described later in the chapter. A problem-solving technique not only unleashes ideas, it sends a message about the kind of behavior that is needed to solve the problem. "Straw votes" can be taken periodically if that helps the group keep moving toward solutions. "Thinking outside the box" and combining ideas are very desirable processes at this stage. Two productive activities are to have brief discussions focusing on benefits and on concerns. These two sharing periods should be initiated with the word stems "I like . . ." (where the benefits are shared), and "I wish . . ." or "How to . . .?" (where the concerns are shared). At this stage, the group should modify, dismiss, or problem-solve each concern.

Step 7: Formulating a Plan

After solutions have been generated, wishes and concerns aired, and modifications made, the revised solution is ready to be formulated into a plan. Participants must remain on task. They need to be reinforced positively for their contributions. Consultants will want to have suggestions available for sharing, but defer presenting them so long as others are suggesting and volunteering. They must avoid offering solutions prematurely or addressing too many issues at one time. Other unhelpful behaviors are assuming the supervisor/expert role, introducing biases, and making suggestions that conflict with existing values in the school context.

As the plan develops, the consultant must make clear just who will do what, and when, and where. Evaluation criteria and methods that are congruent with the goals and plan should be developed at this time, and arrangements made for assessment and collection of data on student progress.

Step 8: Evaluating Progress and Process

This step and the final two steps are frequently overlooked. Consultation and collaboration experiences should be followed by assessment of student progress resulting from the collaborative plan, and also by evaluation of the consultation process itself. Figures 2-2 and 2-3 in Chapter 2, and additional information in Chapter 9, are useful for this purpose.

The consultant will want to make positive, supportive comments while drawing the interaction to a close, and at that time can informally evaluate the consultation with consultee help or formally evaluate by asking for brief written responses. This is a good time also to plan for future collaboration.

Step 9: Following Up the Consultation

Of all ten steps, this may be the most neglected. Ineffective consultation often results from lack of follow-up service (Neel, 1981). It is in the best interest of the client, consultee, consultant, and future possibilities for consultation to reassess the situation periodically. Participants will want to adjust the student's program if necessary, and initiate further consultation if the situation seems to require it. Informal conversations with consultees at this point are very reinforcing. During follow-up, consultants have opportunities to make consultees feel good about themselves. They can make a point of noting improved student behaviors and performance, especially those that relate to the classroom teacher's efforts. Also, they may volunteer to help if things are not going as smoothly as anticipated, or if consultees have further needs. As stressed in an earlier chapter, the sweetest words a consultee can hear are, "What can I do to help you?" However, this question *must* be framed in the spirit of: "What can I do to help you *that you do not have the time and resources to do?*" and *not* as, "What can I do for you that you do not have the skill and expertise to accomplish?" Consultants should follow through immediately on all promises of materials, information, action, or further consultation, and reinforce things that are going well. They also need to make a point of noting improved student behaviors and performance, especially those that relate to the classroom teacher's efforts.

Step 10: Repeating the Consultation If Needed

Further consultation and collaboration may be needed if the plan is not working, or if one or more parties believes the problem was not identified appropriately. On the other hand, consultation also may be repeated and extended when things are going well. The obvious rationale here is that if one interaction helped, more will help further. This is reinforcing for processes of consultation, collaboration, and teamwork. It encourages others to participate in the consultation and collaboration activity.

What to Say during the Consultation

The ten-step consultation procedure, committed to memory or stapled into a plan book, is a good organizational tool and a reassuring resource for the consultant, particularly for those engaging in their first consultations. Of course, the consultant does not want to parrot points from an outline as though reading a manual for programming the VCR! But by practicing verbal responses that are helpful at each step, it will become more natural and automatic to use facilitative phrases when the need arises. For example:

- *When planning the consultation* (The comments in this step are made to yourself.)

     (What styles of communication and interaction can I expect with these consultees?)

     (Have I had previous consultations with them and if so, how did they go?)

     (Do I have any perceptions at this point about client needs? If so, can I keep them under wraps while soliciting responses from others?)

     (What kinds of information might help with this situation?)

- *When initiating the consultation* (In this step and the rest of the steps, say to the consultee—)

  You're saying that...

  The need seems to be...

  May we work together along these lines...?

  So the situation is...

  I am aware that...

  What can we do in regard to your request/situation...?

- *When collecting information*

  Tell me about that...

  Uh-huh...

  What do you see as the effects of...?

  So your views/perceptions about this are...

  Tell me more about the background of...

  Sounds tough...

  To summarize our basic information then,...

- *When isolating the problem*

  The major factors we have brought out seem to be...

  What do you perceive is the greatest need for...

  What circumstances have you noted that may apply?

  Are there other parts to the need that we have not considered?

  So to summarize our perceptions at this point...

  Are we in agreement that the major part of this issue is...?

- *When identifying the concerns*

  You say the major concern is...

  But I also hear your concern about...

  You'd like this situation changed so that...

  How does this affect your day/load/responsibility?

  You are concerned about other students in your room...

  You're feeling... because of...

  This problem seems formidable. Perhaps we can isolate part of it...

  Perhaps we can't be sure about that...

  If you could change one thing, what would you change first?

- *When generating possibilities*

  How does this affect the students/schedule/parents?

Do we have a good handle on the nature of this situation?

We need to define what we want to happen...

How would you like things to be?

What has been tried so far?

What happened then?

How could we do this more easily?

Could we try something new such as...?

What limitations fall upon things we might suggest?

Let's try to develop some ideas to meet the need...

Your idea of... also makes me think of...

- *When formulating a plan*

Let's list the goals and ideas we have come up with...

So, in trying... you'll be changing your approach of...

To implement these ideas, we would have to...

The actions in this situation would be different, because...

We need to break down the plan into steps.

What should come first? Second...

When is the best time to start with the first step?

- *When evaluating progress*

Have we got a solid plan?

One way to measure progress toward the goals would be...

Some positive things have been happening...

How can we build on these gains?

Now we can decide where to go from here...

In what ways did our getting together help?

I can see the student progress every day...

You're accomplishing so much with...

How could I serve you and your students better?

- *When following up and interacting with colleagues*

How do you feel about the way things are going?

We had set a time to get back together. Is that time still O.K., or should we make it sooner?

I'm interested in the progress you have observed.

I'm following up on that material/action I promised.

I just stopped by...

Since we bumped into each other...

I wondered how things have been going for you...

How are things in your corner of the world these days?

I'm glad you've hung in there with this problem.

You've accomplished a lot, which is hard to recognize when you're with it every day...

You know, progress like this makes teachers look very good!

- *When repeating the consultation*

    Should we have another go at discussing...?

    Perhaps we overlooked some information that would help...

    We got so much accomplished last time.

    How about getting together again to...?

    That's a fine progress report.

    Would another plan session produce even more fantastic results?

What to Consider If Group Problem-Solving Is Not Successful

There is no universal agreement on what makes consultation effective, and little empirical support exists to guide consultants as to what should be said and done in consultation (Gresham and Kendell, 1987; Heron and Kimball, 1988). However, the ten steps outlined in this chapter have worked well for many consultants and consulting teachers, with few resultant problems. If this method of ten steps does not work, consultants should ask several questions:

- Were feelings addressed?
- Was the problem defined accurately?
- Were the nitty-gritty details worked out?
- Was the consultation process evaluated?
- Was there follow-up to the consultation?
- Were any hidden agendas brought to light and handled?
- Could any other problem-solving tools facilitate the process?

Tools to Facilitate Group Problem-Solving

The collaborative format of working together and drawing on collective expertise is widely practiced in the business and professional world. In their efforts to use the best ideas of bright, innovative minds, astute business managers employ a number of group problem-solving techniques. These techniques allow individuals to extend their own productive thinking powers and enhance those of their colleagues by participating in structured group problem-solving activities. Such techniques, often utilized in business and industry, are yet to be promoted to any great extent in educational settings, where autonomy and self-sufficiency have traditionally been valued more than collaboration and teamwork.

APPLICATION 5.1   The Ten-Step Consulting Process

1. Select one or more of the following situations and simulate a school consultation experience, using the ten-step process and any of the application verbalizations that are appropriate:

Situation A: A ninth-grade student is considered lazy by former teachers, has failed several courses, and cannot grasp math concepts. He has difficulty locating information but can read and understand most material at his grade level. He is never prepared for class, seldom has pencil and paper, and loses his assignments. Yet he is pleasant, seemingly eager to please, and will try things in a one-to-one situation. His classroom teachers say he will not pass, and you have all decided to meet about this. How will you, the learning disabilities consulting teacher, address the situation?

Situation B: You are attending a conference on behalf of a third-grade student who is emotionally disturbed and classified as borderline educable mentally handicapped. You believe she should be served in a general classroom with supportive counseling service and reevaluated in a year. The other staff participants feel she should be in special education placement with inclusion into music, art, and physical education. The mother is confused about the lack of agreement among school personnel. How will you address the concerns of all in this situation, particularly the mother?

Situation C: A sixth-grade student's mother is known as a perfectionist. Her son did not receive all As on the last report card, and she has requested a conference with you, the classroom teacher, the principal, and the school psychologist. As gifted program facilitator, how will you address this situation?

Situation D: A first-year kindergarten teacher has learned that one of her students is a child with cerebral palsy. Although the child's history to date has included continuous evaluation, home teaching, group socialization experiences, special examinations, and therapy sessions as well as family counseling for three years, the teacher is nervous about her responsibilities with this child. As the speech pathologist, how will you build her confidence in caring for the kindergartner's language needs and her skill in helping the little girl to develop her potential?

2. As a team effort with colleagues who share your grade level and subject area, construct a scenario to demonstrate the ten-step collaborative school consultation process at your teaching level and in your content area(s)... Role-play it for others, stopping at key points—for example, after problem identification and after formulation of the plan, to ask others what they might do at that point... If several promising alternatives are suggested, try each one and follow it to its conclusion. What techniques worked best? How did individual differences influence the consultation? Were these individual differences used constructively, and if not, what could have been done instead?

APPLICATION 5.2   Positive and Not-So-Positive Consultations

Assess which of the following consultation contacts were positive and which were not so positive. Why were the positive consultations successful? Why were some of them less successful than the consultant and consultee wished? What might have been done to improve the outcome? What still might be done?

Primary level teachers and I sat down and discussed what materials they thought would be good to order and place in the resource room, for their use as well as mine. Everyone had a chance to share needs, express opinions, and make recommendations.

An undergraduate asked me about my student teaching and substituting days. She was feeling very down and unsure of her teaching abilities. I reassured her by telling of some things that had happened to me (and why). I encouraged her to find a dependable support system, and gave her some ideas and things to think about.

A kindergarten child was staffed into my program, but the teacher wouldn't let me take her out of "her" class time. So I arranged to keep the child after school. The first night I was late coming down to get the child, so the teacher came in and had a temper tantrum about it.

The music teacher asks students who cannot read to stand up in class and read, and then pokes fun at them. I approached the teacher about the situation, but the teacher wanted nothing to do with me, and made things worse for the students.

One of the teachers I have spent several weeks with stopped me in the hall yesterday to ask for an idea to use in her class that next hour. Before she finished putting her question into words, she thought of an idea herself, but she still thanked me!

In visiting with the principal about alternatives in altering classroom assignments, it ended with his screaming at me for finding fault with his staff, which I had not done.

I give a sticker every day to a student with learning disabilities if he attends and does his work in the resource room. His classroom teacher complained to the principal because "other students work hard and don't get stickers."

I participated in a parent conference in which the parent wanted to kick the daughter out of the house and into a boarding school. It ended with the daughter agreeing to do more work at home, and the mother agreeing to spend one hour a week with the daughter only.

Several easy and convenient problem-solving techniques suitable for group participation are: brainstorming, lateral thinking, concept mapping, idea checklists, and attribute listing. Others are: jigsaw, reciprocal teaching, compare-and-contrast, and incomplete sentences. Ironically, many teachers incorporate these kinds of group problem-solving activities into curriculum planning for their students but overlook the potential that the techniques can contribute to carrying out their own responsibilities more effectively and pleasurably.

Brainstorming

Brainstorming is a mainstay of creative problem-solving methodology. It facilitates generating many unique ideas. When a group is brainstorming, participants should be relaxed and having fun. There are no right or wrong responses during the process, because problems seldom have only one right approach. No one may critique an idea during the brainstorming process. All ideas are accepted as plausible and regarded as potentially valuable. Each idea is shared and recorded. In large group sessions, it is most efficient to have a leader for managing the oral responses and a recorder for getting them down on a board or chart visible to all.

Rules for brainstorming are

1. Do not criticize any ideas at this time.
2. The more wild and zany the ideas, the better.
3. Think up as many ideas as possible.
4. Try to combine two or more ideas into new ones.
5. Hitchhike (piggyback) on another's idea. A person with a hitchhike idea should be called on before those who have unrelated ideas (Osborn, 1963.)

This technique is useful when the group wishes to explore as many alternatives as possible and defer evaluation of the ideas until the options have been exhausted. People who cannot resist the urge to critique ideas during brainstorming must be reminded that evaluation comes later. Leaders should call on volunteers quickly.

When the flow of ideas slows, it is a good idea to persevere a while longer. Often the second wave of thoughts contains the most innovative suggestions. Each participant should be encouraged to contribute.

APPLICATION 5.3   Example of Using the Brainstorming Technique

A brainstorming session might be held for the following situation:

A first-grade student has read just about every book in the small, rurally situated school. The first-grade teacher and gifted program facilitator brainstorm possibilities for enhancing this student's reading options and benefiting the school resources as well.

Lateral Thinking

The conventional method of thinking is vertical thinking, in which one moves forward mentally by sequential and justifiable steps. Vertical thinking is logical and single purposed, digging down more deeply into the same mental hole. Lateral thinking, on the other hand, digs a "thinking hole" in a different place. It moves out at an angle, so to speak, from vertical thinking to change direction, attitude, or approach so that the problem can be examined in a different way (deBono, 1973).

Lateral thinking should not replace vertical thinking, but complement it. While many educators emphasize vertical thinking at the expense of more divergent production, both are necessary to arrive at creative solutions for complex problems. The ability to use a lateral thinking mode by suspending judgments and generating alternatives should be cultivated by school personnel.

APPLICATION 5.4 Example of Using the Lateral Thinking Technique

Lateral thinking might be used in this situation:

A high school student with learning disabilities has a serious reading problem, but teachers in several classes are not willing to make adjustments. The teachers have not discussed any problems with you recently, but the student has. How might you as consultant, and student as consultee, think of ways to approach the situation and modify classroom practices to help this student succeed? To think laterally, the consultant might regard the teachers as clients and consult with the student about ways of reinforcing teachers when they *do* make things easier. The student would be modifying the behavior of teachers, rather than the vertical thinking approach of asking teachers to modify student behavior.

Concept Mapping

Concept mapping (referred to by some as mind mapping, semantic mapping, or webbing) is a tool for identifying concepts, showing relationships between them, and reflecting on the degree of generality and inclusiveness that envelops them (Wesley and Wesley, 1990). The technique allows users to display ideas, link them together, elaborate on them, add new information as it surfaces, and review the formulation of the ideas. The process begins with one word, or issue, written on paper or the chalkboard and enclosed in a circle. Then other circles of subtopics, ideas, words, and concepts are added to that central theme by lines or spokes that connect and interconnect where the concepts relate and interrelate. More and more possibilities and new areas open up as the webbing grows. Relationships and interrelationships that can help verbalize problems and interventions are recorded for all participants to see. If the concept map is not erased or discarded, the process can go on and on as more ideas are generated and added.

APPLICATION 5.5 Example of Using the Concept-Mapping Technique

A classroom teacher has agreed to work with a student new to the district and identified as behavior disordered. The student has acceptable social skills in some instances and is friendly and cooperative. But he also requires individual instruction, is working about two years below grade level, and makes threats impulsively to other students. On one occasion he brought a weapon to school. During previous visits with the teacher, she indicated that things were going well. Now, in the middle of November, she asks to see you, the consultant for behavioral disorders, immediately. She is upset, saying things such as "It just isn't working," and "I've tried so hard," but she has not described the problem. How might concept mapping or webbing help in this situation?

Concept mapping is being taught to students at all grade levels for reading comprehension. Buzan (1983) offers strategies for mind mapping in which learning techniques such as note taking can be structured to show interrelationships easily. Many students in gifted programs have been introduced to the concept of webbing to focus on a problem of interest and plan an independent study. Sometimes college students are encouraged to try mind mapping by combining lecture notes and text reading to study for exams. Concept mapping is a powerful tool. It is useful not only for enhancing individual learning, but for leading to more meaningful and productive staff development (Bocchino, 1991).

Idea Checklist

Checklists that suggest solutions for problems can be created from sources such as college texts, teaching manuals, and instructional media manuals. More unusual checklists include the Yellow Pages of directories, referral agency listings, gift catalogs, and instructional resource center guides. Asking a question such as "How can we help Shawn improve in math proficiency?" and scanning a Yellow Pages section or an off-level teaching manual may generate new ideas. Several chapters of this book contain checklists.

Other Collaborative Activities

Several collaborative activities that Brown (1994) presents for children's learning are just as promising for facilitating interchange, reciprocity, and a community of learning among adults. They include Jigsaw, reciprocal teaching (Brown, 1994), TalkWalk (Caro and Robbins, 1991), and compare-and-contrast, and incomplete sentences (Dobson, Dobson, and Koetting, 1985).

Jigsaw

Participants in this learning method developed by Aronson (1978) undertake independent, collaborative research on a topic of mutual interest. The technique can be used by a school faculty, a school district staff, or other group of teachers and area specialists to find background material and possible alternatives for solutions to academic and behavioral problems. The group decides on the central theme(s) of the issue and several subtopics. Then the large group divides into smaller groups. Each small group conducts research on one subtopic and shares that knowledge by teaching it to others. In this way all have a part in the problem-solving. Time and energy of busy professionals are maximized. Most important, a collaborative synergy develops that improves their ability to problem-solve in other situations.

Reciprocal Teaching

In reciprocal teaching, six or so participants form a group and each member takes a turn leading a discussion about an article, video, position paper, staff development presentation,

---

APPLICATION 5.6   Example of Using the Idea Checklist

A high school sophomore, seventeen years old and in the educable mentally handicapped program, is ready for a vocational training program. As EMH resource teacher, you believe the Vocational Rehabilitation Unit's four-month job-training program would be the most appropriate program for the student. However, the parents feel very protective of their son and are concerned that the environment will be noncaring. They resist suggestions that he leave their home. How might an idea-checklist process help during this consultation?

or other material they need to understand. The leader begins with a question and summarizes the discussion at the end. Clarification for understanding and predictions about future content can be requested by the leader when appropriate (Brown, 1994). With this technique, group cooperation helps ensure understanding by all members, with the less well-informed learning from those who are better informed.

Compare-and-Contrast

Each small group identifies terms and phrases that define differing perspectives of an issue—for example, reading methods, math methods, tracking or mainstreaming, inclusion or pull-out programs, graded or ungraded systems. Feedback to the large group and organization of resulting lists complete the interaction, with all leaving the session more informed and reflective about the issues.

Incomplete Sentences

Each group of five or six is given two or three typical behavior problems and asked to differentiate the handling of the problems by teachers in differing systems—for example, inclusive or separate, classroom conformity or free choice, restrictive or open. After large-group feedback, discussion refocuses on translating the most promising concepts into educational practice.

Other possibilities include role plays (stopping the small role play group at the critical point in the interaction and having the whole group explore options that would be possible from that point), interviews, interrogator panels, readers' theater, structured controversies (with participants assuming different positions on controversial issues) and the lecture/presentation format.

Interaction Formats

Collaborating consultants will want to know a variety of group formats for stimulating interaction among professionals. (See Figure 5-5.) Some of the most useful ones are:

- *Buzz groups*. Buzz groups work well in a group of 50 or fewer. This format ensures total participation and is easy to set up. The leader presents a topic or problem, provides minimal directions for subgrouping by twos or threes, and invites everyone to consider all the aspects of a problem in the time allowed. The main disadvantage is a high noise level if the physical space is small.
- *Huddles*. Huddles work best with groups of five or six discussants. The leader arranges the groups, defines the topic, announces the time limit (six minutes works well), and gives a two-minute warning when time is expiring. Each group designates its own reporter. The leader usually passes from group to group facilitating and encouraging if needed. In this structure the participants tend to build on colleagues' contributions. The reporting process can vary, from a simple "most important points" to ranking of major points, to a written summary that is collected by the leader.
- *Circle response*. Small groups of collaborators sit in a circle. The designated leader begins by stating or reiterating the topic. The response pattern moves to the left, with each taking a turn or saying "I pass." At the end of a stipulated time, the leader summarizes the ideas and integrated thinking of the group.

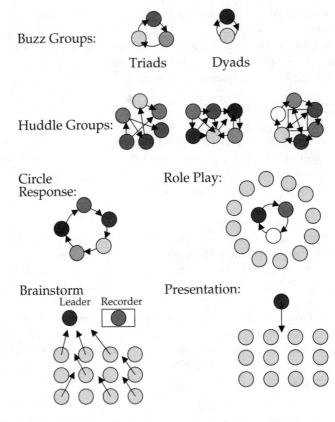

FIGURE 5-5   Interaction Structures

Tips for Consulting and Collaborating

1. Have materials and thoughts organized before consultations. Develop a list of questions that will help ferret out the real problem. Be prepared for the meeting with a checklist of information typically needed. Do not be afraid to say that you do not have *the* answer. If it is something you should know, find out when you can and get back to the person who asked.

2. Have strategies and materials in mind that may be helpful to the situation but do not try to have all the answers. This discourages involvement by others. Do not offer solutions too readily and try not to address too much or too many topics at once. Avoid jargon and shun suggestions that conflict with policies or favored teacher practices.

3. Make it a habit to look for something positive about the teacher, the room, and the student and comment on those things. Use feedback as a vehicle that can provide *positive* information, not just negative comments.

4. Don't try to "fix it" if it is not "broken."

5. Don't wait for the consultee to make the first move. But do not expect that teachers will be enthusiastic or flattered to have questions asked about their classrooms and teaching methods.

6. When a teacher asks for advice about a student, first ask what the teacher has already observed. This gets the teacher involved in the problem and encourages ownership in serving the student's special need. Whenever possible, use the terms *we* and *us,* not *I.*

7. Know how to interpret test results and how to discuss those results with educators, parents, and students.

8. When possible, provide parents with samples of the child's schoolwork to discuss during the conference. Have a list of resources ready to share with parents for help with homework, reinforcements, and study tips. When providing materials, explain or demonstrate their use and then keep in touch so that no problems develop.

9. Maintain contact with teachers during the year. You may find that the teacher has detected an improvement that is directly related to your work, and this reinforcement will be valuable for you and your own morale.

10. Remember that minds, like parachutes, work best when they are open.

Chapter Review

1. While many variants of a problem-solving process exist, basic steps are similar for all. They include problem identification, generating options, analyzing consequences, and developing plans for solutions. When these steps have been taken, implementation of the plan and follow up activity can occur.

2. Communication, cooperation, and coordination are vital components of effective group problem-solving.

3. Problem-identification is the most critical phase of problem-solving. Information from multiple sources, and collaborative input by a team of educators, will help identify the real problem and facilitate its solution.

4. Ten steps important in a problem-solving consultation are planning; initiating the consultation; collecting information; identifying the problem; generating options and alternatives; formulating a plan; evaluating progress; following up; interacting informally; and repeating the consultation if necessary.

5. Consultants will benefit from practicing key phrases to use during each phase of the consultation.

6. Divergent production of ideas during problem-solving can be enhanced by the use of techniques and tools such as brainstorming, lateral thinking, concept mapping, and idea checklists, jigsaw, reciprocal teaching, compare-and-contrast, and incomplete sentences. Teachers often use these techniques with students but overlook their possibilities for contributing to professional activity. Collegiality and collaboration are enhanced by the use of a variety of interaction formats such as buzz groups, huddle groups, circle responses, role plays, panels, and interviews.

To Do and Think About

1. When consultants introduce themselves to consultees, what are four or five things they can mention about themselves in order to develop rapport?

2. Discuss at least five things a consultant does *not* want to happen while consulting and collaborating, along with the conditions that might cause these unwanted events, and how the conditions might be avoided or overcome. Who has the most control over whether these unwanted events will or will not happen?

3. For a challenging assignment, select a school issue or student problem and create a method for engaging in consultation by designating a system, perspective, approach, prototype, mode, and model, as discussed in Chapter 3. Carry out the consultation as a role-play or simulation, using the ten steps and verbal responses suggested in this chapter. In a "debriefing" session with your colleagues, discuss which parts of the development and consultation process were most difficult, possible reasons, and what could be done to make the consultation successful.

For Further Reading

Buzan, T. (1983). *Use both sides of your brain.* New York: E.P. Dutton.

Davis, G.A. & Rimm, S.B. (1989). *Education of the gifted and talented.* Englewood Cliffs, NJ: Prentice Hall. Chapters 10, 11, and 12 on creativity and thinking skills.

deBono, E. (1973). *Lateral thinking: Creativity step by step.* New York: Harper/Row.

Osborn, A.F. (1963). *Applied imagination: Principles and procedures of creative problem-solving.* New York: Charles Scribner.

C h a p t e r **6**

Communication Processes for Consultants and Collaborators

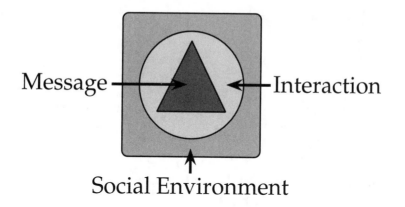

Message ← → Interaction

↑
Social Environment

Introduction

Communication is one of the greatest achievements of humankind. A vital component of human relationships in general, it is also the foundation of cooperation and collaboration among educators.

Communication involves talking, listening, managing interpersonal conflict, and addressing concerns together. Components for successful communication are understanding, trust, autonomy, and flexibility. People who can communicate effectively do so by withholding judgmental behavior and minimizing efforts to control others (Lippitt, 1983).

While problems and conflicts are unavoidable elements of life, good communication skills facilitate problem solving and resolution of conflicts. On the other hand, ineffective communication creates a void that breeds misunderstanding and distrust. Elements of trust, commitment, and effective interaction are critical for conflict-free relationships (Lippitt, 1983). Effective communication becomes a foundation for cooperation and collaboration among school personnel and parents.

Focusing Questions

1. What is a primary reason people fail at work?
2. What are key components of the communication process?
3. How does one establish rapport in order to facilitate effective communication?
4. What are major verbal and nonverbal skills for communicating effectively?
5. What are the primary roadblocks to communication?
6. How can a school consultant be appropriately assertive and cope with resistance when the need arises?
7. What techniques and skills are useful for conflict management?

Key Terms in the Chapter

assertiveness
body language
communication
conflict management
empathy, empathic
high-context communication
low-context communication

nonverbal communication
rapport
resistance
Responsive Listening Checklist
roadblocks to communication
verbal communication

Communication for Effective School Relationships

People typically communicate in one form or another for about 70 percent of their waking moments. They spend about 10 percent of that time writing, 20 to 40 percent speaking, and 45 to 65 percent listening (Bolton, 1986). Unfortunately, as many as eight out of ten people who fail in their work roles do so for one reason—they do not relate well with others (Bolton, 1986).

Communication skills clearly are keys to success in any field, and they are indispensable in consulting with other professionals. A supportive, communicative relationship among special education teachers, general classroom teachers, and parents is critical to the success of mainstreamed children with special learning needs. Trends in education emphasize the necessity for greatly strengthened communication among all who are involved with the student's educational program. Special educators must model and promote exemplary communication and interaction skills if they are to serve as consultants and team members for helping mainstreamed students succeed (Dickens and Jones, 1990).

Scenario

The setting is the hallway of a junior high school in midafternoon, where the general math instructor, a first-year teacher, is venting to a colleague.

MATH TEACHER: What a day! On top of the fire drill this morning and those forms that we got in our boxes to be filled out by Friday, I had a disastrous encounter with a parent.

COLLEAGUE: Oh, one of those, huh?

MATH TEACHER: Jay's mother walked into my room right before fourth-hour, and accused me of not doing my job. It was awful!

COLLEAGUE: (frowns, shakes head)

MATH TEACHER: Thank goodness there weren't any kids around. But the music teacher was there to see me about next week's program. This parent really let me have it. I was stunned, not only by the accusation, but by the way she delivered it. My whole body went on "red alert." My heart was pounding, and that chili dog I had for lunch got caught in my digestive system. Then my palms got sweaty. I could hardly squeak out a sound because my mouth was so dry. I wanted to yell back at her, but I couldn't!

COLLEAGUE: Probably just as well. Quick emotional reactions don't seem to work very well in those situations. I found out the hard way that it doesn't help to respond at all during that first barrage of words. Sounds like you did the right thing.

MATH TEACHER: Well, it really was hard. So you've had things like this happen to you?

COLLEAGUE: Um-humm. I see we don't have time for me to tell you about it, because here come our troops for their next hour of knowledge. But I can tell you all about it later if you want. Come to my room after school and we'll compare notes—maybe even plan some strategies for the future just in case. And, by the way, welcome to the club!

Consulting is not a one-person exercise. A consultant will pay a high price for a "Rambo" style of interaction ("My idea can beat up your idea," or "I'm right and that's just the way it is"). Communication that minimizes conflict and enables teachers to maintain self-esteem may be the most important and most "delicate" process in consulting (Gersten et al., 1991.) Unfortunately, development of communication skills is not usually included in the formal preparation of educators. Because the development and use of "people skills" is the most difficult aspect of collaboration for many educators, more and more educators are stressing the need for specific training in consulting and communication skills to serve special needs students.

Challenges of Communication

Communication requires three elements:

- a message;
- a sender of the message, and
- a receiver of the message.

Semantics play a fundamental role in both sending and receiving messages. A person who says, "Oh, it's no big deal—just an issue of semantics" is missing a major point. The semantics frequently *are* the issue and should never be taken for granted. The vital role of semantics in consultation, collaboration, and teamwork was introduced in Chapter 1, revisited in Chapter 3, and will be important in this chapter, with its focus on communication skills.

In order to communicate effectively, the message sender must convey the purpose of the message in a facilitative style with clarity to the receiver. Miscommunication breeds misunderstanding (Ozturk, 1992). A gap in meaning between what the message sender gives and what the message receiver gets can be described as distortion at best, or as communication trash in severe cases. A person may send the message, "You look nice today," and have it understood by the receiver as, "Gee, I rarely do look very good." A classroom teacher wanting to reinforce the learning disabilities teacher might say "Gerry certainly gets better grades on tests in the resource room," but the resource teacher may hear, "You're helping too much and Gerry can't cope outside your protection."

Vague semantics, distorted messages, and the psychological filters disrupt the message as it passes (or doesn't pass) between the sender and the receiver. Examples of filters are differing values, ambiguous language, stereotypes and assumptions, levels of self-esteem, and personal experiences. Static from preconceived ideas works constantly to prevent people from hearing what others are saying and provide only what people want to hear (Buscaglia, 1986). This can be demonstrated with the well-known game of "Gossip." Players stand in a long line or a circle, while one of them silently reads or quietly receives a message. Then that person whispers the message to the next one, and that message continues to be delivered to each one in turn. After passing through the filters of many people and stated aloud by the very last one, the message in most cases is drastically different from the original message. The game results are usually humorous. Real-life results are not so funny.

Ethnic and Gender Differences in Communication

Language is the window through which the reality of others' experiences is revealed. Gender and ethnicity are other factors that may cloud that window and lead to systematic misjudgments in interpreting communication. Misunderstanding may not be due simply to miscommunication. Other factors such as the sex or cultural background of the sender or the receiver may be responsible. Examples of gender differences in conversational style affecting both sender and receiver of the message are discussed by sociolinguist Deborah Tannen (1994; 1991). Her research describes differences in communication styles between females (both girls and women) and males (both boys and men):

- amount of time listening versus talking;
- interrupting;
- physical alignment during conversation;
- use of indirectness and silence; and
- topical cohesion.

For example, men's and boys' conversations tend to be diffuse, while those of women and girls are tightly focused with minimal topics. Educational consultants should be aware that communication style differences may lead them to be misunderstood or cause them to misunderstand their consultees.

Conversational style is a major component of ethnicity (Tannen, 1994). Different cultures use silence, interruption, proximity, eye contact, facial expression, and intonation to communicate ideas and feelings that consultants may not perceive. For example, in the Midwest it may be considered rude to interrupt; however, overlap or simultaneous group talk is the norm in some ethnic cultures or regional areas of the United States. The Athabaskans in Alaska value silence highly and devalue what they perceive as excessive talk (Scollon, 1985). Unwary educational consultants in such cases could lose much esteem for engaging in consultations as they might do elsewhere. As discussed in Chapters 4 and 13, consultants will continue to be challenged by the cultural diversity of collaborators. Increasing diversity of colleagues, families, and communities requires that educational consultants recognize and continuously consider the impact of culture on communication in their work.

In order to be effective communicators, senders and receivers of messages need skills that include rapport-building, responsive listening, assertiveness, tools for dealing with resistance, and conflict-management techniques. After effective communication skills have been cultivated, consultants and consultees are able to engage more effectively in collaborative problem-solving.

Roadblocks to Communication

Roadblocks (Gordon, 1977) are red flags to interaction, halting the development of effective collaborative relationships. They may be verbal behaviors or nonverbal behaviors that send out messages such as, "I'm not listening," or "It doesn't matter what you think," or "Your ideas and feelings are silly and unimportant." Roadblocks discourage the speaker and erode feelings of being able to handle problems, complete tasks, or live up to standards (Gordon, 1977).

Responsible school consultants most assuredly do not intend to send blocking messages. But by being busy, not concentrating, using poor listening skills, or allowing themselves to be directed by filters such as emotions and judgment, well-meaning consultants inadvertently send blocking messages.

Nonverbal Roadblocks

Nonverbal roadblocks include facing away when the speaker talks, displaying inappropriate facial expressions such as smiling when the sender is saying something serious, distracting with body movements such as repetitively tapping a pencil, and grading papers or writing reports while "listening." Interrupting a speaker to attend to something or someone else—the phone, a sound outside the window, or a knock at the door—also halts communication and contributes in a subtle way toward undermining the spirit of collaboration.

Verbal Roadblocks

Gordon (1977) lists twelve verbal barriers to communication. These have been called the "Dirty Dozen," and they can be grouped into three types of verbal roadblocks that prevent meaningful interaction (Bolton, 1986):

- judging;
- sending solutions; and
- avoiding others' concerns.

The first category, judging, includes criticizing, name-calling, and diagnosing or analyzing why a person is behaving a particular way. False or nonspecific praise, and evaluative words or phrases, send a message of judgment toward the speaker. "You're not thinking clearly," "You'll do a wonderful job of using curriculum-based assessment!" and "You don't really believe that—you're just tired today," are examples of judging. (Notice that each of these statements begins with the word "you.") Nonjudgmental communication expresses interpersonal equity (Gibb, 1974), which is a vital component of a collaborative relationship.

Educators are particularly adept with the next category of verbal roadblocks—sending solutions. These include directing or ordering, warning, moralizing or preaching, advising, and using logical arguments or lecturing. A few of these can become a careless consultant's entire verbal repertoire. "Not knowing the question," Bolton (1986, p. 37) says, "it was easy for him to give the answer." "Stop complaining," and "Don't talk like that," and "If you don't send Jim to the resource room on time . . ." are examples of directing or warning. Moralizing sends a message of "I'm a better educator than you are." Such communication usually starts with "You should . . ." or "You ought to. . . .". When consultees have problems, the last thing they need is to be told what they *should* do.

Avoiding others' concerns is a third category of verbal roadblocks. This category implies "no big deal" to the message receiver. Avoidance messages include reassuring or sympathizing, such as "You'll feel better tomorrow" or "Everyone goes through this stage," or interrogating to get excessive information and thus delay problem solving. Other avoidance messages include intensive questioning in the manner of the Grand Inquisition, and humoring or distracting, "Let's get off this and talk about something else." Avoiding the concerns others express sends the message that their concerns are not important.

Advising, lecturing, and logical argument are all too often part of the educator's tools of the trade. Teachers tend to use roadblock types of communication techniques frequently with students. The habits they develop cause them to overlook the reality that use of such tactics with adults can drive a wedge into an already precarious relationship. Consultants must avoid tactics such as assuming the posture of the "sage-on-the-stage," imparting wisdom in the manner of a learned professor to undergraduate students, lecturing, moralizing, and advising. Unfortunately, these methods imply superiority, which is detrimental to the collaborative process.

Strong emotions and logic are like air and water—they cannot be in the same space at the same time. Being rational with someone who is emotional leads to frustration. Such tools have no place in the consultant's work box. They create irritation and resistance even if the consultant is "right," and they reinforce the false hierarchy of expert/dumb person. When consultants use roadblocks, they are making themselves, their feelings, and their opinions the focus of the interaction, rather than allowing the focus to be the issues, or concerns of the consultee. When they set up roadblocks, listeners do not listen responsively or encourage others to communicate clearly, openly, and effectively. Because it is so easy to inadvertently use a communication block through speaking, it is wise to remember the adage, "We are blessed with two ears and one mouth, a constant reminder that we should listen twice as much as we talk." Indeed, the more one talks, the more likely a person is to make errors, and the less opportunity that person will have to learn something.

Skills For Communicating

Five major sets of skills are integral to successful communication:

- rapport-building skills
- responsive listening;
- assertion skills;
- conflict management skills; and
- collaborative problem-solving skills.

Rapport building is the first step in establishing a collaborative relationship. Responsive listening skills enable a person to understand what another is saying and to convey that the problems and feelings have been understood. When listening methods are used appropriately by a consultant, the consultee plays an active role in problem solving without becoming dependent on the consultant.

Assertion skills include verbal and nonverbal behaviors that enable collaborators to maintain respect, satisfy their professional needs, and defend their rights without dominating, manipulating, or controlling others. Conflict management skills help individuals deal with the emotional turbulence that typically accompanies conflict. Conflict management skills also have a multiplier effect of fostering closer relationships when a conflict is resolved. Collaborative problem-solving skills help resolve the conflicting needs so that all parties are satisfied. Problems then "stay solved," and relationships are developed and preserved. Problem solving was discussed in Chapter 5.

Rapport-Building to Enhance Communication

Collaboration with other professionals that is in the best interest of students with special needs often means simply sitting down and making some joint decisions. At other times, however, it must be preceded by considerable rapport building. Successful consultation necessitates good rapport between the participants in the consulting relationship. Johnson and Johnson (1987) contend that it is more difficult to reject ideas offered by persons who are liked and respected than by those who are disliked. It is important to keep in mind that both the consultant and the consultee should provide ideas toward solving the problem. Respect must be a two-way condition for generating and accepting ideas. Rapport building becomes a vital need for building an appropriate consultation climate.

What behaviors are central to the process of building a trusting, supportive relationship? When asked this question, many teachers mention trust, respect, feeling that it is O.K. not to have all the answers, feeling free to ask questions, and feeling all right about disagreeing with the other person. People want to feel that the other person is *really* listening.

Respecting differences in others is an important aspect of building and maintaining rapport. Although teachers and other school personnel are generally adept at recognizing and respecting individual differences in children, they may find this more difficult to accomplish with adults. Accepting differences in adults may be particularly difficult when the adults have different values, skills, and attitudes. Effective consultants accept people as they really are rather than wishing they were different. Rapport building is not such a formidable process when the consultant respects individual differences and expects others either to have this respect or to develop it (Margolis and McGettigan, 1988).

Responsive Listening Skills

Plutarch said, "Know how to listen and you will profit even from those who talk badly." Shakespeare referred to the "disease" of *not* listening. Listening is the foundation of communication. A person listens to establish rapport with another person. People listen when others are upset or angry, or when they do not know what to say or fear speaking out will result in trouble. People listen so others will listen to them. Listening is a process of perpetual motion that focuses on the other person as speaker and responds to that other person's ideas, rather than concentrating on one's own thoughts and feelings. Thus, effective listening is *responsive listening* because it is responding, both verbally and nonverbally, to the words and actions of the speaker.

Listening responsively and empathically is associated with the development of trust and understanding (Margolis and Brannigan, 1986; Nichols and Stevens, 1957) and with effective consulting practices (Gutkin and Curtis, 1982). It improves relationships, promotes exploration of prospective solutions (Egan, 1982), minimizes resistance (Murphy, 1987), and fosters collaboration (Idol-Maestas, Lloyd, and Lilly, 1981). Although most people are convinced of the importance of listening in building collegial relationships and preventing and solving problems, few are as adept at this skill they would like or need to be. There are several reasons for this. First, most people have not been taught to listen effectively. They have been taught to talk—especially if they are teachers, administrators, or psychologists. Educators are good at talking and regard it as an essential part of their roles. But effective talkers must be careful not to let the lines of communication get tangled up in a tendency to talk too much or too often.

Reasons for Listening

Listening helps keep the "locus of responsibility" with the one who owns the problem (Gordon, 1977). Therefore, if one's role as a consultant is to promote problem solving without fostering dependence on the part of the consultee, listening will keep the focus of the problem solving where it belongs. Listening is important in showing empathy and acceptance, two vital ingredients in a relationship that fosters growth and psychological health (Gordon, 1977).

Listening can prevent or minimize misunderstandings that occur in schools when educational roles are overloaded with responsibilities. It is very difficult for one person to understand the variety and complexity of another's problems. The receiver of a communication cannot know the sender's experiences or the nuances of the message. Katz and Lawyer (1983) define communication as the exchange of meaning that allows each to influence the other's experience. Listening helps one person "experience" the other's attitudes, background, and problems.

If listening is so important, why is it so hard? First, as discussed earlier, people often are not taught to listen and do not develop the skills needed to be effective listeners. Also, people may be hesitant to listen because they think listening implies agreeing. However, listening is much more than just hearing. A speaker can utter perhaps 125 words a minute, but a listener can process from 400 to 600 words a minute. What happens in the "listener's gap?" Too often listeners think about what they will say next, what they are going to recommend about the problem, or what they are going to do over the weekend.

Listening is also difficult because it is hard to keep an open mind about the speaker. Openness certainly is important in effective communication. Consultants must demonstrate tolerance toward differences and appreciation of richly diverse ideas and values while they are engaged in consulting relationships. A consultant's own values about child rearing, education, or the treatment of children with special needs become personal filters that make it difficult to really listen to those whose values are very different. For example, it may be hard to listen to a consultee parent who thinks it is appropriate for a very gifted daughter to drop out of school at the age of sixteen to help on the family farm because "She'll be getting married before too long and farm work will prepare her to be a wife better than schoolwork ever can." It takes discipline to listen to comments such as this when your mind is reacting negatively and wants to put together some very pointed comments to argue against this kind of thinking. A good rule of thumb to remember in such cases is that "when we add our two cents' worth in the middle of listening, that's just about what the communication is worth!" (Murphy, 1987.)

Feelings of the listener also act as filters to impede listening. Listening is very hard work. If the listener is tired or anxious or bursting with excitement and energy, it is particularly hard to listen carefully. While listening is demanding and difficult, it is vital for the collaborative relationships that are an integral part of the school consultation process. Improving listening skills can help establish collaborative relationships with colleagues, even those with whom it is a challenge to communicate. When consultants and consultees improve their listening skills, they have a head start on solving problems, side-stepping resistance, and preventing conflicts.

There are three major components of responsive listening:

- nonverbal listening;
- encouraging the sending of messages (talking); and
- showing understanding of the message.

Nonverbal Listening Skills

Responsive listeners use minimal and appropriate body language to send out the message that they are listening effectively. Some body language cues reflect ethnic background (Schein, 1969). Hall (1981) discusses a wide range of nonverbal cues that must be understood in order to interpret messages correctly. The high-context communication identified by Hall (1981) relies heavily on nonverbals and group understanding (Sue and Sue, 1990). An example is the communication that develops between twins. Another example is the shortened communication by people who know each other well and can omit much verbal communication without loss of meaning. Low-context communication puts greater reliance on the verbal part of the message.

Studies in kinesics, or communication through body language, show that the impact of a message is about 7 percent verbal, 38 percent vocal, and 55 percent facial. The eyebrows are particularly important in conveying messages. Nonverbal listening behavior of a good listener is described by Tony Hillerman in his 1990 best-seller *Coyote Waits:* "Jacobs was silent for awhile, thinking about it, her face full of sympathy. She was a talented listener. When you talked to this woman, she attended. She had all her antennae out. The world was shut out. Nothing mattered but the words she was hearing" (Hillerman, 1990, pp. 148–149).

Nonverbal listening may be particularly difficult for those amazing people who can do several things at once, such as watch a television show and write a letter, or talk to a colleague and grade papers, or prepare supper while listening to a child's synopsis of the day. This is because nonverbal components of listening should demonstrate to the speaker that the message receiver is respecting the speaker enough to concentrate on the message and is following the speaker's thoughts to find the *real* message. Careful listening conveys attitudes of flexibility, empathy, and caring, even if the speaker is using words and expressions that cloud the message.

A person who is attentive leans forward slightly, engages in a comfortable level of eye contact, nods, and gives low-key responses such as "oh," and "uh-huh," and "umm-humm." The responsive listener's facial expression matches the message. If that message is serious, the expression reflects seriousness. If the message is delivered with a smile, the listener shows empathy by smiling.

The hardest part of nonverbal listening is keeping it nonverbal. It helps the listener to think about a tennis game and remember that during the listening part of the "game," the ball is in the speaker's court. The speaker has the privilege of saying anything, no matter how silly or irrelevant. The listener just keeps sending the ball back by nodding, or saying "I see" or other basically nonverbal behaviors, until he or she "hears" the sender's message. This entails using nonverbal behaviors and "listening" to the nonverbal as well as the verbal message of the sender. The listener recognizes and minimizes personal filters, perceives and interprets the filters of the sender, and encourages continued communication until capable of understanding the message from the sender's perspective. Responsive listeners avoid anticipating what the speaker will say and *never* complete a speaker's sentence.

After listeners have listened until they really hear the message, understand the speaker's position, and recognize the feelings behind the message, it is their turn to speak. But they must be judicious about what they do say. Several well-known, humorous "recipes" apply to this need.

- Recipe for speaking—stand up, speak up, then shut up.
- Recipe for giving a good speech—add shortening.
- It takes six letters of the alphabet to spell the word *listen*. Rearrange the letters to spell another word that is a necessary part of responsive listening. (Did you get *silent?*)
- In the middle of listening, the *t* doesn't make a sound.

Verbal Listening Skills

Although the first rule of the good listener is to keep your mouth shut, there are several types of verbal responses that show that the listener is following the thoughts and feelings expressed by the speaker. Verbal responses are added to nonverbal listening responses to communicate that the listener understands what the other is saying from that speaker's specific point of view. Specific verbal aspects of listening also keep the speaker talking. There are several reasons for this that are specific to the consulting process:

The consultant will be less inclined to assume ownership of the problem.

Speakers will clarify their own thoughts as they keep talking.

More information will become available to help understand the speaker's point of view.

Speakers begin to solve their own problems as they talk them through.

The consultant continues to refine responsive listening skills.

Three verbal listening skills that promote talking by the speaker are inviting, encouraging, and questioning cautiously. Inviting means providing an opportunity for others to talk, by signaling to them that you are interested in listening if they are interested in speaking. Examples are "You seem to have something on your mind," or "I'd like to hear about your problem," or "What's going on for you now?"

Verbal responses of encouragement are added to nodding and mirroring of facial responses. "I see," "Uh-hum," and "Oh" are examples of verbal behaviors that encourage continued talking. These listener responses suggest: "Continue. I understand. I'm listening." (Gordon, 1977)

Cautious questioning is the final mechanism for promoting continued talking. Most educators are competent questioners, so the caution here is to use minimal questioning. During the listening part of communication, the message is controlled by the speaker. It is always the speaker's serve. Intensive and frequent questioning gives control of the communication to the listener. This is antithetical to the consulting process, which should be about collaboration rather than power and control. Questions should be used to clarify what the speaker has said, so the message can be understood by listener—for example "Is this what you mean?" or "Please explain what you mean by 'attitude problem.'"

Paraphrasing Skill

Responsive listening means demonstrating that the listener understands the essence of the message. After listening by using nonverbal and minimal verbal responses, a consultant who is really listening probably will begin to understand the message of the speaker. To show that the message was heard, or to assess whether or not what was "heard" was the same message the sender intended and was not altered by distortion, the listener should paraphrase the message. This has been called active listening (Gordon, 1977) and reflective listening (Bolton, 1986). Paraphrasing is an even more intricate skill than skills discussed earlier. It requires the listener to think carefully about the message and reflect it back to the speaker without changing the content or intent of the message.

There is no simple formula for reflecting or paraphrasing, but two good strategies are to be as accurate as possible and as brief as possible. A paraphrase may begin in one of several ways: "It sounds as if . . .?" or "Is what you mean . . .?" or "So, it seems to me you want (think) (feel). . ." or "Let me see if I understand. You're saying . . ." Paraphrasing allows listeners to check their understanding of the message. It is easy to mishear or misinterpret the message, especially if the words are ambiguous. Correct interpretation of the message will result in a nod from the speaker, who may feel that at last someone has really listened. Or the speaker may correct the message by saying, "No, that's not what I meant. It's this way..." The listener may paraphrase the content of the message. For example, "It seems to me that you're saying..." would reflect the content of the message back to the speaker. "You appear to be very frustrated about..." reflects the emotional part of the message. It is important to use the speaker's words as much as possible in the paraphrase words and to remain concise in responses. By paraphrasing appropriately, a listener demonstrates comprehension of the message or receipt of new information. This aspect of hearing and listening is essential in communication, and in assertion, problem solving, and conflict management as well.

Just by recognizing a consultee's anger, sadness, or frustration, a consultant can begin to build a trusting relationship with a consultee. The listener doesn't necessarily have to agree with the content or emotion that is heard. It may appear absurd or illogical. Nevertheless, the consultant's responsibility is not to change another's momentary tendency; rather, it is to develop a supportive working relationship via effective communication, paving the way to successful cooperation and problem solving while avoiding conflict and resistance.

Parents often comment that they have approached a teacher with a problem, realizing they didn't want a specific answer, but just a kindly ear—a sounding board, or a friendly

	Yes	No
A. *Appropriate Nonverbals*		
1. Good eye contact	_____	_____
2. Mirrored facial expression	_____	_____
3. Body orientation toward other person	_____	_____
B. *Appropriate Verbals*		
1. Door openers	_____	_____
2. Good level of encouraging phrases	_____	_____
3. Cautious questions	_____	_____
C. *Appropriate Responding Behaviors*		
1. Reflected content (paraphrasing)	_____	_____
2. Reflected feelings	_____	_____
3. Brief clarifying questions	_____	_____
4. Summarized	_____	_____
D. *Avoidance of Roadblocks*		
1. No advice-giving	_____	_____
2. No inappropriate questions	_____	_____
3. Minimal solution-sending	_____	_____
4. No judging	_____	_____

FIGURE 6-1   Responsive Listening Checklist (Thurston, 1989)

shoulder. Responsive listening is important in establishing collaborative relationships and maintaining them. It is also a necessary precursor to problem solving in which both parties strive to listen and get a mutual understanding of the problem before it is addressed.

So when is responsive listening to be used? The answer is—*all* the time. Use it when establishing a relationship, when starting to problem solve, when emotions are high, when one conversation doesn't seem to be getting anywhere, and when the speaker seems confused, uncertain, or doesn't know what else to do.

This complex process may not be necessary if two people have already developed a good working relationship and only a word or two is needed for mutual understanding. It also may not be appropriate if one of the two is not willing to talk. Sometimes "communication postponement" is best when you are too tired or too emotionally upset to be a responsive listener. When a consultant cannot listen because of any of these reasons, it is not wise to pretend to be listening, while actually thinking about something else or nothing at all. Instead, a reluctant listener should explain that he or she does not have the energy to talk about the problem now, but wishes to at a later time, for example: "I need a chance to think about this. May I talk to you later?" or 'Look, I'm too upset to work on this very productively right now. Let's talk about it first thing tomorrow." Figure 6-1 summarizes responsive listening skills that help avoid blocked communication.

Assertiveness

By the time the consultant has listened effectively and the collaborative relationship has been developed or enhanced, many consultants are more than ready to start talking. Once the sender's message is understood and emotional levels are reduced, it is the listener's turn to be the sender. Now the consultant gets to talk. However, it is not always easy to communicate your thoughts, feelings, and opinions without infringing on the rights, feelings, or opinions of others. This is the time for assertiveness.

Being assertive involves achieving your goals without damaging the relationship or another's self-esteem (Katz and Lawyer, 1983). The basic aspects of assertive communication (Sundel and Sundel, 1980; Alberti and Emmons, 1974; Thurston, 1987) are

> Use an "I" message instead of a "you" message.
> Say "and" instead of "but."
> State behavior objectively.
> Name your own feelings.
> Say what you want to happen.
> Express concern for others.
> Use assertive body language.

Open and honest consultants say what they want to happen and what their feelings are. That does not mean they always get what they want. Saying what you want and how you feel will clarify the picture and assure that the other(s) won't have to guess what you want or think. Even if others disagree with the ideas and opinions, they can never disagree with the feelings and wishes. Those are very personal and are expressed in a personal manner by starting the interaction with "I," rather than presenting feelings and opinions as truth or expert answer.

Concern for Others during the Interaction

Expressing concern for others can take many forms. This skill demonstrates that although people have thoughts and feelings which differ from those of others, they can still respect the feelings and ideas of others. "I realize it is a tremendous challenge to manage thirty-five children in the same classroom." This statement shows the consultant understands the management problems of the teacher. As the consultant goes on to state preferences in working with the teacher, the teacher is more likely to listen and work cooperatively. The consultee will see that the consultant is aware of the problems that must be dealt with daily. "It seems to me that..." and "I understand..." and "I realize..." and "It looks like..." are phrases consultants can use to express concern for the other person in the collaborative relationship. If the consultant cannot complete these sentences with the appropriate information, the next step is to go back to the listening part of the communication.

How to Be Concerned but Assertive

Assertive people own their personal feelings and opinions. Being aware of this helps them state their wants and feelings. "You" sentences sound accusing, even when that is not intended, which can lead to defensiveness in others. For example, saying to a parent, "You should provide a place and quiet time for Hannah to do her homework," is more accusatory than saying, "I am frustrated when Hannah isn't getting her homework done, and I would like to work with you to think of some ways to help her get it done." Using "and" rather than "but" is very important in expressing thoughts without diminishing a relationship. This is a particularly difficult assertion skill. To the listener the word "but" tends to erase any preceding phrase and prevents the real message from coming through.

It is important to state behavior specifically. By describing behavior objectively, a consultant or consultee sounds less judgmental. It is easy to let blaming and judgmental words creep into language. Without meaning to, the speaker throws up a barrier that blocks the communication and the relationship.

Assertive communication includes demonstrating supportive body language. A firm voice, straight posture, eye contact, and body orientation toward the receiver of the message will have a desirable effect. Assertive body language affirms that the sender owns his or her

---

APPLICATION 6.1   Communicating Positively

Compare the first statement with the second one:

1. "I would like to have a schedule of rehearsals for the holiday pageant. It is frustrating when I drive out to work with Maxine and Juanita and they are practicing for the musical and can't come to the resource room."

2. "When you don't let me know ahead of time that the girls won't be allowed to come and work with me, I have to waste my time driving and can't get anything accomplished."

In reflecting on these statements, which one is less judgmental and accusatory? Can these two contrasting statements create differing listener attitudes toward the speakers? For many listeners the judgmental words and phrases in the second sentence ("you don't let me," "won't be allowed," "waste my time") sound blaming. They introduce a whole array of red flags.

	Usually	Sometimes	Never
1. Conveys "I" instead of "you" message	_____	_____	_____
2. Says "and" rather than "but"	_____	_____	_____
3. States behavior objectively	_____	_____	_____
4. Says what he/she wants to have happen	_____	_____	_____
5. States feelings	_____	_____	_____
6. Expresses concern	_____	_____	_____
7. Speaks firmly, clearly	_____	_____	_____
8. Has assertive posture	_____	_____	_____
9. Avoids aggressive language	_____	_____	_____

FIGURE 6-2   Assertiveness Checklist

own feelings and opinions but also respects the other person's feelings and opinions. This a difficult balance to achieve. Body language and verbal language must match or the messages will be confusing. Skills for being assertive are listed in Figure 6-2.

When consultants and consultees communicate in ways that accurately reflect their feelings, focus on objective descriptions of behavior and situations, and think in a concrete manner about what they want to happen, assertive communication will build strong, respectful relationships. Assertive communication is the basis for solving problems and resolving conflicts.

Managing Resistance and Anger

Sometimes, regardless of how skillful and diplomatic people are in dealing with the emotions of others, they run into barriers of resistance in their attempts to communicate with others. It is estimated that as much as 80 percent of problem solving with others is getting through the resistance. The theme of teacher resistance and how to deal with it is a prominent one in recent school consultation literature (Pugach and Johnson, 1990).

Resistance is a trait of human nature that surfaces when people are asked to change. A wise person once suggested, "How can we ask others to change when it is so hard to change ourselves?" Resistance often has nothing to do with an individual personally or even with a new idea. The resistance is simply a reaction to change of any kind. It requires new ways of thinking and behaving (Margolis and McGettigan, 1988). Change implies imperfection in the way things are being done, and this makes people defensive.

Why Educators Resist

As discussed in Chapter 1, teachers value their autonomy (Parish and Arends, 1983). They tend to interpret instructional modifications for exceptional learners as limits on their freedom to make instructional decisions (Truesdell, 1988). When people experience such threats to their freedoms, they often demonstrate resistance (Hughs and Falk, 1981).

Ample evidence exists that many general education teachers resist mainstreaming and inclusion. Idol-Maestas and Ritter (1985) note that consulting teachers regard the negative attitude of classroom teachers toward mainstreaming students with disabilities as a major obstacle in school consultation. Twenty-two percent of graduates from the early resource/consulting teacher preparation programs reported resistance later from their teaching colleagues toward consultation. It is unrealistic to expect all classroom teachers to adopt instructional modifications comfortably and willingly. A gifted program facilitator explained to a new gifted education staff member, "Before I enter any classroom to confer with a teacher or collect a group of students for the resource room, or make suggestions in special education staffings, I ask myself, 'How would I feel if I were on the other side of this door and a colleague asked me to modify the way I am teaching these students?' This helps me to convey concern and helpfulness rather than judgment and superior expertise."

It is human nature to be uncomfortable when another person disagrees. It is also human nature to get upset when someone resists efforts to make changes, implement plans, or modify systems to be more responsive to children with special needs. The need for change can generate powerful emotions. Most people are uncomfortable when experiencing the strong emotions of others. When someone yells or argues, the first impulse is to become defensive, argue the other point of view, and defend your own ideas. Although a school consultant may intend to remain cool, calm, and collected in the interactions that involve exceptional children, occasionally another individual says something that pushes a "hot button" and the consultant becomes upset, angry, or defensive.

Special education consulting teachers have been asked to describe examples of resistance toward their roles. Their responses include these examples:

Consultees (classroom teachers) won't share how they feel.
They act excited about an idea, but never get around to doing it.
They won't discuss it with you, but they do so liberally with others behind your back.
They may try, but give up too soon.
They take out their frustrations on the students.
They are too quick to say that a strategy won't work in their situation.
They dredge up a past example where something similar didn't work.
They keep asking for more and more details or information before trying an idea.
They change the subject, or suddenly have to be somewhere else.
They state that there is not enough time to implement the strategy.
They intellectualize with a myriad of reasons it won't work.
They are simply silent.

When resistance spawns counter-resistance and anger, an upward spiral of emotion is created that can make consulting unpleasant and painful. Bolton (1986) describes resistance as a push, push-back phenomenon. When a person meets resistance with more resistance, defensiveness, logical argument, or any other potential roadblock, resistance increases and dialogue can develop into open warfare. Then the dialogue may become personal or hurtful. Nobody listens at that point, and a potentially healthy relationship is damaged and very difficult to salvage.

How to Deal with Resistance

An important strategy for dealing with resistance and defensiveness is to handle your own defensiveness, stop pushing so that the other person will not be able to push back, delay reactions, keep quiet, and *listen*. This takes practice, patience, tolerance, and commitment. It is important to deal with emotions such as resistance, defensiveness, or anger before proceeding to problem solving. People are not inclined to listen until they have been listened to. They will not be convinced of another's sincerity and openness, or be capable of thinking logically, when the filter of emotions is clouding their thinking.

Consultants must "hear their way to success" in managing resistance. This may take five minutes, or months of careful relationship building. Colleagues cannot always avoid disagreements that are serious enough to create anger and resistance. A comment or question delivered in the wrong manner at the wrong time may be the "hot button" that triggers the antagonism. Consider remarks such as these:

"If you want students to use good note-taking skills, shouldn't you teach them how to take notes?"

"Not allowing learning disabled students to use calculators is cruel."

"Why don't you teach in a way that accommodates different learning styles?"

"You penalize gifted students when you keep the class in lockstep with basal readers."

Such remarks can make harried, overworked classroom teachers defensive and resentful. If an occasion arises in which a teacher or parent becomes angry or resistant, responding in the right way will prevent major breakdowns in the communication that is needed.

Kroth (1985) suggests several do's and don'ts for dealing with anger:

Do:
> Listen.
> Write down what the other person says.
> Ask what else is troubling, when the other slows down.
> Exhaust the person's list of complaints.
> Ask for clarification of any complaints that are too general.
> Show the list to the person and ask if it is complete.
> Ask for suggestions for solving the problems.
> Write down the suggestions.
> In so much as possible, mirror the other's body posture during the process.
> Speak more softly, as that person speaks loudly.

Don't:
> Argue.
> Defend or become defensive.
> Promise things you can't produce.
> Take ownership of problems that belong to another.
> Raise your voice.
> Belittle or minimize the problem.

Lipshitz, Friedman, and Owen (1989) contend that the power approach to problem solving almost always breeds resistance. They suggest two strategies:

1. *Assume a one-down position.*

   This avoids the power game. An example of assuming the one-down position in a collaborative situation is saying, "Please bear with me if I offer inappropriate suggestions. I don't pretend to understand the organization of your classroom. I know about class-wide management procedures that have been successful with mainstreamed students."

2. *Preempt.*

   This means anticipating a difficulty or emotional block by explaining that while a block may occur, it is normal and temporary, and need not become a serious barrier to problem solving. Just mentioning the possibility of resistance before it occurs can be helpful in managing resistance.

Robinson and Brosh (1980) offer other suggestions for dealing with resistance.

Inquire into resistance. Treat an objection as a learning experience and use questions rather than arguments. Rebutting creates conflict rather than solves problems.

Use the bottom line. Respond to questions with bottom-line answers and be as direct as possible. Never exaggerate and do not "lead up" to potential problems or benefits. Begin with them.

Stop and establish. Stop the talking and take a step back to establish your goal and intention. Seek the goal and intention of others in the situation. For example, you might say, "Let's stop arguing about the merits of this preassessment procedure. My goal is to find a workable solution to John's difficulties in the classroom. What is your goal?" Another example is asking the question, "Can anyone help us understand why we are having trouble finding an acceptable solution? What is impeding our progress?"

Look for understanding. Examine the situation and discover where you agree and disagree. Then start with the agreements (Schindler and Lapid, 1989).

Conflict Management

Conflicts are a part of life. They occur when there are unreconciled differences among people in terms of needs, values, goals, and personalities. If conflicting parties cannot give and take by integrating their views and utilizing their differences constructively, interpersonal conflicts will escalate.

School consultants and collaborators are not exempt from the dysfunction that often accompanies conflict. So it is important to for them to develop tools for transforming vague and ambiguous sources of conflict into identified problems that can be solved collaboratively. Lippitt (1983) suggests that conflict, as a predictable social phenomenon, should not be repressed, because there are many positive aspects to be valued. Conflict can help clarify issues, increase involvement, and promote growth, as well as strengthen relationships and organizational systems when the issues are resolved.

Gordon (1977) contends it is undesirable to avoid conflict when there is genuine disagreement, because resentments build up, feelings get displaced, and unpleasantries such as backbiting, gossiping, and general discontent may result.

Reasons for Conflict among Educators

Teachers, administrators, and parents face many possible occasions for conflict when they are involved with educating children who have special needs. Some conflicts occur because there is too little information or because misunderstandings have been created from incorrect information. These instances are not difficult to resolve because they require only the communication of facts. Other areas of conflict arise from disagreement over teaching methods, assessment methods, goals, and values. Parent goals and teacher goals for the exceptional student may differ significantly, and support personnel may add even more dimensions to the conflict. For example, if a child is instructed by the reading specialist to read more slowly, urged by the learning disabilities teacher to read more rapidly, required by the classroom teacher to read a greater amount of material, and ordered by the parent to get better grades or *else,* communication is tenuous or nonexistent, and conflict is inevitable.

Perhaps the most difficult area of conflict relates to values. When people have differing values about children, education, or educator roles within the learning context, effective communication is a challenging goal. As discussed earlier in this chapter, rapport building, listening, and paraphrasing are significant in building relationships among those whose values conflict. The most important step is to listen courteously until a clear message about the value comes through, demonstrating respect for the value even if it conflicts with yours. Then it is time to assert your own values and, along with the other person, try to reach a common goal or seek a practical issue on which to begin problem solving.

How to Resolve Conflicts in the School Context

Some conflicts, particularly those involving values, are difficult to prevent and may seem at the time to be unresolvable. However, if all can agree to common goals or common ground for discussion, conflicts can be resolved.

Gordon (1977) and many others suggest that conflict resolution can follow one of three paths:

- I win, you lose.
- You win, I lose.
- I win, you win.

The first two paths are frequently taken because people fear conflict and wish to avoid it. The third path, with the win/win outcome, is hard because those involved must confront their emotions and the emotions of others, and work diligently to turn conflict into cooperation. This method focuses on needs rather than solutions. It is based on two-way communication with lots of listening. During conflict situations, the immediate purpose of interaction is improving communication, not changing points of view.

The first step in resolving conflicts within an "everybody wins" philosophy is to use those listening skills described earlier in the chapter to find common ground. In dealing with emotions of the speaker, the listener must concentrate with an open mind and attend to the speaker's feelings as well as the facts or ideas that are part of the message. The listener must strive to hear the whole story without interrupting, even if there are strong feelings of disagreement. Conflict usually means that intense emotions are involved. Only by concentrating on the message with an open mind can all parties begin to deal with the conflict. Emotional filters often function as blinders. If the emotions cannot be overcome, the best tactic is to postpone the communication, using assertive responses to do so.

Listening establishes a common intent and develops a starting attitude. Listening to one who is upset helps that person focus on a problem rather than an emotion. Listening lets people cool down. Bolton (1986) calls this the spiral of resistance, suggesting that if one listens with empathy and does not interrupt, the speaker's anger or high emotion will dissipate. Without saying a word, the listener makes the speaker feel accepted and respected.

It is hard to argue with someone who does not argue back. It is hard to stay mad or upset with someone who seems to understand and empathize. Each time a person listens, a small victory for the advancement of human dignity has been achieved (Schindler and Lapid, 1989). Only after emotions are brought into the open and recognized can all parties involved move on to seek a common goal.

The initial intent for resolving a conflict should be to learn. This enables all factions to increase mutual understanding and think creatively together. Most people could agree to such a start because it does not address goals or values. It does not even require agreement that a problem exists. It simply establishes the intent to learn by working together. Establishing intent for dialogue should follow the reduction of emotional responses. Of course, as discussed earlier, it is important to avoid roadblocks at all stages of the process.

Consultants and consulting teachers must put aside preconceived notions about their own expertise and learn from those who often know the student best—parents and classroom teachers. Such consultees respond positively to open-ended questions that let them know they are respected and needed. When consultants open their own minds, they unlock the potential of others.

After listening constructively, consultants need to help establish ground rules for resolving the conflict. The ground rules should express support, mutual respect, and a commitment to the process. Again, this requires talking and listening, dialoguing, and keeping an open mind. It is important not to dominate the dialogue at this time and, by the same token, not to let the other person dominate the conversation. This part of the communication might be called "agreeing to disagree," with the intent of "agreeing to find a point of agreement." It is important to share the allotted interaction time equitably and in a way that facilitates understanding. Consultants must use precise language without exaggerating points, or, as discussed earlier, flaunting "educationese" and taking inappropriate shortcuts with jargon and "alphabet soup" acronyms.

Dealing with conflict productively also requires asserting your ideas, feelings, or opinions. While listening enables the consultant to understand the speaker's perspectives, wants, and goals, assertion skills allow consultants to present their perspective. This often follows a pattern of listen—assert—listen—assert—listen, and so on, until both parties have spoken and have been heard.

Although there may be resistance after each assertion, it will gradually dissipate so that *real* communication and collaboration can begin to take place. Only after this process has happened can collaborative goal setting and problem solving occur. Figure 6-3 summarizes useful steps for managing resistance and conflict.

There is a well-known story of a man who had three sons. He stipulated in his will that the oldest son should inherit half his camels, the middle son should get one-third of the camels, and the youngest should be the new owner of one-ninth of his camels. When the old man died, he owned seventeen camels. But the sons could not agree on how to divide the camels in accordance with their father's will. Months and months of bitter conflict went by. Finally the three young men sought the advice of a wise woman in the village. She heard their complaints and observed their bitterness and felt sorry that brothers were fighting and putting the family into turmoil. So she gave the brothers one of her camels. The estate then was divided easily according to the father's wishes. The eldest took home nine camels, the second put six camels beside his tent, and the youngest took home two camels. The men were happy, the father's last wishes were honored, and the wise woman took her own camel back and led it home.

A. *Responsive Listening*

    1. Had assertive posture   _____

    2. Used appropriate nonverbal listening   _____

    3. Did not become defensive   _____

    4. Used minimal verbals in listening   _____

    5. Reflected content   _____

    6. Reflected feelings   _____

    7. Let other do most of the talking   _____

    8. Used only brief, clarifying questions   _____

B. *Assertiveness*

    9. Did not use roadblocks such as giving advice   _____

  10. Used "I" messages   _____

  11. Stated wants and feelings   _____

C. *Recycled the Interaction*

  12. Used positive postponements   _____

  13. Did not problem solve before emotions were controlled   _____

  14. Summarized   _____

  15. Set time to meet again, if applicable   _____

FIGURE 6-3   Checklist for Managing Resistance and Conflict

Conflict management is the process of becoming aware of a conflict, diagnosing its nature, and employing an appropriate problem-solving method in such a way that it simultaneously achieves the goals of all involved and enhances relationships among them. If the consulting relationship is treated as a collaborative one in which each person's needs are met (the win/win model), then feelings of self-confidence, competence, self-worth, and power increase, enhancing the overall capacity of the system for responding to conflict in the future (Katz and Lawyer, 1983). The win/win relationship is based on honesty, trust, and mutual respect—qualities stressed earlier as vital to a successful consulting relationship. Win/win allows all involved parties to experience positive outcomes. The model works best when all parties use effective communication skills (Fisher and Ury, 1981).

The opposite of successful conflict management is avoiding conflict, ignoring feelings, and bypassing the goals of others. The relationship becomes adversarial, if it is not already so, because for someone to win, another must lose. When conflicts are approached with responsive listening and dealt with honestly and openly, the underlying problem or need can be resolved.

When engineers stress collaboration, they often use the bumblebee analogy. According to the laws of aerodynamics, bumblebees cannot fly. But as everyone knows, they do. By the same token, some might say that groups cannot function productively because of the conflicts, personal agenda, and individual preferences that exist among the members. But they do. Groups of people play symphonies, set up businesses, write laws, and develop IEPs for student needs. An understanding of adult individual differences, styles, and preferences, as discussed in Chapter 4, will encourage participants in consultation and collaboration to listen more respectfully and value differences among colleagues. This knowledge, when combined with responsive listening, avoidance of roadblocks, and assertiveness, will enable consultants to deal with resistance and conflict productively. Conflict management puts these skills to practical use in educational settings of school and home.

Tips for Consulting and Collaborating

1. Avoid communication roadblocks.
2. Listen. This helps dissipate negative emotional responses and often helps the other person articulate the problem, perhaps finding a solution then and there.
3. Use assertion. Say what you feel and what your goals are.
4. Be aware of your "hot buttons." Knowing your own responses to certain "trigger" behaviors and words will help you control natural tendencies to argue, get defensive, or simply turn red and sputter.
5. Attend to nonverbal language (kinesics, or body language) as well as to verbal language when communicating.
6. Don't "dump your bucket" of frustrations onto the other person. Jog, shout, practice karate, but avoid pouring out anger and frustration on others. Instead, fill the buckets of others with "warm fuzzies" of empathy and caring.
7. Develop a protocol within the school context for dealing with difficult issues and for settling grievances.
8. Deal with the present. Keep to the issue of the current problem rather than past problems, failures, or personality conflicts.

9. Use understanding of individual differences among adults to bridge communication gaps and manage conflicts in educational settings.
10. Advocate for training that focuses on communication, problem solving, and conflict management.

Chapter Review

1. The primary reason people fail at work is because of communication problems. It is too often assumed that communication skill develops with no special attention to the complexities of social interaction.
2. The sender, the message, and the receiver are three key components of the communication process. Each component is vital. When a message is missent or misheard, many distortions occur that prevent open, honest communication. This happens because of differences in values, language, attitudes, perceptions, and gender, ethnicity, and background of sender and receiver.
3. Communication can be hampered by verbal and nonverbal roadblocks. Verbal roadblocks include responses that are judgmental, responses that send solutions, and responses that avoid the concerns of others. Nonverbal roadblocks include body language that conveys lack of empathy and concern.
4. Major skills in effective communication are responsive listening, asserting, managing resistance and conflict, and collaborative problem solving. Both verbal and nonverbal components are included in these skills. The skills form the basis of a respectful, egalitarian relationship and a successful team on behalf of the student with special needs. They pave the way to effective problem solving and mutual collaboration.
5. Listening is the most important skill educational professionals can use to establish rapport with partners in addressing educational goals for children. Responsive listening means using nonverbal and verbal responses to the content of the message and the emotions of the speaker. Verbal responses include brief messages and messages that show understanding. Listening responsively is a challenge because of the temptation to talk about your own thoughts and ideas.
6. Assertive communication allows speakers to state their own views, feelings, and opinions, without impeding the ongoing consulting process. Assertiveness means stating your wants or feelings by starting sentences with "I," using "and" rather than "but," and showing concern for the other person. Resistance sometimes occurs when a speaker is assertive. This resistance is a natural reaction to the request for change. It can be managed by using a combination of assertiveness and responsive listening.
7. Conflict arises when members of educational teams have different feelings, values, needs, and goals. Conflict resolution should follow a win/win model if collaborative efforts are to be maintained. Listening instead of arguing, establishing ground rules, and seeking a common goal help bring teams to the problem-solving stage without any "losers."

To Do and Think About

1. Discuss the following:
What roadblock does each of these comments set up?

What you need is more activity. Why don't you develop a hobby?

You are such a good friend. I can count on you.

Let's talk about something more positive.

I know just how you feel.

Why did you let her talk to you that way?

Which of these lines create resistance and defensiveness?

What you should do is . . .

Do you want to comment on this?

Everyone has problems like that.

That's a good thought.

You mean you'd actually do that?

Let's change the subject.

What should I do?

What assertive statements could be made for each situation?

A colleague talks to you about his personal problems and you can't get your work done.

The paraprofessional comes in late frequently.

During a committee meeting one member keeps changing the subject and getting the group off task.

A colleague wants to borrow some material but has failed to return things in the past.

During a phone conversation with a wordy parent, you need to get some information quickly and hang up soon.

The class next door is so rowdy that your class can't work.

2. Discuss these basic assumptions about communication for consultation and add more to the list.

The reactions of others depend on your actions, word choices, body language, and listening skills.

People generally want to do a good job.

People have a powerful need to "save face."

No one can force another person to change.

Learning to communicate, be assertive, and facilitate conflict resolution is awkward at first.

3. During initial attempts at paraphrasing, the process often feels and sounds awkward and phony. What might be done about that?

4. Practice the following situations:

expressing anger in constructive ways;

getting the interaction back on task;

stating a contrasting view to a supervisor-type;

recommending a better way of doing something;

asking again, and again, for materials you loaned some time ago and you need now.

5. Restate the following message so the language is assertive but nonthreatening to the receiver.

"You penalize gifted students when you keep the class lockstepped in the basal texts and the workbooks."

"If you want students to use good note-taking skills, you should teach them how to take notes."

"Not allowing students to use calculators is poor teaching practice and terribly out-moded."

"It is not fair to insist that learning disabled students take tests they cannot read."

For Further Reading

Bolton, R. (1986). *People Skills: How to Assert Your-self, Listen to Others, and Resolve Conflicts.* New York: Simon and Schuster.

DeBoer, A. L. (1986). *The Art of Consulting.* Chicago: Arcturus.

Fisher, R., and Brown, S. (1988). *Getting Together: Building Relationships as We Negotiate.* New York: Penguin Books.

Fisher, R. and Ury, W. (1981). *Getting to yes: Negotiating agreement without giving in.* New York: Penguin.

Gordon, T. (1977). *Leader Effectiveness Training. L. E. T.: The No-Lose Way to Release the Productive Potential in People.* Toronto: Bantam.

Hall, E. T. (1959). *The Silent Language.* New York: Doubleday.

Chapter *7*

Management Strategies for School Consultation and Collaboration

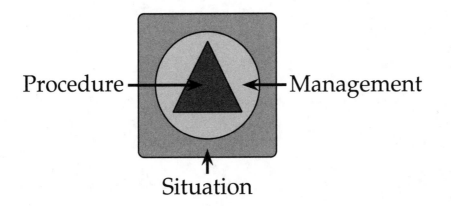

Procedure —→ ▲ ←— Management

↑
Situation

Introduction

Schools are bustling arenas of activities that often seem to have little to do with books and studies. Not only do school personnel teach students in academic settings, they also feed them, transport them, keep records, counsel and advise, dispense materials and resources, address social and health problems, and much, much more. If the services of other school-related roles as diverse as librarian, speech pathologist, school psychologist, social worker, and nurse were included, the list of responsibilities would be even more daunting.

The complexity of contemporary school life is immense. In this daily hubbub the demands on school personnel for efficiency, expertise, and accountability can be overwhelming.

Stress and fatigue take a toll, with burnout and attrition from the field all too frequent results. But role-related stress can be minimized and controlled by managing time and resources wisely and by organizing procedures for carrying out responsibilities of the role efficiently.

Focusing Questions

1. What aspects of their roles cause school personnel to be vulnerable to stress and burnout?
2. What organizational techniques will help consultants and collaborators perform their roles effectively?
3. What procedures for conducting meetings, interviews, and observations contribute to consultation and collaboration success?
4. How can collaborating school consultants manage records and resources efficiently?
5. How do support personnel contribute to collaboration for helping students with special needs succeed in school?
6. What ethical considerations guide the practice of school consultation?

Key Terms in the Chapter

attrition	observation
burnout	related services personnel
consultation log or journal	stress management
ethics of consultation	support personnel
interview	time management

Stress, Burnout, and Attrition of School Personnel

Each year a significant number of teachers experience symptoms of burnout, with feelings of physical and emotional fatigue, loss of enthusiasm for their jobs, and sometimes depression or guilt. Burnout disproportionately affects those in human service professions (Maslach, 1982). High levels of emotional exhaustion and depersonalization, when accompanied by low feelings of personal accomplishment, signal burnout for teachers, social workers, nurses, and others who serve people's needs. They feel used up and exhausted physically, emotionally, and attitudinally. Truch (1980) describes the condition as "chronically miserable" and prone to "rust out." Up to fifty percent of educators have indicated they may leave the profession because of burnout (Raschke, Dedrick, and DeVries, 1988).

Overwhelming responsibilities and pressures in working with special needs students make teachers particularly vulnerable to stress and burnout. In a study of more than six hundred special educators, Zabel and Zabel (1982) found that consulting teachers rank higher in emotional exhaustion and depersonalization than those in other service deliveries. The researchers propose that this occurs because consulting teachers serve large geographic

Scenario

The setting is the kitchen of a home where a middle school student and mother are sitting at the kitchen table.

MOTHER: I see a note here from your teacher saying that you need to make up an important math test you missed yesterday. . . .

CHILD: Uh-huh, I missed it because yesterday was Tuesday.

MOTHER: What does that have to do with the math test?

CHILD: Well, on Tuesdays I'm supposed to see Mrs. Evans, but she wasn't there. So I went to Mr. Bowman instead.

MOTHER: Who is Mrs. Evans?

CHILD: She's the reading teacher. I see her Tuesdays and Thursdays, from 1:30 to 2:30, but she was sick yesterday.

MOTHER: So you saw Mr. Bowman. Who is he?

CHILD: The special education teacher I see for more help with reading, but mostly with spelling and my workbooks. He got called to another school for a meeting, so he sent me to Jeanette.

MOTHER: Now wait a minute—who is Jeanette?

CHILD: Gee, mom, I thought you told the principal you and dad would keep up with my school program.

MOTHER: I'm trying!

CHILD: Anyway, Jeanette is the high school girl who tutors me in reading.

MOTHER: Oh?

CHILD: It's O. K. She's nice. She wants to be a teacher someday. Mrs. Bagley helped me work it out.

MOTHER: And *who* is Mrs. Bagley?

CHILD: The counselor. She says working with Jeanette is good for me, and for her, too.

MOTHER: And just what does Miss Anderson think about all of this?

CHILD: Uh, who's she?

MOTHER: Your *classroom teacher!*

CHILD: Oh, yeah, I forgot all about her.

(This child's schedule underscores the complexity of the school day and accentuates the need for communication, cooperation, and coordination among school personnel.)

(adapted from Michelle Berg.)

areas, many students, and a wide range of expectations of others. As advocates for children with special learning and behavior needs, special education teachers may set unreasonably high expectations for themselves and others. Lack of role clarity and discrepancy between their own role perceptions and expectations of others contribute to this syndrome (Bensky et al., 1980). Dettmer (1982) identifies lack of recognition and reinforcement for their work, along with heavy responsibilities without much decision-making authority, as additional stressors for special education personnel.

Undue levels of stress reduce productivity, motivation, and, eventually, compassion for others (Shaw, Bensky, and Dixon, 1981). Maslach and Pines (1977) have determined that, at the extreme stage of burnout, human service workers are likely to view clients as somehow deserving of their problems.

There may be a cyclical or reciprocal relationship between teacher stress and student behavior (Shaw, Bensky, and Dixon, 1981). For example, short-term results of teacher stress such as irritability, inability to concentrate, disorganization, and poor management of work flow can affect the behavior and performance of students. Teacher stress also affects interactions with other professionals. One unfortunate outcome of burnout is attrition from the field, resulting in fewer professionals available to serve children with special needs.

Stress, Burnout, and Professional Responsibilities

Stress can be said to be the result of disequilibrium. Stress is caused by actions or situations that place special physical or psychological demands on a person. When those actions or situations, called stressors, cannot be balanced by one's coping mechanisms, an imbalance, or disequilibrium, is created (Sapolsky, 1994).

Medical research has shown that although stress is caused by a wide variety of stressors, a person's body responds in a stereotypical pattern (Selye, 1993). The body senses the stressor and prepares for "flight or fight." It responds by releasing hormones into the bloodstream that activate the autonomic nervous system. Energy is mobilized by an increasing heart rate, respiration rate, and other physical reactions. Because this alarm stage cannot be sustained for prolonged periods of time, the body draws on reserves of energy. When stress is diminished, the body recuperates and resistance to stress is increased. If stress does not diminish, however, exhaustion occurs, with negative physical and psychological effects.

Burnout is physical and emotional exhaustion. Prolonged stress or the buildup of stressors causes fatigue and frustration. Up to 50 percent of educators have indicated they may leave the profession because of burnout (Raschke, Dedrick, and DeVries, 1988), and burnout disproportionately affects special education teachers and others in the helping professions (Pines and Aronson, 1988). There are three basic components of burnout (Maslach, 1982):

1. emotional exhaustion ("I'm tired and irritated all the time. I am impatient with my students and colleagues.")
2. depersonalization ("I am becoming emotionally hardened; I start to blame the students or their families for all the problems.")
3. reduced accomplishment ("I feel as if I'm not making a difference for my students.")

The result of burnout is attrition, alienation, cynicism, and physical problems such as heart disease, hypertension, headaches, and psychosomatic illnesses.

The stressors that cause the stress reaction are many. For the consultant, stressors could be a new special education regulation, a change in job description, an angry parent, or a student who is behaving in a violent manner. Teachers usually manage these stressors very well; however, prolonged periods of stress may eventually lead to maladaptive responses. The result may be depression, anger, anxiety, decreased ability to concentrate, distractibility, overeating, or excessive use of alcohol or drugs. Teachers will never be able to reduce or eliminate all the stressors in their lives, but they can develop some positive coping strategies so that a balance between stress and coping can be achieved and burnout can be avoided.

Strategies for Reducing Stress

Developing positive adaptive strategies is crucial to maintaining emotional and physical health. Although stress is unavoidable, behavioral, physical, and cognitive strategies can be used to reduce the impact of stress and to reduce burnout. Educators have adopted stress management strategies such as time management, good nutrition, routine exercise, setting goals and priorities, relaxation, positive self-direction, spiritual development, seeking social support, and developing a positive attitude. Several of these strategies will be described here. The techniques individuals use depend on their preferences, life styles, and skills. Consultants and consultees must learn to "work smarter, not harder" to accomplish goals for students who are at risk of failure in school. Educators also must learn to take care of themselves so they do not lose their commitment and motivation, and students with special needs do not lose their good teachers.

Setting Realistic Goals

School consultants will benefit from developing realistic goals and determining priorities for the many tasks and activities in their daily professional lives. School goals should be established collaboratively with colleagues in the school setting. These are based on school policies, students' IEPs, and other guides. Setting goals will provide a way to gain positive feedback for work. Lack of positive reinforcement and feedback leads to stress. Goals are a yardstick to measure activities and set priorities for daily actions. Goal setting is discussed later in this chapter and also was addressed in Chapter 5.

APPLICATION 7.1   Setting Goals

To check for potential stress factors, use a grid that determines whether your behavior matches your goals (see Figure 7.1). On the left-hand column list your personal goals. Include family, school, personal, community, and organizational goals as appropriate. Across the top, write your most frequent behaviors, such as reading, going to meetings, grading papers, gardening. Then check the behaviors that are helping you meet your goals. If you have behaviors that are not helping meet any of your goals, reflect upon the value of those behaviors at this point in your life. If you have goals you are not accomplishing, examine the behaviors list to see what might be added for helping you accomplish the goals. If you still find gaps, take care, for your flame of enthusiasm and feeling of accomplishment may begin to sputter. Some changes may be in order.

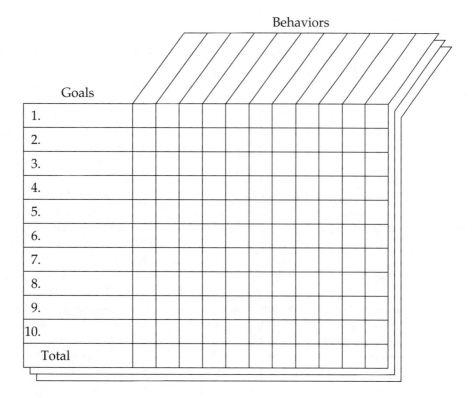

FIGURE 7-1 Stress Management Grid

Taking Time to Relax

Relaxing is crucial to recovery during stress. The body must have time to build up stores of energy and to allow the heart, lungs, and autonomic nervous system to return to normal. Relaxation does not mean sitting down to watch television or to read an exciting book. Real relaxation means physical and emotional inertia. Music helps some people relax. Listening to sixty-cycle music has been shown to increase alpha brain wave, the relaxation wave length (Douglass and Douglass, 1993). Bach, Handel, and Mozart are examples of this type of music.

Others use biofeedback, deep muscle relaxation, yoga, transcendental meditation, massage, or creative imagery to relax. There are many books, video and audio tapes, and courses about these relaxation activities. If being healthy and happy is a goal, one should take time to relax. Put it on a daily "To Do" list. Make a commitment to take care of oneself and relax.

Following a Healthful Diet

Good health also means a balanced diet. The new food guide pyramid consists of five food groups. At the top of the pyramid is the fats and sweets group, and this group should be used sparingly. There are natural fats and sugar in most of the other groups and care must be taken to avoid adding fats or sugars when preparing or cooking foods. The milk group and the meat groups are next. Only a couple servings from these groups are advised, with special care to avoid fats such as fatty meat or cream and regular milk. Two or three servings of fruit are advised and two to five servings are needed in the vegetable group. The base of the pyramid is the bread and grain group, and 6 to 11 servings a day are advised. More information on the food pyramid and serving size is available at libraries or from extension agencies located in towns that are county seats. By adhering to the recommendations in this guide, people will have a well-balanced diet and there will be little need for extra vitamins. Also, consumption of salt, caffeine, and alcohol should be reduced or eliminated.

Developing a Positive Attitude

A positive attitude reduces stress and affects a person's energy level. Studies show that it takes more energy to be grumpy than to be cheerful. Attitudes are the result of the words we use when we talk to ourselves, so positive self-talk is essential for a positive attitude. Zabel and Zabel (1982) describe such self-talk as "I can't change it, so I won't worry about it." One should practice turning every negative thought into a positive one. For example, instead of thinking, "She shouldn't have that attitude toward this student," it is better to think, "I wish her attitude were different." Douglass and Douglass (1993) suggest listening to humorous tapes and programming laughing time into the day. Learn to "let it go," forget harboring grudges and learn to look at the positive aspects of every situation. Stress often makes people feel rushed and negative feelings come with a sense of urgency or frustration. Some ways to reduce stress caused by hurrying are: Slow down. Practice walking slower, talking slower, eating and breathing slower. Adopt a more measured pace. Notice the sunset, a child's smile, the laughter on the playground. Don't add anything to a list without subtracting an old item. More is often achieved by doing less.

Maintaining an Exercise Regimen

Regular aerobic exercise can dissipate stress and build the body's resistance to stress. Morning exercise boosts the energy level for the day. It raises the oxygen level of the blood and makes one more alert. Exercise also builds the cardiovascular system and that is a good protection against many health problems.

The amount of exercise is more important that the type of exercise. Walking, considered by many to be the best overall exercise, can be done at any time, any place, and any age. Twenty minutes of aerobic exercise 3 or 4 times a week is considered adequate to maintain health, to reduce stress, and to control weight. Swimming, running, tennis, cycling, and cross-country skiing are popular activities. Brief periods of exercise, such as walking up the stairs, walking to work, or gardening, can add up to the daily twenty minutes

---

APPLICATION 7.2   Eating Healthfully to Reduce Stress

Exactly what do you eat? Keep a diet diary of your food and beverage intake for a week or two. Examine your diet and develop a plan to eat better. Not only will a nutritious diet help you cope with stress, it will give you more energy. Remember, there is a direct relationship between what you eat and your ability to withstand the effects of stress.

APPLICATION 7.3   **Thinking Positively to Reduce Stress**

Start with a stack of 3 × 5 cards, preferably bright-colored. On five of them write a positive feature about yourself—an ability you are proud of, an accomplishment you have made, or something about yourself that indicates what a wonderful person you are. Then select an activity you enjoy doing every day, such as reading the paper, getting into the car to go home from school, or having that first cup of coffee. Each day before doing this activity, read over your cards. Do this daily and particularly at any time you feel your "flame" starting to burn out. Add to your cards each week. Thinking positively and noting your accomplishments can help prevent burnout.

---

necessary for health. Caro and Robbins (1991) encourage colleagues to "TalkWalk", which is talking and problem-solving while walking together in an unrestricted outdoor environment. One special educator we know held an aerobics session daily after school in her classroom. Colleagues learned what resources were available and got to know each other informally as they improved their health.

Building Networks of Support
Building mutually supportive networks will minimize, if not eliminate, feelings of isolation and helplessness in the demanding role of school consultant. It helps to talk things out with others and to get a new perspective when tackling complex responsibilities inherent in meeting special needs. A support system is an effective outlet for frustration and provides a backup in times of crisis. Talking things out with a friend, family member, counselor, or minister is a good way to relieve stress and will help prevent "dumping," that is, releasing built-up emotions on an unsuspecting colleague.

One special education staff made a commitment to meet each Friday at a centralized place for lunch and lively conversation. Ground rules stipulated there would be no talking about students, schools, or staff in that public place. The camaraderie and conviviality of the weekly event, looked on favorably by district administrators, was an effective support system for teachers whose roles invite stress.

Getting Adequate Rest
Adults generally need from six-and-a-half to nine hours of sleep a night. Stress leads to insomnia. Tired people have an even harder time coping with stress. One's body signals how much sleep is needed. Too much or too little is detrimental to health and productivity.

Taking a nap is a good strategy. Such productive people as Thomas Edison, Harry Truman, Anwar Sadat, and Malcolm Forbes took afternoon naps regularly. During the peak of World War II, Winston Churchill took naps. A brief nap after lunch is the best single thing one can to to make productive use of the rest of the day (Keys, 1991). Weekday naps may not be possible for consultants, but scheduling a brief relaxation time for as few as ten minutes is a proactive strategy for reducing stress.

Making Environmental Changes
Consulting teachers can improve the learning environment by altering it in a variety of ways and at various times during the school year. The classroom or resource area can be set

up so the environmental systems control student behavior (DeShong, 1981). It is helpful to take a critical look at the room arrangement, looking for ways to change the traffic flow and manage trouble spots of congestion efficiently. This may involve moving the pencil sharpener, or having two trash cans instead of one and locating them more strategically. Teachers need to sit momentarily in each area and every desk in the room, asking, "Am I comfortable here? Can I see and hear well? Is there a glare? Are there distractions? Is this a pleasant place?" Comfortable students are happier, more productive students. Learning and teaching are more effective when the environment is pleasant and comfortable.

Consultants will want to structure their consultation areas to increase opportunities for talking with colleagues. Privacy for confidential conversations, room arrangements for collegial interaction, and often-overlooked amenities such as fresh air, comfortable chairs, and attractive displays will encourage collaboration.

APPLICATION 7.4   Controlling One's Life and Role

What if burnout has struck already? What if you feel low self-esteem, emotional and physical exhaustion now? Then these intervention techniques may be helpful.

1. Talk to someone. Say hello, give a positive comment to someone, share ideas.
2. Pretend you are O.K. Remember that problems in life are inevitable and demonstrate that we are alive and still functioning. Smile. Stand up straight and walk with a bouncy step. Wear bright, happy clothes—a funny tie, or long, dangling earrings shaped like dinosaurs or pea pods.
3. Sit in the warm, fresh air. Natural light helps one's body function better.
4. Laugh out loud. Each person should have his or her "laugh ration" every day for mental and physical health. Listen to a comedy tape. Read a joke book. Watch children play.
5. Move. Oxygenate. Mild exercise gets the blood flowing and transports more oxygen throughout the body, helping you feel alert and alive.
6. Play energetic, happy music. Classical music is effective. Rock music is tiring and drains energy from many people.
7. Break that routine. Take a different route to work. Rearrange your schedule or your furniture. Take a vacation if you possibly can. When you do, leave worries and cares behind. Give yourself over to relaxation and rejuvenation.
8. Schedule appointments with yourself. Keep a jar of little treats on your desk, such as encouraging statements, or envelopes with five dollar bills inside, to be good to yourself every now and then.
9. Use reminders to help remember these and other prevention and intervention strategies. They could be colored ribbons, stick-on happy faces, ads from magazines, letters to yourself. Put the reminders on your tote bag or briefcase, on your watch, calendar, or rear-view mirror.
10. Remind yourself often that prevention and remediation of stress and burnout are the concern of the individual, not family or friends or colleagues. Each must become aware of the factors and variables in his or her own personal formula of strategies for keeping the flame of motivation alive.

Management of Time and Energy

When school consultants are asked about the biggest obstacle to their roles, the majority respond, "Time, time, time!" Time is a critical factor in the plans and purposes of educators, particularly for school consultants in their complex, multifarious roles. Studies have shown that school consultants spend time attending meetings, preparing and planning, administering tests, communicating, observing, evaluating, and problem solving (Tindal and Taylor-Pendergast, 1989; Nelson and Stevens, 1981). School consultants have many roles and responsibilities. Time is a precious commodity and many school consultants are prone to "time-lock," the condition that occurs when claims on your time have grown so demanding that you feel it's impossible to wring one more second out of the crowded calendar (Keys, 1991).

Managing time and schedules in order to conduct consultation and collaborate effectively is one of the biggest challenges for school consultants. Caseload is a critical factor in managing time and arranging schedules. The experience of Idol (1988) and others suggests that special education consultants should serve a maximum of 35 students. Those having both direct and indirect service roles should have their ratios classified for each category, and students receiving consultation services as well as direct services should be counted twice.

Problems concerning time management contribute to teacher stress and burnout, and possibly to attrition from the field. Since time is not replaceable or expandable, it must be allocated judiciously to provide the most service for the greatest number of people.

Time management strategies can reduce stress, increase confidence, maximize productivity, and help make sense out of the systems in which we live and work. Time management is about choices. A person just cannot do everything. The problem with time is not a shortage of time, for we have all there is. The problem is how we choose to use the time available to us. Time management is really self-management. Time is not adaptable, but people are. There's an old Chinese proverb that says, "You cannot change the wind, but you can change the sail." Time management (or self-management) skills can be learned and improved. Personality differences and cultural diversity affect the value and use of time and everyone responds to pace and pressure in a different way. Because time management is about choices, it is very personal and the best management plan for one is not the choice of another.

A basic five-step plan is useful for developing and maintaining efficient use of available time:

1. Analyze current use of time.
2. Establish goals and priorities.
3. Plan your time and your work.
4. Use positive time management techniques.
5. Review and reinforce yourself for success.

Analyzing Current Use of Time

In order to make significant improvements in time management, busy consultants must accurately observe their use of time and must analyze their use of time by asking, "Does what I am doing help me achieve my professional or personal goals? Does what I am doing right now enhance the education of students with special needs?" Time logs are a valuable way to observe personal use of time. Consultants may choose to use a diary time log, recording everything they do, when they do it, and how long it takes. Another option is to record time in 15 minute segments, or use a matrix that lists times of the day in segments and lists elements of the consulting role. The matrix can be used to quickly check off those responsibilities that were being done in each segment. Then time spent on each activity can be totaled at the end of the day. When recording use of time, remember to reflect on use of time as the day progresses, rather than at the end of the day.

At the end of several days of observation, the consultant is ready to diagnose the problem. Douglass and Douglass (1993) suggest asking such questions as:

- What patterns and habits are apparent?
- What was the most productive period of my day and why?
- What was the least productive period of my day and why?
- How much of my time was spent on high-value activity and how much was spent on low-value activities?
- What activities need more time?
- What activities could I spend less time on and still obtain acceptable results?

It is also helpful to analyze personal use of time by looking at what you think you're doing, look at what you actually are doing, and look at what you ought to be doing to achieve your goals. These methods of observing and analyzing use of time can be the first step to managing time and energy.

Establishing Goals and Priorities

Goals are the basis of better time utilization. Without well-defined goals, it is impossible to make choices about use of time. Goals help a person evaluate whether one activity is a better or worse use of time than another activity. Goals provide the map to where a person wants to go in her or his life. Reflecting on such questions as "What do I value?", and "Where do I want to go in my life?" helps the busy consultant focus on future goals. The consultant might think about a perfect day five years into the future—and what that day would contain. Further education? Another home? A new car? A stimulating school day with happy, successful students and colleagues who work together enthusiastically? After reflecting on this perfect day and thinking of words that describe it, the consultant can formulate long-term goals for attaining such a day and many more. These goals may be personal or professional, related to educational degrees, home, family, work setting, or job description. Once established, these goals become the measure of which activities are essential and which are nonessential to attaining them. Establishing priorities for daily planning and making choices about use of time becomes easier when using the yardstick of goals.

It is helpful to review long-term goals daily. They should be posted on the wall or in a planner. This simple activity, according to Douglass and Douglass (1993), helps one stay focused and "sort out all the trivia that fills your days." Long-term goals should be subdivided into short term goals, weekly goals, and daily goals. To minimize the gap between long-term and short-term goals, Douglass and Douglass (1993) suggest:

1. Keep a master "to do" list with priority codes that match the items to your goals.
2. Assign a due date to each project. Due dates keep tasks from being put off and foster a sense of completion when accomplished.
3. Estimate time required to complete the task or the project.

There is information about goals elsewhere in this chapter and in Chapter 5.

Planning Time and Work

Time-use analysis leads to planning. Planning assures that time is used to achieve short-term goals and that every day leads closer to long-term goals. Planning assures that daily actions are proactive rather than reactive.

Consultants in educational settings must plan developmental work and maintenance work. Maintenance work is made up of the difficult and time-consuming tasks required to keep the organization and program functioning. This includes meetings, paperwork, and communication with colleagues, students, and families. Developmental work includes observations, program planning and development, evaluations, and curriculum and resource development. Both of these types of work are vital to the success of students with special needs, but often the maintenance work has a greater sense of urgency and demands much time and energy. Planning is the best strategy for balancing these two types of consulting work.

Using Positive Time Management Strategies

There are many books, tapes, and workshops about time management strategies. School consultants should use the ones that are best for them and their roles and preferences. This section will describe six strategies that consultants have found helpful in their self-management efforts.

1. *Identifying and eliminating time wasters* is high on every consultant's list. Time wasters make activities take longer than they should, or they may be activities that have no purpose. Examples of teacher time wasters are phone interruptions, over-scheduling because of an inability to say "no," ineffective communication, excessive socializing, indecision, procrastination, confusion about responsibilities, and fretting about unfinished tasks. The consultant role is particularly vulnerable to all of these factors. The time use analysis described above is helpful in identifying time wasters.
2. *Weekly and daily planning* are crucial for successful time management. A weekly plan should include the goals for the week, the activities necessary to achieve those goals, and the priorities for the activities. A weekly plan takes about 30 minutes for most consultants, and they report that their plan saves them at least an hour a day during the week. Weekly plans help in several ways: avoiding over-scheduling, making decisions, coordinating with others, getting more done, avoiding problems, and thinking of long-range goals. Weekly plans are also successful with teams because they keep the group focused, help them balance priorities, increase shared information, and promote good teamwork. Daily plans evolve from weekly plans and should include tasks, meetings,

paperwork, priorities, and time estimates for each activity. Flexibility is the key in daily planning so it is not good to schedule every minute of the day. Careful planning allows for the spontaneity and flexibility needed in consulting work.

3. *"To Do" and "Not To Do" lists* are helpful time management tools. These lists help consultants manage essential activities and prioritize agendas. A "To Do" list is a work plan. After listing work activities to be completed, analyze them according to your weekly goals. Prioritize using the *ABC* method (Lakein,1973), with *A* as the top priority. Then add time estimates of how long each activity will require. Low priority items can be transferred to the "Not To Do" list. These activities can be delegated, done less often (newsletters can be biweekly rather than weekly), or just ignored. Making decisions about what not to do motivates ignoring the nonessentials and focusing on goals.

4. *Learn to say "no."* Avoid saying "Well, . . ." or "I'll think about it." Perhaps the very worst response is, "I will if you can't find anyone else." Being asked to do "everything" is the price effective consultants pay for being good at their jobs. Inability to say no is a common time waster and can be very stressful. Say no, give a brief reason, and offer an alternative if one comes to mind easily. Saying no is difficult for many consultants and should be practiced until it feels comfortable and guilt-free. Other helpful responses are: "Yes, if you will do something for me," or "This is so important that it needs more attention than I can give it now," or "Please take a number and get in line, because I'm inundated right now." Use your assertiveness as described in Chapter 6.

5. *Managing the paperwork* is every consultant's biggest headache. Organize your desk and office area. MacKenzie (1975) describes the "stacked desk syndrome," in which the desk is so cluttered with things that you want to keep handy that you can't find anything. Ask yourself, "Why do I have this on my desk?" "What do I need this for?" and "Where shall I keep this?" The answers are often "No reason," "Nothing," and "In the recycle box/trash." If you can't decide about keeping a paper, toss it in a box and look over your "maybe" box once a month—or just toss it! Analyze the paperwork you need to do with the same questions you ask about your schedule. And attempt to reduce paperwork. Think information, not paper. Use electronics and computer networks for communication and for data files. Save time, save energy, and save a tree.

6. *Travel time* takes up valuable hours in the rural consultant's week. Planning ahead helps reduce the feeling of wasted time when you're going to a meeting or a home visit in the next county. Driving time can be used to listen to tapes about personal development, stress management, conference sessions and lectures, and time management. Consider using a tape recorder to dictate reports or record creative thoughts and new ideas. Dictate a journal article or a conference presentation to submit. Listen to relaxing music or a tape of bird calls. Listen to the latest best seller, which can often be checked out at your local library, bookstore, or grocery store.

7. *Be prepared for emergencies.* Keep your spare tire in good shape and take water, candles, blankets, a good book, and whatever else the weather in your area dictates. Let being detained overnight by a storm serve as an opportunity to relax or get some work done in peace and quiet. Be prepared and keep a positive attitude.

These strategies are just a few of the many that educators can use to manage their time and their lives. It takes self-discipline to identify and avoid situations that lead to inappropriate use of time. Managing time carefully enhances both productivity and personal well-being and is an important professional goal.

Reviewing and Reinforcing Success

Periodically review your long-term goals and your time analyses. Have you accomplished a goal? Have you incorporated a new time management strategy into your life? Celebrate. Reinforce yourself for your persistence and your accomplishment. The social and professional systems in which consultants work may not reinforce goal achievement so arrange your own celebrations. Take a break, plan time for yourself, get a massage, visit a friend, read a book, get out your camera or watercolors. Plan treats to reinforce your own efficiency and your measurable progress toward goals. Many teachers are quite goal oriented but fail to build self-rewards into their planning schedules (Davis, 1983).

One additional benefit educators can obtain from effective self-management is the ripple effect it has for students. Not only do students profit from more organized and productive teachers, they benefit from modeled techniques they can apply in their own lives.

A basic four-step plan is useful for achieving productive time management practices:

- Establish goals and make plans.
- Identify and eliminate time-wasters.
- Use positive time management strategies.
- Take care of yourself.

When these steps are followed, educators are more able to achieve greater satisfaction with their work, progress toward their goals, and enjoy feelings of self-worth and accomplishment. They also have more time for fun and leisure activities.

Techniques for Meetings, Interviews, and Observations

Who has not winced at the thought of yet another meeting? Meetings, interviews, and classroom observations command precious time as well as physical and mental energy. Tremendous amounts of collective time and energy are wasted when many people are trapped in unproductive meetings. Educators aiming to "work smarter, not harder," should strive for group interactions that are efficient and productive for all.

Conducting Efficient Meetings

School consultants are busy, but classroom teachers may be the most overextended of all. Furthermore, many classroom teachers such as Miss Anderson in this chapter's scenario find the total time for having all their students together for a class period is appallingly short. Consultation and collaboration will be accepted more readily when consultees know that consultants respect their time and their students' time. So a meeting should be planned only if it promises to contribute significantly in serving client needs.

The first rule of thumb in planning an efficient meeting is to ask, "Do we really need to have this meeting?" If the answer is not a resounding "Yes," then the business probably can be handled a more efficient way, perhaps by memo, phone, or brief face-to-face conversations with individuals. Good reasons for having a meeting are

- meeting legal obligations (such as an IEP conference);
- problem solving with several people representing a variety of roles;
- brainstorming so that many ideas are put forth;
- reconciling conflicting views; or
- building a team to implement educational decisions.

Unnecessary meetings waste school time. They also erode participants' confidence in the value of future meetings that may be called. Sigband (1987) recommends that meetings be held only when there is verifiable need, basing each one on an overall purpose and series of objectives. Only people who can make a definite contribution need to be there. An agenda should be prepared, and the meeting room and any needed equipment should be ready. Most important, the meeting must begin on time and end on time, or early if possible.

Preparing for the Meeting

Leaders or chairs of meetings will be more prepared and organized if they follow a planning checklist (see Figure 7-2 for an example). The planning sheet should include general planning points such as date, time, participants, and goals. Checklists designed to stipulate preparations for the room and to note participant needs also will be useful.

Participants

After determining a need for a meeting, leaders and chairs will want to request attendance from only those who can contribute. They should keep the group as small as possible, adhering to the rule of thumb that the more people involved, the shorter the meeting should be. Experts on group interaction recommend that the maximum to have for problem solving is five, for problem identification about ten; for hearing a review or presentation, as many as thirty; and for motivation and inspiration as many as possible. If a group includes more than six people, it is likely someone will not have an opportunity to speak.

Agenda for the Meeting

Chairpersons for meetings should develop an agenda that reflects the needs of all participants. If the agenda is distributed beforehand, participants will be more productive and less apprehensive. (See Figure 7-3 for an example of a premeeting communication to prepare participants.) Sometimes leaders of large group meetings draw on a teaching technique of placing a short, high-interest activity, related to the topic but needing little explanation, on the chalkboard or overhead screen. Participants focus on the task as they arrive, becoming focused on the meeting topic.

It is important to allocate time for each item on the agenda. Estimating the time needed will allow the chair to monitor progress during the meeting. It is counterproductive to focus too long on early items and fail to get to the last ones. If more important items are placed far down the agenda, it might even appear, if time becomes limited, that they have been put there by the convener to avoid action or decision making. Consultants seeking to build collaborative interactions among their colleagues will not want that to happen.

Date: _____   Place: _____

Time: _____   Topic: _____

Participants: _____

Goals For Meeting: _____

_____

_____

Preparation For Room: Preparation For Participants:

_____ Overhead projector   _____ Nametags

_____ Screen, bulbs, cord   _____ Pads and pens

_____ Chalkboard, chalk   _____ Handouts

_____ Charts, pens, tape   _____ Agenda

_____ Tape recorder, tapes   _____ Ice-breaker activity

_____ Podium, lectern   _____ Map of location

_____ Tables, chairs   _____ Refreshments

_____ Breakout arrangements   _____ Follow-up activity

_____ Other?   _____ Other?

Room Arrangement: _____

_____

_____   (Sketch Of Room)

_____

_____

FIGURE 7-2   Checklist to Prepare for Meetings

Seating Arrangements

Comfortable chairs and seating arrangements that facilitate interaction are important factors in the success of a meeting. Full size chairs (not kindergarten furniture) with a little padding, but not too much, should be provided. For best interaction, there should be an arrangement where all can face each other. A circle for six to ten people, a U shape with peripheral seating if there is to be a visual presentation, and a semicircle of one or more rows for large groups work well (Lawren, 1989).

Date: _____   Place: _____

Time Start: _____ Time End: _____ Topic: _____

Roles: Facilitator: _____

Recorder: _____

Timekeeper: _____

Other Participants: _____

Agenda For Meeting: _____

_____

_____

_____

_____   Minutes of Prior Meeting Attached _____

_____   Advance Preparation Needed _____

_____   Next Planned Meeting _____

At the Meeting

Action	Person(s) Responsible	Target Date	Done

FIGURE 7-3   Checklist to Prepare Participants

Participant Responsibilities

Along with the responsibility of each participant to interact and help problem solve, brainstorm, or decide, three other responsibilities are important—chair, recorder, and timekeeper. In many cases the consultant will take care of all three roles, particularly if the meeting includes only two or three people. However, if the meeting is long, or the issues are complex and there is much discussion and brainstorming, it is efficient for the chair to ask another participant to record the plans and decisions.

During the Meeting

Whether the meeting involves two persons or twenty, all participants should be made to feel they have important contributions to make. All should listen attentively to each other, think creatively and flexibly, and avoid disruptive communication such as jokes, puns, sarcasm, or side comments (Gordon, 1974). Talking and whispering in subgroups can be particularly distracting. Ironically, some teachers who will not tolerate such behavior by their students in the classroom are the biggest offenders. Astute group leaders have various ways of handling this disagreeable occurrence. They might go over to the offenders and stand alongside or between them, direct questions to them, or request information from them. In the right circumstance, a touch on the arm or shoulder can bring a talker back into focus toward the business of the group. Each participant in a meeting should be thinking at all times, "What will help move us ahead and solve the problem?" and "What does the group need and how can I help?" (Gordon, 1974).

Minutes of the Meeting

Sometimes a committee is accused of keeping minutes to waste hours! Minutes should reflect the group's decisions about what is to be done, by whom, and by what date, but need not include each point of the discussion. Minutes are a record for naming those who will have a responsibility, for describing plans and decisions, and for listing projected dates for completion of tasks. This is an important aspect of the consultation that should not be slighted.

Assessment of the Meeting

Some time should be reserved at the end of the meeting to discuss progress made and to evaluate the effectiveness of the meeting. If a meeting agenda becomes sidetracked, leaders should redirect the group's attention by making a point to refocus the discussion (Raschke, Dedrick, and DeVries, 1988).

Compromise for consensus is not always the best solution. It may signify a weak decision, a watered-down plan, or a failure by some participants to express their concerns as firmly as they should. During the meeting leaders should encourage opposing views to be aired, so that these do not surface later when the matter has been closed. If any participant wishes to dissent, the time to do so is in the meeting, not in hallways after the matter has been decided.

Of course, many consultations and collaborations involve only two individuals—consultant and consultee. But these procedures recommended for groups of several or more are often pertinent to interactions between only two individuals as well.

Conducting Effective Interviews

School consultants often need to interview school personnel, community resources, and family members to plan programs for helping students with special needs. Interviewees can provide information for case studies and formulation of learning goals. They help generate options and alternatives for special needs and provide data for program evaluation.

Successful interviews require effective communication skills (see Chapter 6), and postures of onedownsmanship, parity, and cooperativeness. Queries such as "Tell me more," and "Could you expand on that?" and "Let me see if I understand what you are saying . . ." are examples of the responsive listening and paraphrasing that help to elicit the most useful information.

The interviewer should take notes, allowing interviewees to look them over at the conclusion of the interview. If a tape recording is desired, the interviewer must ask permission beforehand to make one. Some feel it is best to avoid taping, because respondents are often less candid if their comments are being recorded.

Interviews must be conducted ethically, collegially, and for a purpose not attainable by less intrusive, time-consuming methods. Keys to a successful interview by the school consultant are asking the right questions and valuing the expertise of the interviewee. A follow-up interaction soon after the interview session is affirming and reassuring, thus facilitating further collaboration.

Making Prudent Observations

Consultants often need to observe a student, groups of students, or an entire program in operation. This is not an easy professional task. Consultants who go into classrooms to observe can expect some discomfort and anxiety on the teacher's part. There may be latent resentment because the consultant is free to visit in other classrooms, something many teachers would like but are rarely given the opportunity to do.

Consultants can facilitate the process of observation and ease the minds of those being observed in several ways. First, they should provide a positive comment on entering the room and then sit unobtrusively where the teacher has designated. They should avoid getting involved in classroom activities or helping students. Effective observers can blend into the classroom setting so they are hardly noticed. Regular visits minimize the likelihood of having students know who is being observed and for what reason. It is a sad thing to hear a student say, "Oh, here's that learning disabilities teacher to check up on Jimmy again." Records of behaviors must be done in code so the physical aspects of writing, watching, and body language of the consultant do not reveal the intent of the observation. Each consultant should develop a personal coding system for recording information. Sometimes observers watch the targeted student for one minute, and then divert their attention to another student for one minute, continuing the process with other peers. In this way the student's behavior can be compared with that of classmates. The consultant may teach a lesson and have the classroom teacher observe. This can be helpful for both consultant and consultee.

An observer should exit the room with a smile and a supporting glance at the teacher. Then very soon after the observation, the observer will want to get back to the classroom teacher with positive, specific comments about the classroom, feedback on the observation, and suggestions for entering into problem solving. Although consultants do not observe in classrooms for the purpose of assessing teacher behaviors and teaching styles, it would be myopic to assume they do not notice teaching practices that inhibit student success in the classroom. In a nonthreatening, nonexpert way, the consultant might ask the consultee if the student achieved the goals of the lesson. If not, is there something the teacher would like to change so this could occur? Then what might the consultant do to help?

To avoid gathering inaccurate information, consultants will want to make repeated observations. In doing so, they can also obtain additional information on antecedents to the problem (Cipani, 1985).

Achieving rapport with a consultee while targeting a teaching strategy for possible modification requires utmost finesse by consultants. This underscores the need for providing feedback and continuation of the problem solving process as soon as possible after a classroom observation.

Management of Consultation Records and Resources

A prominent scientist for space research commented that physicists can lick anything, even gravity, but the paperwork is overwhelming. Special education teachers can relate to that. They cite excessive paperwork and record keeping, along with insufficient time in which to do them, as major causes of stress and burnout. Writing and monitoring IEPS, individual pupil record keeping, and completion of records and forms rank high as major usurpers of their personal and professional time (Davis, 1983). When asked to estimate the amount of time they spend performing their responsibilities, resource teachers often overestimate the time spent on direct pupil instruction and staffings and underestimate their time preparing for instruction and performing clerical duties such as record-keeping.

Nevertheless, if teaching is to be an important service profession, careful record keeping is essential. Record keeping must be written into the consultant's role description as a significant responsibility, with time allowed for its accurate completion. Who would want to be treated by a doctor who did not write down vital information after each visit, or served by a lawyer who failed to record and file important documents? The key for educators is to manage their paperwork so it does not manage them. Developing efficient systems and standardized forms for record keeping will help educators, and consultants in particular, work smarter and not harder.

Using a Consultation Log

One of the most important formats for consultants to develop is a consultation log or journal. Consultants can record the date, participants, and topic of each consultation on separate pages, along with a brief account of the interaction and the results agreed on. Space should be provided for follow-up reports and assessment of the consultation (see Figure 7-4 for a sample format). Records should be kept noting the time spent in consultation and any positive results accomplished, if consultation is to gain credibility as an essential educational activity. While consultants cannot control the type of records required, they can determine processes and procedures for collecting and using information (Davis, 1983).

One caution must be noted about consultation logs. Important points of the discussion about student needs and progress might be entered in the log. However, no diagnostic classification or plan that requires parent permission should be recorded (Conoley and Conoley, 1982). Confidentiality of the information must be preserved. Consultants will want to develop procedures for coding that will ensure confidentiality yet identify pertinent information efficiently.

Creating a Logo for Consultant Memos

A consultation memo is a communication tool and also a record of that communication. Consultants will find it helpful to include a personalized logo on the memo forms they use

Client (coded): _____   Consultee (initials): _____

Initiator of Consultation: _____

General Topic of Concern: _____

_____

Purpose of Consultation: _____

_____

_____

Brief Summary of Consultation: _____

_____

_____

_____

Steps Agreed On—By Whom, by When: _____

_____

_____

_____

Follow-up: _____

_____

Most Successful Part of Consultation: _____

_____

Consultation Areas Needing Improvement: _____

_____

Satisfaction with consultation process (1 = least, 5 = most)

1. Communication between consultant and consultee   _____

2. Use of collaborative problem-solving   _____

3. Consultee responsiveness to consultation   _____

4. Effectiveness of consultation for problem   _____

5. Impact of consultation on client   _____

6. Positive ripple effects for system   _____

FIGURE 7-4   Consultation Log Format

to communicate with consultees. This logo identifies the memo at a glance as coming from the consultant. A busy recipient immediately recognizes its source and can make a quick decision about the need to respond now or at a later time. It personalizes professional interaction by providing a bit of information about the consultant, a humorous touch, or the creative element that educators enjoy and appreciate. A carefully designed logo can put consultation, collaboration, and team effort in a positive light. (See Figure 7-5 for an example of a personalized memo pad designed by a consulting teacher whose hobby is quilt-making.)

Another item that improves consultant efficiency is the professional card. Business cards have been a mainstay for communicating basic information in many professions, and it is surprising that they are so seldom used in education. Administrators can increase the visibility of their staff and enhance morale as well by providing them with attractive, well-designed professional cards. Educators find these cards helpful when they interact with colleagues at other sites, or when they attend conferences and conventions. The cards are convenient for quickly jotting down requests for information. They help build communication networks among colleagues with similar interests, and can even promote one's own school district.

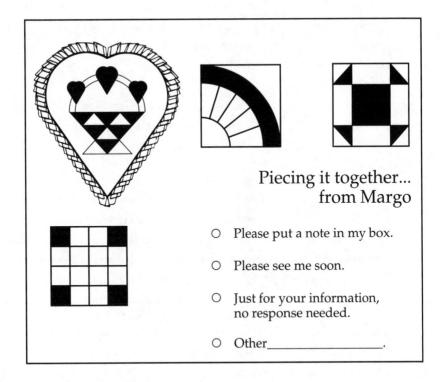

FIGURE 7-5   Consultation Logo Design

Organizing a Consultation Notebook

Consultants often use a loose-leaf notebook divided into sections with index tabs. The sections can be categorized by buildings served, students served, or teachers served. One very organized consulting teacher had a section, "Best Times to Meet with Teachers," listing days and times available for every teacher with whom she collaborated. Each consultant will want to develop the style that works best in his or her school context and role. Figure 7-6 is a list of suggestions for a special education consultant's notebook sections. Consultants may not want or need all of these sections and may come up with others of their own they would like to include. Here again, personalization for the role and school context is recommended.

A primary responsibility of the consultant is to ensure confidentiality of information for both student and staff. This can be accomplished in at least two ways—coding the

Appointments:	One for week, one for year.
"To-do" lists:	By day, week, month, or year as fits needs. List commitments.
Lesson plans:	If delivering direct service, outline of activities for week.
Consultation logs:	Chart to record consultation input and outcomes (Figure 7-5)
Phone call log:	Consultation time by phone.
Observation sheets:	Coded for confidentiality.
Contact list:	Phone numbers, school address, times available.
Faculty notes:	Interests, social and family events and dates, teaching preferences of staff.
Student list:	Coded for confidentiality, birth dates, IEP dates, other helpful data.
Student information:	Anecdotal records, sample products, events, awards, interests, birthdays, talents.
Medication records:	If part of responsibilities.
Materials available:	Title, brief description with grade levels, location.
Services available:	School and community services for resources.
State policies:	Guidelines, procedures, names and phone numbers of agencies/personnel.
School policies:	Brief description of school policies regulations, handbook.
Procedural materials:	Forms, procedures, for standard activities.
Evaluation data:	Space and forms to record data for formative and summative evaluation (see Chapter 9, and coded if confidential).
Idea file:	To note ideas for self and for sharing with staff and parents.
Joke and humor file:	To perk up the day, and for sharing with others.
Three-year calendar:	For continuity in preparing, checking, and updating IEPs.
Pockets:	For carrying personalized memos, letterhead, stamps, hall passes, paper, professional cards.

FIGURE 7-6   Consultation Notebook Format

names with numbers or symbols while keeping the code list in a separate place, and marking person-specific files as confidential. A 'Confidential" rubber stamp prepared for this purpose can be used to alert readers that the information is not for public viewing. These practices, along with the usual protection of information and data, and the practice of seeing that the recorded information is as positive and verifiable as possible, are common-sense rules that should be sufficient for handling all but the most unusual cases.

An itinerant consulting teacher who serves several schools may want to prepare a simple form stating the date, teacher's name and child's code, along with the topic to be considered, for each school. The list can be scanned before entering the building, so no time is lost in providing the consultative or teaching service. Some consulting teachers block off and color-code regular meeting times and teacher responsibilities. This practice permits a clearer picture of available consultation times.

Another helpful strategy is development of a comprehensive manual that includes standard procedures and forms used in the school district and required by the state. An example of a frequently used message form that was made into a pad by the consultant is shown in Figure 7-7.

Consultation Schedules

The consultation schedule is a vital tool. It not only allows the consultant to organize time productively, but demonstrates to administrators and other school personnel that the school consultant is goal directed, productive, and facilitative. Schedules should be left with secretaries of all buildings assigned to the consultant and posted in teacher workrooms, so colleagues have easy access to the information.

Consultations and collaborative experiences can be keyed on the consultant's schedule with code letters, for efficiency. One consulting teacher uses these codes in her notebook:

- ID—informal discussion, spontaneous meeting;
- PM—planned, formal meeting;
- PC—phone conversation;
- MM—major meeting of more than two people;
- FT—follow-through activity; and
- SO—scheduled observation.

Standardized forms are helpful for collecting and using basic information. The forms that produce multiple copies may be more expensive in the short run but can save valuable time and energy in the long run. A story is told of a miser who took overly long strides in his $80 shoes in order to save his shoe leather, but in doing so ripped the cloth of his $100 trousers. In similar fashion, the time spent on developing systems and standardizing conventional forms will be well spent. It frees up more time and energy for individualizing and personalizing the instruction for special needs of the students.

Commercial resources are available that provide sample letters and forms adaptable to a variety of educational purposes, from writing a letter of congratulations to answering concerns and criticisms (Tomlinson, 1984). Although educators will not want to use these patterns verbatim, they can get a "jump start" in preparing some of the more difficult communications.

(tear-off messages)

HIGH SCHOOL PASS

STUDENT'S NAME: _____ HOUR: _____

TEACHER'S NAME: _____ DATE: _____

Test Directions:

_____ 1. Student will work independently on test.

_____ 2. Teacher will read test to student.

_____ 3. Student will answer orally. Teacher records answer.

_____ 4. Can use textbook on test.

_____ 5. Can use notes on test.

_____ 6. Can use review sheets on test.

_____ 7. Give test with these modifications: _____

_____ Yes _____ No   Should student return before period ends?

_____ Time dismissed from class to come to resource room.

_____ Time dismissed from the resource room.

FIGURE 7-7   Message Pad Format

by Wendy Dover (adapted from Farmers Branch ISD, Texas)

Coordination and organization of student files, consultation logs, school procedures, and schedules will necessitate more time for paperwork at the outset, but once the procedures are set up, they will be time efficient and cost effective in the long run.

Organizing and Distributing Materials

Many school districts now have extensive instructional resource centers where school personnel can check out a variety of material for classroom use. Even with the busiest resource center in full operation, consultants usually have their own field-related materials and information about special areas that teachers want and need. With little or no clerical help, and oftentimes little storage space available beyond the seats, floor, and trunk of their own vehicles, traveling school consultants need to develop a simple, orderly checkout system for loaned materials. Without such a system, consultants will soon have little left to use and share.

Materials belonging to the schools should be marked with a school stamp, and personal materials should be labeled with a personal label. Library pockets and checkout cards facilitate checkout and return. The consultant should keep an up-to-date inventory of available personal and school library materials that are loanable and specific to student needs. Before traveling to a school, the consultant can scan the checkout file for materials that are due, and stop by classrooms or put memos into message boxes asking for their return. Efficient consultants leave request cards so school staff can let them know of their needs. They also periodically assess the usefulness of their materials by querying teachers and students who used them. These kinds of interactions build positive attitudes toward collaboration and teamwork, promote the effectiveness of school consultation, and extend the ripple effect of special services.

Related Services and Support Personnel as Partners in School Consultation

An ancient proverb reminds us a child's life is like a piece of paper on which every passerby leaves a mark. Several years ago Bronfenbrenner (1973) stressed that all members of society have the responsibility to teach society's children. A typical community has three kinds of social agencies for educating children—informal, nonformal, and formal (Seay, 1974). Families and neighborhoods are informal agencies for education. Churches, media, and cultural centers are nonformal educator agencies, and schools and universities represent formal agencies. A multitude of educator roles exists among the informal, nonformal and formal agencies, ranging from Scout leaders, to 4-H leaders, to private music and art instructors, to church school teachers. Doctors and dentists teach within their professional roles. Some request information from schools and seek interaction with teachers. One frequently overlooked educational role that more and more schools are learning to value and use is senior citizens, including grandparents of students.

Schools and universities house a variety of support personnel who can assist with student needs. These people also are catalysts for the increasingly popular use of community resources to accentuate learning among students (Dettmer, 1980). Related services and support personnel for students include those serving in areas such as transportation, speech pathology, audiology, psychological services, physical and occupational therapy, recreation, counseling, medical and school health, social work, parent counseling and training, cultural agencies, and mentors or internship supervisors. Each school also has a number of ancillary personnel without whom school life would be disorganized and ineffective. These include people in roles such as food-service staff, secretaries, librarians and media specialists, transportation staff, paraprofessionals, custodians, and volunteer aides.

Related services and support personnel offer services and guidance in academic, emotional, social, physical, career, and transition areas. Support also is provided by coordinators, supervisors, evaluators, and building administrators. Special resource services outside the school include media, speakers, mentors, tutors, judges of events and products, and community partners. Extender services can be provided by libraries, parks, colleges, industries, businesses, and professions. Special activities, managed through clubs, workshops, interest or travel groups, and the like, are an important part of special services for special needs.

Most students with special needs are assigned to general classrooms, even though they may attend resource rooms or work with consulting teachers for a portion of the school day. In order to serve their special learning and behavioral needs, support services and classroom extender services should be integrated into their educational programs. Teachers in a special project who include students with severe disabilities in their general education classrooms reported that the most helpful part of the specialist support they received included shared framework and goals, physical presence, validation of the teacher's contribution, and teamwork (Giangreco, Dennis, Cloninger, Edelman, and Schattman, 1993).

Just as the roles of consultant, consultee, and client are interrelated and interchangeable according to the focus of the consultation, the roles and responsibilities of related, support, and ancillary services personnel interrelate and interchange according to the part each plays in the student's education. For example, transportation personnel are integral to the programs of special education students. They are a key link between home and school. They sometimes play an active role in a referral process for special education, and they can help determine the effects of interventions. They may be involved as partners in reward and reinforcement systems for students, or to extend learning activities beyond the classroom.

The teacher for an educable mentally handicapped student might be a consultee for a bus driver in a consultant role. A librarian might be a consultant to help a gifted program teacher, as consultee, select and locate resources. The school psychologist can contribute valuable information about the purposes, interpretation, and uses of tests. The training of counselors in both individual and group guidance techniques makes them helpful resources in staff development activities and problem-solving sessions. An understanding custodian has always been regarded as a teacher's best friend and helpmate in the school setting. This is especially relevant to the special education teacher's responsibilities. Consultants can encourage custodians to be involved in planning and monitoring special programs for students with special needs.

School nurses and social workers contribute valuable data in consultations and staffings. They are often able to target seemingly insignificant data toward important aspects of problem identification. Transportation staff provide support when they collaborate on scheduling, reinforcement plans, and other special arrangements. One driver of the special education bus displays schoolwork in the bus. She also has a chart for the "star" bus student of the week. She explains that because it is the special education bus, she wants to make their bus ride special. She makes an effort to collaborate with teachers, adapting to special schedules so students are not late or left stranded at a building.

Paraprofessionals and teacher aides interact frequently with other staff members and often are able to view students in different ways. They can share their concerns and contribute information that helps teachers and consultants provide appropriate learning experiences for their students.

Building principles have roles and responsibilities that are just short of overwhelming. So many school issues compete for their time and energy that, when the consultants ask for their participation in consultation and collaboration, special efforts must be made to accommodate administrator schedules. Administrators can assist immeasurably by freeing up teacher time, staggering schedules, and arranging for substitute staff, so that consultation and collaboration among school personnel can take place. Administrators can work with consultants to clarify roles and ensure consultants obtain parity among the school staff. One of their most significant contributions is to encourage interaction and staff development among school personnel. When in-service and staff development are arranged, promoted, and attended by building principals, the multiplier ripple effects are profound. It is vital that all related services and support personnel are included in in-service and staff development sessions, so they are aware of special needs and the programs being implemented to serve those needs.

Labels and categories for school personnel are relatively unimportant within a collaborative climate. The service provided for a child's need determines the role. Thousand et al. (1986) emphasize that schools have many natural, untapped pools of skills and interests across a wide range of unassigned areas. When teachers can form teams and move among roles, positive ripple effects occur. Examples are an increased adult-to-pupil ratio in a learning program and the ability of the school to provide more personalized instruction (Nevin, Thousand, and Paolucci-Whitcomb, 1990).

In order to facilitate appropriate support services for students, consultants can do several things:

- Become knowledgeable about the roles and responsibilities of support personnel.
- Strive for IEPs and informal learning plans that include all facets of the student's learning and involve all roles that will help the student succeed.
- Within the bounds of necessary confidentiality and ethical school practices, ask support personnel for their viewpoints and opinions about helping students with special needs.
- Inform support personnel about the consultation role, schedule, and responsibilities.
- Monitor the student's performance across all kinds of school, home, and community learning in a variety of situations.
- Include support services personnel in staff development activities, encouraging their involvement and collaboration.
- Have specific in-services for them, to provide awareness and encourage collaboration.

Referral Agencies

Every community, large or small, urban or rural, accessible or isolated, wealthy or poor, has agencies and potential resources for contributing to learning programs that serve special needs of children and adolescents. The consulting teacher will find it helpful to develop a directory of referral agencies, with addresses and phone numbers, to have available for consultations and staffings. As one example, a consultant in a mid-size town in the Midwest prepared a referral directory containing more than one hundred sources of assistance. Some were national sources that could be called with a hot line or an 800 number, such as the Missing Children's Network. Others were state-level agencies, including the Resource Center for the Handicapped. Still others were county agencies, such as the County Family

Planning Clinic. But within this average town, many sources were available "just down the street," including a crisis center and a community theater. Resourceful consultants will regularly involve personnel from a variety of agencies to collaborate in planning and implementing student programs that provide support to students' special needs.

Ethics of Consulting and Collaborating

Consultation and collaboration in the school setting require particular emphasis on ethical interaction for several reasons:

Special needs of students are involved.

Confidential data must be shared among several individuals.

Consultants are out and about much more than classroom teachers, interfacing with many people in several buildings.

Parent permission may not be required, but many of the issues approximate the sensitivity of special education issues that do require parental consent.

Consultants have complex roles with many demands on them, but often receive little or no training in how to adapt to those roles.

Consultation implies power and expertise until the collaborative spirit can be cultivated.

Consultants may be asked, on occasion, to act inappropriately as a middle person, or to form alliances or carry information, and they must respond ethically.

Adults often have difficulty adapting to individual differences in teaching styles and preferences of colleagues, and many of them demonstrate resistance.

The persuasive aspects of consultation require a close, careful look at ethical practice (Ross, 1986). Ethical consultation is demonstrated by adhering to principles of confidentiality in acquisition and use of information about students, families, and individual school settings. It also includes a high regard for individual differences among colleagues and the constructive use of those differences to achieve concern and empathy for all, onedownsmanship in the consultative role, and mutual ownership of problems and rewards in the school environment in order to serve students' special needs.

Consultants and collaborators should review legal requirements relating to confidentiality, such as the Family Educational Rights and Privacy Act of 1974 (Buckley Amendment), and truth-in-testing laws within states that legislate them. Requirements such as these stipulate the need for confidentiality of student data and regulate parental access to information about their children.

Hansen, Himes, and Meier (1990) present several suggestions for school consultants to follow in order to exercise ethical behavior in their roles:

1. Promote professional attitudes and behaviors among staff about confidentiality and informed consent.
2. Take care with the quality of information you enter in written records.

3. Take care in discussing problems of children and their families.

4. Focus on strengths of clients and share information only with those who need it to serve the student's needs.

School consultants will be more successful in their roles and more widely accepted by their professional colleagues if they base consultation, collaboration, and teamwork on a code of consultation ethics that includes the following recommendations:

> Avoid any activity that might embarrass colleagues.
>
> Do not violate confidences or carry tales.
>
> Limit the consultative activities to things for which you are trained.
>
> Take care not to distort or misrepresent information.
>
> Openly share helpful data, but only in ways that protect the rights of students and families.
>
> Make as few remarks about specific teaching practices as possible.
>
> Know when to stay in the consultation and when it would be best to get out and seek another approach.
>
> Be open to new ideas and knowledge.
>
> Give colleagues the benefit of wanting to help.
>
> Leave therapy to therapists who are trained for it.
>
> Maintain good records that provide confidentiality.
>
> Keep consultative channels and doors open.
>
> Refrain from taking issues personally.
>
> Above all, advocate for the child, letting student needs guide your actions and decisions.

Several well-known maxims apply to the implementation of planful, efficient, collegial, and ethical practices for consultation:

- "What breaks in a moment may take years to mend."
- "Keep your words sweet, for you may have to eat them."
- "Better to bend than to break."
- "Only a fool would peel a grape with an ax."

Tips for Consulting and Collaborating

1. At the end of the year, write thank-you notes to school personnel you have worked with, including principals, secretaries, and custodians. When writing notes to colleagues, sign your name in a distinctive color on pads of an individualized design. Send a note on a "reminder" memo and staple a bag of nuts, or a valentine cookie, or a doughnut, to it. Remember those who collaborate with you in special ways by delivering a treat to their room and a brief note of appreciation.

2. Color code folders for schools if you serve several. Use a file box with a card for each day to list reminders, and a schedule book. Keep an idea file of filler activities.

3. Use tubs for storage of materials. Plan ahead and put materials in the tub for one week, one month, a season, or a thematic unit.

4. Have a retrieval box in a certain place for receiving borrowed items that are returned. Keep a checkout catalog so you will know where your materials are. When materials are due, remove due cards for the buildings where you will be that week and collect the materials while there.

5. Listen to conversations in the workroom, lunchroom, and faculty meetings. When a topic surfaces for which you have materials, offer to share. Prepare a list of instructional material that is for loaning and distribute copies of it. Make sure grade level and sample objectives of the material are given.

6. Don't schedule yourself so tightly that you have no time for informal interactions and impromptu consultation. These can open the door for more intensive and productive collaboration. Also, be more protective of colleagues' time than you are of your own, and make good use of it.

7. Furnish treats often. For diet-conscious schools, make the treats vegetables or fruit.

8. Develop rapport with librarians. Give advance notice of upcoming topics and try not to make too many spur-of-the-moment requests. Make friends with custodians and refrain from making excessive demands on their time and energy.

9. Keep public remarks about colleagues on a positive, professional level. If you must vent, try using a journal at home. Reviewing it now and then may show you the way to improve the situation.

10. Remember special things about the faculty in each school, and start a card file with comments that will be useful in personalizing the interactions. If you find a news article pertaining in a positive way to a colleague or a student, clip it out and send it along with a congratulatory note.

11. Send a note weekly to classroom teachers of mainstreamed students.

12. Make efficient checklists for procedural activities, such as general items to tell parents at conferences or items to tell new students and their parents.

13. If doing a demonstration lesson, give the classroom teacher a paper stating the name and type of activity, and learning objectives. State your name at the bottom and specify that it comes from "Consultant _____'s Lesson Plan," thereby establishing your identity.

14. Go to classroom teachers and ask them for help in their area of expertise. Ask for a copy of something you have seen that would be a good addition to your file, but be sure a teacher means for you to use it or share it before you do so.

15. Generate alternatives to having more and more meetings, try them out, and get input from colleagues on their value. When a meeting is needed, and it promises to be a difficult one, on the night before the meeting, try visualizing a successful one in which everything goes very well.

16. Visit other schools and take notes on organizational systems and management techniques that could be incorporated into your system. Then prepare a summary sheet for colleagues on your return.

17. Find time to collaborate by exploring innovative ways of "making" more time and using it wisely. Schedule common lunch or preparation periods; in large districts increase class size by just one and use surplus funds to hire substitutes; have teachers match a period of early dismissal time with their contribution of equal time; have students involved in community service one afternoon a week while teachers meet (Raywid, 1993).

18. Develop ways of "working smarter, not harder" such as having information-exchange pools with other teachers, sharing learning centers and packets with colleagues in other attendance centers, and gathering free resources from commercial business and industry.

19. Make a weekly plan called "completion focus," and in that week curtail interferences, get reports up-to-date, grade papers, and on Friday get rid of everything that really doesn't matter anyway.

20. Remember Ralph Waldo Emerson's words, "It is one of the most beautiful compensations of this life that no man can sincerely try to help another without helping himself."

Chapter Review

1. Stress that is encountered in many human service roles can lead to burnout and subsequent attrition from the field. Positive attitudes, health maintenance, supportive networks, realistic goals, relaxation, environmental changes, and taking control of your life will minimize stress and help prevent burnout, fizzle out, rust out, and coast out among consultants and teachers.
2. Careful management of time and energy decreases stress and increases productivity for those in consultative roles. School personnel will want to establish goals to manage their resources, identify and remediate time wasters, use positive time management strategies, and take good care of themselves.
3. Meetings, interviews, and observations must be kept as efficient and positive as possible. With careful planning, each of these activities can be more productive for consultants and collaborators. It is important to provide a comfortable meeting environment, prepare an agenda, keep minutes of decisions and plans, and assess the success of the meeting. When consultants observe in classrooms, they should demonstrate caring attitudes and provide positive support for those being observed.
4. Record-keeping systems and resource management systems are necessary for busy consultants who serve many schools. Consultants must keep records and materials in order, maintain confidentiality, and be on the lookout for helpful material with which to consult and collaborate. Consulting journals and notebooks are tools that facilitate management of complex responsibilities. Personalized touches for memos and messages help develop rapport with consultees.
5. Support personnel are key components in constructing a complete plan for serving students who have special needs. They can be involved as consultants, consultees, and clients in identifying problems, setting goals, planning and implementing programs, reinforcing success, and evaluating outcomes. Consultants should have updated lists of referral agencies available for their use and for sharing with consultees and parents.
6. Ethical and conscientious considerations must guide consultants in every consultative and collaborative effort. The primary aim of any school interaction is the welfare of the student.

To Do and Think About

1. Discuss some record-keeping and managerial tasks that most people really don't like to do, such as preparing income tax returns, and consider ways the activities could be made less unpleasant and more manageable. Then consider how these techniques could be used creatively by school consultants.
2. Describe "The Perfect Meeting." What would need to be done in order for this meeting to transpire?
3. How many support services, related services, and ancillary personnel categories can you list, and how many ways can you find for individuals in these categories to become educational partners with teachers, students, and parents?
4. Design a weekly and daily planning sheet that has space for stating goals, listing activities in categories, prioritizing the list, and estimating times for accomplishing the activities. Try your planning sheets, and share them with others if you found them helpful.
5. Conduct a time analysis to diagnose time management problems you may have. Use one of the methods described in this chapter or develop your own.
6. Create ideas for the following management tools, and if your present situation warrants, construct them and try them out:

a logo for personalized note pads or memo sheets that will identify you and will feature school consultation in a positive, collaborative spirit

an observation checklist that would work in your school situation

a consultation log or journal format to record the consultation and follow-through, as well as a brief assessment of the consultation

a table of contents for a notebook in which to organize information, data, and material needed to carry out the school consultation role

a system for cataloging materials to be shared with consultees, and for checking the material in and out

7. Find out more about several related services roles that you are not familiar with—for example, the occupational therapist, the audiologist, the social worker, or the school psychologist. What are their responsibilities? What preparation did their roles require? What does a typical day entail for each of them? Interview them and ask their views about consultation and collaboration.

8. Develop a plan for ways in which at least three related services and support personnel could be involved in consultation and collaboration to provide a team effort toward serving students with special needs.

9. Compile a reference list of referral agencies, support groups, and community resources in your area that could be helpful in meeting special needs of students. Preface the list with a brief description of the community where the school is located. Then compare your list with a colleague's list that represents a different type of geographic area.

10. Think ahead to your own professional growth and future. Where do you see yourself five years from now? What will it take to get there? Develop some steps that can help you attain your vision.

For Further Reading

Collins, C. (1987). *Time management for teachers: Practical techniques and skills that give you more time to teach.* West Nyack, NY: Parker.

Conoley, J. C., & Conoley, C. W. (1982). *School consultation: A guide to practice and training.* New York: Pergamon. Chapter 9, on Ethical Considerations in Consultative Practice.

Davis, W. E. (1983). *The special educator: Strategies for succeeding in today's schools.* Austin, TX: PRO-ED. Chapter 2 on burnout, chapter 5 on meetings, chapter 6 on paperwork, record-keeping, and time management, and chapter 8 on ethical, legal, and professional dilemmas.

Douglass, M. E., & Douglass, D. N. (1993). *Manage your time, manage your work, manage yourself.* New York: AMACOM.

Jusjka, J. (1991). Observations. *Phi Delta Kappan, 72*(6), 468–470.

Keyes, R. (1991). *Timelock: How life got so hectic and what you can do about it.* New York: HarperCollins.

Lippet, G. & Lippitt, R. (1978). *The consulting process in action.* San Diego: University Associates. Chapter 5 on ethical dilemmas and guidelines for consultants.

MacKenzie, A., & Waldo, K. C. (1981). *About time: A woman's guide to time management.* New York: McGraw-Hill.

Maher, C. A. (1982). Time management training for providers of special services. *Exceptional Children, 48,* 523–528.

Newman, J. E. (1992). *How to stay cool, calm and collected when the pressure's on: A stress control plan for business people.* New York: American Management Association.

Sapolsky, R. (1994). *Why zebras don't get ulcers: A guide to stress, stress-related diseases, and coping.* New York: W. H. Freeman.

Sugai, G. (1986). Recording classroom events: Maintaining a critical incidents log. *Teaching Exceptional Children,* Winter 1986, 98–102.

Chapter *8*

Technology to Facilitate Consultation, Collaboration, and Teamwork

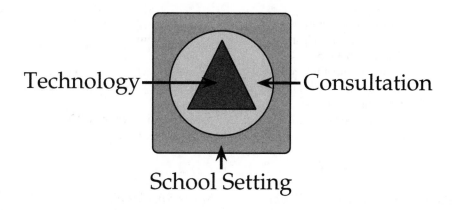

Technology ← ▲ → Consultation

School Setting

Introduction

What do you think about when someone refers to "technology in schools?" If you are like most educators you think about students in a computer lab. Few educators think about themselves using technology, but that is very short sighted. Use of technology can dramatically change the way teachers teach. Moreover, technology can make the processes of consultation, collaboration, and teamwork more efficient and effective than they would be otherwise.

Focusing Questions

1. How can telecommunications and electronic networks make consultation, collaboration, and teamwork more efficient and effective?
2. What time-consuming routine tasks can be done more efficiently with the use of technology?
3. How can computer software be used to make student records more accessible to team members?
4. How can computer software help consultants with assessment and evaluation processes?
5. How can consultants provide leadership in schools to assure effective use of technology to accommodate the needs of students with disabilities in general classrooms?
6. What might a technology-infused inclusive environment look like?
7. How can consultants provide leadership in schools to assure effective use of technology for professional uses and to accommodate the needs of students with disabilities in general classrooms?

Key Terms in the Chapter

assistive technology	scan
computer-assisted instruction	shell or template
electronic bonding	software
electronic bulletin board	spreadsheet
electronic mail (E-Mail)	technology-infused environments
emerging technology	telecommunications
local area network (LAN)	wide area network (WAN)
FAX	word processor

Technology for Enriching Collaboration to Serve Special Needs

Technology is revolutionizing the processes of consultation, collaboration, and teamwork in school settings. Educators in technology-rich environments are able to engage in many of their collaborative efforts continuously throughout the day without leaving their classrooms or offices. Information can be exchanged instantly rather than waiting until a later time or day for face-to-face meetings. Technology, of course, does not eliminate the need for face-to-face interaction; rather, it frees the team members' time together to deal with major issues instead of day-to-day background information. It improves the efficiency of other routine tasks such as writing, material development or data collection so more time will be available for collaborative activities.

Use of technology along with team efforts may be a major reason that full inclusion of students with disabilities in general classroom settings is a feasible option (Lipsky, 1994;

Scenario

CONSULTANT: Mr. Wilcox, please.

SECRETARY: I'm sorry, but Mr. Wilcox is in a meeting right now. May I take a message?

CONSULTANT: This is Mrs. Spencer the school psychologist in Centennial School. I need to speak with him about one of the students in his class.

(The consultant makes similar calls to team members with similar results.)

Later that morning:

WILCOX: I'm returning a call to Mrs. Spencer.

SECRETARY: I'm sorry, but Mrs. Spencer is away from her desk. May I ask her to return your call?

WILCOX: Yes, please do.

That afternoon:

CONSULTANT: Mr. Wilcox, please.

SECRETARY: I'm sorry, but Mr. Wilcox is away from his desk. May I ask him to return your call?

CONSULTANT: No, I will try to reach him later, thank you.

After installation of computer network:

See Figure 8.1 for successful communication through E-Mail.

Male, 1994). Educators who are concerned about students with special needs can be powerful influences in providing leadership for the use of technology in inclusive classrooms to accommodate the special instructional needs of all students.

Use of technology also can improve achievement and self-esteem of many students with disabilities and can be a powerful motivator for students who have experienced failure and frustration in school. It can empower students with disabilities by enabling them to accomplish things never before thought possible. "Telecommunications and multimedia technologies such as interactive video bring the world into the classroom. Electronic communication devices allow students to speak and add their voices to those of their classmates. And adapted computers provide access to instruction in myriad subject areas from learning-to-count, to calculus" (Lewis, 1993, p. 3).

Much has been written about using assistive technology for classroom instruction (Blackhurst & Berdine, 1993; Lewis, 1993; Male, 1994; Edyburn & Majsterek, 1993). This topic will be addressed only briefly in this chapter. Instead, the primary emphasis will be on ways technology can make the processes of consultation, collaboration, and teamwork in schools more efficient and effective.

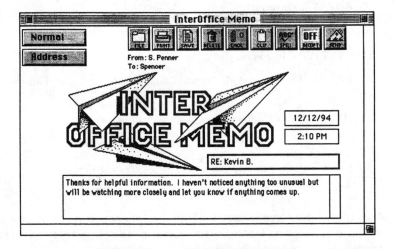

FIGURE 8-1 Electronic Mail

Technology for Managing Consultation and Collaboration Processes

As discussed in Chapter 7, consultation and collaboration processes require careful management. Emerging technology can make this management process far more efficient and effective than traditional methods.

The commercial marketplace of the 1990s embraces the use of emerging technologies for managing organizations and delivering their services. Many corporations are using "electronic bonding" as a means of teaming through technology. Interdisciplinary teams that cross organizational boundaries, sometimes even including customers and vendors, use technologies such as electronic mail, broadcast FAX, teleconferencing and video conferencing to communicate with one another consistently and quickly. Digital pagers and cellular phones make team members accessible regardless of their location and mobility. Information is gathered rapidly and exchanged through databases and electronic bulletin boards.

Schools can become just as efficient, and the walls of classrooms and offices can be opened and expanded through technology. Consider the common stumbling block to collaboration that was described in Chapter 1—the need for time. Computers and telecommunications can be major time-savers in many ways. Messages can be sent at the convenience of one party while others read and respond to them at their convenience. Databases and information on student progress can be stored in a file-server and accessed by any team member at a convenient time. All team members can add notes or other forms of information that keep everyone on the team apprised of information or items of concern. Teachers or resource personnel can use computers to readily adapt student work to meet their needs. Copies of special instructions or worksheets can be sent by a consultant in one building to a teacher in another by way of computer to FAX. The possibilities are unlimited. Lewis (1993) states "technology can increase teachers' professional productivity and reduce the amount of time that must be spent in non-instructional classroom duties" (p. 126).

Telecommunications and Electronic Networks

Computer networks and electronic mail might be the most useful applications of technology for school consultants. Many schools are beginning to use wires or cables to link computers within the building, known as a local area network (LAN), or outside to other areas, known as a wide area network (WAN). Users can share software and communicate with one another in an efficient manner. With electronic networks, a consultant can be in an office or resource room, prepare an adapted lesson or test, and send it to the classroom where needed. The adapted lesson or test would be "waiting" for the teacher or students in the classroom to access at the appropriate time without the presence of the consultant. Conversely, a student might prepare a product in the classroom and send it to the consultant for review and feedback. In other words, a computer network can provide opportunity for monitoring students' work without the consultant or co-teacher always being present in the classroom, making feedback to the student more immediate.

Another advantage of the electronic network is facilitation of interaction among the users, in this case consultants, co-teachers or team members. In some systems users can work simultaneously with the same program. For instance, team members could use a word processor to collaborate in developing a lesson plan, with each team member accessing the work of others and making changes or adding notes. Thus, the number of time-consuming, face-to-face meetings for team members can be reduced significantly with a comparable or even better outcome.

Electronic mail (E-Mail) is another use of the network that can save time and make collaboration more efficient. The scenario at the beginning of this chapter illustrates the change in accessibility that can take place when electronic mail becomes available to team members. Irritating "phone tag" is curtailed, and communication is exchanged more efficiently. E-mail allows information prepared on one computer to be sent by network to another computer.

The power of E-Mail lies in the breadth of connected participants. Individuals are assigned an "address," and sending messages to other individuals in the system simply requires using the appropriate address. A message can be sent to many individuals—for example, the entire team, or all teachers in the building, or one or two individuals. When all members of a collaborative team are connected to the E-Mail system and regularly access it, a message can be sent to one or more persons faster than it takes to walk down the hall to speak to those individuals.

Although it is possible for individuals to arrange for E-Mail, most educators have the E-Mail service facilitated through internal networks set up by the school system. This ensures that all district E-Mail participants are using the same or compatible systems. For collaborators not on a district's E-Mail system, it is possible to deliver an E-Mail message as a FAX.

Some advanced E-Mail systems are capable of providing real time conferencing. An IEP conference or team planning meeting could use such a system, thus saving the time and expense of everyone's traveling to a single location. If team members could have only one of the technologies discussed in this chapter, E-Mail might be the one of choice.

Information Services

Consultants, teachers, and students can use computers with modems to engage in communication with large host computer information systems. These systems offer a variety of options to users ranging from electronic bulletin boards to conferencing capabilities. Potential uses for consultants and teachers include library searches and information bulletins relating to special needs of students with disabilities. Special bulletin boards can be created to address unique audiences. It is even possible to create local bulletin boards that are used by teachers in a single building or school district. A creative consultant or teacher might consider developing such a bulletin board where ideas that have worked in other classrooms can be shared with fellow teachers and consultants.

The Handicapped Users' Database on CompuServe contains a reference library as well as information about computer products designed for users with disabilities. The Disabilities Forum is a bulletin board where people with or interested in disabilities can exchange information. The IBM/Special Needs Forum focuses on special education applications for IBM-compatible computers (Lewis, 1993). Technology specialists and many librarians in a school district usually can provide currently available information services and bulletin boards.

Electronic Scheduling Programs

Many consultants find a scheduling program useful. These programs are electronic calendars in which appointments and other commitments are entered. One special advantage is the way the program can handle recurring appointments. For example, if a team planning meeting is scheduled for every Friday afternoon at 2 P.M., the consultant can enter that information; the program will automatically write in meeting reminders on the appropriate dates. Another advantage is the ability to view (and print out) different types (daily, weekly, monthly) of calendars. These calendars can be shared through the network if desired. Sharing privileges can be customized to allow one or many individuals the right to view or schedule appointments for all or part of a colleague's calendar.

FAX Communication

FAX (facsimile) machines represent yet another form of technology that can enhance the consultation and collaboration processes. Many school buildings have at least one FAX machine. Consultants who serve more than one building can make efficient use of the machines by sending letters, reports and other written products for use in another building, city or state, over telephone wires. As previously discussed, computers on an electronic network can FAX a document directly from a computer, without requiring a printout.

Monitoring Student Records

Databases and other types of management software can help teachers keep track of important information. Databases are most useful for organizing large amounts of information. Being equivalent to electronic filing cabinets, they allow great flexibility in sorting and retrieving data. For example, a consultant might set up a database file on her caseload of students. That file would be made up of individual records, each containing a separate entry for categories she chooses, such as: Name, address, phone number, type of disability, family members' name(s), address, and phone number. Once the format is established the consultant or an assistant can enter the information for each record. It then can be searched and sorted for different types of reports. This search-and-sort capability is what gives databases their flexibility, an advantage over traditional paper filing systems.

Grades and Attendance Records

Several software programs are available to manage records of students' grades. Most allow the teacher to enter students' scores, determine the weight of each assignment or quiz, and set standards for assigning grades. Final grades can be computed automatically. Many programs provide options for printing class rosters, grade reports by student or by assignment, and statistics and graphs that summarize. If special software is not available to a teacher or consultant, a standard spreadsheet can be used to accomplish many of these purposes.

Individual Educational Plans

Many special educators use computers to assist in the laborious process of writing Individual Educational Plans (IEPs). Software programs for producing IEPs have been developed and are available commercially. These programs are special types of databases tailored to the needs of special education professionals. The programs usually contain an IEP shell and a collection of suggested annual goals and short-term objectives. While the availability of these goals and objectives can alleviate much of the drudgery of writing IEPs, they are also the source of most of the criticism of computerized IEPs. Critics argue that the goals and objectives provided in the software are often isolated skills that are not relevant to an individual student or inconsistent with the local school curriculum. Effective software does not require that the IEP team use the goals and objectives provided in the program. It allows them to develop their own if they choose. Some systems even enable users to generate administrative reports and notices to teachers and family members.

Assessment and Evaluation

Assessment and evaluation issues in collaboration and consultation will be discussed more fully in Chapter 9. The data gathered in these processes can be stored in database or spreadsheet applications. They can be readily summarized in various formats, including meaningful graphs and charts. However, when educators store confidential information in computers, *careful steps must be taken to protect confidentiality of student information.* This issue is a major concern if data are to be shared with team members by way of computer networks. Computer technicians should be consulted to determine the safest and most efficient ways to make files secure.

Test-Scoring

One of the most time-consuming parts of the assessment process is scoring standardized tests. Many test-developers provide software programs to assist in this task. "These programs are quick, accurate, and an excellent way for busy teachers to save time" (Lewis, 1993, p. 134). Monitoring Basic Skills Progress, by PRO-ED, Inc., is an example of a program that assists educators in generating, administering, and scoring probes that monitor student progress when using the Curriculum-Based Measurement techniques discussed in Chapter 9. The results are graphed by computer over time so progress can be compared with the expected rate of improvement. The program also analyzes the results and makes recommendations about possible changes in instruction.

Consultants and collaborating teachers need to monitor student performance on computer tasks, especially when use of computers is specified on a student's IEP. Integrated learning systems (ILS) can be beneficial for this purpose. These systems provide instructional software for students and management tools for teachers. They are available in subject areas such as reading, writing, language arts, math, and science. Teachers or consultants can easily monitor student progress and prescribe individualized activities based on the results of previous performance. These systems are growing in popularity with school districts as a measuring tool for Outcomes Based Education (OBE). When available, and when relevant to student goals, these systems should be chosen by teachers and consultants for students in inclusive classrooms. Teachers and/or consultants then can refer to such data to make collaborative decisions about student progress and make changes as may be appropriate. If the software does not have built-in record-keeping capability, the student or paraprofessional can be taught to enter data in a database or spreadsheet that can then be used to prepare summaries or graphs. A skilled consultant can provide valuable assistance to the classroom teacher in making these decisions and setting up the record-keeping tools.

Portfolios

Use of portfolios is yet another way to monitor and evaluate student progress and document consultation activities. However, organizing and maintaining portfolio information can be very time-consuming. The convenience of filing information on a computer should not be overlooked. Products developed on the computer are easily filed. Other products and information can be scanned into the computer to be added to the portfolio. It is even possible with some computers to add audio and video products. Many interesting possibilities exist for the innovative educator and students.

Several formats for recording consultation activities are discussed in Chapters 7 and 9. This type of information could be kept on the computer and would be more efficient than the paper-pencil format. Some of the information such as date, time, or name of student could be automatically entered, and the information searched and sorted in various ways, to provide valuable information for making decisions about students and collaboration processes. For example, if one wanted to know how many times a certain consultant or service provider worked with the student during the year, the data could be sorted to have all the entries for the service provider appearing together. Later, if one wanted to know who provided services on a particular date, the information could be sorted by the date field. Data can be sorted to produce valuable reports for making decisions about programs and services for students. Data also can be added to larger information bases for more extensive district-wide reports. Figure 8-2 illustrates a form that could be kept in a classroom to record services provided for students with special needs. Figure 8-3 shows the information when recorded in a database and sorted by service provider.

Student *Francisco, W.*		Teacher *P. Webber*	
Date	**Time**	**Service Provider**	**Comments**
9-16-94	9:46 a.m.	N. Carney	Scripted paper for English
9-16-94	1:46 p.m.	L. Baker	Checked points earned, made
			suggestion to teacher
			about time-on-task
9-18-94	9:15 a.m.	K. Foster	PT—Worked on small motor
			during handwriting activity
9-18-94	1:44 p.m.	N. Carney	Helped with math instruction.
			Difficult. Try more manipulatives
9-19-94	2:27 p.m.	N. Carney	Paraprofessional helped him
			with math. Spoke to
			teacher about next week's work.

FIGURE 8-2   Service Provider Log

Student: Francisco, W.		**Teacher:** P. Webber	
9/18/84	9:15 AM	**Service Provider:**	K. Foster

Comments:

    PT - Worked on small motor during handwriting activity

9/16/94	1:46 PM	**Service Provider:**	L. Baker

Comments:

    Checked points earned, made suggestion to teacher about time-on-task

9/19/94	2:27 PM	**Service Provider:**	N. Carney

Comments:

    Paraprofessional helping him with math. Spoke to teacher about next week's work.

9/18/94	1:44 PM	**Service Provider:**	N. Carney

Comments:

    Helped with math instruction - difficult for him today Try more manipulatives.

9/16/94	9:46 AM	**Service Provider:**	N. Carney

Comments:

    Scripted paper for English

FIGURE 8-3 Service Provider Log Sorted by Service Provider

Significant advances in technology-based assessment within special education have been made as a result of the Technology-Related Assistance for Individuals with Disabilities Act of 1988 (Greenwood, 1994). A special issue of *Exceptional Children* (October/November, 1994) that addresses this issue is but one example of the importance of this topic. "Advances in software designs enable expert-level assessment knowledge to be employed automatically in the context of data collection, data analysis, decision making, and prescription. . . .Advances in the portability of computers (notebook and subnotebook computers) support classroom observational assessments by practitioners using quality instruments that routinely integrate data collection and numerical analyses with observer training and reliability assessment" (Greenwood, 1994).

Adapting Materials and Tests

Another time-consuming activity for co-teachers and consultants is adapting written products for individuals with disabilities as discussed in Chapter 9. A common example is to adapt a worksheet used to supplement a math or science lesson. It is often thought that there are too many items for students with disabilities to complete in one setting. Moreover, the graphic material might be distracting from the relevant stimuli and need to be removed. The old-fashioned way to deal with this situation is to make a copy of the worksheet, cut it apart with scissors and paste it back together in a more usable format. However, if a scanner and computer with graphics software are available, the project can be completed more efficiently. The worksheet is scanned into the graphics program. The "cut and paste" function of the program is used to eliminate portions that are distracting or too difficult. Then the remaining portions are rearranged as needed and the "new" worksheet printed out. This approach allows for making different adaptations for many different students in a relatively short amount of time.

Text also can be scanned into the computer if OCR software is installed. A consultant might scan a teacher-made test, for example, and then make adaptations as needed for different students with disabilities in the class. The print can be enlarged if needed or more space provided between items when appropriate. Even better, if a classroom teacher prepares the test on the computer, the file can be shared with a consultant or co-teacher to make the adaptations as needed. Of course the ideal situation is when the teacher makes the adaptations without the assistance of the consultant.

There are a number of software programs that can be used to develop written tests. Test banks often accompany classroom texts. Teachers and consultants might find that the use of such programs is an efficient way to adapt a classroom test. For example, some software can produce several types of tests—matching, true-false, completion, and multiple choice. When questions have been typed into the program, they can be easily transferred from one of the formats to another. Other software can create paper-and-pencil tests as well as quizzes that students take at the computer.

Preparing Reports and Other Written Products

Word processors and desktop publishing programs are a *must* for busy consultants and other team members. Once text has been entered in a word processor, it can be changed easily, edited, added to, modified, or reformatted. This capability is particularly useful for routine writing such as consultation logs, letters to parents, memos to other team members, assessment reports, newsletters and classroom materials with adaptations made for specific students with disabilities.

Consultants and collaborating teachers might want to develop "shells" or "templates" for frequently used products. A shell or template is a word processing file that contains the portions of a document that do not change. For example, most of the forms and checklists recommended in this book could be scanned in or retyped to form shells. McLoughlin and Lewis (1990) suggest a shell for assessment reports. Permanent information would include the title, spaces for identifying information and headings such as "Reason for Referral," "Test Behavior," "Results," and "Recommendations." Brief descriptions of commonly administered tests could be included in the shell and simply omitted if not appropriate for a particular report. Male (1994) provides an example of a shell for homework assignments. When using a shell, the file is loaded into the word processor and relevant information is added before saving the file under a new name.

Integrated software that combines word processing and database may be the most powerful tool for enhancing personal productivity of school personnel (Male, 1994). Software of this type allows the user to create a database such as the student information previously described. Any part or all of these data can be merged (or inserted) into word processing documents such as form letters or reports. Once the data for each student have been entered, a consultant can print out any lists needed. Academic or behavioral progress reports can be prepared for specific parents, or for all the parents in the caseload, with personalized information inserted automatically by the computer (Male, 1994).

Technology for Instruction

If mainstreaming and inclusive classrooms are going to work for students with disabilities, the environment and curriculum must change to include the same individualized opportunities for accommodation and effective learning experiences as previously provided in self-contained special education classrooms. Technology can be an effective way to provide at least some of this individualized instruction. Although many types of technologies are used to assist individuals with disabilities in schools, computers are probably the most common. "One major use [of computers] is computer-assisted instruction. In this application, computers deliver instruction and/or provide students with opportunities for practicing new skills or information. In addition, computers are used as tools for accomplishing tasks such as writing, drawing, or composing music" (Lewis, 1993, p. 5). However, educators must look beyond the limits of traditional computer-assisted instruction models that involve primarily drill and practice activities (Edyburn & Majsterek, 1993; Majsterek & Wilson, 1993). O'Sullivan (1990) argues that educators should teach the basic concepts, principles, and systems of technology that underlie technology. The importance of preparing students with disabilities for transition to the world of work is discussed in Chapter 1 of this book. Teachers and consultants should take O'Sullivan's advice seriously and resist the temptation to limit instructional uses of technology to drill and practice activities.

A number of authorities have suggested that emerging technologies are the only tools powerful enough to transform the way general and special educators manage the information explosion and prepare students for productive futures. But emerging technology tools alone are not sufficient to cause this transformation. A whole new paradigm of education must be applied (Edyburn & Majsterek, 1993; Skrtic, 1993). Teachers and consultants need to guide and facilitate students to develop information literacy, a lifelong learning process of accessing, applying and creating information (Edyburn & Majsterek, 1993). To do so, educators need more than emerging technology tools. They need an organizational infrastructure that supports the use of emerging technologies, and professional development programs that enable them to apply emerging technology to their teaching methods.

Figure 8-4 lists the applications reported to the United States Congress by The Office of Technology Assessment (1988) as the most promising for general education students, their peers with disabilities and their teachers.

Technology for Students in Gifted Education

Emerging technologies have much to offer students in gifted education. Computers are used in much the same way as in other types of educational programs but the emphases are different (Pendarvis, 1993). Instead of emphasizing drill and practice or assistive uses,

- drill and practice to master basic skills
- development of writing skills
- problem solving
- understanding abstract mathematics and science concepts
- simulation in science, mathematics, and social studies
- manipulation of data
- acquisition of computer skills for general purposes and for business and vocational training
- access and communication for traditionally unserved populations of students (e.g., students with disabilities)
- access and communication for teachers and students in remote locations
- individualized learning
- cooperative learning
- management of learning activities and record keeping (Office of Technology Assessment, 1988, p. 12–16).

FIGURE 8-4   Promising Computer Applications in Schools

students in gifted education often are taught computer programming, use of Hypertext and other applications requiring higher-order thinking. While knowledge of computer programming languages is not an integral part of most school applications of technology, it is seen as essential for talented high school students who plan to major in computer science or in another field that requires knowledge of computers and programming. An introductory course has been developed by the College Entrance Examination Board (1983) as part of its Advanced Placement program. Students are required to learn PASCAL programming language. They also learn how to design programs that solve different types of problems. They master the basic components and functions of computer hardware and software. They learn how to design programs that solve different types of problems. Using basic statistical packages, they might test data from their own projects or those of peers for statistical significance. Many colleges and universities grant college credit for a passing grade on the Advanced Placement examination on computer knowledge (Pendarvis, 1993).

Computers provide opportunities for students with high ability to learn individually at a more rapid pace than others in the school. In addition, the use of network information services provides a wide array of enrichment in a readily accessible form. Students can subscribe to information services in specific subject areas that interest them and can become involved in receiving and sharing information with individuals around the world. They can easily access the Library of Congress and other such data sources. They can find rich sources of information in the encyclopedia contained on a CD-ROM and other up-to-date, recently developed information. With special software, they can be introduced to subject matter not normally in the school curriculum.

Limitations of Technology for Instruction

Careful monitoring of student progress with computer-assisted instruction is essential. Educators must not be "mesmerized by the technology to a point that they ignore the established principles of effective instructional design" (Majsterek & Wilson, 1993, p. 19). These authors suggest that teachers use computer-assisted instruction to augment teacher instruction. "The day when a student sits down at a terminal for her lesson without any preliminary preparation by a teacher remains in the future" (Majsterek & Wilson, 1993, p. 21). Yet the future is bright, and the potential for helping individuals with special needs is exciting.

Technology-Infused Inclusive Environments

When planning for the future needs of inclusive schools, educators should think of infusing technology in classrooms as part of the essential context for inclusion. A technology-infused classroom is one in which students have maximum access to multiple technology tools at any location. Literally, it means anyone learning anything, anytime, anywhere, with any combination of emerging technologies (Lumley & Bailey, 1993).

Male (1994) cites the work of Via who had success with a technology-infused environment in an inclusive school:

> Students and teachers are using technology to work directly with source materials to explore areas of interest within the general curriculum. They are learning to research and gather information from a variety of sources, synthesize it, and create original reports and presentations. They control the technology for their own purposes, rather than being controlled by it for purposes established by software houses. Can you imagine a better way to integrate special students into "regular" settings? When students can work at their own pace, there is no "norm." Each individual can work to his or her potential and contribute to others' learning. And there can be expanded flexibility to include specialists or therapists in small groups. A classroom can be a resource room for everyone (Via, 1991, p. 6–7 as cited in Male, 1994, p. 3).

A federally funded grant program called "Project K. I. S. S." was conducted in Norfolk, Virginia, schools. Technology was used to promote inclusion of students with disabilities in the general classroom. A technology team made up of one family member of a child with a disability and two special education teachers was assigned to work in the schools with the staff, students, and parents. These team members disseminated information about innovative software to promote group learning, problem-solve with the teachers, and demonstrate how to use cooperative learning methods with computers. The "teachers teaching teachers" model was encouraged to help expand the knowledge of technology uses. Modems were made available to parents of students with disabilities so they could access information about homework assignments and other information provided by the school. The home and school were able to maintain immediate and on-going communication with each other. Students were encouraged to use the modems to submit homework (Shubert 1994).

A technology-infused environment must be paired with good instruction in the classroom; it is not a panacea. It will not cure a disability, nor will it turn an ineffective classroom program into an exemplary one. Although computers and other technologies can work magic with some students, teachers' expectations should remain realistic (Male, 1988).

Even though new and emerging technology introduces new ways to use technology in classrooms, Lewis (1993) has pointed out that it is not always necessary or even desirable to have the latest technology for classroom use. For example, when new computers are introduced, there is often very little software available for them. It is also difficult to find the funds to continually upgrade technology hardware and software. Even though it is desirable to have more equipment, it is also the case that some of the equipment now available in schools is not being utilized effectively. Consider the following example of one creative special education resource teacher/consultant:

> *The teacher/consultant noticed several laptop computers sitting in a storage room gathering dust. Even though they were a bit out-dated she thought she could make use of them in a productive way. She decided to teach some of the students with learning disabilities to use the word processors and spell check applications. After they had developed limited skill in setting up the computers and using the application (from plug-in to shutdown), she approached the classroom teachers to suggest allowing the students to use the laptop computers for their written work in the classroom. Once the teachers agreed to give the approach a try, they began to see that it was a great way to accommodate for writing difficulties of the students. They became strong supporters of the approach. Now they are asking for more computers so more students can benefit from their use. The self-esteem of the students and their written products have improved significantly.*

Assistive Technology

Federal special education legislation refers to an assistive technology *device* as

> *Any item, piece of equipment, or product system, whether acquired commercially off the shelf, modified, or customized, that is used to increase, maintain, or improve functional capabilities of individuals with disabilities (PL 100–407; PL 101–476).*

Federal special education legislation refers to an assistive technology *service* as

> *Any service that directly assists an individual with a disability in the selection, acquisition, or use of an assistive technology device (PL 100–407; PL 101–476).*

These devices and services often are varied and individualized, depending on the type of disability involved. Assistive technology devices can include

- sound enhancement;
- large print;
- braille print;
- sound activation;
- communication boards;
- alternative keyboards;

- magnification devices;
- talking optical character recognition systems (Kurzweil Reader);
- telecommunications devices for the deaf (TDDs); and
- many other less common tools.

Such assistive devices now make it possible for many individuals with severe and multiple disabilities to benefit from activities in general classroom settings.

When selecting assistive technology devices, Lewis (1993) recommends the use of the ABC model to categorize particular benefits for students with disabilities:

> *augment* abilities, and
> *bypass,* or
> *compensate* for disabilities.

Technologies that augment abilities of students include magnification systems to enlarge print materials. Technologies that bypass disabilities can be voice commands or eye gaze instead of commands that use manual keyboards. Compensatory technologies help the student decrease the effects of the disability. They might use spell or grammar checks for individuals with reading and spelling disabilities or keyboarding instead of handwriting for individuals with fine motor disabilities. Special educators are sometimes unsure whether to include use of assistive technology in a student's IEP. Figure 8-5 provides guidelines to help the IEP team make the appropriate decisions about this matter.

Assistive technology should be included in a student's IEP only when it

- enables a student to perform functions that can be achieved by no other means;
- enables a student to approximate a level of accomplishment that could not be achieved by any other means;
- provides access for participation in programs or activities that otherwise would be closed to the individual;
- increases endurance or ability to persevere and complete tasks that otherwise are too laborious to be attempted on a routine basis;
- enables students to concentrate on learning tasks, rather than mechanical tasks;
- provides greater access to information;
- supports normal social interactions with peers and adults;
- supports participation in the least restrictive educational environment

(Adapted from materials developed by Parents Let's Unite for Kids (PLUK) Parent Training & Information Center, Billings, Montana)

FIGURE 8-5 Guidelines for Including Assistive Technology in a Student's IEP

Most school districts have specialists who have been trained in selecting assistive technology for individuals with disabilities. Collaborating teams should include these individuals in their team meetings whenever assistive technology is needed.

Planning for Use of Technology

Consultants should provide leadership in schools to assure effective use of technology for professional uses and to accommodate the needs of students with disabilities in general classrooms in three important ways:

- Participating in schoolwide planning groups;
- Providing a role model in the use of technology; and
- Engaging in collaborative activities where technology is being used.

As one can see from the vast array of technology applications discussed in the preceding pages, there are many decisions to make about what, when, and how to invest in emerging technology. Right now, most schools do not have technology-rich environments to support consultation and collaboration. Thoughtful planning and investment decisions are needed to ensure that team members have the right technologies in their classrooms and offices for both managing and instructional purposes.

Many decisions in education are based on reactions to problems or historical trends (Cain, 1985). This decision-making method does not work well for decisions about technology because of the rapid pace of change in the technology itself. Instead, a holistic and visionary method of planning is needed. Cain recommends a planning process for technology use in which individuals responsible for different program elements are brought together to pose certain questions, such as those in Application 8.1.

The entire process of technology planning 1) looks forward, not backward; 2) looks across all disciplines, not just within each; and 3) includes applications for professional collaboration as well as instructional and student uses.

APPLICATION 8.1   Envisioning Computer Technology

Ask a team of educators the question, "What is your vision of computer technology in this school district 5, 10, or 20 years in the future?" (Remember, the team needs to include the technology specialist as well as the teachers, consultants and administrators.) Participants are then charged with the task of dividing the path into smaller attainable projects to achieve that vision. The smaller projects and futuristic vision can be revisited and adjusted from year to year to reflect changes that develop in the industry or school district.

Tips for Consulting and Collaborating

1. Before sending confidential information through electronic networks make sure steps have been taken to keep hackers and other would-be "technology thieves" from gaining access to the information.
2. Constantly monitor your habits of protecting confidential information. Make sure you do not carelessly leave information in files that are accessible to individuals who are not authorized to see them. When you use E-Mail, be careful when selecting addresses for mail. It is very easy to accidentally include an unauthorized person. Most breeches of confidentiality result from carelessness of people and not from lack of technology safeguards.
3. Consult a technology specialist on a regular basis to remain current in the ever-changing uses of technology.
4. Join or form a computer user's group to learn from one another about new uses for computers.

Chapter Review

1. Telecommunications and electronic networks are possibly the most valuable elements of technology that can revolutionize the way consultants and collaborating teachers engage in collaborative activities.
2. Many time-consuming, routine tasks such as organizing schedules, keeping and sorting records, adapting materials, and developing IEPs can be done more efficiently with the use of technology.
3. Databases can be sorted in various ways and stored on a file server where they can be more accessible to team members (providing steps have been taken to secure confidentiality of the files).
4. Computer software is available to help consultants score tests and prepare reports of assessment and evaluation data. Some programs for student use include monitoring systems that provide useful assessment information. Portfolios can also be kept in computer files. Checklists and other forms used to gather data can be made into "shells" or "templates" for convenient use.
5. Consultants can provide leadership in schools to assure effective use of technology to accommodate the needs of students both with disabilities and with advanced abilities in general classrooms by providing information that goes beyond the use of common drill-and-practice activities. They can guide teachers to help students in the development of information literacy, a life-long learning process of accessing, applying, and creating information. Promising applications include development of writing skills, problem solving, and manipulations of data. The most able students should have opportunities to learn computer programming skills and test scientific data with basic statistical programs.
6. A technology-infused inclusive environment is one in which students have maximum access to multiple technology tools at any location. Students control the technology for their own purposes rather than being controlled by it for purposes established by software houses.
7. Consultants should provide leadership in schools to assure effective use of technology for professional uses and to accommodate the needs of students with disabilities in general classrooms by participating in schoolwide planning groups, providing a role model in the use of technology, and engaging in collaborative activities in which technology is being used. Planning should include applications for professional collaboration as well as instructional and student uses.

To Do and Think About

1. Survey your school building to determine the extent to which staff members are using telecommunications and electronic networks to engage in their collaborative activities. Then think about

how you can get involved in this type of collaboration in your building, or interview a person who uses electronic networks extensively and write a plan for yourself to learn more about their use for your work.

2. Develop "shells" or "templates" on your computer for some of the forms suggested in other chapters of this text.

3. Develop a database that would be helpful to you as a consultant or co-teacher. Enter real or imaginary data and practice sorting it and preparing reports that would be useful to you.

4. Use a computer to adapt an instructional material or a test.

5. Create a computerized portfolio for yourself.

6. Read a journal article about ways to promote development of information literacy.

7. Describe what you would want in a technology-infused inclusive environment if money were no object.

8. Consult a technology specialist in your school district and discuss the possibilities for expanding the uses of technology to facilitate consultation, collaboration, and teamwork in your school.

9. Join or form a computer user's group to learn about new uses for computers from one another.

For Further Reading

Exceptional Children (October/November, 1994) Special issue: Technology-based assessment within special education, *61*(2).

Lewis, R. B. (1993). *Special education technology: Classroom applications.* Pacific Grove, CA: Brooks/Cole.

Male, M. (1994). *Technology for inclusion: Meeting the special needs of all students.* 2nd ed. Boston: Allyn & Bacon.

Majsterek, D. & Wilson, R. (1993). Computer-assisted instruction (CAI): An update on applications for students with learning disabilities. *LD Forum, 19:1* 19–21.

Phi Delta Kappan. (1992, December). A special section on "Technology in the schools," *74*(4).

Chapter **9**

Assessment and Evaluation of School Consultation and Collaboration

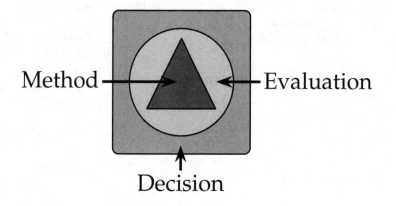

Method ——→ Evaluation

Decision

Introduction

Setting goals and evaluating the achievement of those goals are integral parts of education. This was most vividly illustrated in the requirements of Public Law 94-142 stipulating the development of individual education programs (IEPs). The basic philosophy that supports IEP development and evaluation is also the backbone of all good program development. A critical part of any educational program is the evaluation plan. Without such a plan, it is impossible to determine whether or not the goals have been achieved.

A consultation program requires evaluation just as any other educational program does. Indeed, evaluation is particularly important in programs which strive for abstract skills and intangible outcomes.

Focusing Questions

1. How are evaluation data helpful in developing and improving consultation programs? Who will want to see data from the consultation program for accountability purposes?
2. When should evaluation plans for school consultation and collaboration be developed? When should evaluation procedures for consultation be implemented?
3. Why do school consultants need to evaluate aspects of classroom environments that might affect student behavior? What are classroom environments that might affect student behavior? What are variables that might affect assessment?
4. What are the important processes in consultation? How can the effectiveness of these processes be evaluated? How might objective information be obtained to help consultants improve specific process skills? Are there parallels to the way teachers gather data about student skills?
5. What is the important content of consultation? What types of data might be collected to document the effectiveness of using this content?
6. What data might a consulting teacher collect about student (or client) progress that could be included as part of an evaluation plan? How might that type of information indicate whether or not the consulting teacher is doing a good job in the consultation?
7. How can a consultation program be justified, considering all possible sources of information available in the school and other information that might be gathered for this purpose?

Key Terms in the Chapter

accountability
assessment
behavioral observation
Curriculum-Based Assessment
Curriculum-Based Measurement
evaluation
evaluation plan
formative evaluation

ongoing systematic assessment
outcomes-based education
portfolio assessment
rating forms
self-assessment
self-monitoring of behavior
summative evaluation

Assessing and Evaluating the Consultation

Assessment and evaluation—the words produce apprehension and uneasiness over the use of tests, observations, and rating scales. Who has not dreaded the prospect of having one's work and progress evaluated? Yet in these days of accountability, evaluation is an essential part of professional responsibilities. Consultants cannot know if the consultation activities are effective unless they conduct some type of evaluation. Administrators and policymakers cannot support their programs unless meaningful data are available.

Conoley and Conoley (1982) articulate the critical importance of evaluation to consultants with the following statement:

It will make little difference to a consultee organization if the consultant does everything with textbook perfection. The decision-makers are interested in positive outcomes in terms of cost, increased services, or staff feedback. Consultants must be prepared not only to provide assistance to others who are planning, implementing, and evaluating programs (i.e., program consultation) but must also give priority [emphasis added] to such activities in their own service delivery systems. (p. 82)

Engaging in an on-going systematic assessment process is the best way to make sure appropriate decisions are made.

Scenario

The setting is the conference room of a special education program office where the principal, the director of special education, the special education consulting teacher, and a parent are seated.

PRINCIPAL: Mrs. James, I have asked Mrs. Garcia, our director of special education, and Mr. Penner, our special education consulting teacher, to meet with us today to help address your questions. I've explained to them that you're concerned about the new program for your daughter. As I understand your concerns, you feel she is not learning as much as she did last year when she went to the resource room for special help. Is there anything you would like to add?

PARENT: Well, I don't like to complain, but I just don't understand this new way of doing things for her. I was glad when she qualified for special education, because I thought she would finally get some help. Now she isn't getting it any more. Besides that, I wonder how this consulting program affects the other children. As you know, I am president of the local Parent Teachers Association, and questions about the special education program have come up at several of our meetings. I told parents I would try to get more information from you.

CONSULTING TEACHER: I've been working closely with your daughter's classroom teacher this year, and we've worked out some special learning activities in the classroom such as cooperative learning. She loves that, and when she needs a little extra help, we have arranged for a sixth-grade girl to tutor her. Besides that, she goes to the resource room for math.

SPECIAL EDUCATION DIRECTOR: I understand that the placement team agreed to all these special experiences at the IEP meeting last spring.

PARENT: Yes, I know we agreed to try them, but I don't think they are working. I would like more evidence that this is a good way to educate children who have special learning needs.

PRINCIPAL: Mr. Penner, do you have data that we can show Mrs. James?

CONSULTING TEACHER: Well, I could get some test scores from teachers, I guess.

SPECIAL EDUCATION DIRECTOR: Our consultation program is rather new. I believe it is already producing some positive outcomes, but it is evident that we must provide more documentation of the results. We will need a more structured evaluation plan to get the appropriate data for assessing our results.

PRINCIPAL: I agree. Thank you, Mrs. James, for being involved with your daughter's program and helping us to think through what we need to do. After we do some further work on this topic, may we call on you to collaborate with us on developing a plan?

Components of Consultation Evaluation

A model of consultation evaluation is shown in Figure 9-1. The model features the accumulation of information for two primary purposes—formative evaluation and summative evaluation. Formative evaluation is used when making decisions to modify, change, or refine a program during its implementation. Summative evaluation documents the attainment of program goals and is used most often by administrators in determining whether or not programs should be started, dropped, maintained, or chosen from among several alternatives (Scriven, 1967; Popham, 1988; Posavac and Carey, 1989).

Data gathered during formative evaluations are often included as part of summative evaluations (Tuckman, 1985). The key in selecting evaluation procedures is to consider the purposes of assessment—the questions that need to be answered. Formative assessments provide information for making changes and improvements. The focus is upon individual concerns and the local school context. Summative evaluations are used to make decisions about program goals; therefore, they require collection of data from larger groups. Formative and summative evaluations also differ in the audiences to whom the results will be targeted and the way in which those results will be communicated (Popham, 1988). The authors of this book propose that a good consultation evaluation will include context, processes, and content of consultation. These three elements are used for both formative and summative purposes. Examples of questions that might be answered in each situation are presented in Figure 9-2.

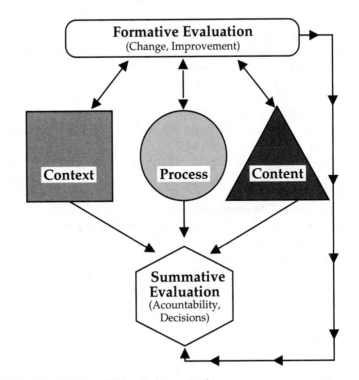

FIGURE 9-1   Evaluation of School Consultation

	Focus on:	FORMATIVE Change/improvement	SUMMATIVE Accountability
Context	**Program success**	**Development/change** What program aspects should be changed to fit this school and community?	**Status decisions** Should the consulting program continue next year?
Process	**Consultation skills**	**Growth/development** What interpersonal management skills need to be changed?	**Self-analysis** Do I have the skills to be an effective consultant?
Content	**Student/client progress**	**Growth/progress** Are achievement and behavior improving?	**Placement decisions** Does the student need more or less restrictive service?

FIGURE 9-2   Purposes of Assessment and Evaluation

Evaluation of Consultation Context

Formative evaluation of the context yields information about all elements that are expected to have an impact on the effectiveness of the consultation, such as students, teachers, family, or home and classroom environments. This information helps in selecting and modifying consultation processes and content, and is particularly useful during the initial stages of a consultation episode. Summative evaluation of context provides information to help decide whether or not the program should be continued in a particular school or district.

Evaluation of Consultation Processes

Formative evaluation of consultation processes provides information about skills and procedures that the consultant should develop or improve during the consultation process. Summative evaluation of processes gives information that demonstrates whether or not the skills and procedures used by the consultant were appropriate and effective.

Evaluation of Consultation Content

Formative evaluation of the content of consultation provides information about effectiveness of the interventions planned by the consultant and consultee and, when the interventions are not effective, provides data to guide school personnel in making program changes. Summative evaluation of content indicates whether or not the student is receiving the appropriate level or type of service. For example, a student might need more in-depth psychotherapy than the school counselor can provide.

Developing an Evaluation Plan

Consultants should identify data-collection methods clearly in the initial stages of program development and at the beginning of each school year thereafter. A consultant who does not determine how to evaluate the program until the end of the school year will be working "harder, not smarter." Summative evaluation procedures should be extensive enough to document achievement of each annual goal. This language probably sounds familiar, for that is exactly what is required when an IEP is developed. The similarity is not coincidental. Principles guiding IEP development must guide all good program development.

Once goals are determined, consultants can begin to list the types of data needed and determine ways of obtaining the data. Much of the data will exist within classrooms, in student files, or in school computer data banks. The challenge is to know what is needed and plan a strategy for collecting and summarizing the data in a meaningful, time-efficient way.

Example of an Evaluation Plan

Anita, a certified learning disabilities teacher, was excited about the prospects for the coming school year. Her school had set goals to address the educational needs of students at risk and to decrease the number of students labeled as disabled. Since many of these formerly labeled students were placed in LD programs, she volunteered to change her program delivery model to consultation and collaboration, with only limited resource room services. It was a challenge for which she hardly knew where to begin.

Anita had studied literature on consultation and collaboration and she knew that the first step was to think through the program goals. She also knew it would be important to gather appropriate data so she and her administrators could decide whether or not their goals were met by this program change. She carefully considered the types of data that she would gather throughout the school year in order to make a good decision about the effectiveness of the program. As she thought about her evaluation plan, she also wanted to make sure she continued to improve her consultation skills during the year. So she included several goals that addressed that need.

Her plan is shown in Figure 9-3.

Components of a Good Evaluation Plan

The evaluation plan should contain at least one measure to document achievement of each program goal and a projected time line for gathering the information. Many different sources of information should be used, including but not limited to: direct observations of behavior; portfolios of student work; long-term projects; logs and journals of consultation activities; interviews; videotaped conferences; anecdotal records; and student grades.

Assessment methods and procedures should be as objective and unbiased as possible. Sometimes unbiased opinions and objectivity are not easily attained. For example, a consultant might ask consultees to complete checklists such as the ones presented in this chapter, but respondents may not be willing or able to offer objective opinions. As noted in earlier chapters, lack of objectivity was cited by Caplan (1970) as theme interference in working with the special needs of students. Consultees sometimes give high ratings indiscriminately. This failure to discriminate may be due to fear of the consequences of being truthful (such as losing a colleague's friendship) or not knowing enough about the questioned behavior to offer a constructive opinion. High ratings are of little benefit for evaluation, and if inaccurate, they may be another example of an iatrogenic effect, compounding problems rather than creating solutions. For these reasons, consultants need information

Program Goals	Evaluation Procedures	Dates
Student progress in general classroom, with grades no less than D in classroom	Curriculum-Based Measurement Grade reports Student portfolios	Daily 9-wks On-going
Increase in skills of teachers for teaching special needs students	Inservice evaluation	Each session
Student use of study skills classroom	Classroom observation Teacher reports	9-wks 9-wks
Positive interaction with peers and teachers in classroom settings	Classroom observation Behavior rating scale	On-going 9-wks
Parent satisfaction with child's school experiences	Questionnaire	Dec.–May
Teacher satisfaction with consultation services	Self-assessment checklists and rating forms	9-wks
Teacher use of suggested materials and methods in teaching	Classroom Environment Checklist	Sep., Jan., May
Consultant use of effective communication and problem-solving	Video-tapes, behavior rating form, consultation verbal analysis system	9-wks
More student service with less labeling	Consultation activity report Consultation log	Daily By need

FIGURE 9-3   Consultation Evaluation Plan

from multiple sources, in different circumstances within the context, and at varying times throughout the school year.

The following points list key elements in developing an effective evaluation plan:

1. It should be an ongoing process.
2. Multiple sources of information should be used.
3. Valid and reliable methods of gathering information should be used.
4. It should be limited to gathering data that will answer pertinent questions and document attainment of consultation goals.
5. It should be realistic, diplomatic, and sensitive to multicultural considerations.
6. Legal and ethical procedures, including protection of rights of privacy, should be followed.
7. Anonymity of respondents should be maintained whenever possible.
8. It should be cost-effective in time and money. For example, whenever possible, existing data should be used.

Evaluating the Context of Consultation

Contextual evaluation is a relatively new conceptual framework through which consultants can examine their efforts. This approach to evaluation grew in importance as part of the educational reform of the 1980s. It is based on the premise that educational events occur in a context and the elements of the context play important parts in determining whether or not educational processes result in the desired outcomes (Field and Hill, 1988).

Contextual evaluation acknowledges the interdependence of all aspects of the school experience, including teachers, parents, students, administrators, classroom environment, school facilities, policies, procedures, and legal requirements. Contextual evaluation should consider the impact of students on teachers as well as the impact of teachers on students. It must assess the effect of teachers on consultants as well as the effect of consultants on teachers. It also should provide information on the professional interactions among individuals involved within the consultation environment(s).

Contextual evaluation is discussed here as it might be applied by individual consultants or collaborators. Administrators interested in a more extensive discussion of contextual appraisal for special education evaluation will find the work of Field and Hill (1988) a helpful reference.

Part I of this book discusses many contextual elements that play a part in school consultation, including societal values, legal requirements, community climate, home environment, school reform movements, teacher attitudes, and student characteristics. That information can provide background for appraising all elements when evaluating a consultation program. Evaluators will want to give careful attention to environmental factors that are related to student outcomes (Ysseldyke and Christenson, 1987). These factors include

- *school district conditions* such as teacher-pupil ratio, extent of emphasis on basic skills, amount of homework, emphasis on test taking, or grading policies;
- *within-school conditions* such as class size, school ambience, leadership from the principal, cooperative environment, collaborative staff relations, degree of structure, or classroom rules and procedures; and
- *general family characteristics* such as socio-economic status, educational level, use of out-of-school time, and peer groups outside the school.

Assessment of student characteristics and general classroom conditions is needed in order for a consultant to determine whether or not any mismatch between student characteristics and classroom situation is a factor in the problem. If the classroom environment is a problem, analysis of the information can be used to formulate appropriate solutions. Information about student progress will be discussed later under content of consultation, because student academic and behavior change is the most valid measure of the effectiveness of content.

Assessment of Classroom Environments

The major contextual element to be assessed is the classroom learning environment in which the student is expected to function. Bender (1988) suggests that educational placement teams conduct extensive evaluations of every classroom in the building at least every five years, keeping the information available for the use of preassessment team members, consultants, and other school staff. He articulates the importance of this type of assessment information for consultants:

> *. . . some of the most useful services presently performed by special education consultants depend on knowledge about the standard functioning of general classrooms. When a consultant visits a class to observe the student and to consult, prior knowledge of what general types of strategies are commonly used in that class is likely to greatly enhance the consultant's ability to make meaningful strategy suggestions. (Bender, 1988, p. 19)*

Other reasons for including this type of assessment in the evaluation plan are: (1) it is recognized that planning for instruction based on student learning styles and characteristics alone has been unsuccessful (Bender, 1988; Bursuck and Lessen, 1987; Ysseldyke and Christenson, 1987); (2) research on effective instruction now provides useful information for determining which elements of the classroom environment should be evaluated (Bursuck and Lessen, 1987; Ysseldyke and Christenson, 1987); and (3) the assessment has the potential to help classroom teachers better understand their own needs in facilitating learning for students with special needs (Bender, 1988).

Classroom elements (Bender, 1988) that should be assessed appear in Figure 9–4. This list of elements will be helpful for consultants who wish to prepare their own checklists or rating forms. The forms should be completed by classroom teachers and discussed in consultations with the teacher. Other sources of rating forms and checklists that can be used for this purpose are cited in the section for further reading.

Evaluating the Process of Consultation

One of the most important reasons for conducting process evaluation is to glean information for professional development. According to some authorities, self-assessment and self-direction are preferred methods of professional development for teachers (Bailey, 1981). The rationale for self-assessment applies even more to school consultants than to teachers, because in most school contexts there will be few, if any, opportunities for consultants to receive any assistance from administrators or supervisors. Without some type of self-assessment, a consultant may perpetuate ineffective processes and the quality of the consultation may decline over time. The value of engaging in self-assessment of one's consultation is illustrated by this journal entry of a graduate student in consultation:

> *Before involvement in the consulting project at this university, I had never seriously examined my communication skills. The video-taping has been the hardest for me; however, I have come to realize the importance of it and I have gained a better insight into areas that can be improved.*
>
> *The first video-tape recording was a real eye-opener, revealing lack of skill in handling resistance. The second recording surprised the consultee, as she realized*

Teaching Strategies and Approaches

Analysis in this category determines types of effective teaching practices used by the teacher, such as:

1. Precision teaching
2. Cooperative learning
3. Self-monitoring
4. Peer tutoring
5. Use of learning strategies
6. Use of alternative or supplementary reading materials, alternative testing and grading strategies

Typical Modifications Made in the Classroom

Analysis in this category includes strategies for effective teaching behaviors, such as:

1. Pacing
2. Monitoring
3. Providing feedback and follow-through
4. Using alternative presentation modes, including visual and auditory presentations
5. Alternative classroom organizations
6. Use of cognitive organizers for reading
7. Use of individualized instruction

Unusual Aspects of the Local Curriculum

Elements assessed in this area include:

1. Average achievement levels of the school
2. Type of curriculum presented to students in prior years
3. Reading level of classroom texts

FIGURE 9-4   Classroom Elements to be Assessed

that during the consultation she had thought of a solution to the problem for herself. The third video-tape revealed more areas in need of work: Conflict resolution, assertiveness, and controlling facial responses. I feel I did a good job of using the problem-solving technique, and the best part was to hear two consultees say they were going to use it themselves in problem situations. They feel it helped them focus on the problem and think of real solutions. It gave them a base from which to work.

Setting time limitations is something I'm not comfortable doing. I would rather allow the consultee enough time to work through feelings and identify the issues. However, looking back over my consultation log, I see that six of the consultations took more than 45 minutes and might well have concluded earlier if I had set time limits.

Now that I have identified this baseline of strengths and weaknesses, I have set the following goals to achieve by the end of the school year:

1. Reduce resistance from consultees to no more than 95% of the time.
2. Resolve conflicts at least 80% of the time.

3. *Use assertive behavior during consultation 100% of the time.*
4. *Eliminate inappropriate facial responses. I will video-tape consultation episodes every nine weeks and tabulate the target behaviors to see if I am making progress in reaching my goals. In addition, I will use a simplified version of the Consultant Behaviors Checklist to get feedback from my consultees every nine weeks. I will periodically interview consultees after consultation episodes to gather more immediate feedback about the target behaviors I am trying to improve.*

Consultant Self-Assessment Procedures

While many individuals engage in some self-appraisal or mental reflection, few do so systematically. Thus, the assessment or appraisal might not lead to meaningful improvement. Effective self-assessment should consist of a systematic, comprehensive program in which the consultant can gain information that leads to improvement or to a change of behavior.

The following suggestions for developing a self-assessment program are adapted from the work of Bailey (1981).

1. *Gain a philosophical overview of self-assessment.* Understand that self-assessment is not synonymous with the accountability required by administrators. Its purpose is personal change and improvement, and you should not share the results with supervisors unless you want to. The activities may not be easy to do, and some are rather time-consuming. They require selection of objective methods to gather data, in order to be most effective. Data should be collected in several consulting sessions with different types of consultees and various problem situations.

2. *Use media for self-assessment.* An objective way of gaining feedback about your behavior is to monitor it through use of audio- or videotaped material. Students in consulting preparation programs have been reluctant initially to use this type of feedback, but most are grateful later for its helpfulness. These tips for preparing and analyzing videotapes are helpful:

2.1 Set the consultee at ease by explaining the purpose of the videotape recording.
2.2 Do a few "trial runs" before involving a consultee, in order to become comfortable with the video camera and accustomed to seeing yourself on tape.
2.3 Don't focus on traits that have nothing to do with the quality of consultation. Taping distorts your voice and visual image, so don't worry about them.
2.4 Observe or listen to the tape several times, each time focusing observations on just one or two behaviors.
2.5 Tabulate behavior using a systematic observation method so the information can be interpreted meaningfully and progress followed objectively.
2.6 Be sensitive to the rights of privacy of the consultee. Arrange the seating during a videotape-recording session so that you face the camera and the consultee's back is to the camera.
2.7 Do not show the tape to an audience without receiving signed permission from the consultee.

3. *Identify the important consultation skills to be observed.* Merely watching and listening to oneself with the help of media will not provide enough information to guide personal development. Specific skills must be designated for recording the observation. Checklists and rating forms such as the Consultant Behaviors Checklist (Figure 9-5) can be used to identify behaviors to observe while viewing or listening to the taped consulting sessions. These checklists were developed from lists of important consulting behaviors described by researchers in the field.

4. *View or listen to taped consulting sessions and tabulate observation data.* Systematic behavioral observation techniques discussed later in this chapter are useful for observing consultant behavior, just as they are useful in observing student behavior in the classroom. Tabulate only one or two behaviors in each viewing, perhaps starting with a verbal behavior such as the number of times you said "O. K." or a nonverbal behavior such as looking away from the consultee. After tabulating the target behaviors, summarize strengths and behaviors that should be improved.

5. *Write down goals and objectives.* Prioritize the behaviors needing change and write behavioral objectives for them. Remember to state some type of criterion such as saying "O. K." no more than two times in a 20-minute consultation session. Include dates for achievement of each objective.

6. *Select strategies to help make the needed changes.* Formulate the strategies from material presented in other chapters of this text.

7. *Gather feedback and chart progress in achieving goals.* Periodic checks to determine whether or not you are making progress in the self-selected area for change is essential. It is very easy to believe falsely that the change has taken place if this step is bypassed. If goals focus on verbal skills, audio tapes probably will be sufficient for follow-up data, but if they include nonverbal skills, use of videotapes should continue. Perhaps it would be most efficient to reevaluate consultation skills at every marking period for students. The advantage of using consultee feedback is that consultee information can be contrasted with the consultant's own information. If there is much discrepancy between the two sets of information, causes of the discrepancy need to be determined.

8. *When a criterion is met, a self-reward is due for a job well done!* The objective data can be shared with a supervisor. The consultant may wish to chart consultation growth just as student progress growth is documented. Charts tell the story much more quickly than a list of numbers or a narrative description. Self-assessment should be an on-going process propelled by realistic expectations.

Records of Consultation Activities

Administrators are interested in more than how effectively consultants communicate or engage in problem-solving. They want to know about practical issues such as how the consultant uses time, how many consultees have been helped, the types of problems addressed, and whether or not the consultation services were helpful to the consultees.

Consultants should keep records of consultation activities in order to answer these types of questions. The consulting log in Chapter 7 is a useful form for documenting these data. Those who want to develop their own forms would find the work of Tindal and Taylor-

Consultant _____   Observer _____   Date _____

	yes	needs work	does not apply

1. Welcome

	yes	needs work	does not apply
Sets comfortable climate	_____	_____	_____
Uses commonly understood terms	_____	_____	_____
Is nonjudgmental	_____	_____	_____
Provides brief informal talk	_____	_____	_____
Is pleasant	_____	_____	_____

2. Communication Exchange

	yes	needs work	does not apply
Shares information	_____	_____	_____
Is accepting	_____	_____	_____
Is empathic	_____	_____	_____
Identifies major issues	_____	_____	_____
Keeps on task	_____	_____	_____
Is perceptive, providing insight	_____	_____	_____
Avoids jargon	_____	_____	_____
Is encouraging	_____	_____	_____
Gives positive reinforcement	_____	_____	_____
Sets goals as agreed	_____	_____	_____
Develops working strategy	_____	_____	_____
Develops plan to implement strategy	_____	_____	_____
Is friendly	_____	_____	_____

3. Interpretation of Communication

	yes	needs work	does not apply
Seeks feedback	_____	_____	_____
Demonstrates flexibility	_____	_____	_____
Helps define problem	_____	_____	_____
Helps consultee assume responsibility for plans	_____	_____	_____

4. Summarizing

	yes	needs work	does not apply
Is concise	_____	_____	_____
Is positive	_____	_____	_____
Is clear	_____	_____	_____
Sets another meeting if needed	_____	_____	_____
Is affirming	_____	_____	_____

FIGURE 9-5   Consultant Behaviors Checklist

Pendergast (1989) a helpful reference. It may be productive also to check with one's administrator to find out what specific information would be most desired. Busy consultants should not spend time collecting information that is not wanted or needed.

One special education consultant in an inclusive school avoided the confusion that resulted from many people going in and out of each classroom every day by devising a system to record these activities. In each classroom she placed record forms that were completed by each person who went into the classroom to consult or provide special services to a student with disabilities. These individuals were asked to "log in" by entering the date, time, name, and a brief comment regarding the student(s) with disabilities during the time in the classroom. Later, the data were sorted in various ways for final reports (see Chapter 8 for further discussion of sorting data using a computer database).

Evaluating the Content of Consultation

The content of consultation consists of the problem solutions, instructional techniques, or behavioral interventions selected through the consultation process. The content can be judged effective if the goals of the consultation are achieved. In school consultation the goals usually address improved achievement or behavior.

Assessing Student Academic Performance

School consultants need training in the traditional approach of examining students through use of formal and informal testing procedures to identify their special learning needs. Skill in observing classroom performance, as differentiated from performance in a testing situation, is also necessary. The most functional approach to making these observations is Curriculum-Based Assessment (CBA).

Curriculum-Based Assessment (CBA)
It is important to identify accurately the student's current level of performance in the classroom and monitor progress in a systematic, on-going manner. Standardized tests are not designed for this type of monitoring. Curriculum-Based Assessment is the most appropriate approach for the purpose (Bender, 1988; Bursuck and Lessen, 1987; Deno, 1987; Wang, 1987).

"There is nothing new about Curriculum-Based Assessment. In many respects it is like coming home to traditional classroom instruction" (Tucker, 1985, p. 199). What *is* new are more precise and practical ways of examining student progress in the classroom curriculum. The basic concept of CBA is use of the actual curriculum materials, or the course of study adopted by a school system, in making the assessment (Tucker, 1985). CBA differs from traditional testing, which uses material representing a composite of items taken from many different curricula. While standardized tests tell us how students perform in relation to a large reference group, CBA tells us how students perform in the classrooms where they are expected to function. Since most school consultants will be addressing problems that occur in general classrooms, they will need this type of information to formulate good solutions to problems and to document effectiveness of their efforts.

Consultants can choose among several ways to conduct CBA. Figure 9-6 illustrates the purposes for some of these ways to conduct CBA. Although teacher-made tests and criterion-referenced tests provide information about content mastery, portfolios and Curriculum-Based Measurement provide information to monitor progress in larger domains over time. All the procedures have valid uses. The method chosen will depend on the circumstances within the school and should be the most valid, reliable, and efficient method for a given purpose. Although Curriculum-Based Measurement meets these criteria, it is limited to measurement of basic skills and cannot be used to monitor many other valuable educational goals. Caution should be taken in adopting commercially prepared CBA measures because they probably will not be accurate measures of the curriculum in a particular school. Criterion-referenced tests that accompany the textbooks adopted by school personnel would be appropriate CBA measures for a consultant to use.

Some school districts and states require a type of CBA for all students. A term commonly used for this practice is *outcomes-based education* (OBE). OBE requires schools to state the outcomes they expect from their efforts. These outcomes are often stated as processes as well as products. Although school districts might state very broad outcomes, such as "all students will be good communicators in a complex world," the outcomes become more narrow as they are stated at the building and classroom levels. For special educators, the IEP is an outcomes-based document for a single individual. For a school that utilizes

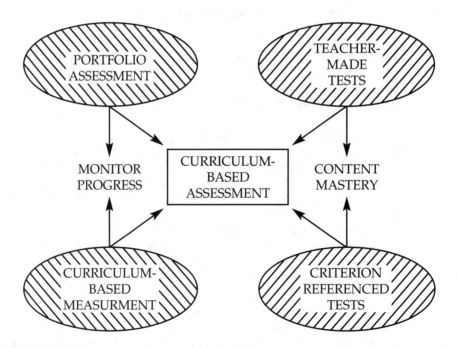

FIGURE 9-6   Purposes of Various Types of CBA

the principles of outcomes-based education, the information generated for that program might be sufficient for evaluation needs. The consultant would need only to gain access to the information as it applies to the program being evaluated.

Other CBA measures are informal reading inventories (assuming the reading materials are taken from school texts), and mastery tests in content subject matter. "CBA is the ultimate in 'teaching the test,' because the materials used to assess progress are *always* drawn directly from the course of study" (Tucker, 1985, p. 200). The disadvantages of teacher-made CBA procedures are the time it takes teachers to develop them, and the unknown reliability and validity of the measures (Fuchs, Fuchs, and Hamlett, 1990).

Many special educators are familiar with approaches to evaluation of student learning such as Precision Teaching (Lindsley, 1964) and Data-Based Instruction (Mercer and Mercer, 1993). These approaches require specification of observable and measurable objectives which can be recorded as the number of correct and incorrect movements or responses per minute. One-minute probes are given daily and the scores are plotted on charts. The charts are analyzed frequently to observe trends which indicate whether or not instructional program changes are needed. A variation of this approach was developed and refined at the University of Minnesota (Deno, 1987). This CBA system is called Curriculum-Based *Measurement* (CBM), emphasis added to differentiate it from other forms of CBA.

Deno (1987) specified two distinctive features of Curriculum-Based Measurement: (1) the procedures possess reliability and validity to a degree that equals or exceeds that of most achievement tests; and (2) growth in each curriculum area is measured on a single global task performed repeatedly across time. This approach differs significantly from criterion-referenced testing, which uses many different tasks, each measuring a different skill in a sequence. CBM has been widely researched in elementary schools using different types of curricula. It measures effectively the growth in academic areas of reading, writing, math, and spelling. The research has not singled out particular situations where it is most appropriate, but CBM is likely to be more useful than criterion-referenced tests for students in classrooms where whole language instruction is being used, because of its emphasis on global measures. It is very appropriate for use with students who have learning problems. It might also be an attractive approach to use with gifted students when basic skill development is of less interest to the evaluator than progress on more global measures.

A major disadvantage of CBM is the time needed to keep records and chart results. However, this process can be facilitated by use of computer software that automatically generates, administers, and scores tests; saves student scores and responses to the items on the tests; graphs scores; and automatically analyzes the student's rate of progress in comparison to the goal line (Fuchs, Hamlett, and Fuchs, 1990).

Portfolio Assessment

Other types of student performance, including sample worksheets, copies of projects, extra-credit reports, and samples of artwork, can be collected to help document the content of consultation. Evaluation of such products is an alternative that has much potential for assessing a wide range of student abilities and needs. A number of educational pioneers are leading the movement toward alternative assessment by promoting portfolios as a means for attesting to student progress over time (Maeroff, 1991).

Many classroom teachers guide students in developing "working portfolios" and "showcase portfolios." The first is used to monitor progress toward specified goals (usually defined mutually by the student and teacher); the second presents the "best" of the products pulled from the working portfolio to show to parents, other teachers, and future employers. Special educators should consider preparing another working portfolio referenced to IEP goals. CBM charts and teacher-made tests can be part of the portfolio, but the strength of using the portfolio is the opportunity to present products such as writing samples, tape-recorded spoken language samples, and observation data that do not lend themselves to being tested in traditional ways.

Paulson, Paulson, and Meyer (1991) describe the portfolio as a purposeful collection of student work that exhibits efforts, progress, and achievements in one or more areas. They propose that students participate in selecting the contents to put into their portfolios, and in developing the criteria for selection and for judging merit. Such processes are arenas for involving students in collaborative experiences to improve their learning and productivity.

A portfolio is larger and more elaborate than a report card, but smaller and more focused than a trunkful of artifacts (Valencia, 1990). A convenient storage device is the expandable file folder. This is to be a working folder; therefore, it should be easily accessible to the student owner and the teacher. Suitable products to be added to the portfolio, after self-assessment by the student and consultation with the teacher, might include: progress charts; completed learning packets, artwork; a student-made book; lists of mastered vocabulary or spelling words; notes on informal conversations; research reports; clever doodles; original songs; creative writing samples; descriptions of good deeds and helpful behavior; an autobiography; journal entries; tests; records of scores; teacher observational notes; audio- or video-tapes; solutions to problems; and much more. It is helpful to have a summary sheet, table of contents, or other organizing format. The construction of this format provides another valuable opportunity for the teacher and student to collaborate and discuss learning.

Portfolio assessment is a procedure that focuses on both process and the product of learning. It is authentic in purpose and task, multidimensional, and contributes to an ongoing learning process. The material can be continuously evaluated, streamlined, and sent with the student from grade level to grade level as visible evidence of growth and improvement. It provides an effective vehicle for partnership in learning between teacher and student and contributes valuable support material for staffings and parent conferences.

Problems to be overcome in using this alternative form of assessment center around the additional work, storage space, patience, and time for teacher interaction with each student. A school consultant can ease the load of a teacher who wishes to use portfolio assessment by working as a team member to consult with students as they reflect on their work, and by collaborating with the teacher to develop ways of organizing and using the procedure.

Portfolios must provide some measure of objectivity to be reliable indicators of growth or progress toward goals in a working portfolio. Teachers need to guide a systematic process of securing samples to put into the portfolio. For example, writing samples might be gathered once each month, dated, and placed in chronological order in the portfolio. Then the samples can be easily viewed to show progress toward the goal. Additional objectivity and evaluation are provided with use of a rubric. Rubrics are lists for standard or outcomes that guide the evaluation process. They are often in the form of rating scales. Figure 9-7 provides an example of a rubric for the product, process, and content of writing. Ideally, the rubric is completed and discussed in a conference between the student and teacher at regular intervals during the school term. The completed rubrics are kept in the portfolio for future reference and modified as growth takes place (Swicegood, 1994).

WRITTEN EXPRESSION RUBRIC

	EMERGING	GROWING	MASTERED	EXPANDED
WRITING PRODUCT				
Handwriting				
Grammar				
Spelling				
Capitalization				
Paraphrasing				
WRITING PROCESS				
Idea generation				
Brainstorming				
Organization of ideas				
Editing skills				
Error correction				
Final draft				
WRITING CONTENT				
Sentence development				
Paragraph organization				
Paragraph development				
Overall length of writing				
Use of words				
Fluency of writing				
Variety of purposes				

COMMENTS:

FIGURE 9-7 Example of Rubric for Portfolio Assessment

Implementation of a portfolio assessment system in collaboration with students and colleagues includes the following steps:

1. Inform students and involve them.
2. Determine types of contents to be included (with flexibility for adding new types that may be determined later).
3. Prepare formats to organize portfolio contents, such as a table of contents or a summary sheet.
4. Determine criteria for evaluating the contents.
5. Determine the final destination of the portfolio and its contents.

Maintaining Student Academic Records

If consultants have been using curriculum-based assessment and systematic behavioral observation procedures, a summary of the information can provide a summative record of consultation content. This information can report the number of goals met or not met, student grades or test scores, and interviews with teachers and parents.

As suggested earlier, one disadvantage of collecting and maintaining records generated by types of assessment such as student portfolios is the amount of space needed for filing them. Minner, Minner, and Lepich (1990) illustrate this point by stating, "If a teacher had a caseload of 15 students and each student worked in four academic content areas, the teacher would collect over 2,000 work samples in an academic year if he or she collected only one sample per week in each area" (pp. 32–33). The volume of papers would be even greater for a consultant who wished to monitor the progress of a caseload of thirty or more students. One solution to this dilemma is to require students to keep their own portfolios of their work (Wolf, 1989). This strategy seems especially valuable for use by consultants for gifted and talented students in content areas of art, music, design, written expression, computer programming, and other subjects which do not lend themselves easily to conventional forms of assessment.

APPLICATION 9.1   Developing a Teacher Portfolio

Educators who plan, develop, and maintain their own portfolios derive several benefits from the activity. They model the process for their colleagues who are not yet participating in this assessment technique and they demonstrate to students the value and importance they place upon portfolios. The portfolio can be presented as an example of their productivity when they are evaluated by a supervisor or an administrator. Last but not to be overlooked—it can be fun.

Possibilities for portfolio products abound. A few are lesson plans that worked well; videotapes of classroom activity highlights; sample tests; effective worksheets or packets; rainy-day ideas that went over well; an original teaching or grading technique; sketch of an unusual bulletin board so it won't be forgotten; list of professional books read; any articles published in newsletters, newspapers, or other professional outlets; documentation of consultation episodes (coded for confidentiality); descriptions of team teaching activities; photos of special class sessions; original computer software that worked well; a highly effective management technique; notes from parents or students that were reinforcing; goals for the semester or school year; special achievements by students. The list could go on and on.

Another method involves collaboration among classroom teacher, special education consultant, *and student* to develop criteria for assessing portfolio products, selecting the best or most representative ones, and removing others. Thus the portfolio volume is reduced while the student is gaining valuable self-assessment skills. Students skilled in using computers can store their products in a computer file as discussed in Chapter 8.

Assessing Student Behaviors

Finding solutions to classroom behavior problems constitutes one of the major content areas of consultation. Consultants will need to gather objective information to document behavior changes. Systematic behavior observations, as well as subjective measures such as rating scales and checklists, should be used for this purpose.

Behavior Observations

Many students with learning and behavior problems, as well as some gifted and talented students, demonstrate social difficulties, lack of motivation, poor work habits or other behaviors that need to be monitored as part of the consultation evaluation program. Several researchers have studied general classroom settings and have identified the emotional, social, and work skills most important for success in that setting (Bursuck and Lessen, 1987; Fad, 1990; Wood and Meiderhoff, 1989). These data can be used to develop a checklist or rating scale most appropriate for your level of service. An alternative is to use one of several commercially developed rating scales and checklists that are available—for example, the Walker Problem Behavior Identification Checklist (Walker, 1976) or the Behavior Problem Checklist (Quay and Peterson, 1987). Caution should be exercised when selecting from existing rating scales, so that those chosen will be appropriate for the classroom situation in which they are to be used.

Several individuals, such as classroom teachers, parents, teacher aides, or peer tutors, can be asked to complete the rating scales. There are two advantages in asking the classroom teacher. First, the behaviors to observe can be more closely targeted. Second, teachers can be encouraged to focus attention on behaviors not previously considered. Bursuck and Lessen (1987) emphasize that a combination of behavioral observation by a consultant and completion of a behavior checklist by the teacher will be preferable to either one alone.

It is not sufficient to observe that the student does not pay attention or is noisy. The educator needs to know precisely the rate and frequency of the behaviors and under what conditions the student displays the behaviors. Systematic, direct observation of the student in the environments in which the problems occur is the best assessment procedure for gathering the information.

Data collected on specific behaviors can help collaborators set goals, plan programs, and evaluate interventions. In preassessment and problem solving, it is much easier to deal with "is at least 15 minutes tardy 85 percent of the time," or "screams and kicks heels on the floor an average of six times per day," or "writes 90 percent of the 4s, 5s, and 7s backward," than it is to collaboratively work on problems described as "irresponsible," "aggressive," and "has problems writing her numbers."

Consultants may select from among several types of ongoing measurement of behavior when they wish to observe a student's behavior in the classroom, on the playground, or in the halls. There are many excellent resources about the methodology of behavior observation (Alberto and Troutman, 1990; Wolery, Bailey, and Sugai, 1988; Rusch, Rose, and Greenwood, 1988).

Documenting Changes in Student Behavior

Several methods of behavior measurement are useful for consultants:

- frequency recording,
- interval recording,
- time sampling,
- duration.

Each method begins with identifying and defining a specific, concrete behavior or a set of behaviors to be observed.

Behavior should be defined so precisely that when measured by two different people, the numbers will be virtually the same, assuring reliability of the measurement. Two people measuring "aggression" or "irresponsibility" would not have very high interrater reliability of the measurement! Sometimes it will take several visits to the classroom to develop an observable and measurable definition of the behavior.

Frequency recording determines the number of times the event happens. It is used to measure discrete behaviors that can be discriminated, such as swearing in class or episodes of crying. Consultants will want to observe in the environment in which the behavior occurs for a number of times to get a representative sample of the behavior. It may be necessary to spend time in the classroom before observation, so that the student becomes accustomed to the observer's presence and is not "on best behavior." Then the measurement will be more realistic. Teachers and students themselves can record frequency of specific behaviors. Trial recording is a variation of frequency recording. This method adds the dimension of recording the opportunities a student has to perform a behavior. For example, if the observer uses frequency recording to measure "compliance with teacher instructions," it will be necessary to know how many teacher instructions were presented before a compliance rate or percent can be obtained. A tally mark could be made on the data sheet for every instruction, and those that are followed would then be circled. A sample data sheet for frequency recording is provided in Figure 9-8.

In interval recording and time sampling, the observation period is marked into intervals such as fifteen-second sections, two-minute sections, or ten-minute sections. Although the measure is more precise with smaller sections of time (intervals), it is not always possible to do this when the observer is teaching the class or leading a discussion. For interval recording, the observer would mark whether or not the behavior in question occurred during the interval. Did Jay spit at another student during that five-minute period (mark +), or refrain from doing so (mark -)? Did Tracy work on the workbook lesson during the interval (mark +), or did she get up and wander around, look out the window, or comb her hair (mark -)? After the observation period, the consultant or teacher should divide the number of intervals in which the behavior occurred by the total intervals observed to get a percent of intervals (or time) that the behavior in question happened.

Student _____   Observer _____

Dates _____   Time _____   Place _____

Definition _____

_____

_____

_____

_____

Date	Time		Behavioral Episodes Tally	Total
	Start	Stop		

FIGURE 9-8   Sample Data Sheet for Frequency Recording

Time sampling is similar to interval sampling, and usually is easier because it does not require looking at the student for the entire observation period. After the observation time is divided into blocks of time (intervals), the observer only marks whether or not the behavior is occurring at the end of the interval. For example, at the end of fifteen seconds, the observer checks to see if Ryan is carving on the desk, the learning materials, or his flesh with a pencil, pen, or some other instrument. If so, the observer would mark +, and if not, the observer would mark -. Although some teachers might wish to stop Ryan's behavior rather than measure it, for the purposes of behavior observation, an observational posture rather than a disciplinary posture is needed. A percent of intervals is reported in order to describe the behavior.

Duration recording requires using a watch or clock to measure how long a behavior occurs. This type of behavior measurement is often used with time on task, time in seat, or time required to complete an assignment or task. The observer starts the stopwatch or notes the time the behavior begins and ends. Using a stopwatch to measure accumulated time performing a specific behavior is an alternative to interval recording or time sampling.

When such measures are used to assess a behavior, and used again after an intervention to reassess the same behavior, observed changes can be very obvious and dramatic. Then the results of collaboration are precise. It is a real boost to a collaborative partnership when a student's homework completion rate soars from 10 percent to 85 percent, or when the number of times a student puts on her coat independently changes from zero percent of opportunities to 100 percent after some work at home by parents.

Audio or Video Tape Records
Another possibility for accumulating records of student behavior, particularly social behavior in the classroom, is the use of audio- or video-taped sessions (Minner et al., 1990), which can be part of a student's portfolio. "Teachers have told us that tapes are especially useful when showing parents how their son or daughter has progressed" (p. 33). This approach to data collection, while very effective, is often difficult to arrange. The suggestions discussed for using video-tapes in self-assessment are applicable for this situation. Consultants should be very cautious about protecting the confidentiality of the observed student as well as other students in the classroom.

Tips for Consulting and Collaborating

1. Evaluate consultations in order to improve upon effectiveness.
2. Suggest to teachers a variety of evaluation tools for monitoring student progress.
3. Acknowledge that less-than-desirable consultations occur occasionally, and build on the experience.
4. Share results of evaluation with key groups as appropriate—consultees, administrators, decision makers, parents—maintaining confidentiality and rights of privacy for those involved.
5. Celebrate even small gains in consultation success.
6. Promote instances of high-quality consultation and collaboration, not just the frequency and time spent in the activities.

Chapter Review

1. An evaluation program is essential for documenting the effectiveness of any educational program. Evaluation is necessary to make program improvements and to defend the quality of the program to administrators and other decision makers.
2. During the initial stages of program development, consultants should create a plan for ongoing evaluation. Formative and summative information of the context, processes, and content of consultation must be gathered in the most efficient manner possible. Methods of gathering data should come from multiple sources and should be as objective and unbiased as possible.

3. Consultants should evaluate the context that has the most impact on student performance, with emphasis on student characteristics and their relationships to classroom environmental conditions. Context evaluation is used primarily for formative evaluation and should include careful appraisal of classroom setting demands.

4. Formative and summative evaluation should include evaluation of consultation processes. Consultants need to engage in systematic self-assessment, in order to gain information for improving their consultation skills, because it is not likely most will have the administrator feedback and monitoring needed for professional growth in this area. They should also keep careful records of their activities, to justify the program to decision makers.

5. No matter how good the processes of consultation may be, the program will not be effective unless students make progress in learning or behavior goals. The content of the consultation must work. It will be critical for consultants to keep records of student achievement and behavior change, in order to document the effectiveness of the program.

6. Data collected on learning achievement and specific behaviors can help collaborators set goals, plan programs, and evaluate the effectiveness of interventions. The desired student behavior should be defined precisely. Data collection methods from which to select include Curriculum-Based Assessment, student portfolio assessment, frequency recording, interval recording, time sampling, duration recording, and audiotape and videotape records.

7. Consultation effectiveness is three-dimensional. The consulting will be a great success if it results in:

   - consultee satisfaction;
   - problem resolution for the client's need(s); and
   - a strengthened consultation system.

To Do and Think About

1. Evaluation is an essential aspect of education. While classroom teachers assume responsibility for evaluating student learning, it is administrators who usually are responsible for evaluating the effectiveness of programs and educational methods such as school consultation. Discuss how the role of school consultants requires that they become actively involved in evaluating consultee satisfaction, problem resolution, and the strength of the consultation system.

2. Name several consumer and decision-making target groups within a school district who are likely to ask for data to support a consultation program. What would be the most effective formats for presenting the data to each target group for its purposes?

3. Study the evaluation model in Figure 9-1 and the example of one consultant's plan described in this chapter. Then develop an evaluation plan for consultation service during the coming school year in your school setting.

4. Work with a group of other consultants or teachers. Have each person make a copy of one of the checklists or rating scales of classroom environment cited in this chapter's section for further reading. Collaborate to compare the rating scales, and create a rating scale that would be useful in a typical school setting.

5. Conduct a self-assessment of consultation skills. Give careful attention to each step of the process as described in this book. Make an effort to videotape the consultation in a real or simulated experience at least every nine weeks throughout an entire school year. Chart behavioral data to demonstrate progress on at least two specific objectives.

6. Use the Consultation Log in Chapter 7 for at least six weeks. Meet with other consultants to modify the forms as needed, and then use the revised forms for the remainder of the school term.
7. Read the references about Curriculum-Based Measurement cited in the section for further reading. Then work with other consultants and teachers to see if this type of assessment could be implemented in a way that would be beneficial to all involved.
8. Practice using the behavior observation techniques described in this chapter. Refine those that are most useful to you.

For Further Reading

Behavior Observation

Cautela, J. R., Cautela, J., and Esonis, S. (1982). *Forms for Behavior Analysis with Children.* Champaign, IL: Research Press.

Hall, R. V., and Houten, R. V. (1980). *The Measurement of Behavior.* Austin, TX: PRO-ED.

Maag, J. W. (1989). Assessment in social skills training: Methodological and conceptual issues for research and practice. *Remedial and Special Education, 10*(4): 6–17. Discusses criticisms of assessment of social skills training, and suggests procedures to improve this type of assessment.

Checklists and Rating Scales of Classroom Environments

Bender, W. N. (1988). The other side of placement decisions: Assessment of the mainstream learning environment. *Remedial and Special Education, 9*(5), 28–33.

Renzulli, J. S., and Reis, S. M. (1985). *The Schoolwide Enrichment Model: A Comprehensive Plan for Educational Excellence.* Mansfield Center, CT: Creative Learning Press. Contains figures, charts, checklists, and text for assessing enrichment activities, process development, and independent study for gifted and talented students.

Salend, S. J., and Viglianti, D. (1982). Preparing secondary students for the mainstream. *Teaching Exceptional Children, 14:* 137–140.

Wood, J. W., and Miederhoff, J. W. (1989). Bridging the gap. *Teaching Exceptional Children, 21*(2): 66–68.

Ysseldyke, J. E., and Christenson, S. I. (1987). Evaluating students' instructional environments. *Remedial and Special Education, 8*(3): 17–24.

Comprehensive Classroom Assessment Programs

Bursuck, W. D., and Lessen, E. (1987). A classroom-based model for assessing students with learning disabilities. *Learning Disabilities Focus, 3*(1): 17–29. Describes the elements of Curriculum-Based Assessment and instructional design, a well-designed, comprehensive system utilizing academic probes, work habit perception check, and environmental inventory.

Steele, J. (1982). *The Class Activities Questionnaire.* Mansfield Center, CT: Creative Learning Press. Evaluates skills and factors related to the instructional climate that indicate the presence of enrichment opportunities for students. Obtains feedback from both teachers and students.

Ysseldyke, J. E., and Christenson, S. I. (1987). Evaluating students' instructional environments. *Remedial and Special Education, 8*(3): 17–24. Discusses the rationale for assessing a student's instructional environment and describes The Instructional Environment Scale (TIES), a set of assessment tools produced by PRO-ED.

Contextual Appraisal of Special Education Programs

Field, S. L., and Hill, D. S. (1988). Contextual appraisal: A framework for meaningful evaluation of special education programs. *Remedial Education, 9*(4): 22–30. Explains the importance of contextual appraisal for special education programs. Of primary interest to administrators.

Curriculum-Based Assessment

The next four references, a set of short papers, explain different aspects of CBM, such as how to develop and administer measurement devices, how to graph performance and practical suggestions for teachers when using the system.

Deno, S. L. (1987). Curriculum-based measurement. *Teaching Exceptional Children, 20*(1): 41–47.

Fuchs, L. S. (1987). Program development. *Teaching Exceptional Children, 20*(1): 42–44.

Tindal, G. (1987). Graphing performance. *Teaching Exceptional Children, 20*(1): 44–46.

Wesson, C. L. (1987). Increasing efficiency. *Teaching Exceptional Children, 20*(1): 46–47.

Fuchs, L. S., and D., and Hamlett, C. L. (1990).Curriculum-Based Measurement: A standardized, long-term goal approach to monitoring student progress. *Academic Therapy, 25*(5): 615–32. Provides a reasonably detailed description of how CBM can be used to help teachers formulate effective instructional programs using the charted data to make relevant decisions.

Portfolio Assessment

Edyburn, D. L. (1994). *An equation to consider: The portfolio assessment knowledge base + technology= The Grady Profile, 19, 4,* 35–38. Discusses a software package for using the computer for portfolio assessment.

Swicegood, P. (1994). Portfolio-based assessment practices. *Intervention in School and Clinic,* 30, *1,* 6–15. Provides an overview of portfolio assessment practices and their application for students with disabilities.

Evaluation of Consultation Processes

Conoley, J. C., and Conoley, C. W. (1982). *School Consultation: A Guide to Practice and Training.* New York: Pergamon Press. Contains more than a half-dozen forms to be used or adapted for gathering consultee feedback about the effectiveness of the consultation process.

Work Habits and Social Skills

Fad, K. S. (1990). The fast track to success: Social behavioral skills. *Intervention in School and Clinic, 26*(1): 39–43. Reports the results of a survey of classroom teachers to identify the social and behavior skills considered essential for classroom survival. The author lists the ten most critical skills. A helpful resource for developing behavior checklists.

C h a p t e r **10**

Consultation, Collaboration, and Teamwork for Student Success in Inclusive Schools

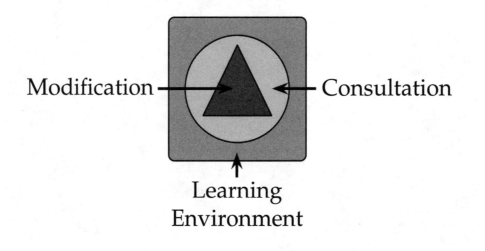

Modification — ▲ — Consultation

Learning
Environment

Introduction

One of the most significant changes to be made in the school reform movement of the 1990s and beyond is collaboration for full inclusion of students with special learning and behavior needs in a unified educational system (see Chapter 1). Many of the changes in the way schools function will need strong efforts in consultation, collaboration, and teamwork among school personnel and parents. Teachers will need to engage in new ways to provide instruction to students. New concepts of accommodating individual student needs within inclusive school environments will be required. Without knowledge of these methods and procedures, consultation and collaboration will result in nothing but talk. The interaction will facilitate process, but will be somewhat empty. Recall the quote in an earlier chapter, for describing consultations that are long on process but short in content, "The emperor has no clothes" (Britt, 1985, p. 30). Relevant content is needed to engage in substantive collaborative efforts for all students in inclusive school settings.

Many new ideas and innovations were developed as part of the school reform movement of the 1980s. Guskey (1990) identified seven major innovations: cooperative learning, the effective schools model, critical thinking, mastery learning and outcomes-based education (OBE), mastery teaching, Teacher Expectations and Student Achievement (TESA), and learning styles. The National Center on Educational Restructuring and Inclusion (NCERI) identified multi-level instruction, cooperative learning, activity-based learning, mastery learning, use of technology, and peer support and tutoring (Lipsky, 1994) as the most useful for inclusive programs. This chapter provides information about many of these innovations and other instructional strategies that are effective in inclusive schools.

Focusing Questions

1. What characteristics distinguish inclusive schools that are effective?
2. How does co-teaching help accomplish the goals of inclusive schools?
3. What other classroom practices contribute to the success of inclusive schools?
4. How do para-educators help accomplish the goals of inclusive schools?
5. What teaching methods increase opportunities for all students to learn effectively in inclusive classrooms?
6. How can the classroom setting be arranged and the learning tasks modified so students with special learning needs have a better chance to succeed in learning tasks?
7. What factors need to be considered when consulting and collaborating with classroom teachers to plan interventions for those with special instructional needs?

Key Terms in the Chapter

classroom modification
co-teaching
cooperative learning
cross-age peer tutoring
curriculum compacting
enrichment
flexible pacing
inclusion
learning styles
mastery learning
modified testing
outcomes-based education (OBE)
para-educators

parallel curriculum
parallel teaching
peer tutoring
strategies
Speak and Add
Speak and Chart
station teaching
Teach and Monitor
team teaching
test-taking skills
textbook adaptation
unified educational system

Scenario

The setting is the LD teacher's office (once the resource room where LD students came for special instruction in the former "pull-out" program). The principal arrives first, followed by two behavioral disorders (BD) teachers, two learning disabilities (LD) teachers, and a speech pathologist. Teacher A assumes the facilitator role, teacher B functions in the recorder role and, teacher D has the timekeeper role (with these roles being rotated in subsequent meetings).

TEACHER "A" (facilitator): "Who has agenda items today?"

PRINCIPAL: "I want to discuss CBM and a discipline policy procedure."

TEACHER "A" (facilitator): "How much time do you need for your agenda item?"

TEACHER "A" (facilitator): (Writes the agenda item and time needed (varying from anywhere from 1 to 10 minutes) on a form.)

TEACHER "C": "I need ideas for working with Jason."

TEACHER "A" (facilitator): (Continues to write agenda items and time needed as each person states them.)

TEACHER "A" (facilitator): "All right, let's start with item 3—Jason.

TEACHER "C": "I'm concerned about Jason because he can't read the fourth-grade materials. He has a wonderful background in science and social studies. I really think his problem is that he can't read and write the material used in the classroom."

TEACHER "B" (recorder): (Writes the main points of the discussion, pertinent decisions and future agenda items related to issue.)

TEACHER "D" (timekeeper): (Starts stopwatch at beginning of each item discussion and notifies when the allocated time has been used.)

TEACHER "A" (facilitator): (After most of the items have been discussed the time for the meeting has almost ended.) "I will put the last two items on the agenda for next week. Are there other items for that meeting?"

Characteristics of Effective Inclusive Schools

Inclusion is a concept that emerged as part of the school reform movement of the 1980s. Inclusion describes an educational context and process that is more than a place where education takes place. It is a philosophy that "celebrates diversity; promotes accountability and professional collaboration; recognizes the importance of strong social relationships among children; and explores strategies for pursuing excellence without sacrificing equity" (Schrag and Burnette, 1994, p. 64). All members of the educational community must change their roles and provide support for inclusive schools to be effective. Much of the content in this book provides guidance in making these role changes. In this chapter we will focus on the elements most closely related to providing instruction in the inclusive environment.

Co-Teaching Methods

A new approach to delivering instruction is needed when students with special needs are no longer receiving special instruction in resource rooms or self-contained classrooms. Co-teaching is one example of such a change in delivery. Co-teaching (sometimes referred to as collaborative teaching or cooperative teaching) involves two or more teachers (often a general education teacher and a special education teacher) who plan and deliver instruction as co-equals within one educational setting to one group of students. It is *not* consultation, nor is it a para-educator taking over a classroom activity, although para-educators can be involved in co-teaching. A key element of co-teaching is the shared responsibility of the teachers in both planning and delivering instruction. There are several ways to engage in co-teaching.

Teach and Monitor

One of the most common approaches is for both teachers to be in the classroom during instruction but for one of them to take primary responsibility for lecturing or presenting the lesson. The other teacher helps monitor performance of students and provides additional assistance to the students who need it. This approach does not require as much advanced planning as other approaches and is simple to implement. However, the teacher who circulates around the room can easily begin to feel like a "teacher's aide." One parent recently reported a situation in which her child came home from school saying they had a new "student teacher" in her room. In reality, the "student teacher" was the special education teacher who was co-teaching in the classroom. This remark is not provided to minimize the role of "student teachers" but to illustrate the point that both teachers might not be recognized as co-equals by the students and as such may not be equally effective in providing instruction. In order to minimize potential limitations of the Teach and Monitor approach to co-teaching, Cook and Friend (1994) suggest that teachers should alternate roles regularly.

Variations of this approach are "Speak and Chart" or "Speak and Add." With "Speak and Chart," one teacher lectures while the other writes the outline or notes on the chalkboard. With Speak and Add one teacher lectures while the other jumps in to add or clarify points from time to time. "Duet" might be considered a planned variation of Speak and Add, where each teacher takes a turn presenting portions of the material in a coordinated fashion. These co-teaching structures often become blended as the following example illustrates:

> *Lori and Mark decided to co-teach a lesson in American history. Their first step was to find time to develop a plan (no small matter!). At the first planning meeting Mark provided his lecture materials from past lessons. They reviewed the lecture outlines, student materials, and assignments. Then they discussed what could be eliminated or added to the original lecture. Although Lori was the assigned teacher for the course, they decided Mark should present the lecture since he had done it many times previously. However, Lori would be in the class and would feel free to add information whenever it seemed appropriate to help clarify a point. Then they decided to revise the student study materials. Lori felt some of it was inconsistent with material previously emphasized in the course. She recommended several changes and Mark thought of some other items that could be eliminated or*

added to help the students in the class who had learning difficulties. He then volunteered to make the revisions since he had the original study guides on his computer. Lori wanted to use cooperative learning techniques and felt they needed a summative experience that would require the students to demonstrate individual accountability. They discussed what the activity would be and Lori agreed to prepare it (a test).

The next week both teachers were in the classroom for the first day when Mark presented the lecture. Lori "jumped in" from time to time to clarify information. At one point she walked up to the chalkboard and drew a diagram to more clearly illustrate a point that seemed to be confusing to the students. The next day it was time to break into teams for team study in the cooperative learning format and Lori took over. She had already formed teams in the class. She instructed students to get into their teams, gave instructions for team activities and told how they could earn bonus points in teams. Once students were engaged in teamwork, both teachers "cruised" the classroom, stopping to help individuals or teams that needed it and providing positive reinforcement for team effort. The third day was time for individual accountability. Both teachers were present while students took the test. Mark closely monitored the students with learning disabilities. He noticed two students were having difficulty writing their answers. He pulled them aside one-by-one and let them dictate answers to him. Then he asked them to do an additional task while the rest of the class finished their tests. As students began finishing the test, Lori involved them in other activities in the center of the classroom while Mark continued to monitor the test-takers. The teachers divided the tests, each grading half. When the tests were graded, Lori recorded the scores in her grade book and Mark gave team rewards.

Parallel Teaching

A second form of co-teaching that is commonly practiced in inclusive schools is parallel teaching (NCERI, 1994). While both teachers co-plan a lesson, they split the class and each delivers the lesson to a smaller group at the same time. Parallel teaching might also involve parallel curriculum, that is, both teachers teach a similar topic but one teacher teaches it at a more advanced level than the other. For example, after having read a story to the entire class, one teacher takes the highest achievers and works on a dramatization of the story while the other teacher works with the other students on vocabulary meaning and retelling the story sequence.

Station Teaching

A third method of co-teaching is station teaching. This approach occurs when teachers co-plan instructional activities that are presented in "stations" or learning centers. While the teachers are stationed at some of the centers, others require independent work or involvement of peer teachers or para-educators. Each station presents a different aspect of the lesson and allows teachers to work with small groups of students. This way each teacher works with all students in the class as they rotate through the stations.

Team Teaching

This approach is sometimes used as a synonym for co-teaching. However, the NCERI study (1994) identified it as a model in which the special education teacher teams up with one or more special education teacher(s) to form a team. This team is responsible for all the children in a classroom or at a particular level. A variation of team teaching observed in an inclusive school involved ignoring the categorical labels for service of students. Instead, all students identified for special education services were assigned to special educators according to their age or grade level placement. The special educators, regardless of categorical specialization, were assigned to grade-level teams and assumed primary responsibility for all students with special needs at the assigned grade level. The special educators met weekly to discuss matters of concern. In addition, each special educator was a member of a grade level team and met regularly to discuss common issues with those team members. The special educators moved in and out of the classrooms at that grade level to co-teach as needed, to adapt materials, or sometimes to present a special lesson. The teaming processes to manage such a system are extensive. According to the teachers involved in the approach, it will not work unless there is *trust* among all the teachers and efficient *teaming* practices. The scenario at the beginning of this chapter provides an example of the system used for team meetings at this school.

Para-educators

Para-educators, often called *paraprofessionals,* play an important role in most inclusive schools. Sometimes para-educators are assigned full-time to assist students with multiple disabilities. They become the "hands," "feet," "eyes," or "ears" for these students. They go wherever the student goes—in the classroom, playground, or lunchroom. They help the student accomplish the tasks in the classroom and provide assistance in any way needed by the student.

Other para-educators serve more or less as co-teachers, although most do not become involved in the planning stages. The Teach and Monitor approach described above is the most common co-teaching model when para-educators are involved. Generally, the para-educator is the monitor all the time when this model is used.

Para-educators also assist teachers in preparing materials, especially adaptations for students with special needs. Para-educators can assume most of the duties of the professional educators but under the guidance of a professional educator. They are not responsible for diagnosing problems nor for planning interventions.

Teacher-Directed Instruction and Mastery Learning

Research has shown that teachers who are most effective in fostering student achievement engage in a number of common practices, many of which are critical for students with low achievement or disability (ERIC, 1987*a;* 1987*b;* Bickel and Bickel, 1986; Morsink, et al., 1986). Effective teachers will do the following:

Direct classroom learning by using structured materials and solicit high levels of academically focused, engaged learning time among students.

Use teaching activities centering on academic issues, with clear goals communicated to students.

Allocate sufficient time for instruction.

Provide extensive content coverage.

Monitor student performance continuously.

Provide many opportunities for correct responses to appropriate teacher questioning.

Provide immediate and academically oriented feedback to students.

Effective Lesson Structure

Research demonstrates that one set of effective teacher practices relates to lesson structure and another set addresses presentation of the lesson. Steps for developing an effective lesson structure, briefly stated, are (ERIC, 1987*b;* 1987*a*)

1. Gain the learner's attention. Use verbal prompts such as "look here" and "listen." Maintain 90 percent task engagement during teacher-directed activities.
2. Review relevant past learning. Teacher review, or correcting of homework, is recommended.
3. Communicate the goal of the lesson. Tell what is being learned and why it is important. Keep the goal statement brief.
4. Model the skill to be learned. Proceed in small steps that are not too difficult and give explicit verbal directions. Exaggerate steps to call attention to the critical features.
5. Prompt for correct response. Let students practice with many correct responses. Continue until very high levels of proficiency are demonstrated. The teacher should do each step as the students are doing it, providing modeling and verbal prompts.
6. Check for skill mastery. Students perform the behavior under teacher supervision without prompting. The teacher provides feedback after every trial and watches for many successful repetitions.
7. Close the lesson. Review the skill, discuss what will be in the next lesson, or introduce independent work.

Effective Presentation of the Lesson

The following presentation skills are summarized from ERIC documents which are in the public domain and can be obtained from Council for Exceptional Children (ERIC 1987a; ERIC 1987b):

1. Elicit frequent responses. Responses can be verbal or written, and can be in unison or given individually. Non-volunteers should be called on in most instances, to insure active involvement of all students.

2. Maintain an appropriate pace. A suitable pace is facilitated when teachers are well-prepared, elicit many responses, and move quickly to questions or teacher input.
3. Maintain student attention. Strategies that are helpful when attention wanes include soliciting more responses from students, moving closer to the student whose attention is lost, or gaining eye contact with students.
4. Monitor student responses and adjust instruction. Keep correct response rates to 80 to 90 percent. Immediately acknowledge correct answers and then move quickly to new input.
5. Ensure that all students have an equal chance to learn. Make sure all students are called on, not just those who volunteer. Use good eye contact with all students, and allow time for them to formulate answers.

Mastery learning and outcomes-based education also have been identified as important elements of instructional programs to foster achievement of low-achieving and at-risk students (Bloom, 1984; Guskey, 1988; Reisberg and Wolf, 1988; Slavin and Madden, 1989; Wang, 1987). The terms refer to the process of setting explicit learning objectives for students and measuring progress toward attainment of the objectives by using frequent Criterion-Referenced Tests. Students who have not achieved mastery of an objective are provided with reteaching and additional practice until mastery is met. This process is not new to special educators, who are required by law to use it in developing individual education programs. However, the procedures are now being advocated for use in general classrooms (Guskey, 1990).

Most special education consultants will have no difficulty working with classroom teachers in use of mastery learning techniques. When consultants are able to provide general education teachers with a set of procedures for mastery learning that is easily implemented using their existing curricula, teachers are more likely to overcome many of the negative attitudes toward low-achieving students (Reisberg and Wolf, 1988). (See Chapter 9 for further discussion of mastery learning techniques using Curriculum-Based Assessment.)

Peer-Assisted Strategies

Classroom teachers often feel the most limiting aspect of their charge is not having enough time to give students with disabilities the individual attention they need. The research about effective teaching identifies "academic engaged time" as highly related to the achievement (Rosenshine and Berliner, 1978). Jenkins and Jenkins (1985) state it this way, "If teachers desire to increase academic engaged time through one-to-one instruction, they must expand their reserve of instructional personnel. They need not look far. Some of the best helpers are other students who can be recruited from inside their own school" (Jenkins and Jenkins, 1985, p. 2).

Researchers have studied several ways of using peers to help one another learn. When one or a combination of these peer-assisted approaches is used, the teacher or consultant manages and monitors the performance of peers as they engage in learning together. Cooperative learning and peer tutoring are two of the most common ways of using peers to help one another learn.

Cooperative Learning

Cooperative learning methods have gained widespread attention for use in many classrooms. When used appropriately, the methods result in improved student achievement and improved social relationships at the same time (Johnson and Johnson, 1987; Lloyd et al., 1988; Madden and Slavin, 1983). The term *cooperative learning* has become associated with a variety of structured approaches that arrange classrooms so students study in heterogeneous groups to meet academic goals (Johnson and Johnson, 1987; Slavin, 1986). In most of the models, all students in the classroom are assigned to heterogeneous groups and, under the guidance of the teacher, help one another master content previously presented by the teacher. Students are held individually accountable for the content, with individual performance scores pooled to determine group rewards. Thus, all students are rewarded for helping, sharing, and working together.

When students with behavior problems are included in the classroom, special educators will need to closely monitor the experiences. It is possible that the classroom teacher will need assistance to teach social skills needed for successful cooperation, developing and posting class rules for cooperative learning such as those shown in Figure 10-1.

Resources for further reading about cooperative learning methods are listed at the end of this chapter. Special educators might need to participate in planning modifications so students with special needs can successfully participate in the cooperative learning activities. If a modification is made, teachers or consultants should make sure that these two elements are present (Slavin, 1990):

1. **Group goals or positive interdependence.** The members within a group must work together in order to earn recognition, grades, rewards, and other indicators of group success.
2. **Individual accountability.** All individuals within the group must demonstrate their learning in order for the group to experience success. This accountability could involve

---

Speak to Each Other

    1. Speak softly.

    2. Take turns talking.

    3. Limit talking to the subject of study.

    4. Look at the person speaking—be a good listener.

    5. Ask teammates for help before asking the teacher.

    6. Disagree agreeably.

Help Each Other

    7. Tell your teammates how to find answers when they need help, instead of telling answers.

    8. Encourage everyone on the team to do his or her best work.

    9. Make sure everyone on your team knows the material before you stop working together.

    10. Don't get yourself or another person off task—pay attention to the assigned work.

FIGURE 10-1   Class Rules For Cooperative Learning

individual test scores that are averaged for group recognition or a report in which each person contributes a specific portion. It should not be a single product without differentiated tasks.

Teaching Social Skills for Cooperation

Some authors (Dishon and O'Leary, 1990; Johnson and Johnson, 1987; Kagan, 1989) recommend direct instruction in the skills needed for cooperative behavior. This instruction probably will be necessary for many special education students and should be monitored closely by the teacher or consulting teacher. Supplemental instruction by the consulting teacher may be needed for children with serious emotional or social problems.

The social skills needed for cooperative learning range from basic skills, such as maintaining eye contact, to complex communication skills. Dishon and O'Leary (1989; 1990) identified the following essential social skills for cooperative learning:

> Task skills for helping the group reach its goals (Checks for understanding, contributes ideas, stays on task), and
>
> Maintenance skills to help build group feeling (Encourages and responds to ideas, and disagrees agreeably).

Suggestions for efficient teaching of social skills for cooperative learning are summarized from tips provided by Dishon and O'Leary (1989):

1. Discuss, describe, brainstorm one skill at a time.
2. Have students identify words and behaviors that might be seen or heard when they practice the skills. For example, prepare charts or transparencies that list what the behavior "looks like" or "sounds like".
3. Have students identify why the skill is important.
4. Observe the skills during team study and discuss them following study time.
5. Focus on the same skill until there is class mastery.
6. Focus on only three or four skills a year.
7. Before class begins, prepare observation forms with names of group members and the skill to be practiced.
8. Copy the forms onto transparencies for recording observations during team study.
9. Walk around class and record observations of social skills. Write down everything that demonstrates the skill.
10. Write only positive words or behaviors and do not identify which individuals or groups demonstrated the behaviors.
11. Give feedback to groups privately.
12. Select words or comments from anecdotal notes and add to the "looks like–sounds like" charts.
13. Post each group's observation form near their station.
14. Listen to and record for more than one group on each occasion.
15. Write a processing statement on the board or on worksheets. For example, write, "We did well on (skill) by (three behaviors)." Always include specific behaviors for students to identify in their responses.

16. Process only one skill during each lesson.

17. Process after each lesson.

18. Process for only five minutes, using a timer.

Addressing Special Problems during Cooperative Learning

Cooperative learning methods were developed for use in general education classrooms with little consideration for the special needs of students. It is possible that special educators will need to collaborate with general classroom teachers to make adaptations for individuals with special needs. When adaptations are made, consultants should be conscious to include the essential elements of effective cooperative learning lessons cited by Slavin (1986): (1) Rewards should be provided to teams rather than individuals; (2) each individual within a team must be held accountable for learning the material; and (3) individuals should have equal opportunities for success. For example, a consultant might suggest providing different material for a student with a learning problem to study with the help of teammates. However, the student's score, or improvement points, would be included in the team average. The team could be awarded bonus points for helping the disabled student. This type of adaptation would provide the individual with a learning problem the opportunity for success while assuring individual accountability and team rewards. A similar approach could be taken for a more able student who needs to be challenged.

Classroom teachers and consultants should engage in systematic problem-solving processes to address the needs of students who are not experiencing success in cooperative learning situations. (See Chapter 5 for more information about problem-solving processes.) Some examples of common problems that can occur during cooperative learning activities and possible solutions are listed in Figure 10-2.

Classwide Peer Tutoring

The Classwide Peer Tutoring approach is a highly structured variation of cooperative learning that involves principles of applied behavior analysis. This approach has been recommended for use with students having special educational needs (Delquadri et al., 1986). Instead of working in heterogeneous teams, students work in pairs in the classroom to monitor and provide feedback in academic tasks such as oral reading, reading comprehension, reading workbook practice, and practice with spelling word lists, math facts, and vocabulary word definitions. The approach requires specialized training in order to be implemented effectively.

Classwide Peer Tutoring is based on the principle of "opportunity to respond." When children are provided with systematic opportunities to respond, such as spelling words aloud, reading, or naming history facts, their achievement will increase. Parents, teachers, paraprofessionals, and peers who have used techniques based on the principle of opportunity to respond report significant gains in student achievement (Hall et al., 1982).

Peer Tutoring

Peer tutoring, including same-age and cross-age tutoring, is receiving renewed attention within the inclusion movement. Peer tutoring is more cost-effective than other tutoring

Learning Problems

Student cannot read and/or write the material.
> Have a teammate read material to the student.
> Have teammates read material aloud "round robin."
> Highlight main ideas and important information.

Student is hearing impaired.
> Have team work in area of room with most sound control.
> Seat student where lips of team members can be seen.
> Provide extra teacher prompting during team study.

Student is visually impaired.
> Provide more time to complete assignment.
> Seat student where team discussion can be heard easily.
> Reinforce efforts of team to explain information.

Student has difficulty making oral presentations.
> Have student write and a team member read the report.
> Allow student to preplan comments by assigning issue.
> Have student work closely with another to offer ideas.

Student cannot do any of the group work.
> Give different material to study and different quiz.
> Form teams by achievement levels (is hard to manage).
> Give direct teacher instruction to provide head start.

Parents of high ability students disapprove of the strategy.
> Meet with parents to explain cooperative learning.
> Stress universal need to learn cooperative strategies.
> Promote the concept of developing leadership skills.

Behavior Problems

Student cannot get along with other team members.
> Give team bonus points based on team cooperativeness.
> Move from team to team, reinforcing right behavior.
> Ignore the behavior (as team sometimes handles it well).

Student is ostracized by team members.
> Use improvement points to provide equal opportunity.
> Select the team for that student with care.
> Place a sympathetic person on that student's team.

Student refuses to become involved in team study.
> Use bonus points often to reinforce involvement.
> Make every effort to involve student in the group.
> Allow student to work alone, but keep door open.

Student is frequently absent or tardy.
> Upon return, have student complete assignment or quiz.
> Use late score for individual grade, but not team score.
> Give creativity bonus if team copes well with absence.

**FIGURE 10-2   Common Problems and Possible Solutions
During Cooperative Learning**

approaches such as the use of paraprofessionals, computer-assisted instruction, and reduced class size (Jenkins and Jenkins, 1985). The benefits of peer tutoring include improved achievement (for tutors as well as tutees), opportunities to learn responsibility, improved social skills, and enhanced self-esteem of tutors and tutees (Gerber and Kauffman, 1981; Scruggs and Richter, 1986).

Classroom teachers occasionally are reluctant to implement peer-tutoring programs despite obvious benefits, because they must spend time and effort in gaining successful results. Since time, energy, and resources for establishing effective peer tutoring programs are considerable, consulting teachers can collaborate with teachers to develop the programs. Peer tutoring programs can be building-wide or limited to one or a few classrooms.

Jenkins and Jenkins (1985) identified the following critical components of a successful peer tutoring program:

1. Provide highly structured lesson formats for tutors to use during the tutoring session, such as packaged programs with teacher instruction.
2. When possible, use content that correlates with the classroom content. Do not expect the tutor to teach material that has not already been presented by the teacher.
3. A mastery model of instruction is preferred because it provides satisfaction to tutor and tutee.
4. Schedule tutoring sessions frequently for moderate lengths of time (about one-half hour every day at the elementary level and daily one-hour sessions at the secondary level).
5. Provide tutor training and supervision, including feedback and reinforcement to tutors and classroom teachers.
6. Keep daily performance data on instructional objectives (as discussed in Chapter 9 concerning Curriculum-Based Assessment). Other types of information can include a daily assignment record, monthly calendar, diary, or log book.
7. Carefully select and pair tutors with learners. The most important selection criteria are individual characteristics such as dependability, responsibility, and sensitivity.

Consideration should be given to personalities and compatibility of the tutor and tutee, congruence of schedules, gender differences (not a critical issue, but perhaps pertinent at the secondary level), tutor knowledge of content to be tutored, interests, and eagerness to participate. More highly skilled tutors are often placed with more difficult-to-teach students (Jenkins and Jenkins, 1985).

One of the most important elements of a good peer-tutoring program is tutor training. The amount and type of training will vary depending on the ages and abilities of the tutors and learners. Training usually addresses topics such as information about the program, tutor responsibilities, measurement procedures, lesson structure, teaching procedures, and personal behavior. The training should include personal relationship skills such as responsive listening, conversing, and praising good effort as described in Chapter 6.

It is important that the tutors be instructed in specific procedures that have been experimentally validated to assure maximum learning and minimum frustration. A systematic, low response-cost set of tutoring procedures for oral reading, math facts, and spelling was validated with parents as tutors (Thurston and Dasta, 1990). The procedures are listed in Figure 10-3.

1. Select material to be used (book, flash cards . . .).
2. Sit in a quiet place.
3. Tell child what response is wanted. ("Let's read this story. Start here." "Read this problem and give the answer.")
4. Praise correct responses.
5. For errors or pauses, tell the answer and ask child to say the answer. Then ask the question again, or restate the problem. For oral reading, have the child go to the beginning of the sentence and reread.
6. Praise correct responses.
7. Enter results on a graph or chart.
8. End on a pleasant note.

FIGURE 10-3   Basic Tutoring Instructions

An example of peer tutoring at the high school level is the H.E.L.P. room in a midwestern high school. The program (Here to Encourage the Learning Process) was developed for students who had difficulties keeping up in general education classrooms, but who did not qualify for special education programs. Although a teacher and a paraprofessional staffed the program, peer tutoring was the principal methodology. Tutors were trained over a period of several weeks in communication skills, study skills, observation skills, writing of behavioral objectives, and tutoring skills.

Evaluations of the H.E.L.P. program show positive results. Parents report that their children are more interested in school, and teachers welcome the assistance. Students say they are less frustrated and more successful in the classroom (Thurston & Dover, 1990).

Student-Directed Approaches

Students with learning difficulties often show marked improvement in general education classrooms after they have been taught strategies for using information presented in the classroom. Many learning strategies resemble processes more commonly recognized as study skills. Some consultants and collaborators have taught learning strategies either in resource rooms or in general education classrooms. Once students learn to use more efficient strategies, it is usually possible for the consultant or collaborator to step back and assist the classroom teacher in monitoring and reinforcing student use of the strategies.

Strategies Intervention Model

The Strategies Intervention Model (Deshler and Schumaker, 1986) was designed to teach secondary-level students how to learn rather than to teach specific content. The learning strategies are techniques, principles, or rules that enable students to learn, solve problems, and complete tasks independently. For example, one strategy involves making several "passes" through a text, each time focusing on a different element and building a cumulative information base for helping retain the content. The strategy is useful for anyone but particularly helpful for slow readers.

The Strategies Intervention Model requires a set of instructional packets that provide materials and procedures needed by a teacher for training the students in use of the strategies. One strand of materials includes strategies that help students acquire information from written materials, such as Word Identification Strategy, Visual Imagery Strategy, Self-Questioning Strategy, Paraphrasing Strategy, and Multipass Strategy. A second strand includes strategies that enable students to identify and store important information, such as Listening and Note-Taking Strategy, First-Letter Mnemonic Strategy, and Paired-Associates Strategy. The third strand includes strategies for facilitating written expression and demonstrating competency, such as Sentence-Writing Strategy, Paragraph-Writing Strategy, Theme-Writing Strategy, Error-Monitoring Strategy, Assignment Completion Strategy, and Test-Taking Strategy.

Deshler and Schumaker (1986) stress the importance of deliberately teaching for generalization across settings. If the special education teacher is collaborating with the classroom teacher, this generalization process will be much more effective than other delivery options. Perhaps the special education teacher will teach the strategies in the resource room, but the regular classroom teacher will want to take over monitoring the generalization. The classroom teacher provides explicit cues that will help the student know when to use a particular strategy and gives periodic probes to determine whether or not the student continues to use the strategy.

> *Central to the entire generalization process just described are regular cooperative planning efforts between the resource and regular classroom teacher. Regular communication is essential to determine the degree to which the newly-acquired learning strategies are being used in the regular classroom. In addition, in such meetings classroom teachers can be encouraged to cue students to use the strategy at the appropriate time (Deshler and Schumaker, 1986, p. 586).*

The significant student gains in academic achievement reported by Deshler and Schumaker (1986) seem to correlate highly with the level of staff training. For more information about becoming certified to use the Strategies Intervention Model, contact:

Kansas Institute for Research in Learning
Department of Special Education
University of Kansas
Lawrence, Kansas 66045

Classroom Survival Skills

The essential strategies for success in elementary schools differ to some extent from those needed at the secondary level, although many strategies can be adapted to serve elementary-age students. Archer and Gleason (1989) provide a set of materials for teaching elementary and middle school students in grades three through six the skills needed for classroom success. The skills included in the materials are based on a survey of five hundred middle school teachers.

Skills for school survival identified by this teacher survey include

- school behaviors and organization skills such as before-class behaviors, during-class behaviors, organization of notebooks, keeping an assignment calendar, getting ready and completing homework, organizing assignments on papers, and organizing desks;
- learning strategies such as completing assignments with directions, memorizing and studying information, answering chapter questions, proofreading written assignments, previewing chapter content, reading expository chapters, taking notes on written material and lectures, and test-taking strategies;
- textbook reference skills such as using the table of contents, glossary, index, and reference lists;
- interpretation skills using graphs and tables; and
- reference skills such as using the dictionary and encyclopedia.

Self-Advocacy Skills

Special educators have long recognized that they cannot be present every time a student with a disability needs special accommodations in school, work, or at home. Students must learn to advocate for themselves. One of the best settings to begin learning these self-advocacy skills is in the inclusive classroom. When teachers collaborate, they can provide instruction for self-advocacy skills as part of other classroom activities. Collaborative plans can be developed to reward students with disabilities when they use appropriate self-advocacy skills. For example, a student with hearing difficulties might not hear all of the relevant material in a classroom discussion and so sit passively, saying nothing. However, if students are taught to assert themselves—for example, to tell other students they need to speak more slowly while facing them so they can understand what is being said—they will be developing a lifelong survival skill. When special educators and classroom teachers collaborate, self-advocacy behavior such as this can be encouraged and praised by the teacher present in the classroom at the time it occurs. Professionals must monitor their own behavior at all times, to make sure they do not advocate for students when students are capable of advocating for themselves.

When students with severe disabilities are included in general classrooms, para-educators are often assigned to assist them. While this assistance is appropriate and necessary, it has the potential of becoming a "self-advocacy barrier." All persons providing assistance for such students must be very cautious in this regard. Other students in the classroom can also become overprotective of an individual with disabilities. It might be wise to provide instructions for classmates about how to help individuals with disabilities develop self-advocacy skills.

Classroom Modifications

One frequently used technique for fostering academic achievement of very able students as well as students with disabilities is to modify general classroom settings or task demands. Ten general areas most amenable to classroom modification (Munson, 1987) are:

- instructional level,
- curricular content,
- instructional materials,
- format of directions and assignments,
- instructional strategies,
- teacher input mode,
- student response mode,
- individual instruction,
- test administration, and
- grading policies.

While classroom modifications may seem to be the most logical way of addressing special learning needs, the consultant should be aware that classroom teachers may resist suggestions for modifying their classrooms and curriculum (Ammer, 1984; Zigmond, Levin, and Laurie, 1985). Teachers seem to be most receptive to adapting the format of directions and assignments and making test modifications (Munson, 1987). Although they view instructional adaptation as desirable, most feel they are not able to do it (Ysseldyke, Thurlow, Wotruba and Nania, 1990). Classroom teachers might believe they do not know how to adapt instruction but the most plausible explanation is that they do not have time to do it. Consultants and collaborators must consider whether or not their suggestions for classroom modifications are reasonable and feasible for the situation. (See Chapter 6 for information about dealing with consultee resistance.)

Many of the resources available for helping teachers make classroom modifications represent the views of special educators rather than the collaborative views of classroom teachers and special education teachers. However, Figure 10-4 contains a list of modifications taken from materials prepared collaboratively by elementary classroom teachers and special education teachers (Munson, 1987; Riegel, 1981). The list is a helpful resource for sharing with classroom teachers during consultations.

Textbook Selection and Adaptation

Very few teachers use modified or adapted texts to accommodate the needs of mainstreamed students (Munson, 1987), although many would agree that most texts written for classroom use are not well suited to serve mainstreamed students with learning difficulties. The need for modified texts in mainstream classrooms was addressed by the Office of Special Education Programs in the U.S. Department of Education, which sponsored a series of projects to adapt widely used texts (Burnette, 1987). The adapted textbook materials are described in a document available from the Council for Exceptional Children. Tape-recorded textbooks can be used on occasion for blind and learning-disabled students. If the student qualifies, tape-recorded texts are available from

Recordings for the Blind
214 East 58th Street
New York, NY 10022

Instructional Level

Let student work at success rate level of about 80 percent.
Break task down into sequential steps.
Sequence the work with easiest problems first.
Base instruction on cognitive need (concrete, abstract).

Curricular Content

Select content that addresses student's interest.
Adapt content to student's future goals (job, college . . .)

Instructional Materials

Fold or line paper to help student with spatial problem.
Use graph paper or lined paper turned vertically.
Draw arrows on text or worksheet to show related ideas.
Highlight or colorcode on worksheets, texts, tests.
Mark the material that must be mastered.
Reduce the amount of material on a page.
Use a word processor for writing and editing.
Provide a calculator or computer to check work.
Tape reference materials to student's work area.
Have student follow text while listening to taped version.

Format of Directions and Assignments

Make instructions as brief as possible.
Introduce multiple long-term assignments in small steps.
Read written directions or assignments aloud.
Leave directions on chalkboard during study time.
Write cues at top of work page (noun =. . .).
Ask student to restate/paraphrase directions.
Have student complete first example with teacher prompt.
Provide folders for unfinished work and finished work.

Instructional Strategies

Use concrete objects to demonstrate concepts.
Provide outlines, semantic organizers, or webbings.
Use voice changes to stress points.
Point out relationships between ideas or concepts.
Repeat important information often.

Teacher Input Mode

Use multisensory approach for presenting materials.
Provide a written copy of material on chalkboard.
Demonstrate skills before student does seatwork.

Student Response Mode

Accept alternate forms of information sharing.
Allow taped or written report instead of oral.
Allow students to dictate information to another.
Allow oral report instead of written report.
Have student practice speaking to small group first.

Test Administration

Allow students to have sample tests to practice.
Teach test-taking skills.
Test orally.
Supply recognition items and not just total recall.
Allow take-home test.
Ask questions requiring short answers.

Grading Policies

Grade on pass/fail basis.
Grade on individual progress or effort.
Change the percentage required to pass.
Do not penalize for handwriting or spelling on tests.

Modifications of Classroom Environment

Seat students according to attention or sensory need.
Remove student from distractions.
Keep extra supplies on hand.

FIGURE 10-4 Suggestions for Classroom Modifications

Some consultants have arranged for volunteers to record textbooks on tape. If consultants and collaborators choose to have volunteer readers tape-record texts, they should instruct the readers to provide advance organizers for the student, to call attention to visual aids, charts, and graphs, and to periodically remind the student to review material just read. Other helpful hints for preparing tape-recorded texts are provided by Mercer and Mercer (1993).

Students with high ability also are served poorly by conventional textbooks. The Educational Products Information Exchange, a nonprofit educational consumer agency, revealed in 1980–81 that 60 percent of the fourth-graders in some of the school districts studied could achieve a score of 80 percent or higher on a test on the content of their math text before opening the books in September. Similar findings were reported for tenth-grade science texts and social studies texts (Reis and Renzulli, 1986). Efforts to locate more appropriate, challenging texts were met with discouraging reports from textbook publishers, who acknowledged that text difficulty had dropped two grade levels during the past decade. When concerned Californians tried to reserve room on the statewide adoption list for textbooks which could challenge the top one-third of students, no publisher had any to present (Kirst, 1982).

Part of the role and responsibility of consultants and consulting teachers is serving on textbook selection committees, in order to provide information that will increase the probability of selecting textbooks appropriate for students with special learning needs. Readability formulas (Fry, 1977) are often used by these committees, to determine whether or not students will be able to comprehend the texts. However, this practice has been questioned by some researchers (Armbruster and Anderson, 1988).

Readability formulas typically measure factors such as sentence complexity, word difficulty, or word length. But there are other, perhaps more important, factors to consider. The readability formulas do not take into account student characteristics such as background knowledge, motivation, interest or purpose, or characteristics of the text that research has shown to facilitate comprehension (Armbruster and Anderson, 1988).

Other elements to be noted when selecting textbooks are:

1. *Organization.*   The text should have a logical, easily identifiable organization using a clearly distinguishable outline; informative headings and sub-headings; format clues such as marginal notations, graphic aids or boldface italics, and signal words and phrases that designate particular patterns of organization.
2. *Coherence.*   The ideas in the text should stick together, as indicated by use of elements such as connectives or conjunctions, clear references, transition statements, chronological sequences that are easy to follow, and graphic aids clearly related to the text.
3. *Content.*   Content should be well-suited to the reader's level of knowledge and skills, as shown by factors such as building carefully on student's prior knowledge, providing substantive explanations of topics about which students are likely to know very little, providing the first sentence in a paragraph as a topic sentence, including preview or summary statements of main ideas, and highlighting main ideas by using underlining and boldface print or color cues (Armbruster and Anderson, 1988).

Modified Testing

Many students with learning and behavior problems have difficulty taking tests over subject matter they have learned. As a student progresses to higher grade levels, the ability to demonstrate knowledge through tests becomes more and more important. Many consultants at upper grade levels will need to give careful attention to the test-taking skills of mainstreamed students with learning and behavior difficulties.

When students have difficulty taking teacher-made tests in content subjects, consultants should give attention to a number of elements about the nature of the tests and ways to either help students take the tests as written, or collaborate with the teacher to make test adaptations. Lieberman (1984) suggests the first week of each school year, beginning at about the seventh-grade level, should be devoted to teaching study skills and test-taking strategies.

Other suggestions to consider when consulting with classroom teachers about alternative test construction and administration include

- Give frequent, timed mini-tests;
- Give practice tests;
- Have students test one another and discuss answers;
- Use alternative response forms (for example, multiple choice rather than essay);
- Back up the written tests with taped tests;
- Provide extra spacing between discussion or short-answer items;
- Underline key words in test directions as well as test items;
- Provide test-study guides featuring a variety of answer formats;
- Provide additional time for students who write slowly;
- Administer tests orally (Mercer and Mercer, 1993).

Curriculum-Based Assessment (CBA), discussed in Chapter 9, is an appropriate testing tool for use at any grade level. It has the most direct application in monitoring growth in basic skill areas such as reading, writing, and mathematics. Standardized test scores and commercially-made criterion-referenced tests usually do not give appropriate information to determine how the student is performing in a particular classroom or whether or not the modification was effective. The consultant or classroom teacher should take frequent measures using the actual materials or content from the classroom.

Teachers are likely to be more resistant to test modifications than to modifications of classroom materials. Likewise, even when they believe it is a good thing to do they are not very likely to make the modifications themselves (Gajria, Salend & Hemrick, 1994; Salend, 1994). Consultants can assist classroom teachers in:

- adapting their tests by adjusting the content to be directly related to the objectives of the class;
- changing the format so the items are easy to read, more space is allowed for discussion, or the order of items is rearranged to make them more predictable;
- rewriting directions or providing cues such as highlighting, underlining, and enlarging;
- providing prompts such as "Start here." or "Look at the sign on this row.";
- adjusting the readability level of the questions;
- providing outlines or advance organizers;
- providing spelling of difficult words; or
- allowing students to use outlines, webs or other visual organizers (Salend, 1994).

As teachers become proficient in using more authentic assessment procedures the need for test modification will lessen. Even then, some type of accommodation is likely to be needed for some students with disabilities.

Assigning Grades

Consultants will need to discuss with the teacher the matter of assigning grades based on modified curriculum or tests. Teachers often hesitate to adapt their grading methods because they fear the adjustments will lower academic standards, deviate from established policy, or become unfair to other students (Carpenter, 1985). Yet it is unfair to mainstreamed students if they are graded in the same manner as other students in the classroom. Grading is an essential part of the educational experience; therefore, eliminating grades for mainstreamed students is unrealistic.

Assigning grades to daily work is a way of providing feedback to students. Grade cards and transcripts communicate messages about the student's progress to parents, prospective employers, or other consumers, as well as to students. If grading policies are not clear, the grades may communicate inaccurately. For example, an interviewed parent said, "I have three children. One is gifted, one is average, and the third is mentally retarded. Which one do you think made the honor roll this quarter? The mentally retarded child! That's hard for me to understand and even harder for my other two children to understand." The mentally retarded child was being graded on progress toward the IEP goals, while the other two children were being graded on performance compared with other students in their classes. Grading policies in the school these three students attended were not made clear to teachers, parents, or students.

Grading policies can vary from one school to another. It is important that teachers, parents, administrators, and students consult and collaborate to establish clear guidelines.

> *In order to grade mainstreamed handicapped pupils fairly and without ambiguities, a fair and clear grading system for all pupils must be operating. If the basic system lacks merit, adjustments for handicapped pupils will suffer the same problem. Particularly where secondary pupils are concerned, educators must be vigilant so that the messages that are sent are clear, accurate, and meaningful (Carpenter, 1985, p. 58).*

Carpenter (1985) reviewed the literature addressing the assignment of grades for mainstreamed remedial and handicapped pupils and found many practical suggestions, including

> basing grades on progress toward IEP goals;
> using lowered grading standards;
> grading process and product separately;
> basing grades on contracts;
> weighting grades, based on difficulty of class or assignments; and
> considering effort in assigning grades.

Some teachers use pass/fail systems, mastery checklists, narrative reports, or a combination of these feedback mechanisms instead of grades. Carpenter (1985) made several recommendations based on a literature review:

1. The school should adopt a reasonable policy for assigning grades to pupils with disabilities. Deviations from standard grading practices should only be used when the pupil's disability is a mitigating factor.
2. When a pupil's disability interferes with learning and performance, a multicategory grading system should be used employing criterion-referenced and self-referenced

methods. Number or letter grades should be based on progress toward, or mastery of, clearly stated objectives. Pass/fail systems should not be used.

3. If the teachers wish to report more than one message, such as both progress and effort, two or more grades should be used.

4. Involve students in grading by including them in setting goals and predetermining how the students' performances will be evaluated in relation to progress toward the goals.

5. Grade frequently. Weekly grades should be considered a minimum time between grade reports to the student.

6. Supplement letter or number grades with narrative reports that invite two-way communication.

7. Consultation and collaboration between teachers is essential when instruction is shared. One purpose of the collaboration is to obtain a broader view of the pupil's overall performance.

8. Separate judgments about effort, attitude, and similar factors from the grading process. In most cases, a grade for effort is appropriate only when a specific objective to that end is clearly stated. For example, if a goal of working alone for twenty minutes has been stated, then progress toward that goal should be reported.

Curriculum Modifications for Very Able Students

Consultants who endeavor to enhance the academic achievement of all students in the classroom must not overlook the needs of very able students. Stimulating learning experiences for gifted students within the general classroom program cannot be provided without extensive modifications to curriculum content, tests, textbooks, and other learning resources.

Several strategies presented in this chapter as effective practices for mainstreamed students with learning and behavioral disorders are identified as less appropriate for gifted students (Schatz, 1990; Robinson, 1990). For example, mastery learning could be a promising approach for developing remarkable talent (Howley, Howley, and Pendarvis, 1986), but to ensure that this occurs it will be necessary to provide exemplary instruction and truly challenging enrichment. As another example, cooperative learning is an effective instructional strategy for a variety of reasons. However, it should not be justified for gifted students by inferring that they require remediation in social skills. Nor should it be used to make gifted students available as handy tutors (Robinson, 1990). While peer tutoring can be challenging and rewarding for the gifted student, it should not be used to set very able students up as surrogate teachers in lieu of modifying the curriculum appropriately for both tutor and tutee.

When gifted students are mainstreamed into general classrooms, as the majority are, their needs as well as the needs of students with learning problems must be considered when any strategy is employed for the entire classroom. These cautions and concerns underscore the need for intensive collaboration and consultation among gifted program facilitators, classroom teachers, and resource personnel, so that classroom modifications and resource adaptations help mainstreamed gifted students develop their learning potential.

Classroom Enrichment

Since most gifted children in elementary schools spend more time with their classroom teachers than with specially trained resource teachers (Gallagher, 1985), the general classroom curriculum should be enriched and adapted to meet their needs. Classroom teachers are responsible for a wide range of student needs and often do not have the time, resources, and facilities to challenge students who can function two, four, or more grade levels beyond their age peers. They want bright students to master the basic skills without falling victim to learning gaps that will impede their progress later. They feel the brunt of parent pressures to provide advanced opportunities, and they wince when their most able students describe lessons as "boring." Some do not feel prepared to teach children who may be as knowledgeable, or more so, in subjects than they.

VanTassel-Baska (1989) notes four mistaken beliefs that need to be overturned regarding educational programs for gifted students. First, consultants and consultees should not assume that differentiated curriculum must always be different from what all learners receive. Neither do all learning experiences need to be product oriented. One curriculum package or a single learning strategy will *not* provide all that is needed.

Acceleration of content for gifted students is *not* harmful as a general rule. VanTassel-Baska promotes a content-based, accelerative curriculum, which contains a process/product/research dimension for in-depth learning, and involves exploration of issues, themes, and ideas across curriculum areas. Activities that can be provided through collaborative efforts of consultants, teachers, family, and resource personnel include

- flexible pacing (appropriate acceleration in content);
- meaningful enrichment (not busywork or enrichment that is irrelevant to their strong abilities and interests);
- group activities (seminars, special classes); and
- individual arrangements (independent study, acquisition of skills in areas needed for pursuing major interests and talents, mentorships, and internships.)

Curriculum Compacting

Curriculum compacting (Renzulli and Reis, 1985) is a strategy that consulting teacher and classroom teacher can plan and implement productively for very able students. Just as teachers condense daily lessons and assignments for children returning to school after an absence, they can compact curriculum for students who learn more quickly and easily than the majority of students. This "buys time" for students to pursue individual interests and independent study in complex areas of regular or accelerated curriculum.

Gifted students need not always accelerate at a fast pace through the curriculum. On occasion they may welcome the opportunity to slow down and study a subject in depth and detail, catching up with the class by completing regular assignments on a compacted basis at a later date.

Some arrangements needed by gifted and talented students are accessible only outside the school setting. When students leave their school campus for enrichment or for accelerated coursework, independent study, internships, or mentorships, special educators and classroom teachers must assume responsibility for collaborating and communicating often, to ensure the students master basic skills and continue to be involved in the life of the school. A list of learning options and alternatives for gifted students is provided in Figure 10-5.

Assistive Technology and Technology-based Instruction

Technology provides another powerful way to help individuals with disabilities benefit from the inclusive classroom instruction. The uses of technology are changing at such a rapid pace that all educators must continually seek more information about its possibilities. Gardner (1994) observes that "What's 'new' in technology is not always what's hot off the production line—it's the discovery of new and creative ways teachers use technology to deliver instruction to students with disabilities through powerful and effective techniques!"

APPLICATION 10.1   Collaborative Assessment of a Student Product

When a student has completed a paper, an exhibit, a computer program, an art work, an invention, or other product, he or she might benefit from seeking the critique of that work by a significant other person. That person might be a content expert in the field, a school administrator, a former teacher, a school board member or other individual interested in the school and qualified to provide feedback on that product. The student could arrange for the critique with a "contract" stating the intent of the request. The process also might create a positive ripple effect for the school curriculum and increased interest by the resource person toward serving in an expanded capacity as an educational resource and consultant.

The following is one example of a contract but should be personalized to fit the student's age, subject area, and context of the request.

I, ___(student's name)___, would like for selected others to critique my ___(type of product)___ on ___(topic)___. I have proofread my work and I am presenting it neatly and clearly. The person(s) I have chosen to critique this work will be:_____
I am requesting:
_____ comments on merits and strengths of the work.
_____ suggestions for additions, deletions, revisions that could improve the work.
_____ comments on weaknesses, inaccuracies, improper procedures, overlooked resources.
_____ ideas for extension of the project.
I will be using your critique to:
_____ revise this work for ___(purpose)___.
_____ work more effectively on my next project.
_____ share with others who are interested in this topic and would value the information.

Thank you for your time and interest!
                    ___(student signature)___
                    ___(teacher(s) signature(s)___
                    ___(evaluator(s) signature(s)___

Exciting, challenging learning activities for gifted and talented students can be provided in the classroom. Collaborators can shop among these basic enrichment options when working together to plan alternatives for very able students.

- Allow students to test out of already-mastered material.
- Compact curriculum to "buy time" for enrichment activity.
- Acquire advanced texts and references for students to use.
- Allow students to study a subject longer than usual.
- Arrange cross-age tutoring between very able with similar interests and learning styles.
- Facilitate independent study.
- Encourage investigations by a small group of able students working as a team.
- Provide learning packs, modules, minicourses, and task cards on topics of interest to gifted students.
- Bring in resource speakers to discuss special issues.
- Cultivate and facilitate mentorships.
- Allow dual coursework for dual credit.
- Permit extended library or laboratory time.
- Schedule time each day for concentrated, uninterrupted work on a project or reflection on an idea.
- Conduct discussions about complex, appealing topics.
- Prepare resource files of community members who could help in the classroom or behind the scenes.
- Provide instruction to students on learning taxonomies and principles.
- Set up mini-seminars for groups of students who share similar interests and abilities.
- Use biographies of exemplary persons to model for and motivate students.
- Set aside an area where student research projects and creative products are showcased and discussed.
- Introduce the world's wisdom through use of quotes, credos, maxims, fables.
- Conduct problem-solving sessions, using real and hypothetical problems.
- Provide discussion time for moral dilemmas, logic, and ethics.
- Make career information and resource persons available.
- Encourage students to keep idea journals, sketchbooks, and idea files.
- Cultivate student self-assessment of learning habits and self-evaluation of learning products.
- Use feedback, grading, and reporting alternatives that do not penalize students for selecting harder curriculum.
- Seek outlets for displaying and publishing exemplary student work.
- Arrange for student participation in appropriate competitive activities.
- Provide instruction in "life tools" such as parliamentary procedure, orienteering, interviewing, research.
- Provide opportunities for developing global awareness.
- Arrange independent study or tutorial in a foreign language.
- Provide "how-to" books on various areas of human endeavor.
- Encourage students to read something from each subject area in the library.
- Recognize and respect unusual, creative questions and ideas.
- Provide liberal, in-depth critiques and comments on work.
- Use intrinsic rewards and appeals to reasoning as much as possible for reinforcement.

FIGURE 10-5 Appropriate Learning Programs for Gifted Students

(Gardner, 1994, p. 10). For example, Gardner (1994) describes ways to use a digital camera to enhance written and oral expression. Another report from the National ERIC Technical meeting reported in *CEC Today* (1994) involved developing a space simulation center.

Technology-based instruction can provide many options and alternatives for the learning programs of students with special needs. All teachers and students can expect to benefit from these learning enhancements, while those with special needs may respond to the particular innovations that deliver stronger representations of the world than traditional approaches to learning now provided. See Chapter 8 for a more extensive discussion of this topic.

Including Students Who Are Deaf or Hard-of-Hearing

Special considerations are necessary when students who are deaf or hard-of-hearing (D/HH) are included in general classroom settings with hearing peers (Afzali, 1994; Luetke-Stahlman, 1994). Children who rely on visual means of communication can be severely isolated at school when others cannot communicate directly with them (Luetke-Stahlman, 1994). All hearing adults and students in the classroom should receive daily sign classes so they can begin to communicate and interact with deaf or hard-of-hearing students. In addition, teachers and para-educators should be extremely sensitive to the student's need to see the lips of oral speakers in the classroom. Even when skilled interpreters are present in the classroom, it is difficult to keep track of speakers, especially when group discussions are taking place. Seating arrangements should be visually organized—for example, in a semicircle. Bright lights shining in the eyes of a D/HH student will also make it difficult to see the lips of the speakers clearly. Loud and obtrusive noises to indicate beginning or passing times for classes should be avoided. Visual safety devices should be present in all classrooms.

In addition, D/HH students need to attend some classes throughout the day with other D/HH students so they can communicate and socialize with one another. Educators must understand that D/HH students who do not require sign in informal situations such as on the playground may need the support services of an interpreter, or systems of oral speech or simultaneous communication during instruction in the classroom.

Support for D/HH students must include parents, siblings, interpreters along with teachers, speech therapists and administrators. These partners should be included in weekly sign classes. It is important to remember that the sign language interpreter is not a para-educator and should not be expected to function in the para-educator role. It is necessary for the interpreter to be available at all times to interpret relevant spoken utterances for the D/HH student. According to Luetke-Stahlman (1994), D/HH students need to be placed in classrooms where teachers are

- facilitative with regard to socialization opportunities;
- using activities such as cooperative learning, team teaching, peer coaching, and peer teaching;
- able to work well with educational interpreters;
- respectful of deaf culture and try to integrate deaf values, history, heroes, and other helpful topics into lessons;
- accepting of a D/HH student as one of the class;
- able to grade the student for more than attendance.

Related Services and Therapies in Inclusive Schools

Much of our discussion to this point has related to teachers' roles in inclusive schools, but roles of other service personnel must also change. When students need services such as physical therapy, occupational therapy, or speech therapy, a decision must be made about where to provide the service. In many inclusive schools the therapist takes the child apart from the group and provides the service directly in the classroom. This arrangement can cause considerable apprehension on the part of other teachers (Schlax, 1994). These fears can be reduced by making sure only one therapist at a time works with the child and by trying to integrate the therapies with the classroom routine. Whenever possible therapists should work with all the students in the class and not single out the individuals with disabilities. When therapies such as physical therapy or occupational therapy require space it might be possible to provide it in the classroom. However, the therapist might consider providing the therapy during recess in the gymnasium. It will also be beneficial if therapists coordinate their activities with a child. For example, Schlax (1994) reported that the physical therapist and occupational therapist assist one another by reinforcing common goals for a student whenever each is in the classroom. Speech therapists can often provide discrimination, language expression, or vocabulary lessons to an entire class of students. Many classroom teachers welcome such a partnership, which can occur as a normal part of the classroom routine such as during "show-and-tell." Support personnel are discussed further in Chapters 7 and 13.

Selecting Instructional Approaches

This chapter includes a menu of ideas and program options shown to be effective for encouraging academic achievement in classroom settings. Which should consultants and consultees select when collaborating to provide service for students with special needs? Any of them, of course, that will serve one student, or a group of students, well.

The options and alternatives should be tested against a number of practical considerations. Idol, West, and Lloyd (1988) suggest a decision-making framework based on the concept of Levels of Intensity of Intervention. The first dimension of the framework addresses the type(s), extent, and content of specialized instruction needed for each student. The second dimension examines the relative responsibilities of the classroom, remedial, and/or special education teacher for implementing the level of instructional modifications needed.

APPLICATION 10.2   Obtaining Resources for Curriculum Modifications

Write sources listed in this book to get more information about the strategies discussed in the chapter. Work with teachers to determine which of these strategies or skills are most needed by the students in your school. Develop a comprehensive plan for including them in a systematic way, and include plans for obtaining training in their use.

An intervention should address both the instructional needs of students with special needs and compatibility with current knowledge regarding effective instruction (Reisberg and Wolf, 1986). Interventions with the best chances for successful adoption by classroom teachers are direct, benefit other children in the classroom, make reasonable time demands on the teacher, and are easy to implement and maintain (Reisberg and Wolf, 1986). Several principles need to be considered when selecting interventions:

1. First, be sure the technique can be applied in the type of classroom organization where the application is needed. For example, individualized instruction where children are provided extensive one-on-one instruction by classroom teachers, as is often done in special education settings, is not stressed here because it is a difficult approach for an overburdened classroom teacher to implement effectively. One of the peer-assisted approaches may be much more appropriate when one-on-one instruction is needed.
2. Select strategies that are based on research demonstrating general classroom effectiveness. Information about some of the more promising research-based approaches is included in this chapter.
3. Give priority to techniques and strategies that do not require extensive reorganization of the classroom or special equipment and materials. The research on classroom modification convincingly argues for this point. Teachers are not likely to follow through on an idea if it requires too much that is incompatible with their normal organizational structure. Select the "least invasive" technique (Idol et al., 1988; Reisberg and Wolf, 1988) and, whenever possible, use the general classroom curriculum.
4. Give priority to ideas that are cost-effective. For example, the use of computers has great potential but might not be cost-effective if the school does not own enough computers. Some other possibilities, such as special books and materials, might also be prohibitive because of cost. Time and effort are other aspects of cost that should not be overlooked.
5. Choose techniques for which you feel competent or can gain the necessary competency. Many of the approaches such as cooperative learning, classwide peer tutoring, or learning strategies model, require extensive training beyond the information presented here.
6. Choose techniques and procedures the teacher feels competent to implement or can learn to implement in a reasonable amount of time. (Staff development for teachers will be discussed in Chapter 12.) Until a teacher has had training for use of the approaches, such techniques should not be looked upon as viable alternatives.
7. Choose approaches that can benefit many children in the classroom. Although the consultation may be precipitated by the needs of one particular student, there are likely to be several more students that could benefit from the same assistance. If the strategies selected can be used with several students at once, the effectiveness of the consultation efforts will be multiplied, and the need for consultation about other students and needs at a later time may be reduced. In addition, these interventions are more likely than other interventions to be accepted by classroom teachers (Reisberg and Wolf, 1988).
8. Be realistic. Consider all aspects of the classroom and select the best approaches for the situation at the particular time.

Tips for Consulting and Collaborating

1. The process of restructuring schools is painful. Begin with small steps and don't get discouraged with your first attempts.
2. Co-teaching *requires* co-planning. Co-planning time must be built into the restructured school day.
3. Co-teachers need to discuss their philosophies about teaching. (Content in Chapter 4 might be helpful for this purpose.)
4. When co-teaching, clarify classroom rules and procedures such as routines for leaving the room, discipline matters, and division of chores such as grading or making bulletin boards (Friend & Cook, 1992).
5. Devise a way to keep track of individuals who are providing services for students, so that monitoring does not become a problem.
6. Portfolios that are passed to the student's next teacher(s) can initiate collaborative consultation among all of a student's teachers and support personnel.
7. Keeping track of individuals to provide services to students can become a major problem. A helpful monitoring form that provides a record of individuals who work in the classrooms is presented in Chapter 8.
8. Time can become a major stumbling block and team members can easily get off the subject unless a structured team planning format is used.
9. Rather than just telling classroom teachers about materials modification, *show* them. Give examples or do one for them.
10. Request demonstration lessons from classroom teachers featuring *their* most outstanding teaching techniques.
11. Offer to retype a test for a teacher (to space, type in large print, or organize it differently) for use with a student who has a learning problem.
12. Before ordering computer software, have students try it out first. This gives them an opportunity to be consultants for teachers, and cultivates student ownership in educational planning and evaluation.
13. When preparing and distributing materials for classroom use, don't just drop them off and run. Help the teacher or student get started, and stay awhile to see how it goes.
14. Keep a supply of materials to send to classrooms for students who need reinforcement, even those with whom you don't work that could use the practice.
15. Have a favorite dozen of successful strategies available for demonstration teaching or sharing.
16. Have students assist in helping make up tests. It teaches them to focus on important things, and perhaps they will study more, too.
17. Compile a list of summer activities, programs, camps, and other opportunities for students. Send it along with the last communication of the year to teachers and/or parents.
18. Be understanding of classroom teachers' daily trials with some mainstreamed students. Celebrate with classroom teachers even the smallest progress by students.
19. When approaching a difficult discussion, sandwich the complaint in between two compliments. First practice saying something positive to a colleague who has been difficult or noncooperative toward consultation, and then *say* it to that person.

Chapter Review

1. Inclusive schools allow all students to work toward the same overall educational outcomes but at different levels or in different ways.

According to research conducted by the National Center on Educational Restructuring and Inclusion (NCERI), successful inclusion requires visionary leadership, collaboration among professionals in schools, use of more authentic assessment measures, systematic staff development, flexible planning time for teachers, changes in funding formulas, and more emphasis on parent involvement than previously.

2. Co-teaching involves two or more teachers planning and delivering instruction as co-equals within one educational setting to one group of students. There are various ways to engage in co-teaching, and all can be effective under certain circumstances.

3. Teachers who are skilled in using effective teacher-directed instruction practices and mastery learning approaches are helpful to students who risk school failure. Consultants and collaborators should be knowledgeable of effective instructional procedures in order to provide assistance and meaningful consultation. Skilled teachers and knowledgeable consultants make a powerful educational team.

4. Paraprofessionals or para-educators play an important role in inclusive schools.

5. Cooperative learning techniques and peer tutoring programs provide a means of extending one-on-one assistance so badly needed by low-achieving students. Improved social relationships are added benefits that accompany academic improvement for all students, both tutors and tutees. Consultants can provide valuable assistance to classroom teachers who wish to use one or both of these instructional approaches. Gifted learners have special needs. In order to develop their potential, they need compacted and accelerated content, appropriate enrichment, nurturant group activities, and opportunities for independent study and production. Many of the effective programs for gifted students require collaboration among teachers, institutions of higher education, and school districts or other community agencies.

   The techniques with potential for the most long-lasting benefit to students are those that help students develop learning strategies and study skills that are generalizable from one classroom setting to another. When special education teachers collaborate with general classroom teachers in teaching and monitoring student use of learning strategies and study skills, the benefits to student learning will be enhanced.

6. The most widely-used consultation approach to fostering student achievement in general classrooms is modification of tasks or setting variables to match student learning styles or other special needs. Consultants should develop a set of guidelines to help in selecting the classroom modifications and suggested techniques. Modified textbooks are not used often enough, although they are very much needed by mainstreamed students. Modified format of work and test modifications are more frequently used. Modifications that can benefit large groups and more children in the classroom usually are well received by teachers. Part of consultation should involve developing plans for testing and grading students with special learning needs. Modifying the test format and extending testing time are common practices. Assigning grades, however, is a problem for many teachers due to concern about fairness, school policy, or lowered academic standards. Consultants should be sensitive to these concerns and help develop grading policies that are fair and reasonable to all students.

   Special considerations are necessary when students who are deaf or hard-of-hearing (D/HH) are included with hearing peers. D/HH students need to attend some classes throughout the day with other D/HH students so they can communicate and socialize with one another. Support personnel, teachers, and family members need to be provided sign classes.

7. When consultants work collaboratively with others in planning, implementing, and evaluating programs and tactics to manage child behavior, all are winners—school personnel, parents, and most of all, students.

To Do and Think About

1. Practice using the different ways to co-teach with another teacher or peer. Make sure you give sufficient time to co-*planning*. After teaching, evaluate the processes and think about what you need to do to improve.
2. Interview a para-educator in an inclusive school setting to find out what types of tasks are required of the person each day.
3. Prepare a list of innovative teaching techniques that teachers in your school, or a hypothetical school, would be interested in using for students at risk. How might you share some of these techniques through consultation and collaboration?
4. Brainstorm possibilities for using collaborative consultation to enhance or modify an activity or lesson you have previously taught or from which you have learned. Talk over your ideas with others to expand and refine them.
5. Develop a plan for implementing a peer tutoring program that could be used in your school.
6. Select a real or hypothetical situation in which you would be consulting about a student with severe learning disabilities. Draft ideas that might come up for discussion regarding testing and grading. The ideas should be consistent with school policy, and fair and honest for the student.

For Further Reading

To obtain information about training in the use of procedures discussed in this chapter, contact the following sources.

On the topic of learning together:
David Johnson and Roger Johnson
Cooperative Learning Center
7208 Cornelia Drive
Edina, MN 55435

On the topic of student team learning:
Robert Slavin
Center for Research on Elementary and Middle Schools
Johns Hopkins University
3505 North Charles Street
Baltimore, MD 21218

On the topic of Classwide Peer Tutoring:
Joe Delquadri
Juniper Gardens Children's Project
1614 Washington Boulevard
Kansas City, KS, 66102

On the topic of classroom survival skills:
Skills for School Success
Curriculum Associates

5 Esquire Road
North Billerica, MA 01862-2589
Telephone: 1 (800) 225-0248

On adapting textbooks for special needs of students:
Adapting Instructional Materials for Mainstreamed Students, by Jane Burnette
Council for Exceptional Children
1920 Association Drive
Reston, VA 22091-1589

On instructional strategies to challenge gifted and talented students:
Instructional Strategies for Teaching the Gifted, by Jeanette Plauche Parker, 1989.
Allyn & Bacon
160 Gould Street
Needham Heights, MA 02194

On co-teaching:
The "House Plan" approach to collaborative teaching and consultation. *Teaching Exceptional Children, 23*(3): 6–10.

Chapter *11*

Family-Focused Home-School Collaboration

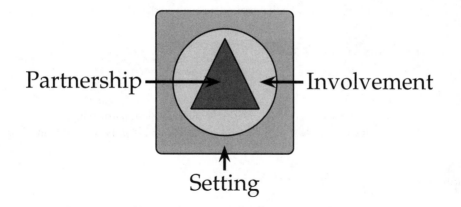

Partnership ——→ ←—— Involvement

↑
Setting

Introduction

Interacting with families of students who have special needs can be one of the most rewarding aspects of an educator's work. It can also be frustrating and discouraging at times. Whether families are supportive and cooperative, or antagonistic and uncooperative, educators must include them in planning, implementing, and evaluating the student's individual educational program.

Family involvement is mandated by federal law and state policy. However, the necessity for family involvement and support is much more than just meeting a mandate. Family members are the child's first and most influential educators. Up to 87 percent of a child's waking hours from birth to age 18 are spent under the control of the home environment, leaving only 13% of the time to be under supervision of schools (Bevevino, 1988). The family setting is critical to a student's performance in school.

While much of the responsibility for a child's learning has been turned over to schools in recent years, it is now time to cultivate home-school collaboration that will allow both school educators and parent educators to fulfill their commitments to develop each child's potential. Home-school partnerships provide students the best opportunity for overcoming risks and handicaps and becoming all that they can be in a complex, challenging world.

Focusing Questions

1. How does involvement by families in partnerships and collaboration with school personnel benefit students and their families?
2. What does family-focused collaboration require?
3. What are barriers to home-school collaboration?
4. How can educators examine their values and attitudes toward families?
5. How can educators build collaborative relationships with families?
6. How should educators initiate home-school interactions?
7. How should educators individualize parent involvement?
8. How can home-school collaboration be evaluated?

Key Terms in the Chapter

cultural competency

empowerment

equal partnership model

family-focused collaboration

home-school collaboration

parent involvement

home-school partnerships

Individual Family Service Plan (IFSP)

Mandates for Family Involvement

The Education for All Handicapped Children Act of 1975 (P.L. 94-142) prescribed several rights for families of children with disabilities. Succeeding amendments have extended those rights and responsibilities. The congressional intent was clearly to assure the educational partnership of home and school, not just to provide a rubber stamp of school decisions. Legislation mandating family involvement is part of P.L. 94-142, the Handicapped Children's Protection Act, Early Intervention for Infants and Toddlers (Part H of P. L. 99-457), and the Individuals with Disabilities Education Act (IDEA, P. L. 101-476).

The passage of P.L. 94-142 in 1975 guaranteed families the right to due process, prior notice and consent, access to records, and participation in decision-making. To these basic rights the 1986 Handicapped Children's Protection Act added collection of attorney's fees for parents who prevail in due process hearings or court suits.

The Early Intervention Amendment was part of the reauthorized and amended P.L. 94-142. Passed in 1986, it makes important provisions for children from birth through five years and their families. Part H addresses infants and toddlers with disabilities or who are at risk for developmental delays. Procedural safeguards for families are continued and the

---

Scenario

The setting is a junior high school. The learning disabilities itinerant teacher has just arrived at the building, hoping to make some contacts with classroom teachers before classes begin, when the principal walks out of her office briskly, with a harried look.

PRINCIPAL: Oh, I'm glad you're here. I believe Barry is part of your caseload this year, right? His mother is in my office. She's crying, and says that everybody's picking on her son.

LD CONSULTANT: What happened?

PRINCIPAL: He got into an argument with his English teacher yesterday, and she sent him to me. After he cooled down and we had a talk, it was time for classes to change, so I sent him on to his next class. But he skipped out. The secretary called and left word with the sitter to inform the mother about his absence. He must have really unloaded on her, because she's here, quite upset, and saying that the teachers do not care about her son and his problems. Could you join us for a talk?

LD CONSULTANT: O. K., sure. (Enters the principal's office and greets Barry's mother.)

MOTHER: I am just about at my wit's end. It has not been a good week at home, but we've made an effort to keep track of Barry's work. Now this problem with his English teacher has him refusing to come to school. Sometimes I feel that we are at cross purposes—us at home and you at school.

LD CONSULTANT: We certainly do not want this to happen. I would like to hear more about your concerns, and the problems Barry and his teachers are having. Is this a good time or may we arrange for one that is more convenient for you?

MOTHER: The sooner, the better. I don't want Barry missing school, but with the attitude he has right now, it wouldn't do him any good to be here.

LD CONSULTANT: Let's discuss some strategies we can work on. We are all concerned about Barry, and we need for him to know that.

---

additional right of participation in the Individualized Family Service Plan (IFSP) is added. The IFSP is developed by a multidisciplinary team with family members as active participants. Part B, Section 691, mandates service to all children with disabilities ages three to five, and permits noncategorical services. Children may be served according to the needs of their families, permitting a wide range of services including parent training. The legislation speaks of families in a broad sense, not just the mother-father pair as the family unit. Families' choices are considered in all decisions.

The 1990 amendments under P.L. 101-476 increase participation in the community by children and adults with disabilities and their families. An example is the formation of community transition councils with the active participation of parents in the groups. Subsequent court decisions and statutory amendments have clarified and strengthened parent rights (Martin, 1991).

Educational Rationale for Family Involvement

Strong home-school relationships support student development and learning (Hansen, Himes, & Meyer, 1990; Reynolds & Birch, 1988). Extensive research about the effects of family involvement demonstrates that involvement with the school by a student's family members enhances the student's chances for success in school (Epstein, 1989) and significantly improves student achievement (Henderson, 1987; Rich, 1987; Kroth and Scholl, 1978). Students improve in terms of both academic behavior and social behavior, with higher attendance rates and lower suspension rates. They have higher test scores, more positive attitudes toward school, and higher completion rates for homework (Christenson & Cleary, 1990).

Children are not the only beneficiaries of family involvement. Family members benefit from improved feelings of self-worth and self-satisfaction, and increased incentive to enhance the educational environment of the home (Murphy, 1981). They have the opportunity to learn skills that help with their child's needs, such as behavior management techniques and communication strategies. As parents work with teachers, they find ways of altering their own behaviors if necessary (Murphy, 1981). They perceive teachers as allies and a readily available source of help (Shea & Bauer, 1985).

Teachers also benefit from family involvement by learning more about their students' backgrounds. They receive support from family members who are valuable sources of information about their children's interests and needs.

School systems benefit from home-school collaboration through improved attitudes toward schools and advocacy for school programs. A positive home-school relationship helps others in the schools and the community. Family involvement increases positive communication among all who are involved on the education team. It augments opportunity for school program success (Shea & Bauer, 1985) and enhances school and community accountability for serving special needs (Turnbull, Turnbull, & Wheat, 1982). These points all provide strong evidence that "reaching the family is as important as reaching the child" (Rich, 1987a, p. 64).

Moving from Parent Involvement to Family-Focused Collaboration

Educational consultants and their colleagues must recognize the realities of today's families. Challenges today in working with families are very different from those faced a decade or two ago. Significant changes have taken place in society. New legislation and new demands for accountability for student outcomes coincide with the emergence of the new American family. In the last decade, there has been an increase in poverty, births to unwed adolescent parents, and rise of non-biological parents as primary caretakers (foster care, grandmothers, extended family, adoptive parents) (Ahlburg and DeVita, 1992; Skolnick, 1991). In addition, there are increasing numbers of families of cultural minority background. Families can include single parents, parents with disabilities, gay and lesbian parents, families in poverty, and extended families. The increase in ethnic diversity is expected to continue (Edelman, 1987; Harry, 1992).

Many families are overwhelmed by family crises and life events; many face multiple and prolonged stressors such as long work hours, illness and disability, and multiple responsibilities. Many are discouraged and burned out. Multiple cultures and languages, differences in perceptions of the role and value of education, multiple stressors, and economic and educational barriers will make collaboration a challenge for many consultants and many families. Educational legislation and social reality call for recognition of all types of families in school-home collaboration for positive educational outcomes for children. This inclusiveness gives educators the opportunity and flexibility to work collaboratively with persons who may be helpful and supportive of the child's success in school.

Broadened Conceptualization of Family

Changing times and changing families require new ideas, new languages, and new models. The first step in these changes is to think in terms of *family* rather than parent. Many children do not live with both parents, or, in many cases, with either biological parent. Part H and Section of 619 of IDEA refer to *families* rather than parents. A broad, inclusive definition of family should be used by consultants who are collaborating with adults responsible for the development and well-being of children with special needs. A new, inclusive definition of the family was suggested to the Office of Special Education and Rehabilitation Services (OSERS) by the Second Family Leadership Conference:

> *A family is a group of people who are important to each other and offer each other love and support, especially in times of crisis. In order to be sensitive to the wide range of life styles, living arrangements, and cultural variations that exist today, family...can no longer be limited to just parent/child relationships. Family involvement...must reach out to include mothers, fathers, grandparents, sisters, brothers, neighbors, and other persons who have important roles in the lives of people with disabilities (Family and Integration Resources, 1991, page 37).*

Beyond Involvement to Collaboration

It is possible for families to be involved in educational activities without being collaborative. Although the two terms—collaboration and involvement—have been used interchangeably in the literature, collaboration goes beyond involvement. Educators too often regard involvement as giving parents information, conducting parenting classes, and developing advocacy committees. However, this kind of involvement does not assure that parent needs and interests are being heard and understood. It does not signify that educators are setting program goals based on parent concerns and input. It might involve parents in a narrow sense but not in *working together* to form a home-school partnership.

It is important to distinguish between parent involvement and parent collaboration in this way:

- Parent involvement is parent participation in activities that are part of their children's education—for example, conferences, meetings, newsletters, tutoring, and volunteer services.

- Collaboration is the development and maintenance of positive, respectful, egalitarian relationships. It includes mutual problem-solving and shared decision-making.

James Comer (1989), at the Yale Child Study Center, reports a decline in student failure after contributions of parents and community members from diverse areas of expertise in the schools, and collaboration among parents and school personnel. Comer also documents improvement in the educational achievement of parents as well as their children (Morsink, Thomas, & Correa, 1991). Parent involvement *can* create possibilities for collaboration and development of relationships essential to student achievement (Christenson & Cleary, 1990).

Values for Home-School Collaboration

Collaboration with families adds a dimension to home-school relationships. Not only should family members be involved with schools, educators must be involved with families. Metaphorically speaking, a one-way street becomes a two-way boulevard to provide an easier road to "Success City" for students. Family-focused home-school collaboration is based on these principles:

- Families are a constant in children's lives and must be equal partners in all decisions affecting the child's educational program.
- Family involvement includes a wide range of family structures.
- Diversity and individual differences among people are to be valued and respected.
- All families have strengths and coping skills that can be identified and enhanced.
- Families are sources of wisdom and knowledge about their children.

Barriers to Collaboration with Parents

School consultants who are aware of potential barriers to home-school collaboration will be better prepared to use strategies that bridge the gap between home and school. Barriers include under-utilization factors, lack of organizational and cultural competence, and family historical, attitudinal, or perceptual factors. Figure 11-1 lists some possible reasons family members may not be involved with home-school collaboration.

Under-utilization of Services

A variety of family demographic factors indicate under-utilization of services provided for children with special needs. Research by Arcia and colleagues (Arcia, Keys, Gallagher, and Herrick, 1992) suggests that families of only 7 out of 100 young children would have no trouble accessing early intervention services. So 93 percent of families will have problems using services allowed by legislation. Analyzing the March, 1991 Current Population Survey, conducted by the U.S. Census Bureau, the researchers examined the distribution of poverty, maternal employment, ethnic minorities, large family size, low maternal education, and teen service under-utilization. Two of the three key factors were poverty and

- illness
- works and cannot leave job
- has little education
- is poor
- feels inadequate
- has no transportation
- cannot read or write
- does not think school is important
- is not assertive
- is single parent
- is burned out

- lives in rural area
- lives in inner city
- is depressed
- does not speak English
- does not trust teachers
- does not understand disability
- does not have a phone
- is from very young family
- is too busy
- fears being blamed
- comes from different culture

FIGURE 11-1   Possible Reasons for Non-involvement in Home-School Collaboration

(Adapted from PEATC, 1991b)

maternal employment. The researchers estimated that twice as many young minority children have at least three of the key factors when compared with the total population of infants and toddlers. These under-utilization factors may be considered barriers to effective collaboration between school and home.

Cultural Competence of Educators

Traditional approaches to reaching out to families are not always appropriate for families from minority groups. Research has demonstrated cultural differences in the utilization of services and the stated needs of families having children with disabilities or other risk factors (Arcia, Keyes, Gallagher, and Herrick, 1992; Sontag and Schacht, 1994). Educators must develop cultural competence (Lynch and Hanson, 1992; Mason, 1994; Anderson and Goldberg, 1991). Cultural competence means accepting, honoring and respecting cultural diversity and differences. Individualizing programs for students must be done in a manner that respects a family's culture. It is important to learn from family members how their beliefs and practices will affect programs for children with special needs. Some families may have culturally based or religiously based views of causes and treatment of disability. In some cultures, what American custom considers a disability or problem is not considered a disability or problem. Discussions of cultural competence and suggestions for developing cultural competence are found elsewhere in this book.

Historical, Attitudinal, and Perceptual Factors

The success of family collaboration activities is based on partnerships developed and maintained by using the relationship and communication skills described in Chapter 6. Parents of children with learning and behavior problems can be effective change agents for their children; therefore, the question is not whether to involve them, but how to do it (Shea & Bauer, 1985). Although family members may want very much to play a key role in encouraging their children to succeed in school, they may be inhibited by their own attitudes or circumstances. Many parents, while very concerned about their child's education, are fearful and suspicious of schools, teachers, and education in general (Hansen, Heimes, & Meier (1990). They may fear or mistrust school personnel because of their own negative experiences as students. Or they may have experienced an unfortunate history of unpleasant experiences with other professionals, with current school personnel falling heir to that history.

Parents of children with special needs face many economic and personal hardships. Work schedules and health concerns prevent some parents from participating in school activities (Leitch & Tangri, 1988). Low-income families may have difficulty with transportation and child care, making it difficult to attend meetings or to volunteer in school even when they would like to do so.

The single parent, already burdened with great responsibilities, is particularly stressed in parenting a child with special needs. The role can be overwhelming at times. When working with the single parent, school personnel will need to tailor their requests for conferences and home interventions, and to provide additional emotional support when needed (Conoley, 1989).

Many types of disability are very expensive for families, and the impact on the family budget created by the special needs of a child may produce new and formidable hardships. Sometimes families arrive at a point where they feel their other children are being neglected by all the attention to the special needs child. This adds to their frustration and stress. In addition, children with special needs and their families are vulnerable to stereotypes of society about physical, learning, or behavioral disabilities. They feel the impact of their family's dependence on others for services (Schulz, 1987). The ways in which families cope with the frustrations and stress influence their interaction with school personnel. Providing support networks can help them cope with the situation (Morsink, Thomas, & Correa, 1991).

Family members may avoid school interactions because they fear being blamed as the cause of their children's problems. Sometimes teachers do blame parents for exacerbating learning and behavior problems—"I can't do anything here at school because it gets undone when they go home!" But blaming does not facilitate development of mutually supportive relationships. Family members are very sensitive to blaming words and attitudes by school personnel.

Judging attitudes, stereotypes, false expectations, and basic differences in values also act as barriers to diminish the collaborative efforts among teachers and families. It is difficult to feel comfortable with people who have very different attitudes and values. Families and teachers should make every effort not to reproach each other but to work together as partners on the child's team. Educators, including teachers and parents, must abandon any posture of blaming or criticism and move on to collaboration and problem-solving. It is important to remember that it does not matter where a "fault" lies. What matters is who steps up to address the problem.

Collaboration requires respect, trust, and cooperation. However, as discussed in Chapter 4 on individual differences and Chapter 6 on rapport-building, collaboration need not require total agreement. Educators cope with value differences in positive ways when they:

1. Remember that a teacher's place is on the parent's side as a team member working for a common goal—the child's success.
2. Become aware of their own feelings of defensiveness. Taking a deep breath and putting the feelings aside will help them continue building positive relationships. If that is not possible, they should postpone interactions until the defensiveness can be handled.
3. Remember that the focus must be on the needs and interests of families and their children, not on their values. It is important to attack the problem, not the person.
4. Accept people as they are and stop wishing they were different. This applies to parents as well as to their children.
5. Remember that most families are doing the best they can. Parents do not wake up in the morning and decide, "I think today I will be a poor parent."
6. Respect parents' rights to have their own values and opinions. Different values do not mean better or poorer values. It is not possible to argue family members out of their values, and teachers do not have the right to do so.

Bridges to Successful Home-School Collaboration

Friendly, positive relationships and honest, respectful communication can help bridge the barriers in home-school collaboration. The goal of collaboration is to promote the education and development of children by strengthening and supporting families. Keeping this in mind, consultants will remember that collaboration is not the goal, but the means to the end. Strategies that have proved to be sturdy bridges to circumvent barriers are focusing on family strengths; using appropriate communication skills; and promoting positive roles for family members.

Focusing on Family Strengths

It is an unfortunate situation for collaborative consultants that the traditional emphasis in education, health, and mental health is the illness-based, or pathology-based, model of human problems (Berg, 1994; Leviton, Mueller, and Kauffman, 1992). The philosophy of family-focused services and collaboration emphasizes the empowerment approach, that is, recognizing, developing, and using whatever resources already exist in the family system. Instead of focusing on what an individual is doing wrong, the family-focused approach emphasizes what he or she is doing right and strengthens that capacity. Instead of focusing on the child's problem, collaborators focus on family members and the strength of their experiences. This encourages the developmental progress of the child as well as healthy reactions to problems and crises, and competent life management (Waters and Lawrence, 1993).

Using Appropriate Communication Skills

Chapter 6 describes communication skills that are important in building and maintaining collaborative relationships with adults in the lives of students with special needs. Consultants will want to use rapport-building skills to build trust and confidence in the collaborative relationship and to recognize and reduce their own language and communication barriers. Those who communicate with family members should use these guidelines:

- Be aware of voice tone and body language.
- Be honest and specific.
- Give one's point of view as information, not as the absolute truth.
- Be direct about what is wanted and expected.
- Do not monopolize the conversation.
- Listen at least as much as talk.
- Do not assume one's message is clear.
- Stay away from educational or psychological jargon.
- Attack the problem, not the person.
- Focus on positive or informational aspects of the problem.
- Have five positive contacts for every "negative" one.
- Always be honest, not soft-pedaling reality.

Promoting Positive Roles for Family Members

Family members play a range of roles from purveyor of knowledge about the child to advocacy and political action. No matter what role is undertaken by individual family members, educational consultants should remember that families are

- partners in setting goals and finding solutions;
- the best advocates and case managers for the child with special needs;
- individuals with initiative, strengths, and important experiences;
- the best information resource about the child, the family, and their culture.

Within any role along the wide continuum of family members, the consultant must respect and support the courage and commitment of family members to struggle with the challenges of daily living faced by all families. Recognizing, supporting, and reinforcing interventions with and on behalf of the child with special needs will promote an increased sense of competency and help create a safe, nurturing environment for children, while maintaining the unique cultural and ethnic characteristics of their family unit (Berg, 1994; Waters and Lawrence, 1993).

Supporting and reinforcing families in their chosen roles is not always easy. Members in multi-problem families often are viewed as having defective or faulty notions of parenting, no problem-solving skills, and an array of psychopathology (Berg, 1994). Even when families have different values and expectations, and face risk factors such as poverty or drug/alcohol involvement, Waters and Lawrence (1993) recommend that professionals focus on strengths. Educational consultants can think of this as the "hero" approach, which recognizes that slaying dragons is courageous. Noting what Joseph Campbell (1990) calls the courageous and natural engagement in the battles in life journeys will help educators recognize the heroic battle instead of counting dragon heads. Figure 11-2 lists other suggestions for developing bridges to overcome barriers in collaboration.

- Keep in mind that the family usually has concerns and issues that have nothing to do with you personally and that you may not know about.
- Be sensitive to the language levels, vocabularies, and background of the family and adjust your language, but be yourself.
- Get enough information, but not more than you need. You don't want to appear "nosy."
- Focus discussions on factors you can control.
- Find out what has been tried before—ask advice.
- Listen so that you are completely clear about the family's concerns.
- Honor confidentiality.
- Remain open to new approaches and suggestions. Each family is different.
- Set concrete, measurable goals. Communication is clearer and measures of success are built in.
- Wait until the family asks for help or until a good relationship is established before making suggestions.
- Help families solve their own problems and allow them to become, or develop the skills to become, their child's own case manager.

FIGURE 11-2   Suggestions for Building Bridges to Successful Home-School Collaboration

(Adapted from PEATC, 1991b)

Developing Home-School Partnerships

The crucial issues in successful learning are not between home *or* school, and parent *or* teacher, but the relationship between each pair of variables (Seeley, 1985). When school personnel collaborate with family members, they nurture and maintain partnerships that facilitate shared efforts to promote student achievement. The more that family members become partners with teachers and related services personnel, the smoother and more consistent the delivery of instruction to the student can be (Reynolds & Birch, 1988). As families and teachers plan together and implement plans of action, they find that working as a team is more effective than working alone (Shea & Bauer, 1985). Each can be more assured that the other is doing the best for the child (Stewart, 1978).

Five Steps for Collaborating with Families

Five basic steps will assist school personnel in developing successful home-school partnerships:

Step 1: Examining one's own values
Step 2: Building collaborative relationships
Step 3: Initiating home-school interactions
Step 4: Individualizing for parents
Step 5: Evaluating parent/school collaboration

Step 1: Examining Own Values

Value systems are individualistic and complex. They are the result of nature and the impact of experiences on nature. People need to apply information and logic to situations that present values different from their own. Kroth (1985) provides an example. He notes that a significant amount of research indicates a positive effect on children's academic and social growth when teachers use a daily or weekly report card system to communicate with parents or guardians. This information provides logical support for interaction among teachers and family members on a regular, planned basis. However, in spite of the evidence, many teachers do not use the system.

School personnel must guard against setting up a climate of unequal relationships. It is vital to recognize that parents are the experts when it comes to knowing about their children, no matter how many tests educators have administered to students, or how many hours they have observed students in the classroom. If professional educators are perceived as *the* experts, and the *only* experts, false expectations may create unrealistic pressure on them. Some family members find it difficult to relate to experts. So a beautiful "boulevard of progress" becomes a one-way street of judging, advising, and sending solutions. (Refer to communication roadblocks in Chapter 6.)

The first step in collaborating with families is to examine one's own values. Figure 11-3 is a checklist for examining values and attitudes toward parents and other family members.

Communicating messages of equality, flexibility, and a sharing attitude will facilitate effective home-school collaboration. The message that should be given to parents of students with special needs is, "I know a lot about this, and *you* know a lot about that. Let's put our information and ideas together to help the child."

The checklist in Figure 11-4 serves as a brief self-assessment to test congruency of attitudes and perceptions with the two-way family collaboration discussed earlier. Inventorying and adjusting of one's own attitudes and perceptions about parents are the hardest parts of consulting with them. Attitudes and perceptions about families and their roles in partnerships greatly influence implementation of the consulting process.

School personnel also must keep in mind that family members are not a homogeneous group; therefore, experiences with one family member cannot be generalized to all other parents and families. There is evidence that mothers and fathers react differently to their exceptional children (Levy-Shiff, 1986). Furthermore, parental stress seems to be related to the child's developmental age and parental coping strengths (Wikler, Wasow, & Hatfield, 1981).

Step 2: Building Collaborative Relationships

The second step in collaborating with families is building collaborative relationships. As emphasized in Chapter 6, basic communication and rapport-building skills are essential for establishing healthy, successful relationships with family members. To briefly review, these are the most important skills for educators in interacting with families:

- responsive listening;
- assertive responding; and
- mutual problem-solving.

Instructions: Rate belief or comfort level, from 1 (very comfortable or very strong) to 5 (very uncomfortable or not strong at all).

How comfortable do you feel with each?

_____ parents or others who are over protective

_____ teachers who think they are never wrong

_____ families who send their children to school without breakfast

_____ teachers who get emotional at conferences

_____ teachers who do not want mainstreamed students

_____ open discussions at parent meetings

_____ parents who have lost control of their children

_____ volunteers in the classroom

_____ conflict

_____ being invited to your students' homes

_____ using grades as a behavior management tool

_____ family members who call every day

_____ teachers who do not follow through

_____ students attending conferences

_____ principals attending conferences

_____ parents who do not allow their children to be tested

_____ different racial or ethnic groups

_____ family members who do not speak English

_____ others who think special needs children should be kept in self-contained classrooms

_____ teachers who think modifying curriculum materials or tests is watering down the lessons

_____ family members who drink excessively or use drugs

_____ administrators who do not know your name

_____ criticism

How strongly do you believe the following?

_____ Family members should be able to call you at home.

_____ Newsletters are an important communication tool.

_____ Family members should volunteer in the classroom.

_____ General classroom teachers can teach students with special needs.

_____ All children can learn.

_____ Family members should come to conferences.

_____ Resistance is normal and to be expected in educational settings.

_____ Children in divorced families have special problems.

_____ Family resistance is often justified.

_____ Teacher resistance is often justified.

_____ Family influence is more important than school influence.

_____ Medical treatment should never be withheld from children.

_____ Children with severe disabilities are part of a supreme being's plan.

_____ Sometimes consultants should just tell others the best thing to do.

_____ Consultants are advocates for children.

_____ Teachers should modify their classrooms for children with special needs.

_____ It is a teacher's fault when children fail.

_____ Consultants are experts in educating special needs children.

_____ Some people do not want children with special needs to succeed.

Do you think all teachers, administrators, counselors, psychologists, parents, grandparents, social workers, and students would have responded as you did? What happens when members of the same educator team have different views?

FIGURE 11-3   Examining Own Values

	Little				*Much*
1. I understand the importance of parent involvement.	1	2	3	4	5
2. I recognize the concerns parents may have about working with me.	1	2	3	4	5
3. I recognize that parents of students with special needs may have emotional and social needs I may not understand.	1	2	3	4	5
4. I recognize and respect the expertise of families.	1	2	3	4	5
5. I feel comfortable working with families whose values and attitudes differ from mine.	1	2	3	4	5
6. I am persistent and patient as I develop relationships with families.	1	2	3	4	5
7. I am comfortable with my skills for communicating with families.	1	2	3	4	5
8. I am realistic about the barriers for me in working with families.	1	2	3	4	5
9. I find it difficult to understand why some families have the attitudes they have.	1	2	3	4	5
10. I recognize that some family members will have problems interacting with me because of their experience with other teachers.	1	2	3	4	5

FIGURE 11-4   Self-Assessment of Attitudes and Perceptions Concerning Families and Family Collaboration

Prudent teachers avoid words and phrases that may give undesirable impressions of the children or the special needs with which they are concerned (Shea & Bauer, 1985). They listen for the messages given by parents and respond to their verbal and nonverbal cues, as discussed in Chapter 6.

In communicating with families, school personnel must avoid jargon that can be misunderstood or misinterpreted. Some professional educators seem unable, or unwilling, to use jargon-free language (Schuck, 1979). Choices of words can ease, or can inhibit, communication with parents, and professional educators must respect language variations created by differences in culture, education, occupation, age, and place of origin (Morsink, Thomas, and Correa, 1991).

Teachers and administrators often find that one of the most important but difficult aspects of developing relationships with parents is listening to them. The challenge lies in listening to parents' messages even though they might disagree strongly with the family members, and their attitudes and values might differ significantly from those of the families. Although the quality of the interaction should be a primary focus in parent relationships, the numbers and variety of initiated communications are important as well. Hughes and Ruhl (1987) found that most teachers averaged fewer than five parent contacts per week, but 27 percent averaged from 11–20 parent contacts per week. Phone calls, introductory and welcoming letters, newsletters, school-to-family calendars, and notepads with identifying logos all have been used effectively by educators to initiate partnerships. Each note, phone call, conversation, or conference, whether taking place in a formal setting or on the spur of the moment at the grocery store, should reflect willingness and commitment of school personnel to work with parents as they face immense responsibilities in providing for the special needs of their child.

An effective partner-educator provides support and reinforcement for family members in their family roles. In addition to listening to family members and recognizing their expertise, it is crucial to support parents by giving them positive feedback about their efforts toward the child's education. Many parents spend more time with their children who have disabilities than with those who do not (Cantwell, Baker, & Rutter, 1979). Parents often get very little reinforcement for parenting, particularly for the extra efforts they may expend in caring for children with special needs.

Too many families hear very few positive comments about their children. They may feel guilty or confused because of their children's problems. Examples of support and reinforcement that teachers use include thank-you notes for helping with field trips, VIP (Very Important Parent) buttons given to classroom volunteers, supporting phone calls when homework has been turned in, and Happygrams when a class project is completed. It is important for teachers to arrange and encourage more regular, informal contacts with parents. Parents often report being put off by the formality inherent in some scheduled conferences, particularly when they are limited to 10 minutes, as they often are, with another child's parents waiting just outside (Lindle, 1989).

One innovative program is the Trans*Parent* Model (Bauch, 1989) in which teachers use a computer-based system called Compu-Call that stores messages in a computer. It directs the autodialer to place calls either to all parents or to specific groups of parents. The purpose of these calls can be to describe learning activities, explain homework assignments, or suggest ways that parents can support the child's home study. Parents call any time from anywhere and get the information they need. The system enables parents to help children keep up who are having problems or have an extended absence from school.

Family members often become frustrated when they do not understand the subjects their children are attempting to master. A program of Family Math encourages parents and children to work together as a team in evening sessions involving a "hands-on" approach to learning math concepts and logical thinking (Lueder, 1989). Family literacy programs that are established in some communities enable parents to help children with their school work (Nuckolls, 1991). Some schools have set up an evening computer literacy program in which parents and students can learn together and reinforce each other as they gain skills in educational technology.

Parents are not the only ones who put energy and time into such programs. The programs require a level of school personnel involvement that challenges the staff and pushes them to the limit. But the positive ripple effect of having family members play more active roles in their child's education makes the effort worthwhile.

Step 3: Initiating Home-School Interactions

Parents, regardless of their educational background and socio-economic status, want their children to be successful in school (Epstein, 1987). Even parents who are considered "hard to reach," such as non-traditional, low-income, and low status families, usually want to be more involved (Davies, 1988). Most parents, however, wait to be invited before becoming involved as a partner in their child's education. Unfortunately, many family members have to wait for years before someone opens the door and provides them the *opportunity* to become a team member with others who care about the educational and social successes of their children. Parent satisfaction with their involvement is directly related to perceived opportunities for involvement (Salisbury & Evans, 1988). They are more motivated to carry on when they are aware that the results of their time and energy are helping their child learn.

School personnel who are in a position to observe these results can provide the kind of reinforcement that parents need so much.

Student Collaboration.   The child has the greatest investment and the most important involvement in a planning conference (Hogan, 1975). It seems counterproductive to engage in plan sessions for the child's development without involving him or her as a member of the team. Shea and Bauer (1985) stress several benefits from having students participate in conferences for their individualized programs:

- Awareness that parents and teachers are interested in them and working cooperatively;
- Information by teachers and family members to evaluate their progress;
- Feeling of involvement in the efforts toward personal achievement;
- A task-oriented view of improving their performance.

Shea and Bauer recommend discussing advantages of the child's participation with parents and encouraging their support but not including the child if there are strenuous parental objections.

Equal Partnership Model.   Family-focused collaboration emphasizes the importance of recognizing strengths that family members have to contribute along with their needs regarding their exceptional children. Family members have a range of strengths, as discussed earlier, and a range of needs. Kroth (1985) suggests a four-tiered model representing a continuum for strengths and needs. There are strengths that all parents have, such as expertise about the child, and needs that all parents have, such as information related to services for their children. Most families spend time with their children and have information related to school functions. Some families volunteer or participate in home tutoring and parent support groups, but probably no more than a few families participate in leadership for political action and fund raising, or parent training or therapy.

Planning workshops, booklets, and classes without assessing parent interest in such activities communicates a message that educators know more about their needs than they do, and parent involvement is not a true partnership. An example of a needs and interests assessment is included in Figure 11-5. Schoor (1988) notes that in a study of 25 successful intervention programs, all were facilitated by professionals who responded to the needs of those they served rather than to the perceptions and demands of professional educators and bureaucrats.

The equal partnership model stresses the importance of providing opportunities for family members to use their strengths and utilize their commitment and skills to contribute as full partners to the education of their children. This relationship is not based on a deficit model of blame and inequality. Families appreciate having their special efforts recognized, just as teachers do.

Tools for assessing parent strengths are similar to those used for assessing needs. Interviews and checklists are useful in determining what types of contributions families can bring to the partnership. Again, these assets can be conceptualized along four levels of involvement, from strengths which all family members have, to skills that only a few family

Families! We want to learn more about you so that we can work together helping your child learn. Please take a few minutes to respond to these questions so your voice can be heard. It will help the Home-School Advisory Team develop programs for families, teachers, and children.

Check those items you are most interested in.

_____ 1. Family resource libraries or information centers

_____ 2. Helping my child learn

_____ 3. Support programs for my child's siblings

_____ 4. Talking with my child about sex

_____ 5. Helping with language and social skills

_____ 6. Mental health services

_____ 7. Talking with another parent about common problems

_____ 8. Respite care or babysitters

_____ 9. My role as a parent

_____ 10. Classes about managing behavior problems

_____ 11. Making my child happy

_____ 12. Managing my time and resources

_____ 13. Making toys and educational materials

_____ 14. Reducing time spent watching television

_____ 15. What happens when my child grows up

_____ 16. Recreation and camps for my child

_____ 17. State-wide meetings for families

_____ 18. Vocational opportunities for my child

_____ 19. Talking to my child's teacher

_____ 20. Talking with other families

_____ 21. Learning about child development

_____ 22. Things families can do to support teachers

_____ 23. Home activities that support school learning

_____ 24. Information about the school and my child's classes

_____ 25. Helping my child become more independent

_____ 26. Others?

_____

_____

_____

Thanks for your help!

Name of family member responding to this form:

_____

Child's name: _____

FIGURE 11-5   Family Needs Assessment

members are willing and able to contribute. For example, all parents have information about their children that schools need. At more intensive levels of collaboration, some family members are willing and able to tutor their children at home, come to meetings, help make bulletin boards, and volunteer to help at school. At highest levels of collaboration, only a few parents can be expected to lobby for special education, serve on advisory boards, or conduct parent-to-parent programs. A number of parent advocates of children with learning and behavior disorders have made impressive gains in recent decades toward state and national focus on the rights of children with special needs. They have formed organizations, identified needs, encouraged legislation, spoken for improved facilities, and supported each other through crises. In many instances they have involved pediatricians, community agency leaders, and businesses in special projects for children with special needs.

Sometimes school personnel involve family members without being collaborative. As stated earlier, involvement is not synonymous with collaboration. Developing a workshop on discipline or a volunteer program without assessing strengths, needs, and goals demonstrates a failure to respect the partnership between school and home. A true partnership will feature mutual collaboration and show respect for the expertise of both parties in the partnership. By considering family member strengths as well as needs and interests, educators will be focusing on the collaborative nature of parent involvement. An example of a strengths assessment form is provided in Figure 11-6.

Family Involvement in IEP Planning.   The Individual Education Plan (IEP) or Individual Transition Planning (ITP) conference can be a productive time or a frustrating experience. Parents may be emotional about their child's problems, and teachers might be apprehensive about meeting with the parents (Reynolds & Birch, 1988). A number of researchers have found that minimal parent involvement in team decision-making, particularly related to IEP and ITP development, is a major problem in special education programs (Pfeiffer, 1980; Boone, 1989).

School consultants will improve school-home collaboration in these areas if they provide family members with information and preparation for the meeting. Consultants can communicate with family members by phone, letter, or informal interview to inform them about

- Names and roles of staff members who will attend;
- Typical procedure for such meetings;
- Ways they can prepare for the meeting;
- Contributions they are encouraged to make;
- Ways in which follow-up to the meeting will be provided.

Figure 11-7 outlines ways parents can be involved in IEP, ITP, or IFSP development and implementation before, during, and after the IEP conference. The lists could be used for conferences or meetings with them.

Step 4: Individualizing for Families

Special education professionals are trained to be competent at individualizing educational programs for student needs. Nevertheless, they may assume that all parents have the same

Families! We need your help. Many of you have asked how you can help provide a high-quality educational program for your children. You have many talents, interests, and skills you can contribute to help children learn better and enjoy school more. Please let us know what you are interested in doing.

_____ 1. I would like to volunteer to help in school.

_____ 2. I would like to help with special events or projects.

_____ 3. I have a hobby or talent I could share with the class.

_____ 4. I would be glad to talk about travel or jobs, or interesting experiences I have had.

_____ 5. I could teach the class how to _____.

_____ 6. I could help with bulletin boards and art projects.

_____ 7. I could read to children.

_____ 8. I would like to help my child at home.

_____ 9. I would like to tutor a child.

_____ 10. I would like to work on a buddy or parent-to-parent system with other parents whose children have problems.

_____ 11. I would like to teach a workshop.

_____ 12. I can do typing, word-processing, phoning, making materials, or preparing resources at home.

_____ 13. I would like to assist with student clubs.

_____ 14. I would like to help organize a parent group.

_____ 15. I want to help organize and plan parent partnership programs.

_____ 16. I would like to help with these kinds of activities:

At school _____

At home _____

In the community _____

Your comments, concerns, and questions are welcomed.

THANKS!

Name: _____

Child's Name: _____

How to Reach You: _____

FIGURE 11-6   Strengths Assessment for Family Members

strengths and needs, thereby overlooking the need to individualize parent involvement programs (Schultz, 1987; Turnbull & Turnbull, 1982). By using the assessments discussed earlier, and taking care to avoid stereotypes and judgments, they will be more able to involve parents in individualizing their child's learning program.

Christensen and Cleary (1990) confirm that successful home-school consultation includes mutual problem identification, mutual monitoring of effects of involvement, and active sharing of relevant information. Successful work with parents calls for establishing respectful and trusting relationships, as well as responding to needs of all partners. The degree to which parents are placed in an egalitarian role, with a sense of choice, empowerment, and ownership in the education process, is a crucial variable in successful collaboration (Cochran, 1987; Peterson & Cooper, 1989).

Throughout the year family members can:

Read about local, state, and national educational issues and concerns.

Learn about the structure of the local school system.

Observe their child, noting in particular the child's work habits, play patterns, and social interactions.

Record information regarding special interests, talents, and accomplishments, as well as areas of concern.

Before the IEP conference family members can:

Visit the child's school.

Discuss school life with the child.

Talk with other parents who have participated in conferences to find out what goes on during the conference.

Write down questions and points they would like to address.

Review notes from any previous conferences or other meetings with school staff.

Prepare a summary file of information, observations, and products that would further explain the child's needs.

Arrange to take along any other persons that they feel would be helpful in planning the child's educational program.

During the IEP conference family members can:

Be an active participant.

Ask questions about anything that is unclear.

Insist that educational jargon and "alphabet soup" acronyms not be used.

Contribute information, ideas, and recommendations.

Let the school personnel know about the positive things school has provided for the child.

Ask for a copy of the IEP or other plan made, if it is not offered.

Ask to have a follow-up contact time to compare notes about the child's progress.

After the IEP conference family members can:

Discuss the conference proceedings with the child.

Continue to monitor the child's progress and follow up as agreed on.

Continue to reinforce school staff for positive effects of the planned program.

Keep adding to the notebook of information, observations, and products.

Serve as an active participant in efforts to improve schools.

Say supportive things about the schools whenever possible.

FIGURE 11-7   Checklist for Family Members for Developing IEPs

When school consultants and collaborators solicit information from parents, they should use the communication skills discussed in Chapter 6. Interviews must not seem like interrogations. The types of questions consultants ask are important in preserving respectful relationships. Inappropriate types of questions would be yes-or-no questions, "why" questions, forced-choice questions, double-binds that result in no-win responses, and questions that solicit agreement with the educator.

On the other hand, questions that are appropriate for parent interviews explore feelings and focus on the what, when, where, and how dimensions of child learning and behavior. Only questions that provide essential information and nurture the collaborative spirit should be asked. Figure 11-8 demonstrates inappropriate questions that have been restated in a more appropriate manner.

Families From Culturally Diverse Populations.   At times the consultant's communication and collaboration skills are challenged by ethnic and differences. Language and cultural differences can be barriers that must be overcome by understanding the knowledge and skills needed to provide "culturally competent services" (Cross, 1988).

Lynch and Hansen (1992), Huff and Telesford (1994), and Cross (1988) suggest that school personnel use these strategies when collaborating with families from diverse cultural groups:

1. Acknowledge cultural differences and become aware of how they affect parent-teacher interactions.

Appropriate	*Inappropriate*
I'd like to hear your thoughts on Ramona's progress.	I think Ramona is doing much better, don't you?
What problems do you have with Jim's teacher?	Why don't you like Jim's teacher?
What thoughts have you had about you and Kay talking with a counselor?	When are you and Kay going to see a counselor?
What are some strategies we can work on to make sure Sherry gets to her first hour class?	Don't you think you should curtail Sherry's late nights on weekdays?
What is the history of Lionel's hearing problems?	Didn't you take Lionel to the doctor about his persistent earaches?
What kinds of concerns do you have?	Do you have any questions?
What are the behaviors that you worry about? What does the scene look like when it happens?	What do you mean, he is always in trouble?

FIGURE 11-8   Appropriate/Inappropriate Questions to Ask Parents

2. Examine one's own personal culture, such as how one defines family, desirable life goals, and behavior problems.
3. Recognize the dynamics of group interactions such as etiquette and patterns of communication.
4. Explore the significance of the child's behavior in relationship to his or her culture.
5. Adjust collaboration to include culturally specific activities.
6. Learn about the families. Where are they from and when did they arrive? What cultural beliefs and practices surround child-rearing, health and healing, and disability and causation?
7. Recognize that some families may be surprised by the extent of home-school collaboration expected in the United States.
8. Learn and use words and forms of greetings in the families' languages.
9. Work with cultural mediators or guides from the families' cultures to learn more about the culture and facilitate communication between school and home. Examples are: relative, church member, neighbor, or older sibling.
10. Ask for help in structuring the child's school program to match her or his home life, such as learning key words and phrases used at home.

Well-publicized policies at the district level encouraging home-school collaboration are vital in providing opportunities for minority family members to become full partners with teachers, but effective structures and strategies often do not exist (Chavkin, 1989; Lynch & Stein, 1987). Lightfoot (1981) suggests that traditional methods of parent involvement such as Parent Teacher Association (PTA) meetings, open house or newsletters permit little or no true collaboration, constructing instead a "territory" of education which minority parents are hesitant to invade. Concern, awareness, and commitment on the part of individuals in the educational system are a beginning in collaboration between teachers and families who have language, cultural, or other basic differences.

Step 5: Evaluating Home-School Collaboration

Evaluation of efforts to provide opportunities for collaboration in schools can indicate whether families' needs are being met and family strengths are being utilized. Evaluation also shows whether needs and strengths of educational personnel are being met. Assessment tools used after a workshop, conference, or at the conclusion of the school year allow school personnel to ask parents, "How did we do in facilitating your learning of the new information, or accessing the new services?" Some teachers use a quick questionnaire, to be completed anonymously, to see whether the activity or program fulfilled the goals of the home-school collaboration. If the data show that the activity gave families the information they needed, provided them with the resources they wanted, and offered them the opportunities they requested, educators know whether to continue with the program, offer the activity again, or modify the plans.

Educators also should evaluate their own involvement with families. This means assessing the use of family strengths and skills to facilitate educational programs with children who have special needs. Did teachers get the information they needed from families? How many volunteer hours did parents contribute? What were the results of home tutoring upon the achievement of the resource room students? What changes in family attitudes about the school district were measured? Chapter 9 contains information about procedures for evaluating collaboration efforts. Note again that the purpose of parent collaboration is to utilize the unique and vital partnership on behalf of their children. (See Figure 11-9.)

In proposing guidelines for interagency collaboration, Melaville and Blank (1991) have several useful suggestions for successful home-school collaboration:

- Involve all key players.
- Choose a realistic plan or strategy.
- Establish a shared vision.
- Agree to disagree on some issues and processes.
- Make promises you can keep.
- Keep your "eyes on the prize."
- Build ownership for all individuals and units.
- Avoid technical difficulties (language problems, getting hung up on paperwork or details).
- Share the success.

Home-school collaboration is mandated, it is challenging, and it is rewarding. Students, schools, and families are strengthened with appropriate outreach efforts and partnership activities when they are based on the values and practices of the family-focused approach.

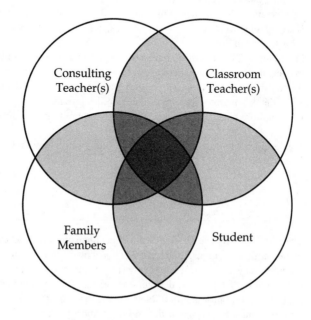

FIGURE 11-9 Interaction in Home-School Collaboration

Tips for Consulting and Collaborating

1. Establish rapport with families early in the year. Call right away, before problems develop, so that the first family contact is a positive one.
2. Invite families to school to talk about their traditions, experiences, hobbies, or occupations.
3. Send home "up slips" as opposed to "down slips." Have a parent conference because the student is *performing well* in the classroom.
4. When sharing information with families, "sandwich" any necessary comments about problems or deficits between two very positive ones.
5. During interaction with families, notice how your actions are received, and adapt to that.
6. When interacting with families, never assume anything.
7. When several staff members will be meeting with family members, make sure each one's role and purpose for being included in the meeting are understood by the parents.
8. Introduce families to all support personnel working with the child.
9. Some family members shy away from being handed sample work, preferring to have the work laid out on a surface to view without forced attention. Do not continue talking when they are reading their child's work.
10. Send out monthly newsletters describing the kinds of things the class is doing, and school news or events coming up. Attach articles families would be interested in. Have a "Family Corner" occasionally, for which families provide comments or ideas.
11. Encourage volunteering in the classroom, to read stories, help with art lessons, listen to book reports, or give a lesson on an area of expertise such as their job or a hobby.
12. Invite families to help students find resource materials and reference books on research topics in the library.
13. Send follow-up notes after meetings. Put out a pamphlet about home-school collaboration in IEP planning conferences.
14. Provide classroom teachers with handouts that can be used during conferences.
15. Have a Home Book notebook of pictures, activities, and stories about class that students take turns sharing at home.
16. Put a Family Board at the entrance of the building for posting ideas of interest to families, examples of class activities, and pictures.
17. Invite parents and siblings, sitters, and grandparents to all class parties.
18. Write thank-you notes for suggestions families provide.
19. Have families from other countries or culture groups talk to students about their customs and culture.
20. Ask families what their family goals are, and discuss how those goals can be met by the classroom curriculum.

Chapter Review

1. The variable with the most significant effect upon children's development is family involvement in their child's learning. Although educational professionals come and go in children's lives, and school settings change often for many students, families are the link of continuity in the lives of most children. They are the decision-makers for their children, whose futures are largely dependent on the continued ability of their parents to advocate for them.
2. Educators must be partners with families of students with special needs. While this is a demanding and challenging responsibility, educators are committed to such a partnership because it

fulfills a legal right of families. Research confirms the benefits of the partnership for children, families, and schools. Involvements mean teacher involvement as well as family involvement. This becomes collaboration and mutually respectful, committed teamwork.

3. Educators and families face barriers to home-school collaboration, including under-utilization of services, lack of cultural competency, and differing attitudes, history, values, culture, and language. Examining their own culture and values as potential barriers to understanding will enable them to address diversity during collaboration.

4. Educational consultants have successfully used the bridges of focusing on family strengths, using appropriate communication skills, and promoting positive roles for family members. These are considered empowerment strategies which recognize and promote family competence.

5. Educators must clarify their own values in order to respect the values of others. Checklists and structured value-clarification activities help educators identify their specific values about education, school, and home-school collaboration.

6. Using rapport-building skills and communication skills such as responsive listening, assertive responding, and mutual problem-solving will convey respect for family members and willingness to collaborate with them. Patience and calm persistence are needed.

7. Educators should provide a variety of opportunities for families to become involved with the school. These opportunities should be based on family strengths, expertise, and needs. Family strengths represent contributions that they can make to the partnership. The needs of parents are those interests and needs they have concerning their families.

8. Home-school collaboration can be evaluated using informal or formal assessment methods to determine the effects of the program on children's learning and behavior, as well as family members' attitudes and behaviors, and the attitudes and behaviors of school personnel.

To Do and Think About

1. Brainstorm to identify family characteristics that would be encouraging to a consultant or teacher who has students with learning and behavior disorders. Then develop plans for interaction and involvement with families that would cultivate those characteristics.

2. Identify roadblocks in these three interactions. Then suggest what could and should have been said differently by the Teacher in scene A, by the parent in scene B, and by the consultant in scene C.

   Scene A. *PARENT:* What's this about suspending my child from your class for three days? I thought you people were supposed to be teaching kids instead of letting them sit and waste time in the principal's office.

   TEACHER: You're being unreasonable. You don't understand our rules and neither does your child. Your child needs to learn some manners and plain, old-fashioned respect!

   Scene B. *TEACHER:* I'm calling to tell you that your son caused a disturbance again in my class. I would like you to meet with me and his counselor.

   PARENT: He's always been an active kid. Can't you people learn to handle active, curious children without always dragging us parents into it?

   Scene C. *PARENT:* How can I get Bobby to settle down and do his homework without a battle every night? It's driving us crazy.

   CONSULTANT: I'm glad you're concerned, but I think he will be O. K. if you just keep on him. Don't worry, he's a bright kid and he'll snap out of this phase soon. Just be glad your other three aren't dreamers like he is.

3. Plan a booklet that could be used by consultants to improve home-school communication and collaboration. Report on what will be included, how it can be used, and how it will be helpful.

4. Reflect upon the often-told story about three bricklayers being interviewed by a reporter to find out what they were doing. The first retorted, " I'm laying bricks, so don't bother me." The second elaborated a bit, "I'm making a wall, that's what." But the third, with purpose gleaming in his eyes, responded, "Why, we're building a cathedral." In what ways can educators build functional but beautiful relationships with family members, and not just go through the required motions?

For Further Reading

Berg, I. K. (1994). *Family-based services: A solution-focused approach.* New York: W. W. Norton.

DesJardins, C. (1993). *How to get services by being assertive.* Chicago: Family Resource Center on Disabilities.

Martin, R. (1991). Extraordinary children—ordinary lives. Champaign, IL: Research Press.

Sue, C. W., and Sue, D. (1990). *Counseling the culturally different: Theory and practice* (2nd ed.). New York: Wiley.

Turnbull and Turnbull (1985). *Parents Speak Out.* (These are stories written by parents of children with disabilities, with follow-up comments several years later.)

Chapter 12

Staff Development and Resources for Enhancing Consultation, Collaboration, and Teamwork

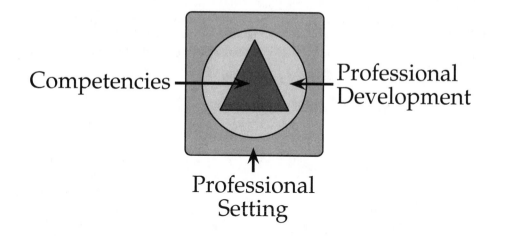

Competencies → Professional Development

Professional Setting

Introduction

Staff development is a prime factor in the success of school consultation and collaboration. When well-planned, well-delivered, and constructively evaluated, it catalyzes consultation services and collaborative activity. Consultation, collaboration, and teamwork have become key concepts in school reform of the 1990s. However, educators have not been prepared, for the most part, to deliver this kind of service (Friend & Cook, 1990; White & Pryzwansky, 1982). Preservice students in teacher education generally do not receive sufficient training and modeling for learning how to collaborate. Nor have many experienced teachers developed the consultation and collaboration skills that they must have to adapt to collaborative roles.

School personnel already in the field need in-service and staff development (ISD) for cultivating their skills to engage productively in collaborative endeavors. Their effectiveness will increase when they become more proficient in finding and sharing resources for learning. In addition, through staff development experiences they can build the professional scaffolding that helps their present and future colleagues engage in professional collaboration. Consultation, collaboration, and teamwork will be enhanced through carefully designed and well-conducted in-service and staff development activities.

Focusing Questions

1. What are the roles, responsibilities, and opportunities for school personnel in providing inservice and staff development?
2. How do in-service and staff development differ?
3. What characteristics and needs of adult learners are important for planning in-service and staff development?
4. How should school personnel needs for consultation and collaboration and teamwork be assessed?
5. What target groups and formats should be considered by staff developers in designing and implementing in-service and staff development?
6. What methods and techniques will facilitate productive in-service and staff development?
7. How should in-service and staff development be evaluated?
8. What external resources can be explored and utilized through consultation and collaboration?

Key Terms in the Chapter

Educational Resources Information Center (ERIC)
Federal Register
Federal Grants and Contracts Weekly
follow-through
follow-up
grant funds
incentives
inservice

job maintenance
mentor
needs assessment
needs sensing
personal growth
professional development
Request for Proposal (RFP)
staff development

Purposes of Staff Development

Staff development serves at least one or more of four overarching purposes:

- *Job maintenance.* Completion of in-service or staff development programs may be required for certification renewal or endorsement for assigned roles.
- *Professional development.* When school reforms such as inclusion and outcomes-based education are initiated, school personnel need information and skills to help them deal with the changes.

- *Personal growth.* As life-long learners, educators seek more knowledge and new skills that will help them facilitate students' learning.
- *Inspiration.* Educators can be energized by uplifting professional experiences.

The ideal staff development includes goals that address all four of these purposes in personalizing the experience for each participant (see Figure 12-1).

Roles, Responsibilities, and Opportunities for Staff Development

Educators are caught up in demands for school reform and restructuring efforts that emphasize consultation, collaboration and teamwork as goals. However, they receive little coaching and preparation for the new roles. Teacher education programs may eventually incorporate

---

Scenario

—(adapted from Dettmer, 1990)

Several teachers at a middle school are conversing in the teachers' work room on Friday afternoon.

SOCIAL STUDIES TEACHER: What a week! I feel as if I've attended to everything this week but my students and the curriculum. Maybe things will slow down a bit next week.

MATH TEACHER: Guess you didn't look at your office memo yet, hmmm? There's a reminder about the staff development sessions next Tuesday and Thursday mornings before school. Something about working with consultants.

SOCIAL STUDIES TEACHER: Consultants? You mean people who drive over from the central office to borrow your clock and tell you what time it is? Or some imported experts from more than fifty miles away?

MATH TEACHER: I believe this group involves our own special education staff. We're supposed to find out about school consultation service and get ready to collaborate with staff who will be consulting teachers.

ART TEACHER: Oh, great. How does that involve me? I had my required course in special education. What I really need is a bigger room and more supplies.

SOCIAL STUDIES TEACHER: And if we are supposed to collaborate with these people, where will we find the time?

PHYSICAL EDUCATION TEACHER: Uh-huh. It will be hard enough just carving out the time to go to the *meeting* about it.

MATH TEACHER: Now you know you'll just *love* sitting in that stuffy room trying to stay awake when you'd rather be in your classroom getting set for the day.

SOCIAL STUDIES TEACHER: Well, let me put it this way. If they don't dismiss by 8:20 sharp, I'm leaving!

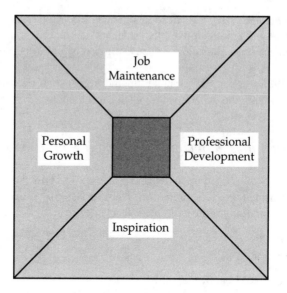

FIGURE 12-1   Purposes of Staff Development

consultation training into preservice and degree programs, but it will be too late for those just completing teacher requirements (novice teachers) and those already on the job (experienced or veteran teachers).

Typical novice teachers, or "rookies," enter the profession having little experience but much enthusiasm. Classroom management has been a big concern for this group even before the inclusive classroom brought special pressures. They ask questions such as "How can I get everything done? Will I be able to control the class? How can I provide for each child's needs? Will my colleagues respect me? Will my students like me?" Short on experience, they tend to be up to date on current educational research and teaching technology. They have little confidence in their ability to analyze individual learning needs and prescribe strategies for those needs. Not knowing what is "normal," they are less secure in pinpointing special needs within the heterogeneous classroom.

Experienced or veteran teachers are more able to recognize student variability and identify strategies that serve a wide range of needs. They have followed the progress of students through one or several years and know more or less what to expect. Their patterns of teaching and classroom organization may accommodate some facets of student achievement range, and keep the learning environment organized, but they need practical information on contemporary issues such as inclusion, transition, cultural diversity, and accountability. They may be resentful of new philosophies such as class-within-a-class, co-teaching, curriculum compacting, or peer tutoring that seem intrusive and disruptive to procedures they have developed through several years of experience (see Figure 12-2).

Educational leader Shanker (1992) notes the irony of having car manufacturers set up production teams and train them to build cars *together,* while people in education assume that school staff members will step right into a team concept of doing things with little or no help. He contends, "If it takes 600 courses and 92 hours a year per employee to make a better automobile, it will take that and more to make better schools. And if we're not willing to commit ourselves to this kind of effort, we are not going to get what we want (Shanker, 1992, p. 3). In more and more schools, staff development is being organized on a total school or district basis and tailored for specific groups of personnel who are engaged in institutional change processes (Reynolds & Birch, 1988). Consultants and consulting teachers should assume an active role in providing leadership for professional development of all school personnel. Their roles are ideal for orchestrating awareness experiences and training activities in a variety of content and process areas, including skills for collaboration and teamwork.

Unfortunately, attitudes toward in-service and staff development (ISD) are not generally positive. They range from indifference to resentment to disdain. Criticisms cited by Davis (1986) and others in regard to in-service and staff development call attention to the lack of

- Clear purpose
- Relevance
- Meaningful objectives

Educator Level	Current Status	Needs
Preservice	Up-to-date information	Reality check
	Enthusiasm	Confidence
	Energy	Practice with "normal"
Novice	Energy	Management skill
	Enthusiasm	Self-esteem
	Motivation	Incentive to take risks
Veteran	Experience	New approaches
	Refined techniques	Morale-booster
	Tried-and-true strategies	Leadership opportunity
Support Staff	Varied roles	Awareness of whole picture
	Skills for needs	Coordination of efforts
	Incentive for success	Satisfaction
Parents	Knowledge of student	Information on education
	Keen interest	Support
	Advocacy effort	Broad view
Community	Multifaceted knowledge	Awareness of issues
	Perspectives on work	Opportunity to contribute services
	Multiple skills	Way to support schools

FIGURE 12-2 Differentiated Needs for Staff Development

- Structure and organization
- Emphasis on quality, not quantity
- Practicality and long-term applicability
- Flexibility and choices
- Interest and intrigue
- Attention to adult learner characteristics
- Support from administrators
- And most of all, follow-up activities.

Specific problems that contribute to ineffectiveness of staff development in general, and inservices in particular, are

1. Too few teacher preparation programs that put strong emphasis on conducting and participating in ISD
2. Few education texts that feature an ISD section
3. Too little attention in journals and other professional resources on techniques and processes that ensure high quality ISD
4. Too little networking by educators with other professional organizations interested in education
5. Adherence to old ways of delivering ISD—"dog and pony show" presentations, "inspirational" speakers
6. Lack of time

In order to provide the most constructive staff development experiences possible, planners and presenters need to address several points:

- What are the characteristics of school personnel as adult learners?
- What are the needs of school personnel in serving students with learning and behavior problems?
- What kind of material is most helpful for them?
- How might the material be presented effectively and efficiently?
- How can follow-up and support be provided after the in-service and staff development experiences?

Differentiating In-service from Staff Development

In-service and staff development are two necessary but distinctly different structures for professional growth. In-service is ordinarily a single event or a series of short sessions on a topic of educational interest or school need. School personnel attend in-services on such topics as assertive discipline, critical thinking skills, cooperative learning, drug awareness, student motivation, and a host of other content and process areas. They participate in in-service days as orientation for the new school year, or as refresher sessions during the school term. These one-shot sessions, on a topic of general appeal, are most often provided by an expert on a topic, who might be a state official, university professor, professional consultant, corporate leader, or educator from another district. In-service goals generally are directed toward awareness and information.

Staff development, on the other hand, is a process of long-term commitment to professional growth across a broad range of school goals. It should involve all school personnel and usually includes local leadership in place of, or at least in addition to, service by outside consultants. Goals are directed toward involvement, commitment, and renewal. School personnel determine their own needs, develop steps to address those needs, and evaluate their professional growth.

Under ideal circumstances in-service is one useful component of a long-range, ongoing staff development program to serve the professional needs of teachers, administrators, and support personnel in the school system. Staff development is a fundamental part of the general plan for improving education for all students.

Characteristics of the Adult Learner

First and foremost, participants in ISD must be approached as the adult learners and professionals they are. Participants in in-service and staff development demonstrate several basic characteristics as adult learners. They have (Knowles, 1978)

a desire and need to be self-directed in the learning;
a wide experience base upon which to draw;
a time perspective for the learning that is oriented to the here and now;
a problem-centered focus on the learning.

In his more recent research, Knowles indicates that the most definitive of these four characteristics for educators is the wide experience base they bring to the ISD (Feuer and Geber, 1988). Those who provide ISD for school personnel must recognize that the recipients will be self-directed, experienced, and interested primarily in material they can use at the present for real problems. They desire ownership in the ISD process, and they will resist aspects of staff development that are perceived as attacks on their competence. They can and should serve as resources for their colleagues during professional development activities. And although some fun and reward are refreshing and necessary, adult learners respond best to intrinsic motivations rather than extrinsic motivations.

Staff developers can use knowledge of adult learner characteristics to work more productively with staff development participants. The first step is to acknowledge that each person's perception of the environment reflects and is filtered through his or her own stage of development (Oja, 1980). Because of learning style preferences and variations in ways people process information, as discussed in Chapter 4, presenters of staff development activities must attend to different types of participants. These include (Garmston and Wellman, 1992)

- Those looking for facts, data, and references;
- Those wanting to relate the topic to themselves through interactions with colleagues;
- Those wanting to reason and explore;
- Those who would like to adapt, modify, or create new ideas and procedures.

With these adult learner characteristics in mind, staff developers will need to:

arrange for participant comfort;
provide participants with options and choices;
manage participants' time well;
deliver practical, focused help; and
follow up on the effectiveness of the experience.

Adult learners value in-service and staff development activities in which they work to-ward realistic, job-related, useful goals. They need to see results for their efforts with fol-low-through and feedback experiences, and most of all, with having success in using the activities within their school context.

Guskey (1985) stresses that ISD for busy school personnel must illustrate clearly ways in which new practices can improve student performance, and how these practices can be implemented without too much disruption or extra work. This is particularly important for ISD that focuses on consultation and collaboration, because this kind of professional activ-ity often involves more time and effort initially. In Guskey's model of teacher change, staff development should be designed for the purpose of modifying classroom teaching practic-es. This change causes changes in student learning outcomes, which result in altered teach-er beliefs and attitudes. This is a promising concept for promoting collaboration to help students with special needs.

Planning In-service and Staff Development

Many professional growth activities can and should take place among practicing teachers right at the school site, particularly activities designed to improve teacher ability in meeting needs of students at risk. However, the experiences will need to have specific personnel roles assigned to the task of preparing the activity and coordinating it (Howey, Bents, and Corrigan, 1981). "Staff development will never have its intended impact as long as it is grafted onto schools in the form of discrete, unconnected projects" (Joyce, 1990, p. 21). Those who conduct staff development should be selected carefully. They have a much more important role in teacher readiness than has been accorded to them (Joyce, 1990; Dettmer, 1986). Staff development planners and presenters need expertise in content, process, and understanding of the school context.

The consultant role is ideal for coordinating useful in-service and staff development activities. Special education personnel often inherit these responsibilities either as a part of a plan or by default. There are disadvantages as well as advantages in being a "prophet in your own land" to conduct professional development activities, but one of the biggest ad-vantages is knowledge of the school context.

Determining In-service and Staff Development Needs

The consultant or consulting teacher who provides staff development will want to assess the needs of other school personnel for the ISD. What do they know about a topic at this point? What do they want to learn? How can they be involved in planning, conducting, and evaluating the staff development for their individual needs? This information should be solicited through needs assessment instruments. Before conducting needs assessment, however, the staff developer should engage in *needs-sensing* activities. In data gathering, it is important to move beyond the surface data to get at what is *really* wanted (Henkelman, 1991). School personnel may assess their needs as wanting classroom strategies for behavior management or for grouping high-ability learners in productive but nonelitist ways. However, the staff developer may sense the need for addressing their concerns about inclusion and accountability for student performance. What do participants *need* to *want* to know? This radar-reading of what the participants-to-be need to know is a subtle but vital precursor to assessing needs. After all, if educators knew what they wanted or needed in every case, they probably would be doing it.

Needs Sensing

Needs-sensing information allows planners to design formal needs assessment procedures that will reflect the true needs of all involved. For example, if a needs assessment questionnaire asks, "Which of the five topics do you want to know more about?" and the list includes discipline, motivation, computer literacy, alternative grouping structures, and mainstreaming, the ranked results will be somewhat predictable in a typical district. Alternative grouping structures probably would rank low, with discipline and motivation high.

Prior to the needs assessment activity, an interviewer or investigator might ask teachers if they would like to explore possibilities for structuring their classrooms to promote better discipline and stimulate student interest. If the answer is affirmative, staff development on modified grouping structures could be offered as an area of interest that facilitates discipline as well as student motivation. As another example of needs sensing, teachers could be asked if they wish to explore ways in which children can work together, learn from each other, and share in the results of the learning. If the answer is yes, staff development on cooperative learning could be implemented. For a third example, it would be less helpful to assess needs with the question, "Do you want to know more about advanced placement possibilities at your high school?" than to sense where needs lie by first asking, "How might we extend learning of very able students beyond courses that cover grade-level material they have already mastered?"

Needs sensing is a very important precursor to needs assessment. It can be carried out best through

classroom observations;

visits to successful programs, followed by a comparative analysis;

dialogues and interviews with students, parents, support personnel, and others in the community;

task force investigations; and

buzz group outcomes.

Staff developers should develop instruments that allow target groups to feel able and willing to contribute information.

APPLICATION 12.1   Conducting Needs Sensing

Conduct a needs-sensing study by interviewing school personnel to obtain information on these concerns:

1. What do we need to know to help students in our schools feel good about themselves?
2. How important are test formats, designs, and reporting procedures in helping students learn to the best of their ability?
3. How can we determine which reinforcers work best for different ages and developmental levels and interests?
4. Do we use ancillary and support personnel to the greatest advantage for our students?
5. Does our current material develop critical thinking, or do we need more effort in this area?
6. Do we have the resources for adapting materials to the needs of low-achieving students?

Needs Assessment

After needs sensing has been conducted, needs assessment instruments and procedures can be developed from the data. Most school personnel have had experience with completing needs assessments. Formats for needs assessments include:

- checklists;
- questionnaires and surveys;
- open-ended surveys of areas of concern;
- interviews; and
- brainstorm session records.

Needs assessment might ask personnel to check topics of need, or to describe their concerns, which can be developed into a staff development activity.

Presenting In-service and Staff Development

Garmston (1988) says that presenting an in-service session or a staff development activity to adult learners might be compared to giving presents. He suggests the "present" should be something participants (presentees) want or can utilize, personalized to individual taste as much as possible, attractively wrapped, and a bit suspenseful. The presenter should

- know audience needs and interests;
- conduct the ISD in interesting, efficient, pleasant manner;
- package the ISD material attractively;
- provide an element of surprise and intrigue; and
- deliver follow-up help, support, and additional information.

Target Groups for In-service and Staff Development

Target groups for school-related in-service and staff development include a wide variety of roles: classroom teachers; administrators; parents of students; librarians and media specialists; food-service, custodial, and secretarial staff; school board members; special education personnel; paraprofessionals, social workers and health workers; mentors, talent instructors, and youth directors; pediatricians and dentists; legislators, community leaders, policymakers, and university personnel for teacher education.

Formal and Informal In-service and Staff Development

Just as there are formal and informal approaches to consultation, as discussed in Chapter 3, there are formal and informal approaches to ISD. Formal ISD can be conducted through scheduled sessions, conferences, programs, press releases, presentations, modules, courses, brochures, retreats, and other planned activities. Informal ISD occurs through conversations, observations, reports about one topic that include another aspect of education, memos, references to media productions, software programs and reading material. One very informal, convenient, and particularly effective in-service technique is to display information, explanations of procedures, invitations to collaborate, and morale boosters on bulletin boards located in places school personnel frequent (see Figure 12-3 as an example). The possibilities for both formal and informal ISD activities are limited only by the imagination of the personnel who provide them. Some special education consultants prepare bulletin boards of information about pertinent topics. Others provide staff members with newsletters or columns within existing newsletters. Some request ten minutes in which to talk to the teachers at faculty meetings.

APPLICATION 12.2   Conducting Needs Assessment

As a needs assessment procedure, ask teachers to check the topics that interest them most:

_____ Assertive Discipline—creating a positive atmosphere in the classroom
_____ Critical Thinking—developing effective skills of analysis and evaluation through course materials
_____ Alternative Assessment Procedures—including portfolios
_____ Behavior Management—techniques for assimilating behavioral-disordered students into the mainstream
_____ Beyond the Basals—guiding very able students in using library and supplementary texts as basals
_____ Working Smarter, not Harder—using consulting teachers and resource personnel to meet the needs of all students more effectively

It is important to leave space on the instrument for open-ended responses, and to encourage them. After the needs assessments have been returned, summarize the information and use it to plan ISD activities that will be meaningful for participants and relevant to the needs they specified.

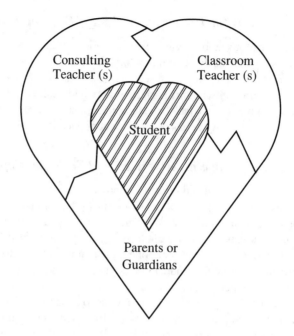

FIGURE 12-3 "Let's Collaborate" (By Kay Wright)

One enterprising group of teachers organized a series of sessions called "THT—Teachers Helping Teachers," in which they took turns delivering short sessions on topics in their area of expertise. Soon the idea caught on among other teachers. A teacher who had a school-related skill to share was excused, with the endorsement of the administration, for one-half day, to prepare for and present to teachers in another school within the district. Teachers truly collaborated and consulted to help other teachers.

A popular practice with some gifted program consultants is to provide calendars of enrichment activities for classroom teachers. As these are used, they become vehicles for carrying out goals of the gifted program, such as creative thinking, independent study, research, and small-group investigations.

A productive inservice could be a brief session to explain the consultant role and what the consultant will be doing. Such endeavors often increase interest in consultation and collaboration dramatically. Consultants also might prepare information sheets of "Questions Frequently Asked About..." and suggest answers for the questions. A bagged treat or a package of peanuts could be stapled on as a friendly, caring gesture.

When consultants work with one key teacher and their colleagues observe the results, that is informal staff development. As they ask what they can do to help teachers, then discuss their needs, and finally deliver on their promises to the best of their ability and the resources of their area, they are cultivating professional development among school personnel.

APPLICATION 12.3   Planning Professional Development for Related Services and Support Personnel

Related services and support personnel were discussed in Chapter 7 as important partners in programs for students with learning and behavior problems. Think of at least two reasons for including each of the target groups on page 319 in awareness and information sessions about an educational topic. For example, pediatricians and dentists may wish to learn more about characteristics of exceptional children, in order to diagnose problems that are brought to their attention. They also may need to know about referral systems in the schools and the possibilities for arrangements such as sheltered workshops for educable mentally handicapped individuals.

Learning is often a spontaneous event, occurring as a synergy of learner interest and need, teacher insight, and a supportive environment. This is the ideal "teachable moment." It is not stretching the comparison too much to suggest that there is an ideal "professional development moment." Perceptive consultants who seek ways of meeting students' special needs will find that in-service and staff development are appropriate tools. They need not expect all ISD experiences to be formal and planned. Both formal staff development and the informal, or "teachable moment for teachers" approaches, are needed. (See Figure 12-4).

The Teachers' Workroom as a Staff Development Forum

Very little has been written about the teachers' workroom. This is surprising, because many teachers spend time there on a fairly regular basis. Of course, some go there quite frequently, and others hardly ever do. Visits usually fall within one of three purposes—physical, social, or personal. There are physical benefits of refreshment, a quick nap, or a restroom break. Social benefits of interaction with adults are important to some. Personal benefits include attending to professional tasks such as grading papers or reading materials; it is a

	Formal	**Informal**
Plan	Typically structured Example: Workshop	Usually casual Example: Newsletter column
Method	Designed with care Example: Speaker/discussion	Somewhat spontaneous Example: Hall chat
Evaluation	Data collection Example: Checklist	Reflection Example: Journal note

FIGURE 12-4   Formal and Informal Inservice and Staff Development

personal decision to accomplish these tasks in the workroom rather than in the classroom or at home (Dettmer, 1989).

Elementary teachers, in particular, often seek the opportunity to have interaction with colleagues and share reflections about teaching practices. Occasionally this is problematic because the discourse can become quite negative and cynical. When workroom talk affects one's morale negatively, going there becomes iatrogenic and should probably be avoided. Nevertheless, the teachers' workroom has long been recognized by special education teachers as a useful hub of interaction. They recognize the opportunity to develop rapport with consultees and learn more about their teaching approaches and student needs.

It is important that consulting teachers spend enough time in the teachers' workroom ("Don't the special ed people want to be a part of our faculty?"), but not too much ("Don't those special ed people have anything to do?"). Of course, care must be taken to keep professional conversation general in nature. Confidentiality and ethical treatment of information are necessary behaviors for all teachers, and special education teachers in particular. But in this room that is provided for relaxation, reflection, and refreshment, a collaborative spirit can be nurtured and then carried out the door to classrooms and offices beyond.

APPLICATION 12.4   Differentiating between Formal and Informal ISD

Determine which of the following staff development activities might be formal and which might be informal. (If two or more people engage in this application exercise, it is not likely there will be complete agreement on the classifications.)

Study groups and problem-solving sessions

Planned interactions between classroom and special education teachers

Demonstration teaching by a consulting teacher

Packets containing program information for administrators

County fair exhibits on disabilities

Seminar programs involving scientists, business leaders, engineers, military personnel, environmental leaders, physicians

Saturday programs for parents

Exchange programs for teachers (from rural to urban and urban to rural)

Grant-writing workshops

Educational television programs

Summer workshops

Interactive video programs

Satellite discussions with leading educational figures

Teaching strategy books and software

A "share fair" in which each staff member brings a favorite idea to share

---

APPLICATION 12.5   Designing a Teacher's Workroom

In your thoughts, or on sketch paper, create a "dream workroom" that would serve school personnel in their physical, social, and personal needs. What would it look like? What would it sound like? How might a consultant nurture the collaborative spirit there? What would it take to construct and appoint such a room? Could some of your suggestions be done right away, with little cost or disruption?

Suggestions for improving the workroom/lounge in general, and for making it more conducive to collegial interaction,in particular, include (Dettmer, 1989):

- having a suggestion box in which staff could put ideas for time-savers, student pleasers, or budget easers.
- having salad luncheon potluck once a month, perhaps on payday. (Set out different salads every half hour or so, if there are many people.) Simpson (1990) describes a "Tuesday Luncheon" concept that has been in effect for many years and supports teachers' efforts to reflect on their instruction.
- holding a Friday afternoon snack time to encourage teachers to recap the week and think ahead to the next.
- posting a "Brag Board" on which commendations could be displayed involving anyone and everyone connected with the school, from students to bus drivers to parents of students.
- providing an "Orientation to Special Education" folder on an accessible table, changing its contents often.

More research is needed on the problems and possibilities of this important facet of school life. However, the consultant will find many opportunities in the workroom for developing rapport with consultees and initiating constructive interactions. This school place must be used wisely and judiciously.

Format for In-service and Staff Development

In-service and staff development plans can be classified as an economy package, a conventional package, or a deluxe package of experiences. For example, a gifted program consultant generated three sets of plans for gifted program staff development to serve the differentiated needs of his six assigned schools. He offered

The Economy Model, featuring

- characteristics of gifted students;
- curricular needs of gifted students; and
- activities to serve the curricular needs.

The Conventional Model, featuring

- characteristics and needs of gifted students;
- curricular implications of those needs;
- program differentiation to meet the needs;
- strategies and activities for serving the needs; and
- community resources for gifted students.

The Deluxe Model, featuring

- characteristics and needs of gifted students;
- curricular implications of those needs;
- gifted program goals and objectives;
- learning theories and teaching models suited to gifted students' needs;
- learning styles and student interests;
- curricular planning for gifted students;
- community resources for gifted students; and
- parental involvement in gifted programs.

There is no single pattern for in-service and staff development format that will be appropriate for every school context. However, the following outline is one that can be adapted to a variety of schools and staff needs.

1. Engage in needs sensing.
2. Conduct needs assessment.
3. Select the topic to be featured.
4. Determine the audience to be targeted.
5. Choose a catchy, upbeat title for the activity.
6. Determine presenters who will contribute.
7. Decide on incentives, promotion, and publicity.
8. Outline the presentation.
9. List the equipment and room arrangement needed.
10. Plan carefully the content to be covered.
11. Prepare handouts and visual materials.
12. Rehearse the presentation.
13. Determine an evaluation procedure for the activity.
14. Plan for the follow-up activity.

Examples of sessions that follow this format are included in Figures 12-5 and 12-6.

Time for In-service and Staff Development

Time is the enemy when planning in-service and staff development activities. There is not enough of it readily available at student-free times when teachers can concentrate and reflect. Before-school hours and after-school hours might seem workable because partici-

Needs Sensing: Interviews with support staff

Needs Assessment: Survey form of questions participants would like to have answered

Topic: Students with special needs

Audience: Paraprofessionals, social and health workers, food service and custodial staff, secretary staff, bus drivers, librarians and media specialists

Title: "Helping All Kids Succeed in Our School"

Presenters: Consulting teachers for learning disabilities, behavioral disorders, mental handicaps, and physical handicaps

Incentives: Door prize, refreshments

Publicity: A basket of treats and an announcement about the meeting, placed in the school office, workroom, and bus barn

Format: A thirty-minute overview of exceptionalities, followed by a short videotape of exceptional children. Then a refreshment break, and a thirty-minute small-group discussion of ways in which each school role contributes to the learning of students with special needs. At the conclusion, a five-minute whole group summary of goals for all school staff

Equipment and room: Videotape player, overhead projector and screen, table for refreshments, semicircles for whole-group, and tables in corners of the room for small-group discussion

Content: To be planned by the consulting teachers, speaking to needs identified in the needs sensing and needs assessment data, goals of special education programs, student needs, curricular modifications that teachers make that affect such school conditions as schedules and rewards, strategies that support personnel can use to help students, and an individual plan by each participant for giving support to meet special needs of students

Handouts: None

Visuals: A high-quality, overview type of videotape on exceptionalities. Basic transparencies for describing exceptional student characteristics and needs

Rehearsal and preparation: At a time all presenters can be there

Evaluation procedure: Modified version of Evaluation Form in Figure 12-11

Follow-up: Brief interviews with participants to check on individual plan progress and any further questions

FIGURE 12-5   ISD Module for Support Personnel

pants are coming to school anyway or are required to stay after school for a specific length of time. But teachers find it hard to focus on their own learning at an early hour, when their thoughts are centered on beginning the school day efficiently. By day's end, energy and emotions may be lagging and other responsibilities beckon. Saturday sessions are no more popular and encroach on the family and community life so necessary for sustaining teacher vitality and support.

The arrangement preferred by most teachers is released time. This means that their responsibilities with students will be assumed by others. Loucks-Horsley et al. (1987) recommend providing released time for ISD participants by using

- substitute teachers;
- a substitute cadre that conducts planned enrichment activities;

- roving substitute teachers; or
- teacher triads where one teacher teaches two classes to free up the second teacher.

The substitute cadre eliminates the necessity for detailed lesson planning by the teacher, because the enrichment activities are planned and provided by the cadre. Roving substitutes allow released teachers to have short periods of time for observing, coaching, gathering research data, or assisting in another classroom. Loucks-Horsley et al. (1987) counsel that the time issue is a "red herring," because the problem often lies in the constructive use of time, not its availability.

Released time to attend professional development activities away from the school district must be supported strongly by school administrators. Permission to attend may be granted more readily if you are slated to make a presentation. If that is not possible, you

---

Needs Sensing: Information gained during regularly scheduled observations in classrooms

Needs Assessment: Questionnaires asking teachers to check major areas of interest and add others if they wish

Topic: Mainstreamed students with special needs

Audience: Elementary-level classroom teachers

Title: "Teamwork Makes Every Child a Winner"

Presenters: Consultants for learning disabilities, behavioral disorders, gifted students, and students with mental and physical handicaps

Incentives: Released time, attendance by administrator, credit on professional growth plan, refreshments

Publicity: School newsletter, personal written invitations

Format: Two one-hour sessions after school. During the first one, held on Tuesday, five-minute presentations by each consulting teacher, and five-minute presentations by key elementary teachers, describing inclusion. Refreshment break. Small-group problem-solving sessions to identify major problems of mainstreaming. The following Thursday, again the five-minute presentations but this time focusing on modifications and alternatives teachers can use to overcome the problems identified during Tuesday's session. Small-group problem-solving sessions to determine best approaches for trying some of the ideas

Equipment: Overhead and screen, samples of materials, table for refreshments. Theatre-in-the-round arrangement for total group, and small work tables for the break-out groups

Content: Prepared specific to the exceptionalities discussed, and including information on student characteristics, learning and behavior needs, curricular implications, and possibilities for collaboration and teamwork among special and general education personnel to meet those needs

Handouts: Color coded, to accompany content

Visuals: Transparencies, samples of student work when using the curricular modifications

Rehearsal: All presenters during the week before the ISD

Evaluation: An instrument similar to Figure 12-11

Follow-up: Individual consultations with each teacher by consulting teachers who have mainstreamed students in those classrooms

---

FIGURE 12-6   ISD Module for Classroom Teachers

might volunteer to facilitate or chair a session, or to work a few hours in some capacity at the conference. Administrators may respond favorably to a plan for attending and bringing back information in the form of a written report or a summarized presentation to be shared with colleagues. If none of these possibilities is viable, professional or personal leave days will have to be used.

Incentives for Participation in ISD

Incentives for attendance and enthusiastic participation at in-service and staff development sessions need to feature interest, humor, and intrigue. They should include both extrinsic and intrinsic reinforcement for adult learners. Intrinsic incentives for long-range staff development are, of course, personal and professional growth, benefits for students, and advancement in the profession. But there are good reasons for providing pleasurable, extrinsic rewards as well. For example, a drawing could be held in which the lucky winner receives a free class period during which the principal substitutes. Teacher aide time could be provided. Participants could be treated to a gala affair upon "graduation" from a program. They might be transported to this gala affair in a limousine provided by local businesses (Robert, 1973). Recognition for their participation could be publicized in local papers and professional magazines. Released time from playground or lunch duty for specified periods could be provided. The best parking spot in the lot (perhaps the superintendent's!) could be awarded, for a week or so, as a door prize. A starter list of incentives is provided in Figure 12-7.

Released time	Child care during the ISD
Paid college credit	Many options and choices
Progress on professional plan	Reduced teaching load
Stipend	Hair stylist demonstrations
Door prize	Badges and buttons
Sabbatical for long-term ISD	Demonstrations of materials
Free food	Free teacher supplies
A plush site for the session	Endorsement by community leaders
Choice parking lot spaces	Drawing for resort weekend
A note on yearly evaluation	Free material from merchants
Have a famous person there	Ticket giveaway (dinner, a banquet, theater,
Faculty performances	sports)
Have a theme party	Lively entertainment
Lots of useful handouts	Funny fashion show
Retreat at a resort	Progressive format—moving from place to
Grab bags	place for parts of the session
Publicity in local paper	A share-fair
Recognition for attending	Controversial topic
Make-and-take products	Assurance of follow-up support
Attendance by administrators	Bring one idea, take home many
Free Xeroxing of materials	

FIGURE 12-7   Incentives for Participating in ISD

Prospective participants should receive information about the ISD through school newsletters, memos, bulletin boards, and public announcements. Publicity spots that are run on radio and T. V. provide the added benefit of calling attention of the community to professional development efforts by the school district. They are a natural prelude for follow-up work to build awareness and support among the public for school improvement issues.

Techniques for Conducting ISD

Consultants who deliver in-service and staff development on their own professional turf may face some difficulty in being accepted as "prophets in their own land" (Smith-Westberry and Job, 1986). They will want to scrutinize their own capabilities and deficits first. Practice sessions can help presenters gain confidence and skill. Smith-Westberry and Job recommend videotaping the practice sessions, discomforting though that may be, and critiquing the taped sessions carefully to correct deficiencies.

Presenter and Participant Responsibilities

Presenters have a responsibility to know their participants well. They should be experienced and confident with the content they are presenting. After assessing participant needs, they should develop the format and content carefully, rehearse for the presentation, plan the closing segment even more carefully, arrange for feedback and evaluation, and form ideas for follow-up to the presentation.

Participants, as presentees, have the responsibility to participate whole-heartedly in the ISD, collaborate and cooperate with the activities and evaluation, and commit themselves to the follow-up activities. One of the most helpful contributions on their part is to defer any negative attitudes toward in-service and staff development and anticipate good experiences from the ISD to come.

Delivery of ISD Content

The ISD may follow one of two basic formats-lecture format, or interactive style (Smith-Westberry and Job, 1986). Lectures should include real-life examples and practical approaches. For lectures, the room arrangement might be configured as semicircles, a theater-in-the-round, or chairs in small semicircles to allow for periodic subgrouping. Stiff formats of straight rows generally should be avoided. For interactive sessions, chairs can be placed in a circle or around individual tables in octagon form. Larger tables might be arranged in a diamond shape. A "maple leaf" format of chairs allows for subgrouping (Knowles, 1970).

Presenters should have with them all supplies that they anticipate needing, such as:

chalk, eraser, pointer;

overhead transparency markers, extra bulb, extension cord, blank transparencies, three-prong adapter;

pens, pencils, writing paper, pad for sign-up requests;

masking tape, thumbtacks, scissors, strong tape for securing cords, clip-on light to read notes in the dark;

other emergency items (tissues, hose, cup for water, stick-on notes, mints or cough drops, string, screwdriver and pliers).

A good way to begin an ISD is to use an icebreaker, particularly if participants do not know one another. However, the icebreaker must not encroach on presentation time. Early arrivers could begin the brief activity, and time could be called when the hour to begin is at hand. An example of a well-known icebreaker technique is provided in Figure 12-8.

It is vital for the presentation to *begin on time.* Also, presenters will want to "begin with a bang." The opening remarks in a presentation should be snappy and to the point. They should "hook" the participants into being interested. Now is the time to stress that the session has been developed from data on needs assessments that participants completed. Presenters should state the goal(s), the procedures to be followed, a *brief* overview of the issue(s) to be addressed, and the range of probable avenues the ISD will take, while remaining somewhat flexible for any circumstances that arise.

ISD content should be presented through more than one sensory channel, just as good teachers present a variety of materials for learners. Handouts, visuals, brief tape-recorded messages, and frequent changes in presenter position and style will be appreciated by adult learners, just as they are welcomed by students in the classroom. A new activity should occur approximately every fifteen to twenty minutes (Britton, 1989). And, of course, presenters do need to be prepared for inevitable contingencies and emergencies—burned-out

---

ICEBREAKER ACTIVITY

Let's Get Acquainted

Move about the room and get a signature from a person who fits each category. Use a person's name only once.

1. Someone who loves chocolate. _____

2. One who has swum in both the Atlantic and Pacific. _____

3. Someone who knows who won the Super Bowl last year. _____

4. Someone who doesn't care who won the Super Bowl._____

5. A person with a birthday in the same season as yours._____

6. Someone who plays a musical instrument. _____

7. One who loves cats. _____

8. An elementary level teacher/student. _____

9. A high school level teacher/student. _____

10. One who traveled more than twenty miles to be here. _____

When your list is complete, sit down and interact with those around you.

FIGURE 12-8   Ice Breaker Activity

bulbs, too few handouts, loud noises, a rude question, or a tornado alert! Presenters can use small-group activities intermittently to encourage involvement and sustain interest. Huddle groups of six people conferring for six minutes, circle response groups in which each person speaks in turn around the small circle, and buzz groups of dyads or triads work well.

Some presenters dread speaking to groups. Would-be presenters may be inexperienced or feel terrified to stand before groups, particularly before their peers. It is a good idea to practice the presentation before the event. A script of remarks can be typed (triple spaced for easy reading) and rehearsed in front of the mirror or a kindly compatriot. Holding private practice sessions before a mirror will allow you to critique gestures and body language. It may help to watch other performers, or to practice with dramatic readings.

Engaging in relaxation exercises before the event has helped some nervous speakers to be at ease. During the presentation the speaker might locate supporters in the audience and key in on them for assurance. If a tense time arises, a cartoon or joke might be brought out to ease the tension, but this must be used with care. The humorous piece must be inoffensive and related to the topic. That is a tall order. At any rate, presenters will find it comforting to remember that most audiences are more interested in the usefulness of the content than in the skills of the presenters; therefore, the key is to provide useful, timely information.

Garmston (1990) stresses that presenters can make or break the success of the session in its last few minutes. Final impressions should encourage participants to sort and store the material. The last comments should stimulate inquiry and support commitment and collegiality. Closing activities need to be planned carefully and calculated precisely. Perhaps the most important criterion of all is to *end on time*. Figure 12-9 contains a brief list of do's and don'ts for conducting successful ISD activities.

Do's and Don'ts for In-service and Staff Development

Do assess needs.	Do use evaluation data to plan better ISD.
Do set goals.	Don't lecture exclusively.
Do arrive early and prepared.	Don't use jargon.
Do be flexible.	Don't schedule at poor times.
Do provide incentives.	Don't read to participants.
Do keep on task.	Don't assume all have same needs and interests.
Do follow up.	Don't try to do too much.
Do start on time.	Don't run overtime.
Do carry a "survival box."	Don't demean efforts and competencies of
Do provide good handouts.	others.
Do be enthusiastic.	Don't allow one participant to dominate.
Do summarize often.	Don't be afraid to say, "I don't know."
Do make eye contact often.	Don't get unnecessarily technical.
Do encourage administrators to attend.	Don't rush through material.
Do be prepared to modify.	Don't overuse the overhead.
Do follow through on promises.	Don't be discouraged.
Do involve the audience.	

FIGURE 12-9   Do's and Don'ts for In-service and Staff Development

Visuals for the Presentation

Many presenters use visuals during presentations—transparencies, films, videotapes, charts, and posters. The visuals should be simple, clear, and visible. They must not be cluttered with infinite detail, but represent the "bottom line" about the topic. The audience will attend more to color graphics than to black-and-white. An effective transparency presents one main idea per sheet, with a maximum of seven words per line and seven lines per visual, and does not contain technical language or jargon. A rule of thumb for the display of figures and graphs is to present only information that the audience could sketch freehand with accurate representation of the main idea. The type on transparencies must be BIG! It should be tested for legibility from the back of the room by a person who has never seen it before.

Presenters should not read from the transparency material, but wait until the audience has time to peruse it. When noting information, speakers should point to the transparency, not to the screen. Expeditious use of the on/off switch allows the presenter to control the audience's attention. It is best to leave room lights on unless the visual is a film. After a point is made, turning off the machine and standing away from it directs attention back to the presenter. Clip-on microphones allow presenter mobility. Imaginative use and variation of space, location, volume, and graphics will enliven the presentation and focus participant attention.

A dramatic effect can be achieved with the use of two overhead machines and screens. The main point might be presented on one screen while subpoints or illustrations are flashed on the other. As a variation, two presenters could collaborate, one at each machine, to dialogue about the material. This technique needs to be rehearsed before it is used.

Handouts for the Presentation

Presentees appreciate good handouts. Handouts are more widely read and better remembered when they are in color. They should be practical, usable, and attractive. There should not be too many nor too few. Unless the handout is needed as a component of participation involvement, it should be distributed at the close of the session. If handed out during the session, an orderly procedure must be preplanned, so that distribution does not consume valuable session time and make the audience restless.

Participants tend to become annoyed when there are not enough handouts to go around. Even with the best planning, this does happen occasionally. Presenters should have a sign-up paper available for those who were short-changed; and must follow through right away by sending the material. It is best not to distribute handouts before the session begins. In order to minimize requests and avoid having to refuse, presenters will want to keep printed material out of sight until it is needed.

Follow-Up Activities

Follow-up to in-service and staff development is the breeze that fans any fires of change that were sparked by the activity (Dettmer, 1990). Educators sometimes avoid trying new concepts and techniques because they are uncomfortable with them or uncertain about the outcomes. It is easy to revert to business as usual, once the ISD activity is over. So follow-up to ISD is vital, just as it is with the consultation process. Follow-up should be a long-term practice of support for the innovation, and as such, might more appropriately be described as *follow-through* (Dettmer, 1990). The possibilities include peer coaching, discussion groups, visits to sites where the innovation is occurring, newsletters, and interviews. Data gathered during follow-up and follow-through can be used to plan future in-services and staff development projects. (See Figure 12-10.)

One caution must be noted regarding ISD outcomes. When educators are introduced to new concepts and challenged to try new approaches, some discomfort is inevitable. Learning new skills involves greater effort than continuing to use old ones (Joyce and Showers, 1983). The adage that training may make you worse before it makes you better is an important point to consider. This accents the need for follow-through efforts and perseverance on the part of the consultant.

Please take a few minutes to respond to these questions about the recent staff development ____(date)____ on the topic of ____(topic)____. In doing so you will be helping staff developers and presenters plan effective staff development experiences for you and your colleagues.

1. Have you implemented any idea or strategy that was presented during the staff development? If so, please describe it briefly and rate the success level:

_____

_____

_____

___1, not effective   ___2, somewhat effective   ___3, very effective

2. Is there something more you would like to learn about this topic? If so, please describe your need.

_____

_____

_____

3. If you did not use the staff development information, please explain your reluctance to do so.

_____

_____

_____

4. This item is *very* important. Did the information or enthusiasm you received have positive ripple effects that you could identify and describe? If so, please do, and also rate the extent to which this happened.

_____

_____

_____

1 = a little   2 = somewhat   3 = to a great extent   4 = profoundly

---

FIGURE 12-10   Follow-up Information for Staff Development

Evaluation of the In-service and Staff Development

The tool used most often for in-service and staff development evaluation is a questionnaire participants complete immediately following the activity. The evaluation should include both objective responses and an invitation for open-ended responses. A Likert scale of five to seven values is preferable to a Yes-or-No format. The evaluation data should be used to design more meaningful activities as well as to improve presentation skills. (See Figure 12-11 for an example of an ISD evaluation tool, and consult Chapter 8 for additional information on evaluation.)

Presenters may want to complete a self-evaluation and evaluate the participants as well. By doing so, consultants ascertain participant preparedness and responsiveness to the topic. This provides information that can help them and their host schools plan further consultation and collaboration directed to the participants' needs.

Benefits of In-service and Staff Development

In-service and staff development for consultation, collaboration, and special needs of students have the potential to create positive ripple effects that have no bounds. They encourage

- increased respect for individual differences, creative approaches, and educational excellence;
- teacher proficiency in innovative curriculum and teacher strategies;

In-service/Staff Development Evaluation

Date _____

Name (optional) _____   Teaching Area and Level (s) _____

Site of the In-service/Staff Development _____   Topic _____

Rate the following with a value from 1 through 5:

1 = None   2 = A little   3 = Somewhat   4 = Considerably   5 = Much

1. The event increased my understanding of the topic. _____
2. The goals and objectives of the event addressed needs I had identified. _____
3. The content was well developed and organized. _____
4. The material was presented effectively. _____
5. The environment was satisfactory. _____
6. I gained ideas to use in my own situation. _____
7. I will use at least one idea from this event. _____
8. Strengths of the event: _____
9. Ways the event could be improved: _____
10. I would like to know more about: _____

FIGURE 12-11   In-service/Staff Development Evaluation

- staff and parent involvement, and satisfaction with the educational system;
- collegiality and collaboration among all school personnel as well as community and parents.

In order to attain these positive outcomes, in-service and staff development must be planned, conducted, and evaluated thoroughly.

Resource-Gathering and Dissemination

Consulting and collaborating teachers are effective catalysts for finding and using resources in and beyond school facilities. Resources for learning include people (experts, models, advocates and supporters); places (sites, sources); and things (data, materials, equipment, systems and procedures). The source of resources to help children and adults learn is virtually unlimited. There are local colleges and universities; business, industry, and professions; special interest groups in the community; city, county, and state officials; talented parents and grandparents; local service organizations; foreign student exchanges; museums; libraries; vocational and technical schools; media; recreation leaders; county agents; senior citizens; even students themselves. When educators consult with others and collaborate in teams, they are more able to locate and coordinate the services of others as mentors, resource speakers, experts, adjudicators (see student product assessment technique in Chapter 10), or technology and media specialists. Networking with these resource personnel can increase the learning opportunities for students greatly.

Rate the following items, using a scale of:

1 = inadequate,   2 = fair,   3 = satisfactory,   4 = good,   5 = excellent

---

____   1. I was well-prepared.

____   2. I was organized.

____   3. My material was on target with their needs.

____   4. I established rapport and got off to a good start.

____   5. Participants seemed interested.

____   6. Participants wanted to know even more about the topic(s).

____   7. I had an accurate perspective of the audience.

____   8. I got participants involved.

____   9. I had the right kind and amount of handouts.

____   10. My presentation materials were high quality.

____   11. I did my very best in this activity.

____   12. I have plans for follow-through with the participants.

____   13. I learned from the experience, too.

____   14. This is my overall rating of the staff development.

FIGURE 12-12   Presenter's Self-Assessment of Staff Development

---

APPLICATION 12.6   Preparing a Staff Development Outline

Prepare an outline of a staff development activity that might be used by special education consultants to cultivate a spirit of collaboration and teamwork among general classroom teachers, special education personnel, and related services and support personnel. Include a list of do's and don'ts that would be pertinent to this ISD activity.

Sources for Assistance in Crisis

One helpful practice is to prepare attractive booklets for student use. One that was developed in Topeka, Kansas, by the Topeka Youth Council is called "Youth Yellow Pages." The shirt-pocket-sized book contains emergency and crisis numbers (drugs, eating disorders, running away, suicide, sexuality, AIDS, sexual abuse, pregnancy, teen parenting, the law, drinking and driving, accidents, violence, and parent-adolescent mediation). It also includes sections of material on education, employment, services for disabled, volunteering, mental health, recreation, and youth organizations and centers. A similar book developed in Pulaski County, Arkansas, contains similar topics along with a wealth of important assistance-center addresses and telephone numbers.

Library and Media Resources

The library and media centers are repositories of tremendous amounts of information. Consultants and collaborators should be familiar with basic education sources, including

- Educational Resources Information Center (ERIC), a U. S. federal information system of 16 clearinghouses throughout the country;
- Education Index, an index of titles and citations arranged by topic headings and author headings;
- Reader's Guide to Periodical Literature, titles and citations covering a wide variety of topics;
- CompuServe, Dialog, and similar on-line data bases
- Educational journals and reviews. [See Vockell and Asher (1995) for a table of the 15 most frequently cited journals by Encyclopedia of Educational Research, along with other helpful information on educational data sources given in the For Further Reading sections at the end of each chapter.]
- Interlibrary loans are another useful source of information for the needs of consulting teachers working with wide ranges of student learning and behavioral needs.

Generating Proposals for Grant Funds

One of the most impressive contributions of resources by school personnel is the funded grant. Several benefits accrue to grant recipients. The first of these benefits—team collaboration—occurs whether or not the grant proposal is funded. Few significant proposals are developed in these times that do not include a number of collaborating colleagues—some in major roles and others with minor but important involvement. Another benefit is the collection of resources and support needed to meet the goals of the grant. As resources are targeted, and letters of support are generated, more and more people become involved and supportive of school programs.

When a grant proposal is funded, benefits soar. Money and resources become available for carrying out projects that were only dreams. This has an energizing, morale-boosting effect that can reverberate throughout a school system. The amounts of money do not need to be sizable for these benefits to occur. Some of the most invigorating projects have resulted from relatively small grant funds. The projects with the highest payoffs are those that generate ripple effects beyond the grant funding.

School consultants and collaborators, particularly those who have significant staff development responsibilities, are in ideal positions to seek grant funds. Even larger districts that employ grant-writers can use the participation of these personnel productively.

School districts should designate individuals to be trained in grant-seeking techniques, for there are a few important procedures that are critical to success.

Successful grant proposals emanate from an identified need. A good match must be found between that need and the goals of an appropriate funding source. The proposal must be prepared correctly and submitted on time. Proposals that are not funded should not be cast aside but critiqued thoroughly for possible revision and resubmission. Proposal development has two phases: (1) planning and (2) preparation. The most productive strategy is to spend about 80 percent of time and energy on planning the project, and the remaining 20 percent on writing the proposal. Those who switch these priorities end up with weak projects that are hard to direct even in the unlikely event that they are funded.

Two general sources of funding are available: public agencies and private foundations. Most companies need to give money away as part of their tax structure, and the grant-developer's challenge is to convince companies to give part of it to them (Zimet, 1993). Experts in grant production advise that requirements for proposals are somewhat different between public and private sources. Grant-writing is a combination of technical writing and creative writing (Zimet, 1993). Three mistakes must be avoided at all costs: failing to read instructions diligently; disregarding specific topic areas and funding source matches; and ignoring deadlines. Because proposal preparation is hard work, astute grant-writers follow basic steps to avoid major pitfalls:

1. Identify a need. What is the problem? Is it potentially fundable? High priority topics for successful grant proposals in the mid-1990s include: gangs, violence, world-class standards, teachers to provide education to meet those standards, math and science education, teen pregnancy, inclusion, integrated curriculum, and computer literacy for both young people and adults.
2. Explore the research base for the identified need. Watch for trends and for connections that link trends and fields.
3. Get together a team of productive people. Note the points in Chapter 4 about having a variety of skills and learning styles on the team. Having multiple perspectives and a wide range of competencies will vastly improve the proposal. Teams are particularly

helpful for collecting the demographic data that will be required for properly executed proposal preparation.

4. Identify possible sources of funding. Funding sources are listed in the Federal Register. However, for some enthusiastic grant-seekers, this source is too little and often too late. Other useful information resources are

Federal Grants and Contracts Weekly;

Catalog of Federal Domestic Assistance

Annual Register of Grant Support

Foundation Grants Index;

The Source Book Profiles

The Foundation Directory

Foundation Reporter Corporate Giving Directory;

The Directory of Corporate Philanthropy;

The Taft Corporate Giving Directory;

Education Funding Research Council;

Education Week.

These and other resources are available at many libraries. With telecommunications software and a modem, other sources can be obtained online.

5. Obtain the guidelines for the selected funding source(s). A guidelines packet is called "Request for Proposal," or RFP. From this point, each step of the process must be preceded with this admonition—READ THE GUIDELINES! At this stage you will read to be sure that there is a good fit between your idea and the funding source, for the ability of that source to meet your budget request, for directions on how to apply, for criteria to be used in evaluating the proposal, and most of all, for the APPLICATION DEADLINE. A proposal submitted late is no proposal at all. That is the first elimination criterion, even for otherwise superior proposals. The second way to guarantee that the proposal will not be considered is failure to stay within the specifications.

6. The next step is to design the project. As stressed earlier, this phase should take up the major part of time and energy that can be directed toward the project. And—read the guidelines, thoroughly and often. Typical parts of a proposal are description of who will manage the project; personnel involved in implementing and maintaining the project; description of project activities; evaluation plan for assessing the project's effectiveness; dissemination of project results; budget justification; continuation of the project beyond funding dates; letters of support; and, of course, the ubiquitous forms that must be filled out accurately and completely. These parts are weighted in varying amounts to determine the proposal's ranking among all submitted proposals, and those weight values are listed in the guidelines.

Subcategories under description of the project include expected outcomes that tie to the problem, objectives that relate to each of the activities, plan of operation, timeline, data-collection procedures, and ways to evaluate each activity.

7. Budgets must be adequate for the project, but not "padded." All items should be tied to the activities of the project and the key personnel costs involved. If set too low, they would signal poor planning that would undermine the project. Budgets provide for indirect costs (overhead), any cost sharing or subcontracting for services, and, primarily, the direct costs of the proposed project—salaries and fringe benefits, equipment, supplies

and materials, travel (which many funding agencies are restricting greatly), consultant fees, computer expenses, printing and duplicating, postage and telecommunication, along with other direct costs specific to the focus of the project.

8. Interagency collaborative support is a very desirable component of most grant projects and is a requirement of some agencies for submitted proposals.

9. Establish contact with the funding agency and put to good use any suggestions their program officers have for proposal development.

10. The most singularly important step is to meet the deadline. If it is not met, the proposal is eliminated, and the time, energy, and costs expended in producing it are wasted.

APPLICATION 12.8   Trying Out the Proposal Plan

As the proposal is being developed, try telling your plan as a three-minute story to some impartial, objective colleagues, or better yet, to individuals outside the educational fields whose perspectives you value. If they do not understand it and become enthusiastic about it, the plan needs more work or a different focus.

If a proposal is not funded, the developers should ask to receive reviews of that package. Reading the reviewer comments is a form of staff development and helps make the next attempt more productive. If the review marks were good, the proposal should be revised or modified as they indicated, and resubmitted. Proposals are funded because:

- the benefits they promise to a targeted population are sound;
- the uniqueness of the proposal is educationally sound;
- it presents a strong case for local need and strong collaborative efforts;
- it contains local efforts to help with funding;
- the potential to benefit both local and state or regional efforts is evident;
- there are strong evaluative components;
- it has the potential for longevity and positive ripple effects; and
- it has justifiable and reasonable budget requests (Stephens, 1994).

Tips for Consulting and Collaborating

1. If an opportunity arises, suggest certain activities to certain teachers who might want them. Don't force. Sometimes, although not often, the distribution of material to teachers backfires because they resent the inference that they need it, so let them decide. Instead of stuffing teachers' mailboxes with things they may not want, lay out new books or activities on tables in the teachers' workroom.

2. Have an in-service on parent-teacher conferences for students with special needs. Ask teachers to submit "stumper" problems. Then use them to determine how to react and deal with those situations. Have lots of ideas to distribute.

3. Do your very best to get administrators to *attend* and *participate* in the ISD activities.

4. About two months after in-service, send teachers a checklist of outcomes derived from the in-service, with a place for them to comment before returning the lists.

5. In the teachers' workroom, have treats and note cards with the directions, "Take a treat and take a sheet," meaning to take a sheet that has tips concerning student needs. A variation is "Take a treat and leave a sheet" in which the sheet is a needs assessment or evaluation you wish to collect.

6. Travel with others to workshops and conferences. The trip provides opportunities for conversation and rapport building.

7. Hand out your school's business cards at conferences, writing your name, educational area, and shared interest on them. This opens up possibilities for future interaction and collaboration.

8. After attending a convention, conference, or other helpful meeting, or after reading an informative piece, write a short note describing it and put a copy in teachers' boxes, spreading the news on things learned.

9. Organize a system so you will know all teachers have been reached through informal or formal ISD.

10. Develop calendars and time lines of program activities to post in teacher areas or to distribute among school personnel. Do not overlook secretaries, for whom such information is particularly important.

11. Prepare teaching videotapes that demonstrate activities appropriate for students with special needs.

12. Bring in the expertise of other school personnel to assist with consultations, especially for specific content areas.

13. Make a personal pledge to read at least one article a week from a professional journal.

14. Join a dynamic professional organization and become actively involved in it.

15. Conduct workshops on topics teachers request. If a topic is outside your line of expertise, find someone who can present it.

16. After each informal or formal ISD, check back to see how the ideas were used, and if there were difficulties, assist in overcoming them.

17. Learn a new technique and infect others with your enthusiasm for using it. Don't just drop off learning centers and activities you have prepared. Ask teachers if you can help get them started.

18. Become acquainted with people in businesses and organizations who are field-testing products, materials, and processes.

19. Observe programs in other schools and share observations with key people in your own school context.

20. Remember that knowing how to consult does not guarantee you the opportunity to do it! Create the opportunity.

Chapter Review

1. Consultants and consulting teachers have ideal roles for planning and implementing in-service and staff development. Through their involvement with ISD activities, they can share content and help build processes that facilitate learning by students with special needs. They also will have the opportunity to develop consultation and collaboration networks in their local school context.

2. In-service is one specialized component within long-range, ongoing staff development programs involving all school personnel.

3. Adult learners have a need to be self-directed in their learning. A group of adult learners represents a wide experience base on which consultants can draw and build. Adult learners want learning that is oriented to the present and that helps them deal with problems they are now facing.

4. In-service and staff development must be designed to address assessed needs of the participants. Before needs assessment is conducted, needs sensing should be undertaken. Teachers may not always know, or verbalize, what they need to know about helping students with special needs.

5. In-service and staff development for facilitating learning by students with special needs should be presented to a wide range of target groups—teachers, administrators, support personnel, policymakers, teacher educators, and others who are involved with learning programs and materials. Finding time, arranging incentives and publicity, and developing the format are important points in planning ISD.

6. Successful ISD activities are created by effective delivery styles, appropriate visuals, helpful handouts, careful evaluation, and commitment to follow-up after the ISD.

7. In-service and staff development can create positive ripple effects for the entire school, through development of teacher proficiency, greater staff involvement, and cultivation of collegiality and collaboration.

8. Grant funds invigorate school programs. Proposals should be planned collaboratively and must follow RFP guidelines.

To Do and Think About

1. Propose several ways a consulting teacher might serve the special needs of students through in-service and staff development activities.

2. Reflect on concerns a classroom teacher might express through needs sensing and needs assessment in regard to learning and behavior needs of students in the classroom.

3. Suppose that an in-service session on alternative grouping techniques is scheduled for an elementary school, with attendance by all building teachers required. The one-hour session is scheduled for Thursday after school, in the kindergarten room. A methods instructor from a nearby university will lecture to the group. Later this evening there is a high-school play performance, and the next day is the end of term before the grading period. How do the in-service topic, time, location, and format violate the principles of good adult learning experiences?

4. Design a teachers' workroom bulletin board that could be considered an informal in-service concerning a disability or an example of students at risk.

5. In a brainstorm session, think up a list of "Things I Don't Want to Happen" with regard to in-service and staff development activities. After having fun with this, it may be a good idea to countermand these "ISD Horrors" with a list of preventives.

6. In a teacher's guide for a particular subject, locate instances where collaboration and use of a consultant are referred to, or better still, encouraged.

7. How might in-service and staff development activities promoted by the special education consulting teachers activate positive ripple effects throughout the school for all students?

For Further Reading

Caldwell, S. D. (Ed.). (1989). *Staff Development: Handbook of Effective Practices.* Oxford, OH: National Staff Development Council.

Journal for Staff Development. Manhattan, KS; Kansas State University. All issues.

Joyce, B. (ed.). (1990). *Changing School Culture through Staff Development.* Alexandria, VA: Association for Supervision and Curriculum Development.

Joyce, B., and Showers, B. (1988). *Student Achievement through Staff Development.* New York: Longman.

Morsink, C. V., Thomas, C. C., and Correa, V. I. (1991). *Interactive Teaming: Consultation and Collaboration in Special Programs.* Columbus, OH: Merrill. Chapter 8, on empowering team members through staff development.

Chapter 13

Looking Ahead with Consultation, Collaboration, and Teamwork in Schools

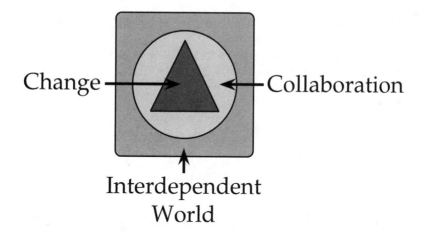

Change — ▶ ◀ — Collaboration

Interdependent World

Introduction

Never before in history have so many elements of people's lives changed so quickly. No one knows for certain where these changes will lead, but trends that have been set into motion should help futurists predict with considerable insight what the world will be like in the twenty-first century. The predictions by these futurists will help educators determine the changes that must occur in schools if they are to meet the demands of the future.

School reform and restructuring movements are addressing the ever-increasing demands for a responsive, responsible educational system. However, schools cannot function as the sole provider of all services needed and still meet their substantial academic responsibilities. Interrelationships must be developed with other public and private sector agencies.

Social and economic trends will place even further demands on schools. These social and economic trends reach around the globe and are reflected in the profound changes of political and cultural structures that erupted in the early 1990s. Changes of such magnitude will ripple throughout social institutions, including schools and the families they serve.

Schools must change dramatically to prepare students for their future. Students who are at risk now because of special learning and behavior difficulties will be placed in even greater jeopardy by ever-accelerating demands on them to keep pace. It is clear that consultation, collaboration, and teamwork among professional and family educators are keys to increasing the opportunities for all students to be successful learners, happy individuals, and productive members of society. This final chapter summarizes key trends that are likely to affect changes in schools and other societal institutions, early in the next millennium, and that signal the need for extensive consultation, collaboration, and teamwork among educators.

Focusing Questions

1. What changes are predicted in society, and how do these predictions relate to the future of students with special needs?
2. What changes are occurring now that will affect schools of the future?
3. How is the nature of student needs changing?
4. What roles will educators play in serving the needs of students and families in the future?
5. Why will interagency collaboration be so important to schools and families?
6. Why are new metaphors needed for education?
7. What are the demands and challenges for consultive and collaborative personnel in schools of the future?

Key Terms in the Chapter

advocacy

change agent

cultural competence

demographic data

futurist

interagency collaboration

metaphor

reification

Zeitgeist

World Trends and Social Concerns Affecting Education

A host of world trends and social concerns is mandating changes in school and home education. Populations are shifting and becoming more diverse. Complex social and health issues affect people of all ages. Critical shortages of skilled, competent workers exist in a

---

Scenario

Another school day is over. The events of the past week are history. What remains beyond the moment is the future. As the teachers in the Chapter 12 scenario conclude their discussion about next week's staff development sessions and head for their rooms to pick up schoolwork they will take home for the weekend, their glances fall on a poster that hangs beside the door:

"The Future Is Now!"

Below the poster in smaller type is an often-quoted maxim—"If we do what we have been doing, we will continue to get what we have been getting." And below that in firm, bold letters, is the question, "Can we do better?" It is a good question to ponder over the weekend...

---

variety of business and service areas. The structure of the family and home has undergone tremendous pressures that affect all members deeply, especially children. Resolutions of these concerns are vital, in order to help children and youth become productive, fulfilled individuals. Although these children and youth are only about one-third of the population, they are 100 percent of the future.

Futurists contribute a wealth of information and ideas to help guide decision making as the twentieth century settles into the history books and the twenty-first century emerges. Their ideas tend to fall into one of four main themes:

- changes in society;
- economic trends;
- family structure changes; and
- demographic trends.

These trends and changes will have a major impact on all aspects of society, including schools.

Changes in Society

The next two decades promise to bring as much change to the world as the previous two hundred years produced. Change is the decisive factor in the structure of the modern world (Benjamin, 1989). Many of the trends point to the need for cooperation, collaboration, and teamwork in making decisions. One of the more obvious trends is interdependency. Societies have become more and more interdependent. It is no longer possible to limit your concerns to the immediate area in which you live. Technology connects individuals, schools, and governments around the world. In this global village of interdependent societies, a decision on one side of the globe can dramatically affect the other side.

In order to survive in an interdependent world, each society must learn to cooperate, collaborate, and communicate with all others. A responsible global citizenry is an expected outcome of the educational system. Tye (1990) suggests that global education can serve as a vehicle for bringing about school improvement. Global education focuses on the importance of involving communities and creating partnerships.

Technology will bring about complex changes at a rapid pace. The capability to store and retrieve information using computer data bases will force businesses, governments, and institutions such as schools to restructure. Toffler (1990b) suggests information networks will allow nonhierarchical communications to pass up and down the corporate ladder. Young employees on the bottom rung of the career ladder will be able to communicate directly with top-level executives working on the same problem. Employees who cannot collaborate within this process are not likely to survive in the workplace. Workers of the future will need to assess critically the information gathered across many cultures.

Knowledge is mushrooming at a pace no one individual can master. Statistics show that, in this country, some two thousand new titles appear on the bookshelves *every* month. It would require reading sixty-six books per day in order to stay abreast of new information in just this one information format. How, then, is one to deal with the overwhelming barrage of new information?

In the future, requirements for knowledge and responsibilities for decision making will be redistributed. In a continual cycle of learning, unlearning, and relearning, workers will master new technologies, adapt to new organizational forms, and generate new ideas. Technology that enhances team decision making will replace old hierarchical and bureaucratic structures. "Five-year-olds today experience more information in one year than their grandparents did in a lifetime" (Gayle, 1990, p. 12). It will be impossible for any one person to know everything needed for making good decisions.

If a student is having difficulty in today's learning environment, what will be the prognosis for that student's survival in tomorrow's world? What will it take for students with special learning needs to be successful lifelong learners? How can students with behavioral disorders be constructive, productive members in increasingly complex social environments? In what ways can the potential of those with special gifts and talents be developed?

It will become more and more necessary for individuals to work in teams and share their knowledge and skills, in order to be effective decision makers. Schools will need to de-emphasize coverage of facts, stressing instead access to information and synthesis of that information. Consultation with others in their areas of expertise, and collaboration to pool the ideas and resources of all, will be key tools for human survival.

Preparing the Future Work Force

Greater ties are being forged between academic and vocational content in education. *Work force 2000* declares that narrow, specific job skills training is not sufficient preparation for workers of the future and calls for the integration of academic and technical education. Another policy statement by the federal government, *Goals 2000,* includes the School to Work Opportunities Act, which outlines educational components of school-based training, paid and unpaid work, mentoring, and community activities. These plans and policies will necessitate new partnerships between educators and employers. Such collaboration will be crucial to the outcomes of the program and the employability of school graduates. Because of the experience of special education personnel in transition programming and in such employability-related skill areas as social skills and self-management, school consultants for students with special needs will be called on to provide leadership in school-to-work programs.

These goals for American students will undoubtedly renew the commitment of special education to focus on transition services for students with special needs. Without consultation, collaboration, and teamwork, transition programming is incomplete. P. L. 101-476 supports secondary special education and requires transition plans in IEPs beginning no later than age 16. The goal is to have more effective outcomes for young people with disabilities. According to Lichtenstein (1993), young adults with disabilities who have dropped out of high school are at the greatest risk of lifelong economic and social harm. About 40 percent of students with emotional and behavioral disorders and an estimated 40 percent of students with learning disabilities drop out of school. This compares with nearly 26 percent of the general population.

Family, culture, and community are vital factors in the transition process (Syzmanski, 1994). These elements, says Syzmanski, are missing from most transition planning and are especially important for people with disabilities. Parents must be proactive partners in the transition process, and the family as a whole is affected by process and outcome. Culture and gender exert great influence on career choices, role models, expectations, and opportunities (Hawks and Muha, 1991). Planning processes and interventions for transition must acknowledge cultural diversity. The best transition programs become part of the community and rely on natural community supports (Syzmanski, 1994). Partnerships with families, employers, and the community are essential to the success of transition programs. The skills for developing and maintaining these partnerships are basic to the role of the educational consultant, thus, the consultant has much to offer in the field of transition.

Cultural Diversity in Schools of the Future

A great deal of work remains to be done as this society enters the twenty-first century. Students, families, and communities served by schools of the future will have a different face than appears today. Education will be required to respond effectively to changes in the cultural nature of American society. Ponterotto and Cases (1991) assert that children of color will be approximately 30 percent of the nation's youth population by the year 2000. These changing demographics create a greater need to improve educational services to culturally diverse groups. Schools of today and of the future must consider cultural factors such as language, race, ethnicity, customs, family structure, and community dynamics in developing programs and practices. Education must acknowledge the role of culture in the educational process.

Attitudes, practices, policies, and structures must be adapted for students in our multicultural society, and, according to Mason (1994), the spirit and process of collaboration are essential for these efforts. Cultural competence is the term used to describe organizations that recognize

- the increasing cultural and racial diversity of students and families;
- culture's role in help-seeking behaviors (Isaacs and Benjamin, 1991);
- diverse perspectives on the origins or etiology of thoughts that the dominant culture describes as mental health problems (Mason, 1994);
- differential service utilization rates of various cultural and racial groups (Mason, 1994)

There are four basic principles of the cultural competence model (Mason, 1994):

1. Valuing diversity
2. Conducting self-assessment
3. Understanding the dynamics of difference
4. Adapting to diversity

Both the Child Welfare League of America (1993) and the Research and Training Center on Family Support and Children's Mental Health at Portland State University have developed cultural competence self-assessments. Staff need to be trained on the differences between majority and nonmajority cultures, and they should examine their own cultural beliefs regarding illness, health, and disability; culturally specific program characteristics and components; and research and theory describing programs that exemplify aspects of the cultural competence model (for example, Isaacs and Benjamin, 1991). Valuable resources for learning about culturally specific perspectives are family members, parents, and natural community helpers such as religious leaders.

Racial categories currently used often lack the necessary details to target the needs of children, youth, and their families. School consultants must be aware within each cultural group there are many other important factors. Care should be taken not to ignore within-group diversity. Examples of such factors are income, education, national origin, social history, levels of assimilation and acculturation, and rural-urban continuum. While these distinctions may appear minor, they can be quite significant when providing services, advocating on behalf of a student and family, and promoting systematic changes (Mason, 1994).

For students with special needs and their families and communities, educators must ask not only, "What do I need to learn about this person culturally to help her or him?" but also "What is the impact of race, family structure, gender, and ethnicity on the problems this person is having?" According to the Regional Research and Training Institute for Human Services (1994), all who deliver human services, including educators, must

- develop culturally appropriate diagnostic methods and tools;
- develop culturally appropriate educational methodology and treatment approaches;
- identify effective outreach efforts to culturally diverse communities;
- identify and utilize culturally diverse natural helpers;
- eradicate nonmajority over-representation in restrictive settings such as special education, foster care, and juvenile justice; and
- evaluate culturally competent services and programs.

Culturally competent organizations such as the school of the near future must acknowledge and protect the right of children to their own culture and to the customs, beliefs, and practices that comprise that culture. They also must affirm that an individual's culture is an integral part of the physical, emotional, intellectual, and overall development and well-being of that individual.

Challenges facing contemporary and future educators are vast; however, so are the benefits to students with special needs and their families. No matter what the education system and structure look like in the future, no matter what roles are assigned to teachers, administrators, social workers, psychologists, and parents, and no matter how children are labeled or grouped, there will be one constant: all will have to work collaboratively, cooperatively, and collectively.

Changes Affecting Schools of the Future

In Chapter 1, current school reform movements were linked to the need for consultation and collaboration among educators. Reform and restructuring movements are a response to societal changes that have placed increased demands on schools to meet the changing needs of students and their families. According to Newmann (1991), the call for drastic changes is related to two issues:

- large numbers of students, especially low-income students of color, who fail in school and score poorly on national tests; and
- students who succeed in school and score well, but are not fully prepared to cope successfully with the demands of contemporary life.

Many key leaders in education are trying to predict and forecast for schools of the future. Thoughtful educators recognize schools will need to be very different from the way they are now, but they do not always agree about changes needed. It is clear that more choices must be available for young people during their high school years, in order to prepare the work force needed for the future. Without an educated work force, the economy will suffer and decline in productivity. Educational changes will be needed in school governance, reform of curriculum and instruction, accountability, and roles of educators (Newmann, 1991). Although there is considerable debate on the meaning of reform and restructuring initiatives, there is agreement on two issues:

- The purpose of changes called for is to provide a quality education for all children, especially those with learning and behavior problems.
- There will be considerable role change, including increased collaboration and consultation (Jenkins, Pious, and Jewell, 1990).

Reform and restructuring call for collaboration in planning and problem solving, and this will require enhanced collegial relationships (West, 1990). Educational collaboration can be an effective catalyst for bringing about needed changes in complex educational systems.

The Future for Students with Special Needs

Family status, ethnicity, and economic level of students in schools of the future will be different from those today. It is necessary to speculate about the nature of the problems students in special education programs for learning and behavioral disorders will have if the dual system of regular education and special education survives. Schools will enroll an increased number of children with severe impairments—for example, cerebral palsy and

---

**APPLICATION 13.1   Matching Predictions to Consultation
and Collaboration Roles**

Consider the following changes in school some educators are predicting for the next century. How do these changes match your ideas? What will be the role of consultation, collaboration, and teamwork in education from "birth to death" if these predictions come to pass?

Total integration for many special education students who are currently served in pull-out programs will continue well into the next century (Wiederholt, 1989).

As the reform efforts bring about restructuring of schools to include integration of academic and technical skills for changing society, vocational education will become more valued in secondary schools (Gayle, 1990).

More emphasis will be given to early childhood education as a preventive measure and, if this is successful, remedial programs will be decreased (Benjamin, 1989). There will be a need for more collaboration among preschool teachers, school psychologists, parents, health service providers, and other personnel within and outside the school.

The Back-to-Basics movement will become Forward-to-Emerging Basics, which will include the use of telecommunications technology in problem solving and other advanced technical skills (Gayle, 1990).

There will be a new collaborative role for teachers and students in which students accept an active senior partnership role in the learning enterprise (Benjamin, 1989).

Professions are products of the Zeitgeist, or the general intellectual and ethical climate and needs of a particular time in history (McGaghie, 1991). This is an important consideration in assessing the competence of educators for performing their roles. Data from educator evaluations will be interpreted in a broader framework, encouraging expanded roles for teachers and support personnel.

"Education will be respected as a valuable and prestigious profession by the 21st century" (Gayle, 1990, p. 13).

---

such syndromes as Trisomy 13 and 18—who will need special services. Medical problems that used to result in death during the first year of life are now being treated; children with these complications are living long enough to become students in public schools. Increasing numbers of premature infants are being saved at even earlier stages of their development. The rapidly increasing group of children whose parents ingested alcohol and other drugs before conception or during pregnancy, or who transferred complications through sexually transmitted diseases will have an alarming impact on education. For example, one of the fastest growing populations at risk for AIDS is young children. These children will greatly tax the physical, emotional, and economic resources of schools and school personnel. The burgeoning population of senior citizens will vie for the same resources that children need.

These problems require up-to-date knowledge on the part of school personnel and ongoing collaboration with professionals in the medical field. In addition to this challenge, schools will face the increasing financial demands made by students with such types of problems.

Changes in Teaching Practices for the Future

"Many concepts in special education are proving increasingly unworkable. Nowhere is this more evident than in our attempts to reify the 'conditions' we decided were evidenced by individuals who failed in school" (Ysseldyke, 1986, p. 22). Reification (converting an abstraction into a concrete thing) of categories, labels, delivery systems based on test scores, and the like, too often has diverted the attention of educators away from improving instruction. As stressed in earlier chapters, a growing number of special education leaders contend that students at risk of school failure in conventional settings are not disabled and deficient students. The problem lies in the misfit between their abilities and the demands made on them in an inflexible school situation. Teachers would do well to examine their teaching practices, curricular requirements, and learning environment structure as a first alternative, if students are not learning and behaving acceptably.

With school consultation and collaboration as an integral part of the educational program, there is hope for creating the flexibility students need, and for enhancing the repertoire of teaching practices that will enable them to succeed. The best teachers have always been those who expand, change, modify, and compact the requirements so that the important material is taught, but in a way and to the extent that serves each student's individual, special needs.

In their book that is widely used in special education courses, Hallahan and Kauffman (1991) include several descriptions of collaborative efforts between a classroom teacher and a special education teacher. For example, when an itinerant teacher for the visually impaired and a third-grade teacher work together to adapt material and team up to provide services, there are three beneficiaries of their efforts: consultant, consultee, and client. Even the roles are somewhat interchangeable, depending on who provides the direct service to whom. When a teacher of emotionally disturbed students and a fifth-grade teacher collaborate on procedures and reinforcements for a seriously disturbed student, all three roles again benefit. Additionally, the student's improved behavior creates a positive ripple effect for other school personnel and students in the school.

Literature on change and the future is evolving from viewing teachers as recalcitrant and resistant to change, toward examining the structure of the school context and the personal attributes of teachers that affect whether or not they implement changes (Richardson, 1990). Hoyt (1991) identifies two kinds of educational change as

- process, or people change; and
- structural, or system, change.

Structural changes will work only after the "people change" creates an attitude of readiness for structural change (Hoyt, 1991).

It will be important for school personnel in the future to participate actively in school improvement projects. Keys to the success of organizational development projects are a genuine investment in the process by the top administrator and skillful involvement of the staff (Conoley, 1989). Conoley emphasizes teachers will need to take some responsibility for achieving the quality of outcomes they desire. However, they must also feel the extra effort they give to committee work, problem identification, or problem-solving teams is not just added to their load of responsibilities. They need to perceive this effort as having a positive effect on their daily lives.

In their commentary on the necessary restructuring of special and regular education, Reynolds, Wang, and Walberg (1987) propose that unless major structural changes are made in the field of special education, special education will become more a problem, and not so much a solution, in providing education for children with special needs. Disjointedness and proceduralism are twin facets of the overall problem these researchers identify as inefficiency in using costly resources. Increasing numbers of students who qualify for special education and an increasingly negative climate for funding to support special projects add to the problems and trends that signal the need for change.

Collaborative consultation is recommended by Phillips and McCullough (1990) as a viable tool for educators to use in coping with a rapidly changing, increasingly complex society. They also suggest that correlates of collaboration such as group morale, cohesion, and increased knowledge of processes and alternatives are important to success in meeting student needs. However, they note

> *Administrative, teaching and support personnel must address matters of conceptual dissonance and reach a consensus regarding the nature and importance of collaborative relations. In short, educational leaders and advocates of consultation-based programming must develop ways to effectively institute a collaborative ethic in schools. (Phillips and McCullough, 1990, p. 295)*

This collaborative ethic is a means of empowering professionals to assist each other in solving problems. Teacher empowerment is threatened when teachers are asked to make changes without the opportunity to reflect on the theoretical frameworks. Opportunities should be provided that allow teachers to interact and have conversations about their work (Richardson, 1990). Richardson cautions that this process must be implemented in an atmosphere of trust.

APPLICATION 13.2   Making Changes through Consultation, Collaboration, and Teamwork

Consider the following typical school needs, and ways that consultation and the collaborative ethic might assist in making school changes:

- Create opportunities to interface special education programs with the general program.
- Institute communication networks among school staff, parents, advocacy groups.
- Contribute to text selections, curriculum revisions, general school reform.
- Identify exemplary, successful teaching practices.
- Coordinate use of community resources for students' needs.
- Help parents identify ways to contribute to school programs.
- Help other educators and parents set realistic goals for students with learning and behavioral problems.
- Contribute to planning and conducting in-service and staff development.
- Conduct formative and summative evaluation to improve school programs.

Hoyt (1991) stresses that collaboration involving school personnel must involve not only shared responsibility, but shared authority and shared accountability as well. As Hoyt puts it, this three-way sharing will help ensure the concept of collaboration fares better in the next ten years than the concept of partnerships did during the past decade.

Interagency Collaboration

As a process, collaboration is a means to an end rather than an end in itself. The desired end is to engender more effective educational outcomes for students with special needs. Schools are not alone in their responsibility for removing barriers that keep students from succeeding in the adult world. Personnel in mental health, employment and training, child development, recreation, health, and welfare services, as well as education, have a vital interest in promoting school success for all children.

Many of the families of children with special needs face a multitude of problems and need services beyond the realm of education. Too often these services are fragmented without a coherent, binding strategy to meet basic family goals (Bruner, 1991). The Education and Human Services Consortium (Melaville and Blank, 1991) proposes that education, health, and human service agencies join each other as co-equals in orchestrating the delivery of services to children and families. System-level collaboration is based on the reality that no one agency can provide all necessary services for children with disabilities and their families. Collaborative strategies can

- Help provide better services to families who are part of several human service systems;
- Keep children and families from falling through the cracks by ensuring that they receive needed services; and
- Reduce environmental risks to children.

When systems collaborate, they reduce service duplication, reduce the total cost of services, ensure fewer gaps in services, minimize conflict, and clarify responsibility.

Interagency collaboration includes these elements (Bruner, 1991):

1. Jointly developing and agreeing to a set of common goals and directions;
2. Sharing responsibility for obtaining those goals;
3. Working together to achieve the goals, using the expertise of each collaborator.

There are some common elements of interagency collaboration that contribute to the effectiveness and efficiency of efforts:

- *Collaborative attitude.* Recognize the need for collaboration and take the time to develop positive relationships within the team. Joint ownership will reduce conflict and problems.
- *Written guidelines.* Form a written statement of philosophy that stands as the measure of all policies and actions. Delineate roles, responsibilities, and agreements for shared resources.

- *Team leadership*. Leadership roles should be assigned but can be shared. Coordination and technical assistance are important roles.
- *Staff development*. Cross-agency training can foster positive relationships and promote the development of the skills and processes of collaboration.
- *Collective input and supportive environment* (Weber, 1994). Clarity of purpose comes from sharing obstacles that individuals and agencies face and solutions they envision. Sharing relevant experiences and insights reduces barriers between cultural differences and promotes understanding and empathy.

"If you think interpersonal and interagency consultation is challenging, wait until you try interagency collaboration!," says one experienced educational consultant. Turf issues, lack of clarity on fiscal responsibilities, and shared personnel, facilities, and equipment agreements are among the barriers to successful interagency collaboration. On the other hand, many educators have had experience with interagency collaboration while working with Interagency Coordinating Councils, as established under Part H of P. L. 99-457 (the Handicapped Infant and Toddler Program), and with Community Transition Councils, as established under P. L. 101-476. Others have valuable experience working with other human service agencies in developing "One-Stop Shopping," and "Wrap-around" programs. These experiences in collaborative efforts, difficult though they may have been, will serve participants well as they assume new roles in interagency collaboration.

Many families face significant environmental risks, including those that contribute to the etiology of developmental disabilities or exacerbation of those conditions. Identifying and implementing collaborative strategies and evaluating their impact is particularly challenging. The ultimate goal is the future success of students with special needs by eliminating or reducing difficulties that place them at risk: infant mortality, delinquency, youth unemployment, child abuse and neglect, drug involvement, suicide, mental illness, and poverty. Interagency collaboration is not a "quick fix." It is time consuming and process intensive. It takes commitment and flexibility to discover new roles and relationships. These new roles and responsibilities utilize collaborative skills that take practice, knowledge, and skills.

Developing New Metaphors for Education

Productive thinking about complex issues can be enhanced by metaphor (Pollio, 1987). Metaphors are mental maps that permit the connection of different meanings through some shared similarity. They appear often in spoken and written communication. "Life is a loom," and "The fog swallowed the ship," and "Last June my flower garden was a paint box of colors," are metaphors. They connect in order to explain. People use metaphors to sort out their perceptions, evaluate, and express feelings, and reflect upon the purpose of things in order to make better sense of their world (Deshler, 1985).

Belth (1977) suggest that, as we create or reject particular metaphors, we form problems. The world's problems, therefore, become what we form them to be. So, through metaphors we can imagine the world as we wish it to be and fashion it accordingly. The majority of our creative ideas and our problem-solving solutions are born in analogical and

metaphorical thinking. We take ideas from one context and apply them elsewhere to produce new ideas or more interesting presentations. We make connections that transform our
thinking to more productive heights. Metaphorical thinking is

> practical (useful and helpful);
> personal (individualistic);
> pleasurable (unconventional, surprising, or humorous);
> powerful (enlarging and attitudinal);
> pedagogical (teaching, exemplifying).

However, metaphorical thinking can be problematic as well. Just as metaphors are
good tools for explaining ideas and achieving new perspectives on both the unfamiliar and
the very familiar, they can limit our thinking if they are simplistic or outdated (von Oech,
1983), and then they become stereotypic and imprisoning.

Schools and education have generated a variety of metaphors, but some of them are
now viewed as uninspiring and somewhat demoralizing to the human spirit. They shackle
our thinking about teaching and learning. Dobson, Dobson, and Koetting (1985) assert that
the outlook on education is imprisoned today within three unfortunate metaphors:

> A military metaphor—characterized by concepts and vocabulary such as target popu-
> lation, strategy, objectives, training, standardized, discipline, schedule, and informa-
> tion systems;

> An industrial metaphor—revealed by language such as cost effectiveness, product,
> feedback, efficiency, quality control, and management; and

> A disease metaphor—reflected in words and practices such as diagnostic, prescriptive,
> treatment, remediation, label, impaired, monitor, deviant, and referral.

In another context, Futrell (1989) used the metaphor of business to describe education,
with knowledge being the commodity, learning an asset, research an enterprise, and intellectual capacity as capital. These kinds of metaphors—military, industrial, disease, and
business—may illustrate schools as we have come to know them, but seem to be counterproductive for the future. We need good, new metaphors in education—metaphors that up-
lift, inspire, and promise positive outcomes.

One promising metaphor is gardening, with concepts and vocabulary that reflect bud-
ding potential, that recognize special needs, and anticipate high production. For example,
the gardening/cultivator metaphor might include:

> Seeds—students
> Climate—learning environment
> Soil—curriculum
> Gardener—teacher, parent, support personnel
> Sunlight—ideas
> Rain—materials, resources, opportunity for learning
> Shade—incubation, protection

Fertilizer—stimulation, interest, curiosity, fun
Weeds—irrelevancies
Pruning/grafting—deficits, talents
Predators/disease—learning and behavior problems
Seasons—time, rhythm and cycle of development
Harvest—achievement, fulfillment.

Positive, nurturant metaphors can be used to highlight the benefits of processes such as collaboration and to overcome obstacles by pointing out faulty perspectives and myopic viewpoints.

A constructive step that an educator could take toward thinking differently about education, schools, and students, would be to envision schools in a new metaphorical way. Development of a powerful new metaphor that features collaboration and encourages teamwork just might intrigue resisting, reluctant colleagues and entice them into trying these complex interactive processes. (See Figure 13–1.)

Stimuli for creating new metaphors can come from many sources:

- Thinking about important student outcomes;
- Finding ways parents, support personnel, and other community members can be involved in learning;
- Engaging in collegial interactions among school educators and parent educators;
- Highlighting examples of teacher satisfaction;
- Carrying out school reform; and
- Acknowledging today's students as society's future.

Developing a Plan Infusing Consultation, Collaborating, and Teamwork

Individual differences abound when adults set about the task of developing personal plans for attaining professional goals. School reform and the student success it is intended to

---

APPLICATION 13.3   A New Personal Metaphor for Education

Create a new metaphor for education that focuses on consulting, collaborating, and teamwork. Make it more positive than the conventional military, industrial, and disease metaphors discussed above. Decide on a way to express your *new* metaphor. For example, you might use a paragraph, poem, drawing, song, or physical movement that releases it from your own inner thoughts into a form that can be shared with others. Share it with colleagues. What new vocabulary does your metaphor contribute to the profession? How is it more enlightening and stimulating than the ones that have been around awhile? Does your metaphor encourage cultural diversity, respect for individual differences of children *and* adults, and processes of communication and collaboration? Could you use it productively as a logo? The theme of a speech? In your everyday conversation about schools and students and professional colleagues?

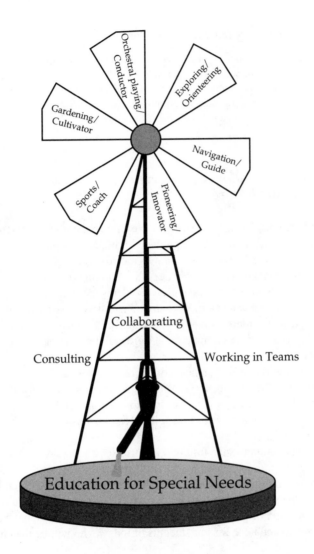

FIGURE 13-1   New Metaphors for Education

generate depend upon both individual and organizational development (Sparks, 1992) Sparks reminds professional educators that staff development is not the answer to all performance problems. "Continuous improvement is truly an inside-out process in which we first seek to change ourselves before expecting the same of others" (Sparks, 1992, p. 2). In order to develop content and processes for consultation services and to initiate collaboration and teamwork in the school context educators will want to construct their own personal plans for fulfilling these roles.

APPLICATION 13.4   A Personal Plan for Collaborative Consultation

Develop a personal plan for using concepts of school consultation, collaboration, and consultation within the school context and the role responsibilities you anticipate for the future. Make a copy of the plan and mail it to yourself at a designated time in the future, to remind you of the commitment you made when you were focused on these issues, setting goals, and reflecting on actions you might take to achieve those goals.

Challenges for Consultation, Collaboration, and Teamwork in the Future

As educational consultants struggle to establish themselves in school classrooms and buildings, they often find they are pioneers in modeling consultation, collaboration, and teamwork. They must serve as consultants and advocates of children with learning and behavior needs when the nature of those needs is changing quickly. They will be collaborating with professionals in fields focusing on problems as varied and alarming as alcohol and other drug abuse, neonatal health, sexually transmitted diseases, disintegration of the family, psychological disorders, poverty, child abuse, English-as-second-language concerns, geographic isolation, environmental hazards, and a host of unresolved or not-yet-recognized needs.

Struggles to establish new collaborative roles for educators will be stressful and time-consuming (Newmann, 1991). No simple solution exists for the complex issues and concerns of the future. Now is the time to develop skills of consultation, collaboration, and teamwork on behalf of students with special needs and the society in which they live (see Figure 13-2).

Collaboration is the future. It is intrinsic to school reform and restructuring, interagency cooperation, responses to changing student needs, and future global, economic, demographic, and technological trends. As consultants facilitate collaboration and teamwork within the school context, to serve special needs each school day, they provide a basis and a framework for continued collaboration throughout the global world. This framework provides help and hope for our students of today, who will be the citizens of tomorrow.

Tips for Consulting and Collaborating

1. Don't try to do it all by yourself.
2. Advertise successes, both yours and those of classroom teachers. Sometimes teachers are amazed that a student or a situation has shown *any* progress whatsoever.
3. Give talks at community clubs and service organizations—about schools, student needs, consultation and collaboration endeavors.
4. Develop a networking system for support and delivery of positive "strokes" to school personnel and parents.
5. Inform teachers of legislative and litigative activity.

6. Host sessions at conferences for policy makers and administrators.
7. Have open house and extend invitations to school board members.
8. Follow up open house with-thank you notes to visitors for their interest and attendance.
9. During the summer, send postcards to teachers saying, "I'm looking forward to working with you this year."
10. Don't appear *too* dedicated—so much so that your involvement is intimidating to others who are still unsure and a bit reluctant.
11. Write a proposal and receive resources for sharing with the schools.
12. Do not expect the same levels of involvement and commitment from everyone.
13. Do not try to "go it alone." Look to colleagues for support and counsel.
14. Be an advocate through serving as officer and committee member of organizations whose goals support your consultation goals and role.
15. Never give up!

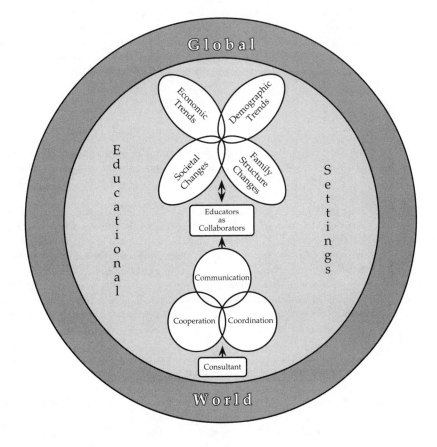

FIGURE 13-2   Educational Settings in a Global World

(By P. Dettmer and L. Katzer)

Chapter Review

1. World trends and societal changes in economics, family structure, and demographics will affect students with special needs in a number of significant ways.
2. Schools of the future will house large numbers of students who are failing and performing poorly on national tests, as well as students who perform better on tests but are not prepared adequately for the demands of the workplace.
3. There will be increasingly large populations of students who have profound learning and behavior problems brought on by social problems, medical problems, and economic hardships.
4. Successful schools of the future will require educators to make changes in role functions and school personnel, and will encourage parents to be actively involved in school reform and restructuring.
5. Successful schools of the future will engage in interagency collaboration, with collaborators working together to achieve goals of serving all students' needs effectively.
6. New metaphors are needed for education. Metaphors help define problems and clarify thinking. Visions for the future of learning and teaching that focus on traditional metaphors for education, such as military, industrial, and disease, are myopic and somewhat demoralizing.
7. Bringing about needed school change requires greater emphasis on collaboration and teamwork. School consultation will be an important tool for coordinating health, social, and educational services to help all students, particularly those with special needs.

To Do and Think About

1. Discuss three to five major concerns regarding social, economic, and environmental issues of the future that will have a major impact on school learning and teaching. How can consultation, collaboration, and teamwork help students with special needs succeed in spite of the pressures they face from these issues?
2. What are the major conditions within school contexts and competencies of school personnel that are needed for successful consultation, collaboration, and teamwork by educators?
3. Select one or more of the issues and concerns discussed in this chapter. Have a panel of four or five members read more about these issues and reflect on them. Then conduct a panel forum, directing questions from the whole group to panel members for their comments.

    As a variation, have a roundtable discussion in which each participant reads about one issue presented in the chapter, and a moderator asks each, in turn, questions having a common denominator of focus—in this case, school consultation and collaboration. (A seating arrangement around tables forming a U shape, with the moderator moving about inside the U shaped space, works well.)
4. Generate a list of possibilities for inclusion in a newsletter to parents, community leaders, or school personnel that reflects consulting teacher roles and the contributions these roles can make to students, school programs, and communities for the future.
5. Create a list of school reform research questions needed for the future that might be explored within the context of strong school consultation programs and competent consulting personnel.
6. Find a forum in which to promote your new metaphor for education.
7. Develop a job description for an educator in the year 2000, using any context for which an educator might be interviewed as a candidate (job title, location, ages of students, content areas, training required). Does your job description reflect the need for communication and coordination among colleagues, parents, and support personnel?

8. Now that you have studied the content, process, and context of collaborative schools that utilize consultation services and promote teamwork, what kind of schools would you build if you could start all over in a place where no schools exist?
9. Create a motivational bumper sticker that will proclaim the importance of professional and parent educators during the 1990's and into the next millennium.
10. Where do we as educators, parents, life-long learners, go from here?

For Further Reading

Naisbitt, J., and Aburdene, J. (1990). *Megatrends 2000.* New York: Morrow.

Toffler, A. (1990). *Powershift.* New York: Bantam.

William T. Grant Foundation Commission on Work, Family, and Citizenship. (1988). *The Forgotten Half. Pathways to success for America's Youth and Young Families.* Washington, D. C.: Author.

References

Afzali, E. (1994). *Inclusion of deaf students in the regular classroom: Perceptions of regular teachers and deaf educators.* Kansas State University: Unpublished dissertation.

Ahlburg, D.A., and DeVita, C.J. (1992). New realities of the American family. *Population Bulletin, 47,* 1–44.

Alberti, R.E., & Emmons, M.L. (1974). *Your perfect right: A guide to assertive behavior* (2nd ed.). San Luis Obispo, CA: Impact.

Alberto, P.A., and Troutman, A.C. (1990). *Applied behavior analysis* (3rd ed.). Columbus, Ohio: Merrill Publishing Co.

Allington, R.L., & Broikou, K.A. (1988). Development of shared knowledge: A new role for classroom and specialist teachers. *The Reading Teacher,* April 1988, 806–811.

Ammer, J. (1984). The mechanics of mainstreaming: Consider the regular educators' perspective. *Remedial and Special Education, 5*(6): 15–20.

Anderson, M., and Goldberg, P. (1991). *Cultural competence in screening and assessment: Implications for services to young children with special needs ages birth through five.* Minneapolis, MN: PACER Center, Inc.

Archer, A., & Gleason, M. (1989). *Skills for school success. Book three; Teacher guide.* North Billerica, MA: Curriculum Associates.

Arcia, E., Keys, L., Gallagher, J.J., and Herrick, H. (1992). *Potential underutilization of Part H Services: An empirical study of national demographic factors.* Chapel Hill, NC: Carolina Policy Studies Program.

Armbruster, B.B., & Anderson, T.H. (1988). On selecting "considerate" content area textbooks. *Remedial and Special Education, 9*(1), 47–52.

Aronson, (1978). The jigsaw classroom. Beverly Hills, CA: Sage Publications.

Babcock, N.L., & Pryzwansky, W.B. (1983). Models of consultation: Preferences of educational professionals at five stages of service. *Journal of School Psychology, 21,* 359–366.

Baca, L.M., & Cervantes, H.T. (1984). *The bilingual education interface.* Columbus, OH: Merrill.

Bailey, G.D. (1981). Self-directed staff development. *Educational Considerations, 8*(1), 15–20.

Baker, P.J. (1991). Metaphors of mindful engagement and a vision of better schools. *Educational Leadership, 48*(7), 32–35.

Banks, J.A. (1988). *Multiethnic education and practice* (2nd ed.). Boston: Allyn & Bacon.

Banks, J.A., & Banks, C.A. (1989). *Multicultural education: Issues and perspectives.* Needham Heights, MA: Allyn & Bacon.

Barstow. (1981). The Talcott Mountain Science Center. In J.N. Nazzaro (Ed.). *Computer connections for gifted children and youth.* Reston, VA: Clearinghouse on Handicapped and Gifted Youth.

Baush, J.P. (1989). The transParent school model: New technology for parent involvement. *Educational Leadership, 47*(2): 32–35.

Beckoff, A.G., & Bender, W.N. (1989). Programming for mainstream kindergarten success in preschool: Teachers' perceptions of necessary prerequisite skills. *Journal of Early Intervention, 13*(3), 269–280.

Belth, M. (1977). *The process of thinking.* New York: Davie McCay.

Bender, W.N. (1988). The other side of placement decisions: Assessment of the mainstream learning environment. *Remedial and Special Education, 9*(5), 28–33.

Benjamin, S. (1989). An ideascape for education: What futurists recommend. *Educational Leadership, 47*(1), 9–14.

Bensky, J.M., Shaw, S.F., Gouse, A.S., Bates, H., Dixon, B.E., & Beane, W.E. (1980). Public Law 94–142 and Stress: A problem for educators. *Exceptional Children, 47*(1), 24–29.

Berg, K.K. (1994). *Family-based services: A solution focused approach.* New York: W.W. Norton.

Bergan, J.R. (1977). *Behavioral consultation.* Columbus, OH: Merrill.

Bergan, J.R., & Tombari, M.L. (1976). Consultant skill and efficiency and the implementation and outcome of consultation. *Journal of School Psychology, 14*(1): 3–14.

Betts, G.T. (1986). The autonomous learner model for the gifted and talented. In J.S. Renzulli (Ed.), *Systems and models for developing programs for the gifted and talented* (pp. 27–56). Mansfield Center, CT: Creative Learning Press.

Bevevino, M. (1988). The 87 percent factor. *Delta Kappa Gamma Bulletin, 54*(3), 9–16.

Bickel, W., & Bickel, D. (1986). Effective schools, classrooms and instruction: Implications for special education. *Exceptional Children, 20*(6), 489–519.

Bietau, L. (1994, December). Personal correspondence.

Blackhurst, A.E., & Berdine, W.H. (Eds.) (1993). *An introduction to special education.* New York: HarperCollins.

Blaylock, B.K. (1983). Teamwork in a simulated production environment. *Research in Psychological Type, 6,* 58–67.

Bloom, B.S. (1984). The search for methods of group instruction as effective as one-to-one tutoring. *Educational Leadership, 41*(8), 4–18.

Bocchino, R. (March, 1991). Using mind mapping as a note-taking tool. *The Developer,* pp. 1, 4.

Bolton, R. (1986). *People skills: How to assert yourself, listen to others, and resolve conflicts.* New York: Simon and Schuster.

Boone, H.A. (1989). Preparing family specialists in early childhood special education. *Teacher Education and Special Education, 12*(3): 96–102.

Braaten, S., Kauffman, J.M., Braaten, B., Polsgrove, L., Nelson, C.M. (1988). The regular education initiative: Patent medicine for behavioral disorders. *Exceptional Children, 55*(1), 21–27.

Britt, S. (1985). Our high priests of process. *Newsweek,* November 18, p. 30.

Britton, N. (1989, May). Training the trainer in Richardson, Texas. *The Developer,* pp. 1, 3.

Bronfenbrenner, U. (October,1973). Tear down the walls. *Scholastic Teacher,* pp. 78–79.

Brown, A.L. (1994). The advancement of learning. *Educational Researcher, 23*(8), 4–12.

Brown, D., Pryzwansky, W.B., & Schulte, A.C. (1991). *Psychological consultation: Introduction to theory and practice.* Needham Heights, MA: Allyn & Bacon. Chapters 6 and 7, on roles of consultants and consultees.

Brown, D., & Schulte, A.C. (1987). A social learning model of consultation. *Professional Psychology: Research and Practice, 18,* 283–287.

Brown, D., Wyne, M.D., Blackburn, J.E., & Powell, W.C. (1979). *Consultation: Strategy for improving education.* Boston: Allyn & Bacon.

Brownwood, A.W. (1987). *It takes all types!* San Anselmo, CA: Baytree.

Bruner, J.S. (1960). The process of education. Cambridge, MA: Harvard University Press.

Bruner, C. (1991). *Thinking collaboratively: Ten questions and answers to help policymakers improve children's services.* Washington, D.C.: Education and Human Service Consortium.

Burnette, J. (1987). *Issue brief 1: Adapting instructional materials for mainstreamed students.* Reston, VA: The ERIC/SEP Special Project on Interagency Information Dissemination, the ERIC Clearinghouse on Handicapped and Gifted Children, Published by the Council for Exceptional Children.

Bursuck, W.D., & Lessen, E. (1987). A classroom-based model for assessing students with learning disabilities. *Learning Disabilities Focus, 3*(1): 17–29.

Buscaglia, L. (1986). *Loving each other: The challenges of human relationships.* Westminister, MD: Fawcett.

Bush, G. (1991). *America 2000: An education strategy.* Washington, D.C.: U.S. Department of Education.

Buzan, T. (1983). *Use both sides of your brain.* New York: E.P. Dutton.

Cain, E (1985). Developing an administrative plan for the implementation of micro-computers. *Selected Proceedings of Closing the Gap's 1985 National Conference,* 14–16.

Caldwell, S.D. (Ed.). *Staff development: Handbook of effective practices.* Oxford, OH: National Staff Development Council.

Calhoun, E.F. (1993) Action research: Three approaches. *Educational Leadership, 51*(2), 62–65.

Campbell, D.E., & Kain, J.M. (1990). Personality type and mode of information presentation: Preference, accuracy, and efficiency in problem-solving. *Journal for Psychological Type, 20,* 47–51.

Campbell, J. (1990). *The hero with a thousand faces.* New York: Work Publishing.

Cancelli, A.A., & Lange, S.M. (1990). Considerations for future research in the institutionalization of school-based consultation. *Journal of Educational and Psychological Consultation, 1*(1), 87–98.

Canning, C. (1991). What teachers say about reflection. *Educational Leadership, 48*(6), 18–21.

Cantwell, D.P., Baker, L., & Rutter, M. (1979). Families of autistic and dysphasic children: Family life and interaction patterns. *Archives of General Psychiatry, 36,* 682–687.

Caplan, G. (1970). *The theory and practice of mental health consultation.* New York: Basic Books.

Carlyn, M. (1977). An assessment of the Myers-Briggs type indicator. *Journal of Personality Assessment, 41*(5), 461–473.

Caro, D.J., & Robbins, P. (1991). TalkWalking—thinking on your feet. *Developer,* November 1991, 3–4.

Carolina Computer Access Center (1991). as cited in Male, M. (1994). *Technology for inclusion: Meeting the special needs of all students.* (2nd ed.) Boston: Allyn & Bacon.

Carpenter, D. (1985) Grading handicapped pupils: Review and position statement. *Remedial and Special Education, 6*(4), 54–59.

Cautela, J.R., Cautela, J., & Esonis, S. (1982). *Forms for behavior analysis with children.* Champaign, IL: Research Press.

Chandler, L.A. (1980). Consultative services in the schools: A model. *Journal of School Psychology, 18*(4), 399–401.

Chase, B. (1994). cited in *Special Education Report 20,* (14), 2.

Chavkin, N.F. (1989). Debunking the myth about minority parents. *Educational Horizons, 67,* 119–123.

Child Welfare League of America. (1993). *Cultural competence self-assessment instrument.* Washington, D.C.: Child Welfare League of America.

Christenson, S.L., & Cleary, M. (1990). Consultation and the parent-educator partnership: A perspective. *Journal of Educational and Psychological Consultation, 1,* 219–241.

Cipani, E. (1985). The three phrases of behavioral consultation: Objectives, intervention, and quality assurance. *Teacher Education and Special Education, 8,* 144–152.

Clark, B. (1988). *Growing up gifted.* Columbus, OH: Merrill.

Clark, G.M., and Knowlton, H.E. (1988). A closer look at transition issues for the 1990's: A response to Rusch and Menchetti. *Exceptional Children, 54*(4): 365–367.

Clinchy, E. (1991). Helping parents make the school system work for them. Buffalo Public Schools Parent Center. *Equity and Choice, 7*(2–3), 83–88.

Cochran, M. (1987). The parent empowerment process: Building on family strengths. *Equality and Choice, 4,* 9–22.

Coleman, P.G., Eggleston, K.K. Collins, J.F., Holloway, G.D., & Rider, S.K. (1975). A severely hearing impaired child in the mainstream. *Teaching Exceptional Children: 3,* 6–9.

College Entrance Examination Board (1983). *Advanced placement course description: Computer science.* Princeton, NJ: Author.

Collins, C. (1987). *Time management for teachers: Practical techniques and skills that give you more time to teach.* West Nyak, NY: Parker.

Comer, J. (1989). Children can: An address on school improvement. In R. Webb & F. Parkay (Eds.), *Children can: An address on school improvement by Dr. James Comer with responses from Florida's educational community* (pp. 4–17). Gainesville, FL: University of Florida, College of Education Research and Development Center in collaboration with the Alachua County Mental Health Association.

Conoley, J.C. (1989). Professional communication and collaboration among educators. In M.C. Reynolds (Ed.), *Knowledge base for the beginning teacher* (pp. 245–253). Oxford, England: Pergamon Press.

Conoley, J.C. (1987). National Symposium on School Consultation. Austin, TX: University of Texas.

Conoley, J.C., & Conoley, C.W. (1988). Useful theories in school-based consultation. *Remedial and Special Education, 9*(6), 14–20.

Conoley, J.C., & Conoley, C.W. (1982). *School consultation: A guide to practice and training.* New York: Pergamon Press, Inc.

Cook, L., & Friend, M. (1993). Educational Leadership for Teacher Collaboration in *Program Leadership for Serving Students with Disabilities,* Project supported by the Virginia Department of Education (through the U.S. Department of Education, Project #H10034–93).

Corey, M. S., & Corey, G. (1992). *Groups: Process and practice,* (2nd ed.). Pacific Grove, CA: Brooks/Cole.

Cosden, M.A. (1988). Microcomputer instruction and perceptions of effectiveness of special and regular education elementary school teachers. *Journal of Special Education, 22,* 242–252.

Covey, S.R. (1989). *The 7 Habits of Highly Effective People.* New York: Simon and Schuster.

Cross, T. (1988). Services to minority populations: What does it mean to be a culturally competent professional? *Focal Point, 2,* 1–3.

Cuban, L. (1986). Persistent instruction: Another look at constancy in the classroom. *Phi Delta Kappan, 68,* (1), 7–11.

Curtis, M.J., & Zins, J.E. (1988). Effects of training in consultation and instructor feedback on acquisition of consultation skills. *Journal of School Psychology, 26,* 185–190.

Curtis, M.J., & Zins, J.E. (1981). *The theory and practice of school consultation.* Springfield, IL: Charles C. Thomas.

Daggett, W.R. (1989). The changing nature of work—A challenge to education. Unpublished speech delivered to the Kansas Legislative and Educational Leaders.

Davies, D. (1988). Low-income parents and the schools: A research report and plan for action. *Equity and Choice, 4,* 51–59.

Davis, G.A., and Rimm, S.B. (1989). *Education of the gifted and talented.* Englewood Cliffs, NJ: Prentice-Hall.

Davis, W.E. (1989). The regular education initiative debate: Its promises and problems. *Exceptional Children, 55*(5): 440–47.

Davis, W.E. (1985). *The special educator: Meeting the challenge for professional growth.* Austin, TX: PRO-ED.

Davis, W.E. (1983). *The special educator: Strategies for succeeding in today's world.* Austin: PRO-ED.

DeBoer, A.L. (1986). *The art of consulting.* Chicago: Arcturus.

de Bono, E. (1973). *Lateral thinking: Creativity step by step.* New York: Harper & Row.

Delquadri, J., Greenwood, C.R., Whorton, D., Carta, J.J., & Hall, R.V. (1986). Classwide peer tutoring. *Exceptional Children, 52,* 535–542.

Deno, S.L. (1987). Curriculum-based measurement. *Teaching Exceptional Children, 20*(1), 41–47.

Deshler, D., & Schumaker, J. (1986). Learning strategies: An instructional alternative for low-achieving adolescents. *Exceptional Children, 52*(6), 583–590.

Deshler, D. (1985). Metaphors and values in higher education. *Academe,* November–December, 1985, 22–29.

Deshler, D.D., & Schumaker, J.B. (1986). Learning strategies: An instructional alternative for low-achieving adolescents. *Exceptional Children, 52,* 583–590.

DeShong, B.R. (1981). *The special educator: Stress and survival.* Rockville, MD: Aspen.

DesJardins, C. (1993). *How to get services by being assertive.* Chicago: Family Resource Center on Disabilities.

Dettmer, P. (Ed.). (1990). *Staff development for gifted programs: Putting it together and making it work.* Washington, D.C.: National Association for Gifted Children.

Dettmer, P. (1989). The consulting teacher in programs for gifted and talented students. *Arkansas Gifted Education Magazine, 3*(2), 4–7.

Dettmer, P. (1989). The teachers' lounge: Professional asset or liability? *The Master Teacher State-of-the-Art Papers, 20*(25), 1–4.

Dettmer, P. (1986). Gifted program preservice and staff development: Pragmatics and possibilities. *Gifted Child Quarterly, 30*(3), 99–102.

Dettmer, P. (1982). Preventing burnout in teachers of the gifted. *G/C/T. 21:* 37–41.

Dettmer, P. (1981). The effects of teacher personality type on classroom values and perceptions of gifted students. *Research in Psychological Type, 3,* 48–54.

Dettmer, P., & Lane, J. (1989). An integrative model for educating very able students in rural school districts. *Educational Considerations, 17*(1), 36–39.

Dickens, V.J., & Jones, C.J. (1990). Regular special education consultation: A teachers education strategy for implementation. *Teacher Education and Special Education, 13*, 221–224.

Dickens, V.J., & Jones, C.J. (1990). Regular/special education consultation: A teacher education training strategy for implementation. *Teacher Education and Special Education, 13*(3–4), 235–239.

Dishon, D., & O'Leary, P.W. (1989). Tips for teachers: Time saver options. *Cooperative Learning, 10*(2):30.

Dishon, D., & O'Leary, P.W. (1990). Social skills and processing. *Cooperative Learning, 10*(2): 35–36.

Dobson, R.L., Dobson, J.E., & Koetting, J.R. (1985). *Looking at, talking about, and living with children: Reflections on the process of schooling.* Lanham, MD: University Press of America.

Dorris, M. (1979). Why I'm not thankful for Thanksgiving. *Midwest Race Desegregation Assistance Center Horizons, 1*(5), 1.

Douglass, M.E., & Douglass, D.V. (1993). *Manage your time, your work, yourself.* New York: AMACOM.

Doyle, D.P. (1991). America 2000. *Phi Delta Kappan, 73*(3), 184–191.

Dragan, E.F. (1994). Transition planning: what schools need to know. *CEC Today, 1*(7), 1, 14–15.

Dunn, R., & Dunn, K. (1978). *Teaching Students Through Their Individual Learning Styles.* Reston, VA: Reston Publishing.

Dyck, N., & Dettmer, P. (1989). Collaborative consultation: A promising tool for serving gifted learning-disabled students. *Journal of Reading, Writing, and Learning Disabilities, 5*(3), 253–264.

Edelman, M.W. (1987). *Families in peril: An agenda for social change.* Cambridge: Harvard University Press.

Edgar, G. 1990. Is it time to change our view of the world? *Beyond Behavior, 1*(1): 9–13.

Educational Leadership. (1994/1995, December/January). *52*(4). Entire topical issue on The Inclusive School.

Edyburn, D., & Majsterek, D. (1993). Technology applications for individuals with LD: What can we say today? *LD Forum, 19* (1): 3–5.

Edyburn, D.L. (1994). An equation to consider: The portfolio assessment knowledge base + technology = The Grady Profile. *LD Forum, 19*(4): 35–38.

Egan, G. (1982). *The skilled helper: A model for systematic helping and interpersonal relating* (2nd ed.). Monterey, CA: Brooks/Cole.

Eisner, E.W. (1988). The ecology of school improvement. *Educational Leadership, 45*(5), 24–29.

Epstein, J.L., (1991). Paths to partnership: What we can learn from federal, state, district, and school initiatives. *Phi Delta Kappan, 75*(5):344–349.

Epstein, J.L. (1989). Building parent-teacher partnerships in inner-city schools. *Family Resource Coalition Report, 8,* 7.

Epstein, J.L. (1987). Parent involvement: What research says to administrators. *Education and Urban Society, 19,* 119–136.

ERIC Clearinghouse on Handicapped and Gifted Children. (1987b). Lesson structure. *ERIC Digest #448.* Reston, VA: Council for Exceptional Children.

ERIC Clearinghouse on Handicapped and Gifted Children (1987a). Critical presentation skills. *ERIC Digest 449.* Reston, VA: Council for Exceptional Children.

Evans, S. (1980). The consultant role of the resource teacher. *Exceptional Children, 46*(5), 402–404.

Exceptional Children (October/November, 1994) Special Issue: Technology-Based Assessment Within Special Education.

Fad, K.S. (1990). The fast track to success: Social behavioral skills. *Intervention in School and Clinic, 26*(1), 39–43.

Family Integration Resources. (1991). *Second Family Leadership Conference.* Washington, D.C.: U.S. Department of Education.

Feldhusen, J.F., & Kolloff, P.B. (1986). The Purdue three-stage enrichment model for gifted education at the elementary level. In J.S. Renzulli (Ed.), *Systems and models for developing programs for the gifted and talented* (pp. 126–152). Mansfield Center, CT: Creative Learning Press.

Feldhusen, J.F., & Robinson, A. (1986). The Purdue secondary model for gifted and talented youth. In J.S. Renzulli (Ed.), *Systems and models for developing programs for the gifted and talented* (pp. 153–179). Mansfield Center, CT: Creative Learning Press.

Feuer, D., & Geber, B. (1988). Uh-Oh . . . second thoughts about adult learning theory. *Training,* December 1988.

Field, S.L., & Hill, D.S. (1988). Contextual appraisal: A framework for meaningful evaluation of special education programs. *Remedial and Special Education, 9*(4), 22–30.

Fisher, R., & Brown, S. (1988). *Getting together: Building relationships as we negotiate.* New York: Penguin Books.

Fisher, R., & Ury, W. (1981). *Getting to yes.* Boston: Houghton-Mifflin.

Friend, M. (1984). Consultation skills for resource teachers. *Learning Disability Quarterly, 7,* 246–250.

Friend, M. (1988). Putting consultation into context: Historical and contemporary perspectives. *Remedial and special Education, 9*(6), 7–13.

Friend, M., & Bauwens, J. (1988). Managing resistance: An essential consulting skill for learning disabilities teachers. *Journal of Learning Disabilities, 21,* 556–561.

Friend, M. & Cook, L. (1990). Collaboration as a predictor for success in school reform. *Journal of Educational and Psychological Consultation, 1*(1), 69–86.

Friend, M., & McNutt, G. (1984). Resource room programs: Where are we now? *Exceptional Children, 51,* 150–155.

Fry, E. (1977). Fry's readability graph: Clarifications, validity, and extension to level 17. *Journal of Reading, 21,* 242–252.

Fuchs, L.S. (1987). Program development. *Teaching Exceptional Children, 20*(1), 42–44.

Fuchs, D., & Fuchs, L.S. (1994). Inclusive schools movement and the radicalization of special education reform. *Exceptional Children, 60*(4), 294–309.

Fuchs, D., & Fuchs, L.S. (December, 1994/January, 1995). Sometimes separate is better. *Educational Leadership, 52*(4), 22–26.

Fuchs, D., & Fuchs, L.S. (1994). Inclusive schools movement and the radicalization of special education reform. *Exceptional Children, 60*(4), 294–309.

Fuchs, D., & Fuchs, L.S. (1988). Evaluation of the adaptive learning environments model. *Exceptional Children, 55,* 115–127.

Fuchs, D., Fuchs, L.S., Dulan, J., Roberts, H., & Fernstrom, P. (1992). Where is the research on consultation effectiveness? *Journal of Educational and Psychological Consultation, 3*(2), 151–174.

Fuchs, L.S., Fuchs, D., & Hamlett, C.L. (1990). Curriculum-based measurement: A standardized, long-term goal approach to monitoring student progress. *Academic Therapy, 25*(5), 5, 615–632.

Fuchs, L.S., Hamlett, C.L., & Fuchs, D. (1990). *Basic math, basic reading, basic spelling [Computer programs].* Austin, TX: PRO-ED.

Fuller, R.B. (1975). *Explorations in the geometry of thinking synergetics.* New York: Macmillan, p.3.

Futrell, M.(1989). Mission not accomplished: Education reform in retrospect. *Phi Delta Kappan, 71*(1), 9–14.

Gajria, M., Salend, S.J., Hemrick, M.A. (1994). Teacher acceptability of testing modifications for mainstreamed students. *Learning Disabilities Research & Practice, 9* (4): 236–243.

Gallagher, J.J. (1985). *Teaching the gifted child* (3rd ed.). Boston: Allyn & Bacon.

Gallessich, J. (1973). Organizational factors influencing consultation in schools. *Journal of School Psychology, 11*(1), 57–65.

Gallessich, J. (1974). Training the school psychologist for consultation. *Journal of School Psychology, 12,* 138–149.

Gardner, J.E. (1994). The technological edge. *CEC Today, 1* (8): 10.

Garmston, R. (1988, October). Giving gifts. *The Developer,* pp. 3, 6.

Garmston, R. (1990, February). Maintaining momentum, Part II: Keeping the train rolling. *The Developer,* pp. 3, 7.

Garmston, R.J., & Wellman, B.M. (1992). *How to make presentations that teach and transform.* Alexandria, VA: Association for Supervision and Curriculum Development.

Gayle, M. (1990). Toward the 21st century. *Adult Learning, 1*(4), 10–14.

Gerber, M., & Kauffmann, J. (1981). Peer tutoring in academic settings. In P. Strain (Ed.), *Utilization of classroom peers as behavior change agents,* (pp. 155–187). New York: Plenum Publishing.

Gersten, R., Darch, C., Davis, G., & George, N. (1991). Apprenticeship and intensive training of consulting teachers: A naturalistic study. *Exceptional Children, 57*(3), 226–236.

Giangreco, M.F., Dennis, R., Cloninger, C., Edelman, S., Schattman, R. (1993). *Exceptional Children, 59*(4), 359–372.

Gibb, J.R. (1974). Defensive communication. In R.S. Cathcart & L.A. Samovar (Eds.), *Small group communication: A reader* (2nd ed.), (pp. 327–33). Dubuque, IA: William D. Brown.

Goldfein, D. (1977). *Every woman's guide to time management.* Millbrae, CA: Les Femmes.

Goodlad, J. (1984). *A place called school: Prospects for the future.* New York: McGraw-Hill.

Gordon, J. (1991). Measuring the goodness of training. *Training, 28*(8), 19–25.

Gordon, T. (1974). *T.E.T.: Teacher effectiveness raining.* New York: Wyden.

Gordon, T. (1977). *Leader effectiveness training, L.E.T.: The no-lose way to release the productive potential in people.* Toronto: Bantam.

Graubard, P.S., Rosenberg, H., & Miller, M.B. (1971). Student applications of behavior modification to teachers and environments or ecological approaches to deviancy. In E.A. Ramp & B.L. Hopkins (Eds.), *A new direction for education: Behavior analysis* 1971 (pp. 80–101). Lawrence, KS: University of Kansas.

Greenburg, D.E. (1987). *A special educator's perspective on interfacing special and general education: A review for administrators.* Clearinghouse on Handicapped and Gifted Children. Reston, VA: The Council for Exceptional Children.

Greenwood, C.R. (1994). Advances in technology-based assessment within special education. *Exceptional Children, 61* 2:102–104.

Gregorc, A.F., & Ward, H.B. (1977). A new definition for individual: Implications for learning and teaching. *NASSP Bulletin, 61,* 20–26.

Gresham, F.M., & Kendell, G.K. (1987). School consultation research: Methodological critique and future research directions. *School Psychology Review, 16*(3), 306–316.

Guskey, T.R. (1988). Mastery learning and mastery teaching: How they complement each other. *Principal, 68,* 1, 6–8.

Guskey, T.R. (1990). Integrating innovations. *Educational Leadership, 47,* 5, 11–15.

Guskey, T. (1985). Staff development and teacher change. *Educational Leadership, 42*(7), 57–60.

Guthrie, G.P., & Guthrie, L.F. (1991). Streamlining interagency collaboration for youth at risk. *Educational Leadership, 49*(1), 17–22.

Gutkin, T.B. (1986). Consultees' perceptions of variables relating to the outcomes of school based consultation interactions. *School Psychology Review, 15* (3), 375–82.

Gutkin, T.B., & Curtis, M.L. (1982). School-based consultation theory and techniques. In C.R. Reynolds & T.B. Gutkin (Eds.), *The handbook of school psychology* (pp. 796–828). New York: Wiley.

Gutkin, T.B., Singer, J., & Brown, R. (1980). Teacher reactions to school-based consultation services: A multivariate analysis. *Journal of School Psychology, 18,* 126–134.

Haight, S.L. (1984). Special education teacher consultant: Idealism versus realism. *Exceptional Children, 50*(6), 507–515.

Hall, E.T. (1981). *The silent language.* Garden City, NY: Anchor Press.

Hall, C.S., & Lindzey, G. (1978). *Theories of personality* (3rd ed.). New York: John Wiley & Sons.

Hall, E.T. (1959). *The silent language.* New York: Doubleday.

Hall, G.E., & Hord, S.M. (1987). *Change in schools: Facilitating the process.* Albany: State University of New York Press.

Hall, R.V., Delquadri, J., Greenwood, C.R., & Thurston, L. (1982). The importance of opportunity to respond in children's academic success. In E. Edgar, N. Haring, J. Jenkins, & C. Pious (Eds.), *Mentally handicapped children: Education and training* (pp. 107–140). Baltimore, MD: University Park Press.

Hall, R.V., & Houten, R.V. (1980). *The measurement of behavior.* Austin, TX: PRO-ED.

Hallahan, D.P., & Kauffman, J.M. (1991). *Exceptional children: Introduction to special education.* Englewood Cliffs, NJ: Prentice Hall.

Hallahan, D.P., Kauffman, J.M., Lloyd, J.W., & McKinney, J.D.(Eds.) (1988). The regular education initiative. *Journal of Learning Disabilities, 21*(1): special issue.

Halpern, A.S. (1992). Transition: Old wine in new bottles. *Exceptional Children, 58*(3), 202–211.

Hammer, A.L. (1985). Typing or stereotyping: Unconscious bias in applications of psychological type theory. *Journal of Psychological Type, 10,* 14–18.

Hansen, J.C., Himes, B.S., & Meier, S. (1990). *Consultation: Concepts and practices.* Englewood Cliffs, NJ: Prentice Hall.

Harris, K.C., & Zetlin, A.G. (1993). Exploring the collaborative ethic in an urban school: A case study. *Journal of Educational and Psychological Consultation, 4*(4), 305–317.

Harry, B. (1992). *Cultural diversity, families, and the special education system: Communication and improvement.* New York: Teachers College Press.

Hawks, B.K., & Muha, D. (1991). Facilitating the career development of minorities: Doing it differently this time. *Career Development Quarterly, 39,* 251–260.

Hay, C.A. (1984). One more time: What do I do all day? *Gifted Child Quarterly, 28*(1), 17–20.

Henderson, A.T. (1987). *The evidence continues to grow: Parent involvement improves student achievement.* Silver Springs, MD: National Citizens Committee in Education.

Henkelman, J. (1991, February). Staff developers as consultants. *The Developer.* Oxford, OH: National Staff Development Council.

Henning-Stout, M. (1994). Consultation and connected knowing: What we know is determined by the questions we ask. *Journal of Educational and Psychological Consultation, 5*(1), 5–21.

Heron, T.E. & Harris, K.C. (1987). *The educational consultant: Helping professionals, parents, and mainstreamed students.* Austin, TX: PRO-ED.

Heron, T.E., & Harris, K.C. (1982). *The educational consultant: Helping professionals, parents, and mainstreamed students.* Boston: Allyn & Bacon.

Heron, T.E. & Kimball, W.H. (1988). Gaining perspective with the educational consultation research base: Ecological considerations and further recommendations. *Remedial and Special Education, 9*(6)21–28, 47.

Hillerman, T. (1990). *Coyote waits.* New York: Harper & Row.

Hodgkinson, H.L. (1985). *All one system: Demographics of education, kindergarten through graduate school.* Washington, D.C.: American Council on Education.

Hodgkinson, H.L. (1989). *The same client: The demographics of education and service delivery systems.* Washington, D.C.: Institute for Educational Leadership, Center for Demographic Policy.

Hogan, J.R. (1975). The three-way conference: Parent, teacher, child. *The Elementary School Journal, 75*(5):311–315.

Holmes Group Forum. (1990). Back to school basics, *The Holmes Group Forum, 5* (1), 1, 3.

Howe II, H. (1991). America 2000: Bumpy ride on four trains. *Phi Delta Kappan, 73* (3), 192–203.

Howey, K.R., Bents, R., & Corrigan, D. (Eds.). (1981). *School-focused inservice: Descriptions and discussions.* Reston, VA: Association of Teacher Educators.

Howley, A., Howley, C.B., and Pendarvis. E. (1986). *Teaching gifted children: Principles and strategies.* Boston: Little, Brown, and Co.

Hoy, W.K. (1990). Organizational climate and culture: A conceptual analysis of the school work place. *Journal of Educational and Psychological Consultation. 1*(2): 149–168.

Hoyt, K. (1991). Education reform and relationships between the private sector and education: A call for integration. *Phi Delta Kappan, 72*(6), 450–453.

Hudson, F. (1992). *Team teaching and academic achievement.* Unpublished manuscript, Kansas State University, College of Education, Manhattan, KS.

Huefner, D. (1988). The consulting teacher model: Risks and opportunities. *Exceptional Children, 54* (5), 403–414.

Huefner, D.S. (1988). The consulting teacher model: Risks and opportunities. *Exceptional Children, 54*(5), 403–414.

Huff, B., and Telesford, M.C. (1994). Outreach efforts to involve families of color in the Federation of Families for Children's Mental Health. *Focal Point, 8,* 10–11.

Hughes, C.A., & Ruhl, K.L. (1987).The nature and extent of special educators' contacts with students' parents. *Teacher Education and Special Education, 10,* 180–184.

Hughs, J., & Falk, R. (1981). Resistance, reactance, and consultation. *Journal for School Psychology, 19*(2):139–142.

Hulsebusch, P.L. (1989). *Significant others: Teacher perspectives of relationships with parents.* Paper presented at the annual meeting of the American Educational Research Association, San Francisco.

Hunter, M. (1985). Promising theories die young. *ASCD Update,* May 1985, *1,* 3.

Idol, L. (1986). *Collaborative School Consultation: Recommendations for State Departments of Education.* The Task Force on School Consultation, Teacher Education Division, Council for Exceptional Children.

Idol, L. (1988). A rationale and guidelines for establishing special education consultation programs. *Remedial and Special Education, 9*(6), 48–58.

Idol, L. (1990). The scientific art of classroom consultation. *Journal of Educational and Psychological Consultation, 1*(1), 3–22.

Idol, L. (1986). *Collaborative School Consultation*. Report of the National Task Force on School Consultation). Reston, VA: Teacher Education Division, The Council for Exceptional Children.

Idol, L., & West, J.F. (1987). Consultation in special education (Part II): Training and practices. *Journal of Learning Disabilities, 20, 474–497.*

Idol, L., Paolucci-Whitcomb, P., & Nevin, A. (1986). *Collaborative consultation*. Austin, TX: PRO-ED.

Idol, L., West, J.F., & Lloyd, S.R. (1988). Organizing and implementing specialized reading programs: A collaborative approach involving classroom, remedial, and special education teachers. *Remedial and Special Education, 9,* 2, 54–61.

Idol-Maestas, L. (1981). A teacher training model: The resource/consulting teacher. *Behavioral Disorders, 6*(2), 108–121.

Idol-Maestas, L. (1983). *Special educator's consultation handbook*. Rockville, MD: Aspen.

Idol-Maestas, L.,& Celentano, R. (1986). Teacher consultant services for advanced students. *Roeper Review, 9*(1), 34–36.

Idol-Maestas, L., & Ritter, S. (1985). A follow-up study of resource/consulting teachers: Factors that facilitate and inhibit teacher consultation. *Teacher Education and Special Education, 8:* 121–131.

Idol-Maestes, L., Lloyd, S., & Lilly, M.S. (1981). Noncategorical approach to direct service and teachers education. *Exceptional Children, 48:* 213–220.

Isaacs, M.R., and Benjamin, M.P. (1991). *Towards a culturally competent system of Care, Vol II*. Washington, D.C.: Georgetown University Child Development Center, CASSP Technical Assistance Center.

Jackson, R.M., Cleveland, J.C., & Merenda, P.F. (1975). The longitudinal effects of early identification and counseling of underachievers. *Journal of School Psychology, 13,* 119–128.

Jenkins, J., & Jenkins, L. (1985). Peer tutoring in elementary and secondary programs. *Focus on Exceptional Children, 17,* 6, 1–12.

Jenkins, J.R., Pious, C.G., & Jewell, M. (1990). Special education and the regular education initiative: Basic assumptions. *Exceptional Children, 56,* 479–491.

Jersild, A.T. (1955). *When teachers face themselves*. New York: Teachers College Press, Columbia University.

Johnson, D.W., & Johnson, F.P. (1987) *Joining together: Group theory and group skills* (3rd ed.). Englewood Cliffs, NJ: Prentice-Hall.

Johnson, D.W., & Johnson, R.T. (1987). *Learning together and alone: Cooperative, competitive, & individualistic learning* (2nd ed). Englewood Cliffs, NJ: Prentice Hall.

Johnson, L.J., Pugach, M.C., & Hammittee, D.J. (1988). Barriers to effective special education consultation. *Remedial and Special Education, 9,* (6), 41–47.

Johnson, S. (1992). *"Yes" or "No": A guide to better decisions*. New York: Harper Collins.

Journal of Educational and Psychological Consultation, 1990. All issues.

Journal of Psychological Type (formerly named *Research in Psychological Type*). All issues.

Journal of Staff Development, 15(4), 1–88. Entire issue. Topical issue on Results-Oriented Staff Development.

Joyce, B. (Ed.). (1990). *Changing school culture through staff development*. Alexandria, VA: The Association for Supervision and Curriculum Development.

Joyce, B.R., & Showers, B. (1988). *Student achievement through staff development*. New York, NY: Longman.

Joyce, B.R., & Showers, B. (1983). *Power in staff development through research on training*. Alexandria, VA: The Association for Supervision and Curriculum Development.

Jung, C.G. (1923). *Psychological types*. New York: Harcourt Brace.

Jung, C.G. (1954). *The development of personality* (R.F.C. Hull, trans.). New York: Pantheon.

Jusjka, J. (1991). Observations. *Phi Delta Kappan, 72*(6), 468–470.

Kagan, S. (1989). *Cooperative Learning: Resources for Teachers*. San Juan Capistrano, CA: Resources for Teachers.

Katz, N.H., & Lawyer, J.W. (1983). Communication and conflict management skills: Strategies for individual and systems changes. *Nonviolence and Change National Forum, 63:* 31.

Kauffman, J.M. (1994). Places of change: Special education's power and identity in an era of educational reform. *Journal of Learning Disabilities, 27*(10), 610–618.

Keefe, J.W., & Ferrell, B.G. (1990). Developing a defensible learning style paradigm. *Educational Leadership, 48*(2), 57–61.

Keirsey, D., & Bates, M. (1984). *Please understand me: Character and temperament types.* Del Mar, CA: Gnosology.

Keller, H.R. (1981). Behavioral consultation. In J.C. Conoley (Ed.), *Consultation in the Schools* (pp. 59–100). New York: Academic Press.

Keys, R. (1991). *Timelock: How life got so hectic and what you can do about it.* New York: HarperCollins.

Kirst, M.W. (1982). *How to improve schools without spending more money. Phi Delta Kappan, 64*(1): 6–8.

Knight, M.T., Meyers, H.W., Paolucci-Whitcomb, P., Hasazi, S.E., & Nevin, A. (1981). A four-year evaluation of consulting teacher service. *Behavioral Disorders, 6,* 92–100.

Knowles, M. (1970). *The modern practice of adult education.* New York: Association Press.

Knowles, M. (1978). *The adult learner: A neglected species.* Houston, TX: Gulf Publishing.

Kolb, D.A. (1976). *Learning-style inventory: Technical manual.* Boston: McBer & Co.

Kratochwill, T.R., & VanSomeren, K.R. (1985). Barriers to treatment success in behavioral consultation: Current limitations and future directions. *Journal of School Psychology, 23,* 225–239.

Kroth, R.L. (1985). *Communication with parents of exceptional children: Improving parent-teacher relationships.* Denver: Love.

Kroth, R.L., & Scholl, G.T. (1978). *Getting schools involved with parents.* Arlington, VA: Council for Exceptional Children.

Kummerow, J.M., & McAllister, L.W. (1988). Team-building with the Myers-Briggs Type Indicator: Case studies. *Journal of Psychological Type, 15:* 25–32.

Lakein, A. (1973). *How to get control of your time and your life.* New York: McKay.

Lanier, J.E. (1982). Teacher education: Needed research and practice for the preparation of teaching professionals. In D.C. Corrigin, D.J. Palmer, & P.A. Alexander (Eds.), *The Future of Teacher Education.* College Station, TX: Dean's Grant Project, College of Education, Texas A & M University.

Lawren, B. (1989). Seating for Success. *Psychology Today,* September 1989, 16, 18–19.

Lawrence, G. (1982). *People types and tiger stripes.* Gainesville, FL: Center for Applications of Psychological Type, Inc.

Lawrence, G. (1984). A synthesis of learning style research involving the MBTI. *Journal of Psychological Type, 8,* 2–15.

Lawrence, G. (1988, September). *Type and Stereotype: Sorting out the Differences.* Speech presented at the 1988 conference of Association for Psychological Type-Southwest, Albuquerque, NM.

Lawrence, G., & DeNovellis, R. (1974). Correlation of teacher personality variables (Myers-Briggs) and classroom observation data. Paper presented at American Educational Research Association conference.

Leitch, M.L., & Tangri, S.S. (1988). Barriers to home-school collaboration. *Educational Horizons, 66,* 70–75.

Leviton, A., Mueller, M., & Kauffman, C. (1992). The family-centered consultation model: Practical application for professionals. *Infants and Young Children, 4,* 1–8.

Levy-Shiff, R. (1986). Mother-father-child interactions in families with mentally retarded young child. *American Journal of Mental Deficiency, 91,* 141–142.

Lewis, A.C. (1992). All together now: Building collaboration. *Phi Delta Kappan, 73*(5), 348–349.

Lewis, R.B. (1993). *Special education technology: Classroom applications.* Pacific Grove, CA: Brooks/Cole.

Lichtenstein, S. (1993). Transition from school to adulthood: Case studies of adults with learning disabilities who dropped out of school. *Exceptional Children, 59,* 336–347.

Lieberman, A. (1991). Accountability as a reform strategy. *Phi Delta Kappan, 73*(3): 219–220.

Lieberman, L. (1984). *Preventing special education . . . for those who don't need it.* Newtonville, MA: GloWorm.

Lieberman, L. (1986). *Special educator's guide . . . . to special education.* Newtonville, MA: GloWorm.

Lightfoot, S. (1981). Toward conflict and resolution. Relationships between families and schools. *Theory into Practice, 20*(2), 97–104.

Lilly, M.S. (1987). Lack of focus on special education in literature on educational reform. *Exceptional Children, 53*(4), 325–326.

Lilly, M.S., & Givens-Ogle, L.B. (1981). Teacher consultation: Present, past, and future. *Behavioral Disorders, 6*(2), 73–77.

Lindle, J.C. (1989). What do parents want from principals and educators? *Educational Leadership, 47*(2), 12–14.

Lindsey, J.D. (Ed) (1993). *Computers and exceptional individuals,* 2nd ed. Austin TX: PRO-ED.

Lindsley, O. (1964). Direct measurement and prosthesis of retarded children. *Journal of Education, 147:* 62–81.

Lippitt, G.L. (March, 1983). Can conflict resolution be win-win? *The School Administrator,* pp. 20–22.

Lippitt, G., & Lippitt, R. (1978). *The consulting process in action.* San Diego: University Associates. Chapter 5, on ethical dilemmas and guidelines for consultants.

Lipshitz, R., Friedman, V., & Owen, H. (December, 1989). Overcoming resistance to training and a nonconfrontive approach. *Training and Development Journal,* pp. 46–50.

Lipsky, D.K. (1994). National survey gives insight into inclusive movement. *Inclusive Education Programs 1*(2): 4–7.

Lloyd, J.W., Crowley, E.P., Kohler, F.W., & Strain, P.S. (1988). Redefining the applied research agenda: Cooperative learning, prereferral, teacher consultation, and peer-mediated interventions. *Journal of Learning Disabilities, 21,* 43–52.

Loucks-Horsley, S., Harding, C.K., Arbuckle, M.A., Murray, L.B., Dubea, C., & Williams, M.K. (1987). *Continuing to learn: A guidebook for teacher development.* Andover, MA: The Regional Laboratory for Educational Improvement of the Northeast and Islands.

Lueder, D.C. (1989). Tennessee parents were invited to participate—and they did. *Educational Leadership, 47*(2): 15–17.

Luetke-Stahlman, B. (1994). Inclusion of students who are deaf or hard-of-hearing. Paper presented at Kansas Special Education Institutions of Higher Education meeting, Wichita, Kansas, April 22, 1994.

Luft, J. *Group processes: An introduction to group dynamics* (3rd ed.). Palo Alto, CA: Mayfield.

Lumley, D., & Bailey, G.D. (1993). *Planning for technology: A guidebook for school administrators.* New York: Scholastic, Inc.

Lynch, E.W., & Hanson, M.J. (1992). *Developing cross-cultural competence: A guide for working with young children and their families.* Baltimore: Paul H. Brooks.

Lynch, E.W., & Stein, R.C. (1990). Parent participation by ethnicity: Comparison of Hispanic, black, and anglo families. *Educating Exceptional Children* (5th ed.). Guilford, CT: Dushkin.

Lynch, E.W., & Stein, R.C. (1987). Parent participation by ethnicity: A comparison of Hispanic, black, and Anglo families. *Exceptional Children, 54,* 105–111.

Maag, J.W. (1989). Assessment in social skills training: Methodological and conceptual issues for research and practice. *Remedial and Special Education, 10*(4), 6–17.

MacKenzie, R.A. (1975). *The time trap.* New York: McGraw Hill.

MacKenzie, A., & Waldo, K.C. (1981). *About time! A woman's guide to time management.* Yew York: McGraw Hill.

Madden, N.A., & Slavin, R.E. (1983). Cooperative learning and social acceptance of mainstreamed academically handicapped students. *Journal of Special Education, 17,* 171–182.

Madden, N.A., Slavin, R.E., Karweit, N.L., & Livermon, B.J. (1989). Restructuring the urban elementary school. *Educational Leadership, 46*(5), 14–18.

Maeroff, G.I. (1993). Building teams to rebuild schools. *Phi Delta Kappan, 74,* (7), 512–519.

Maeroff, G.I. (1991). Assessing alternative assessment. *Phi Delta Kappan, 73*(4), 273–281.

Maher, C.A. (1985). *Professional self-management: Techniques for services providers.* Baltimore: Paul H. Brookes.

Majsterek, D., & Wilson, R. (1993). Computer-assisted instruction (CAI): An update on applications for students with learning disabilities. *LD Forum, 19* (1): 19–21.

Male, M. (1994). *Technology for inclusion: Meeting the special needs of all students.* 2nd ed. Boston: Allyn & Bacon.

Margolis, H., & Brannigan, G.G. (1986). Building trust with parents. *Academic Therapy, 22,* 71–74.

Margolis, H., & McGettigan, J. (1988). Managing resistance to instructional modifications in mainstream settings. *Remedial and Special Education, 9,* 15–21.

Martin, R. (1991). *Extraordinary children—ordinary lives.* Champaign, IL: Research Press.

Maslach, C. (1982). *Burnout: The cost of caring.* Englewood Cliffs, NJ: Prentice Hall.

Maslach, C., and Pines, A. (1977). The burnout syndrome in the daycare setting. *Child Care Quarterly, 6,* 100–113.

Mason, J.L. (1994). Developing culturally competent organizations. *Focal Point, 8,* 1–8.

McCarthy, B. (1990). Using the 4MAT system to bring learning styles to schools. *Educational Leadership, 48*(2), 31–37.

McCormick, L., & Kawate, J. (1982). Kindergarten survival skills: new directions for preschool special education. *Education and Training of the Mentally Retarded, 17*(3): 247–252.

McDonald, J.P. (1989). When outsiders try to change schools from the inside. *Phi Delta Kappan, 71*(3), 206–212.

McGaghie, W.C. (1991). Professional competence evaluation. *Educational Researcher, 20*(2), 3–9.

McGlothlin, J.E. (1981). The school consultation committee: An approach to implementing a teacher consultation model. *Behavioral Disorders, 6*(2), 101–107.

McKenzie, H.S., Egner, A.N., Knight, M.F., Perelman, P.F., Schneider, B.M., & Garvin, J.S. (1970). Training consulting teachers to assist elementary teachers in the management and education of handicapped children. *Exceptional Children, 37,* 137–143.

McLoughlin, J.A., & Kass, C. (1978). Resource teachers: Their role. *Learning Disability Quarterly, 1*(1), 56–62.

McLoughlin, J., & Kelly, D. (1982). Issues facing the resource teacher. *Learning Disabilities Quarterly, 5,* 58–64.

McLoughlin, J., & Lewis, R. (1990). *Assessing special students* (3rd ed.). Columbus, OH: Merrill.

Medway, F.J., & Forman, S.G. (1980). Psychologists' and teachers' reactions to mental health and behavioral school consultation. *Journal of School Psychology, 18,* 338–348.

Melaville, A.I., & Blank, M.J. (1991). *What it takes: Structuring interagency partnerships to connect children and families with comprehensive services.* Washington, D.C.: Education and Human Resources Consortium.

Mercer, C.D., & Lane, H. (1994). Principles of responsible inclusion. *LDA Newsbriefs, 29* (4): 1.

Mercer, C.D., & Mercer, A.R. (1993). *Teaching students with learning problems* (4th ed.). Columbus, OH: Merrill.

Meyen, E.L., & Skrtic, T. (Eds.). (1988). *Exceptional children and youth: An introduction,* (3rd ed.). Denver: Love.

Michaels, K. (1988). Caution: Second-wave reform taking place. *Educational Leadership, 45*(5), 3.

Miller, T.L., & Sabatino, D. (1978). An evaluation of the teacher consultant model as an approach to mainstreaming. *Exceptional Children, 45,* 86–91.

Milne. A.A. (1926). *Winnie-the-Pooh.* New York: E.P. Dutton.

Minner, S., Minner, J., & Lepich, J. (1990). Maintaining pupil performance data: A guide. *Intervention in School and Clinic, 26*(1), 32–37.

Mokros, J.R., & Russell, S.J. (1986). Learner-centered software: A survey of microcomputer use with special needs students. *Journal of Learning Disabilities, 19,* 185–190.

Morsink, C., Soar, S., Soar, R., & Thomas, R. (1986). Research on teaching: Opening the door to special education classrooms. *Exceptional Children, 53*(1), 32–40.

Morsink, C.V., Thomas, C.C., & Correa, V.I. (1991). *Interactive teaming: Consultation and collaboration in special programs.* Columbus, OH: Merrill.

Munson, S.M. (1987). Regular education teacher modifications for mainstreamed mildly handicapped students. *Journal of Special Education, 20*(4): 489–502.

Murphy, A.T. (1981). *Special children, special parents: Personal issues With handicapped children.* Englewood Cliffs, NJ: Prentice Hall.

Murphy, E. (1987a). *I am a good teacher.* Gainesville, FL: Center for Applications of Psychological Type.

Murphy, E. (1987b). *Questions children may have about type differences.* Gainesville, FL: Center for Applications of Psychological Type.

Myers, I.B. (1962). *The Myers-Briggs type indicator manual.* Palo Alto, CA: Consulting Psychologists Press.

Myers, I.B. (1974). *Type and teamwork.* Gainesville, FL: Center for Applications of Psychological Type, Inc.

Myers, I.B. (1980a). *Gifts differing.* Palo Alto, CA: Consulting Psychologists Press, Inc.

Myers, I.B. (1980b). *Introduction to type.* Palo Alto, CA: Consulting Psychologists Press, Inc.

Myers, I.B. (October 16, 1975). Making the most of individual gifts. Keynote address at the first national conference on the uses of the Myers-Briggs Type Indicator. Gainesville, FL: University of Florida.

Myers, I.B., & McCaulley, M.H. (1985). *Manual: A guide to the development and use of the Myers-Briggs type indicator.* Palo Alto, CA: Consulting Psychologists Press.

Naisbitt, J., & Aburdene, J. (1990). *Megatrends 2000.* New York: Morrow.

Nazzaro, J.N. (1977). *Exceptional timetables: Historic events affecting the handicapped and gifted.* Reston, VA: The Council for Exceptional Children.

Neel, R.S. (1981). How to put the consultant to work in consulting teaching. *Behavioral Disorders, 6*(2), 78–81.

Nelson, C.M., & Stevens, K.B. (1981). An accountable consultation model for mainstreaming behavioral disordered children. *Behavioral Disorders, 6,* 82–91.

Nevin, A., Thousand, J., & Paolucci-Whitcomb, P. (1990). Collaborative consultation: Empowering public school personnel to provide heterogeneous schooling for all—or, who rang that bell? *Journal of Educational and Psychological Consultation, 1*(1), 41–67.

Nevin, A., Thousand, J.S., & Villa, R.A. (1993). Establishing collaborative ethics and practices. *Journal of Educational and Psychological Consultation, 4*(4), 293–304.

Newman, J.E. (1992). *How to stay cool, calm, and collected when the pressure's on: A stress control plan for business people.* New York: American Management Association.

Newmann, F.M. (1991). Linking restructuring to authentic student achievement. *Phi Delta Kappan, 72,* 458–464.

Nichols, R.G., & Stevens, L.A. (1957). *Are you listening?* New York: McGraw-Hill.

Nuckolls, C.W. (1991). Culture and causal thinking: Diagnosis and prediction in a South Indian fishing village. *Ethos, 19*(1): 3–51.

Oja, S.N. (1980). Adult development is implicit in staff development. *Journal of Staff Development, 1*(1), 9–51.

Okolo, C.M. (1993). Computers and individuals with mild disabilities. In J. D. Lindsey (Ed.), *Comput-*

ers and Exceptional Individuals, 2nd ed. Austin TX: Pro-Ed.

O'Neil, John. (December, 1994/January, 1995). Can inclusion work: A conversation with Jim Kauffman and Mara Sapon-Shevin. *Educational Leadership, 52*(4), 7–11.

Osborn, A.F. (1963). *Applied imagination: Principles and procedures of creative problem-solving.* New York: Charles Scribner.

O'Sullivan (1990) as cited by Daggett, W.R. (1990). The changing nature of work—A challenge to education. Unpublished speech delivered to community college and educational leaders.

Ozturk, M. (1992). Education for cross-cultural communication. *Educational Leadership, 49*(4): 79–81.

Parent Educational Advocacy Training Center PEATC (1991a). *Partnership series 1: Teachers' strategies for involving hard-to-reach families.* Alexandria, VA: Parent Educational Advocacy Training Center PEATC.

Parent Educational Advocacy Training Center PEATC (1991b). *Partnership series 10: Trading places: Improving understanding between parents and teachers.* Alexandria, VA: Parent Educational Advocacy Training Center PEATC.

Parish, R., & Arends, R., (1983). Why innovation programs are discontinued. *Educational Leadership, 40:* 62–65.

Parker, J.P. (1989). *Instructional strategies for teaching the gifted.* Needham Heights, MA: Allyn & Bacon.

Paulson, F.L., Paulson, P.R., & Meyer, C.A. (1991). What makes a portfolio a portfolio? *Educational Leadership, 48*(5), 60–63.

Pelletier, J. (1982). Consultation model for students with behavior disorders. Unpublished manuscript, Kansas State University, Special Education Department, Manhattan, KS.

Pendarvis, E.D. (1993). In A.E. Blackhurst and W.H. Berdine, (Eds.), *An Introduction to Special Education.* New York: HarperCollins.

Perelman, L.J. (1992). *School's out—Hyperlearning, the new technology and the end of education.* New York: Morrow.

Peterson, N.L., & Cooper, C.S. (1989). Parent education and involvement in early intervention programs for handicapped children: A different perspective on parent needs and parent-professional relationships. In M.J. Fine (Ed.), *The Sec-*

ond Handbook on Parent Education (pp. 197–234). New York: Academic Press.

Pfeiffer, S. (1980). The school-based interprofessional team: Recurring problems and some possible solutions. *Journal of School Psychology, 18*(4): 388–394.

Phi Delta Kappan (1992, December). A special section on "Technology in the Schools," *74*(4).

Phillips, V., & McCullough, L. (1990). Consultation-based programming: Instituting the collaborative ethic in schools. *Exceptional Children, 56*(4), 291–304.

Phillips, W.L., Allred, K., Brulle, A.R., & Shank, K.S. (1990). The regular education initiative: The will and skill of regular educators. *Teacher Education and Special Education, 13*(3–4), 182–186.

Pines, A., & Aronson, E. (1988). *Career burnout: Causes and cures.* New York, NY: Macmillan.

Pollio, H. (1987). Practical poetry: Metaphoric thinking in science, art, literature, and nearly everywhere else. *Teaching-Learning Issues,* Fall 1987, 3–17.

Polsgrove, L., & McNeil, M. (1989). The consultation process: Research and practice. *Remedial and Special Education, 10*(1), 6–13, 20.

Ponterotto, J.G., & Casas, J.M. (1991). *Handbook of racial/ethnic minority counseling research.* Springfield IL: Charles C. Thomas.

Popham, W.J. (1988). *Educational Evaluation* (2nd ed.). Englewood Cliffs, NJ: Prentice Hall.

Posavac, E.J., & Carey, R.G. (1989). *Program evaluation: Methods and case studies* (3rd ed.). Englewood Cliffs, NJ: Prentice Hall.

Preston, D., Greenwood, C.R., Hughes, V., Yuen, P., Thibadeau, S., Critchlow, W., & Harris J. (1984). Minority issues in special education: A principal-mediated inservice program for teachers. *Exceptional Children, 51,* 112–121.

Price, M., & Goodman, L. (1980). Individualized education programs: A cost study. *Exceptional Children, 46*(6): 446–454.

Pryzwansky, W.B. (1974). A reconsideration of the consultation model for delivery of school-based psychological services. *American Journal of Orthopsychiatry, 44,* 579–583.

Pryzwansky, W.B. (1986). Indirect service delivery: Considerations for future research in consultation. *School Psychology Review, 15*(4), 479–488.

Pryzwansky, W.B., & Noblit, G.W. (1990). Understanding and improving consultation practice: The qualitative case study approach. *Journal of Educational and Psychological Consultation, 1*(4), 293–307.

Public policy. (1994, fall). *Teaching Exceptional Children, 27*(1), 78–80.

Pugach, M.C. (1988). The consulting teacher in the context of educational reform. *Educational Children, 55*(3), 273–275.

Pugach, M.C., & Johnson, L.J. (1995). *Collaborative practitioners, collaborative schools.* Denver, CO: Love.

Pugach, M.C., & Johnson, L.J. (1990). Fostering the continued democratization of consultation through action research. *Teacher Education and Special Education, 13*(3–4), 240–245.

Pugach, M.C., & Johnson, L.J. (1989). Prereferral interventions: Progress, problems, and challenges. *Exceptional Children, 56,* 117–126.

Pugach, M.C., & Johnson, L.J. (1989). The challenge of implementing collaboration between general and special education. *Exceptional Children, 56*(3), 232–235.

Pugach, M.C., & Johnson, L.J. (1990). Fostering the continued democratization of consultation through action research. *Teacher Education and Special Education, 13,* 240–245.

Pugach, M.C., & Johnson, L.J. (1989). Prereferral interventions: Progress, problems, and challenges. *Exceptional Children, 56,* 117–126.

Pugach, M., & Sapon-Shevin, M. (1987), New agendas for special education policy: What the national reports haven't said. *Exceptional Children, 53*(4): 295–299.

Quay, H.C., & Peterson, D.R.(1987). *Manual for the revised behavior problem checklist.* Coral Gable, FL.

Ramirez, B.A. (1990). Culturally and linguistically diverse children. *Educating Exceptional Children* (5th ed.). Guilford, CT: Dushkin.

Raschke, D., Dedrick, C., DeVries, A. (1988). Coping with stress: The special educator's perspective. *Teaching Exceptional Children, 21*(1), 10–14.

Raymond, G.I., McIntosh, D.K., & Moore, Y.R. (1986). *Teacher consultation skills (Report No. EC 182–912).* Washington, D.C.: U.S. Department of Education. (ERIC Document Reproduction Service No. ED 170–915).

Raywid, M.A. (1993). Finding time for collaboration. *Educational Leadership, 51*(1), 30–34.

Regional Research and Training Institute for Human Services (1994). Cultural competence: New frontiers. *Focal Point, 8,* 8–10.

Reis, S.W., & Renzulli, J.S. (1986). The secondary triad model. In J.S. Renzulli (Ed.), *Systems and models for developing programs for the gifted and talented* (pp. 267–305). Mansfield Center, CT: Creative Learning Press.

Reisberg, L., & Wolf, R. (1986). Developing a consulting program in special education: Implementation and interventions. *Focus on Exceptional Children, 19,* 3, 1–14.

Reisberg, L., & Wolf, R. (1988). Instructional strategies for special education consultants. *Remedial and Special Education, 9,* 6, 29–40.

Remedial and Special Education Journal. Issues focusing on school consultation and collaboration.

Renzulli, J.S. (Ed.). (1984). *Technical report of research studies related to the Revolving Door Identification Model.* Bureau of Educational Research, University of Connecticut.

Renzulli, J.S. (Ed.). (1986). *Systems and models for developing programs for the gifted and talented.* Mansfield Center, CT: Creative Learning Press.

Renzulli, J.S., & Reis, S.M. (1985). *The schoolwide enrichment model: A comprehensive plan for educational excellence.* Mansfield Center, CT: Creative Learning Press.

Renzulli, J.S., & Reis, S.W. (1986). The enrichment triad/revolving door model: A schoolwide plan for the development of creative productivity. In J.S. Renzulli (Ed.), *Systems and models for developing programs for the gifted and talented* (pp. 216–266). Mansfield Center, CT: Creative Learning Press.

Reynaud, G., Pfannenstiel, T., & Hudson, F. (1987). *Park Hill Secondary learning disability project: An alternative service delivery model implementation manual.* Kansas City, MO: Park Hill School District 7703 N.W. Barry Road.

Reynolds, M.C. (1962). A framework for considering some issues in special education. *Exceptional Children, 28,* 367–370.

Reynolds, M.C. and Birch, J.W. (1988). *Adaptive mainstreaming: A primer for teachers and principals.* White Plains, NY: Longman.

Reynolds, M.C., Wang, M.C., & Walberg, H.J. (1987). The necessary restructuring of special and regular education. *Exceptional Children, 53*(5), 391–398.

Rich, D. (1987). *School and families: Issues and actions.* Washington, D.C.: National Education Association.

Richardson, V. (1990). Significant and worthwhile change in teaching practice. *Educational Researcher, 19*(7), 10–18.

Riegel, R.H. (1981). Making modifications in the mainstream: A consultant's guide to cooperative planning. Unpublished manuscript. Plymouth, MI: Model Resource Room Project.

Ritter, D.R. (1978). Effects of a school consultation program upon referral patterns of teachers. *Psychology in the Schools, 15*(2), 239–243.

Robert, M. (1973). *Loneliness in the schools (What to do about it).* Niles, IL: Argus Communication.

Robinson, A. (1990). Cooperation of exploitation? The argument against cooperative learning for talented students. *Journal for the Education of the Gifted, 14*(1): 9–27.

Robinson, III, E.H., & Brosh, M.C. (1980). Communication skills training for resource teachers. *Journal of Learning Disabilities, 13,* 55–58.

Rogers, J. (1993). The inclusion revolution. *The Research Bulletin, Phi Delta Kappa, 11,* 1–6.

Rosenfield, S. (1985). Teacher acceptance of behavioral principles: An issue of values. *Teacher Education and Special Education, 8*(3): 153–158.

Rosenshine, B.V., & Berliner, D.C. (1978). Academic engaged time. *British Journal of Teacher Education, 4:* 3–16.

Ross, R.G. (1986). *Communication consulting as persuasion: Issues and implications. (Report No. CS506–027).* Washington, D.C.: U.S. Department of Education. ERIC Document Reproduction Service No. ED 291–115.

Rule, S., Fodor-Davis, J., Morgan, R., Salzberg, C.L., & Chen, J. (1990). An inservice training model to encourage collaborative consultation. *Teacher Education and Special Education, 13*(3–4), 225–227.

Rusch, F.R., & Menchetti, B.M. (1988). Transition in the 1990s: A reply to Knowlton and Clark. *Exceptional Children, 54*(4), 363–364.

Rusch, F.R., Rose, T., & Greenwood, C.R. (1988). *Introduction to behavior analysis in special education.* Englewood Cliffs, NJ: Prentice Hall.

Safran, J.S. (1991). Communication in collaboration/consultation: Effective practices in schools. *Journal of Educational and Psychological Consultation, 2*(4) 371–386.

Safran, S.P. (1991). The communication process and school-based consultation: What does the research say? *Journal of Educational and Psychological Consultation, 2*(4), 343–370.

Salend, S.J. (1994). *Effective mainstreaming: Creating inclusive classrooms* (2nd ed.). New York: Macmillan.

Salend, S.J., & Salend, S. (1984). Consulting with the regular teacher: Guidelines for special educators. *The Pointer, 25,* 25–28.

Salend, S., & Viglianti, D. (1982). Preparing secondary students for the mainstream. *Teaching Exceptional Children, 14,* 137–140.

Salisbury, C.L., & Vincent, L.J. (1990). Criterion of the next environment and best practices: Mainstreaming and integration 10 years later. *Topics in Early Childhood Special Education, 10*(2), 78–89.

Salisbury, G., & Evans, I.M. (1988). Comparison of parental involvement in regular and special education. *Journal of the Association for Persons with Severe Handicaps, 13,* 268–272.

Sapolsky, R. (1994). *Why zebras don't get ulcers: A guide to stress, stress-related illness, and coping.* New York: W.H. Freeman.

Schatz, E. (1990). Ability grouping for gifted learners. *Educating Able Learners. 15*(3) 3, 5, 15. Denton, TX: Gifted Students Institute.

Schein, E.H. (1969). *Process consultation: Its role in organization development.* Reading, MA: Addison-Wesley.

Schein, E.H. (1978). The role of the consultant: Context expert or process facilitator? *Personnel and Guidance Journal,* February 1978.

Schenkat, R. (1988). The promise of restructuring for special education. *Education Week,* November 16, 1988.

Schindler, C., & Lapid, G. (1989). *The great turning: Personal peace, global victory.* Santa Fe: Bear and Company.

Schlax, K. (1994). Eight tips for effective integration of therapists. *Inclusive Education Programs 1*(2): 11.

Schlichter, C. (1986). Talents unlimited: Applying the multiple talent approach in mainstream and gifted programs. In J.S. Renzulli (Ed.), *Systems and mod-els for developing programs for the gifted and talented* (pp. 352–390). Mansfield Center, CT: Creative Learning Press.

Schmuck, R.A., & Schmuck, P.A. (1979). *Group process in the classroom,* (2nd. ed). Dubuque, IA: Wm. C. Brown.

Schoor, L.R. (1988). *Within our reach: Breaking the cycle of disadvantage.* New York: Anchor Books.

Schrag, J., & Burnette, J. (1994). Inclusive schools. *Teaching Exceptional Children,* Spring, 64–68.

Schuck, J. (1979). The parent-professional partnership: Myth or reality? *Education Unlimited, 1*(4): 26–28.

Schulz, J.B. (1987). *Parent and professional in special education.* Newton, MA: Allyn & Bacon.

Scollon, R. (1985). The machine stops: Silence in the metaphor of malfunction. In D. Tannen and M. Saville-Troike (Eds.), *Perspectives in Silence.* Norwood, NJ: Ablex.

Scriven, M. (1967). The methodology of evaluation. In R.W. Tyler, R.M. Gagne, & M. Scriven (Eds.), *Perspectives of Curriculum Evaluation.* Chicago: Rand-McNally.

Scruggs, T.E., & Richter, L. (1986). Tutoring learning disabled students: A critical review. *Learning Disability Quarterly, 9*(1): 2–14.

Seay, M. (1974). *Community Education: A Developing Concept.* Midland, MI: Pendell.

Seeley, D.S. (1985). *Education through partnership.* Washington, D.C.: American Enterprise Institute for Public Policy Research.

Selye, H. (1993). History of the stress concept. In L. Goldberger and S. Brevitz (Eds.), *Handbook of Stress* (2nd ed.). New York, NY: Free Press.

Semmel, M.I., & Gerber, M.M. (1990). If at first you don't succeed, bye, bye again: A response to general educators' views on the REI. *Remedial and Special Education, 11*(4), 53–59.

Sewall, G.T. (1991). America 2000: An appraisal. *Phi Delta Kappan, 73*(3), 204–209.

Shanker, A. (1994). Full inclusion is neither free nor appropriate. *Educational Leadership, 52*(4), 18–21.

Shanker, A. (1993, November). Ninety-two hours. *The Developer* Oxford, OH: National Staff Development Council.

Shaw, S.F., Bensky, J.M., & Dixon, B. (1981). *Stress and burnout: A primer for special education and special services personnel.* Reston, VA: Council for Exceptional Children.

Shea, T.M., & Bauer, A.M. (1985). *Parents and teachers of exceptional students.* Boston: Allyn & Bacon.

Shepard, L.A. (1987). The new push for excellence: Widening the schism between regular and special education. *Exceptional Children, 53* (4), 327–329.

Sheridan, S.M. (1992). What do we mean when we say "collaboration"? *Journal of Educational and Psychological Consultation, 3*(1), 89–92.

Shubert, P. (1994). Keys include special students. Unpublished paper. Denver: Council for Exceptional Children conference.

Sigband, N.B. (1987). The uses of meetings. *Nation's Business,* February 1987, 28R.

Sileo, T., Rude, H., & Luckner, J. (1988). Collaborative consultation: A model for transition planning for handicapped youth. *Education and Training in Mental Retardation, 23*(4): 333–339.

Simpson, G.W. (1990). Keeping it alive: Elements of school culture that sustain innovation. *Educational Leadership, 47*(8), 34–37.

Skolnick, A. (1991). *Embattled paradise: The American family in an age of uncertainty.* New York, NY: Basic Books.

Skrtic, T. (1993). The crisis in special education knowledge: A perspective on perspective. In E.L. Meyen, G.A. Vergason, & R.J. Whelan, (Eds.), *Challenges Facing Special Education.* Denver: Love Pub.

Slavin, R. (1988). *The School Administrator, 45,* 9–13.

Slavin, R.E. (1986). *Using student team learning* (3rd ed.). Baltimore, MD: Center for Research on Elementary and Middle Schools, The Johns Hopkins University.

Slavin, R.E. (1990). Research on cooperative learning: Consensus and controversy. *Educational Leadership,* December *47*(4), 52–54.

Slavin, R.E., & Madden, N.A. (1989). What works for students at risk: A research synthesis. *Educational Leadership, 46,* 4–13.

Slavin, R.E., Madden, N.A., Dolan, L.J., & Wasik, B.A. (1994). Roots and wings: Inspiring academic excellence. *Educational Leadership, 52*(3), 10–13.

Slesser, R.A., Fine, M. J., & Tracy, D.B. (1990). Teacher reactions to two approaches to school-based psychological consultation. *Journal of Educational and Psychological Consultation, 1*(3), 242–258.

Smith, S.C. (1987). The collaborative school takes shape. *Educational Leadership, 45*(3), 4–6.

Smith-Westberry, J., & Job, R.L. (1986). How to be a prophet in your own land: Providing gifted program inservice for the local district. *Gifted Child Quarterly, 30*(3), 135–137.

Sondel, B. (1958). *The Humanity of Words.* Cleveland, OH: The World Publishing Co.

Sontag, J.C., & Schacht, R. (1994). An ethnic comparison of participation and information needs in early intervention. *Exceptional Children, 60,* 422–433.

Sparks, D. (1992, September). Some basic understandings. *The Developer.* Oxford, OH: National Staff Development Council.

Speece, D.L., & Mandell, C.J. (1980). Resource room support services for regular teachers. *Learning Disability Quarterly, 3,* 49–53.

Staff. "I don't think it's right to type people." *The Type Reporter,* No. 37, pp. 1–4.

Staff. (1989), April). Staff development in the journals. *The Developer,* p. 6.

Stainback, S., & Stainback, W. (1985). The merger of special and regular education: Can it be done? A response to Lieberman and Mesinger. *Exceptional Children, 51*(6), 517–521.

Stainback, S., & Stainback, F.M. (1988). In M.C. Reynolds (Ed.), *Adaptive mainstreaming: A primer for teachers and principals.* White Plains, NY.

Stainback, S., Stainback, W., & Forest, M. (1989). *Educating all students in the mainstream of regular education.* Baltimore, MD: Brookes.

Stainback, W., & Stainback, S. (1984). A rationale for the merger of special and regular education. *Exceptional Children, 51*(2), 102–111.

Steele, J. (1982). *The class activities questionnaire.* Mansfield Center, CT: Creative Learning Press.

Stephens, P. (1994, October). Developing a successful grant application. Presented at United School Administrators, Emporia, KS.

Stephens, T.M. (1977). *Teaching skills to children with learning and behavioral disorders.* Columbus, OH: Merrill.

Stewart, J.C. (1978). *Counseling parents of exceptional children.* Columbus, OH: Merrill.

Sue, D.W., & Sue, D. (1990). *Counseling the culturally different: Theory and practice* (2nd ed.). New York: John Wiley.

Sugai, G. (Winter, 1986). Recording classroom events: Maintaining a critical incidents log. *Teaching Exceptional Children,* pp. 98–102.

Sundel, S.S., & Sundel, M. (1980). *Be assertive: A practical guide for human service workers.* Beverly Hills: Sage.

Swicegood, P. (1994). Portfolio-based assessment practices. *Intervention in School and Clinic. 30*(1): 6–15.

Symanski, E.M. (1994). Transition: Life-span and life-space considerations for empowerment. *Exceptional Children, 60,* 402–410.

Tannen, D. (1994). *Gender and discourse.* New York: Oxford University Press.

Tannen, D. (1991). *You just don't understand: Women and men in conversation.* New York: William Morrow.

Teagarden, J. (Spring,1988). Acres wrap-up from a teacher's perspective. *Take Heart,* p. 4. Manhattan, KS: Kansas State University.

Tharp, R. (1975). The triadic model of consultation. In C.A. Parker (Ed.), *Psychological consultation in the schools: Helping teachers meet special needs.* Reston, VA: The Council for Exceptional Children.

Tharp, R.G. (1975). The triadic model of consultation: Current considerations. In C.A. Parker (Ed.), *Psychological consultation: Helping teachers meet special needs* (pp. 135–151). Minneapolis, MN: Leadership Training Institute/Special Education.

Tharp, R.G., & Wetzel, R.J. (1969). *Behavior modification in the natural environment.* New York: Academic Press.

Thousand, J., Fox, T., Reid, R., Godek, J., Williams, W., & Fox, W. (1986). *The homecoming model: Educating students who present intensive educational challenges within regular education environments* (Monograph No.7–1). Burlington, VT: University of Vermont, Center for Developmental Disabilities.

Thousand, J.S., Villa, R.A., Paolucci-Whitcomb, P., & Nevin, A. (1992). In W. Stainback & S. Stainback (Eds)., *Controversial issues confronting special education: Divergent perspectives.* Boston: Allyn & Bacon.

Thurston, L.P. (1989). *Rural special education teachers as consultants: Strategies, practices, and training.* Presented at American Council for Rural Special Education national conference, Ft. Lauderdale, FL.

Thurston, L.P. (1987). *Survival skills for women: Facilitator manual.* Manhattan, KS: Survival Skills and Development.

Thurston, L.P., & Dasta, K. (1990). An analysis of in-home parent tutoring procedures: Effects on children's academic behavior at home and in school and on parents' tutoring behaviors. *Remedial and Special Education, 11*(4): 41–52.

Thurston, L.P., & Dover, W. (October, 1990). *Rural at-risk students.* Paper presented at the 12th annual Rural and Small Schools Conference, Manhattan, KS.

Thurston, L.P. & Kimsey, I. (1989). Rural special education teachers as consultants: Roles and responsibilities. *Educational Considerations, 17*(1), 40–43.

Timar, T. (1989). The politics of school restructuring. *Phi Delta Kappan, 71*(4), 265–275.

Tindal, G. (1987). Graphing performance. *Teaching Exceptional Children, 20*(1): 44–46.

Tindal, G., & Taylor-Pendergast, S.J. (1989). A taxonomy for objectively analyzing the consultation process. *Remedial and Special Education, 10*(2): 6–16.

Tindal, G., Shinn, M., Waltz, L., & Germann, G. (1987). Mainstream consultation in secondary settings: The Pine County model. *Journal of Special Education, 21*(3), 94–106.

Todnem, G., & Warner, M.P. (1994, September). Demonstrating the benefits of staff development: An interview with Thomas R. Guskey. *Kansas Direct Connection,* September 1994. Hays, KS: Kansas Staff Development Council.

Toffler, A. (October 15, 1990). Power shift: Knowledge, wealth and violence at the edge of the 21st century. *Newsweek,* pp. 86–92.

Toffler, A. (1990). *Powershift.* New York: Bantam.

Tomlinson, G. (Ed.). (1984). *School administrator's complete better book.* Englewood Cliffs, NJ: Prentice-Hall.

Treffinger, D.J. (1986). Fostering effective, independent learning through individualized programming. In J.S. Renzulli (Ed.), *Systems and models for developing programs for the gifted and talented* (pp. 429–460). Mansfield Center, CT: Creative Learning Press.

Truch, S. (1980). *Teacher burnout and what to do about it.* Novato, CA: Academic Therapy.

Truesdell, C.B. (1983). The MBTI: A win-win strategy for work teams. *MBTI News, 5,* 8–9.

Truesdell, L.A. (1988). Mainstreaming in an urban middle school: Effects of school organization and climate. *Urban Review, 20*(1): 42–58.

Tucker, J.A. (1985). Curriculum-based assessment: An introduction. *Exceptional Children, 52*(3): 199–204.

Tuckman, B.W. (1985). *Evaluating instructional programs* (2nd ed.). Boston: Allyn & Bacon.

Turnbull, III, H.R., & Turnbull, A.P. (1985). *Parents speak out: Then and now* (2nd ed.). Columbus, OH: Merrill.

Turnbull III, H.R., Turnbull, A.P., and Wheat, (1992). Assumptions about parental participation: A legislative history. *Exceptional Education Quarterly, 3*(2), 1–8.

Turner, R.R. (April, 1987). Here's what teachers say. *Learning 87,* 55–57.

Tye, K.A. (Ed.). (1990). *Global education: From thought to action.* Alexandria, VA: Association for Supervision and Curriculum Development.

Tyler, V.L. (1979). *Intercultural interacting* Provo, UT: Brigham Young University, David Kennedy Center for International Studies.

U.S. Department of Education. (1985–1986). *Patterns in special education service delivery and cost.* Washington, DC: Department of Education, Office of Special Education Programs.

Valencia, S. (1990). A portfolio approach to classroom reading assessment: The whys, whats, and hows. *The Reading Teacher, 43* (4)338–340.

Van Tassel-Baska, J. (1989). Appropriate curriculum for gifted learners. *Educational Leadership, 46*(6): 13–15.

Vasa, S.T. (1982). *The special education resource teacher as a consultant: Fact or fantasy?* Paper presented at the Sixth Annual Meeting of the Council for Exceptional Children, Houston. (ERIC Document Reproduction Service No. ED 218 918).

Via, S. (1991). How much technology is enough? *The Catalyst, 8*(3), 6–8.

Vockell, E.L., & Asher, W.J. (1995). *Educational research,* 2nd ed. Englewood Cliffs, NJ: Prentice-Hall.

Voltz, D.L., Elliott, Jr., R.N., Cobb, H.B. (1994). Collaborative teacher roles: Special and general educators. *Journal of Learning Disabilities, 27*(8), 527–535.

von Oech, R. (1983). *A whack on the side of the head.* New York: Warner.

Walker, H.M. (1976). *Walker problem behavior identification checklist manual.* Los Angeles: Western Psychological Services.

Waltz, L. (1990). Mainstream consultation and training. *The Consulting Edge, 2*(1), 5–6.

Wang, M. (1987). Toward achieving educational excellence for all students: Program design and student outcomes. *Remedial and Special Education, 8*(3), 25–34.

Wang, M.C. (1987). Toward achieving educational excellence for all students: Program design and student outcomes. *Remedial and Special Education, 8,* 25–34.

Wang, M.C. (1986). The adaptive learning environments model: Design and effects. Paper presented at Association for Children with Learning Disabilities Conference.

Wang, M.C., & Birch, J.W. (1984). Effective special education in regular classes. *Exceptional Children,.* February, 1984, pp. 391–398.

Wang, M.C., & Walberg, H.J. (1988). Four fallacies of segregationism. *Exceptional Children, 55,* 128–137.

Waters, D.B., and Lawrence, E.C. (1993). *Competence, courage, and change: An approach to family therapy.* New York: W.W. Norton.

Weber, L. (1994). Diversity and collaboration. *Center News.* Memphis: Center for Research on Women, University of Memphis, *13,* 2, 10.

Webster's new collegiate dictionary (8th ed.) (1981). Springfield, MA: Merriam-Webster.

Webster's third new international dictionary, unabridged: The great library of the English language. (1976). Springfield, MA: Merriam-Webster.

Wesley, W.G., & Wesley, B.A. (1990). Concept-mapping: A brief introduction. *Teaching Professor, 4*(8), 3–4.

Wesson, C.L. (1987). Increasing efficiency. *Teaching Exceptional Children, 20*(1), 46–47.

West, J.F. (1990). Educational collaboration in the restructuring of schools. *Journal of Educational and Psychological Consultation, 1,* 23–41.

West, J.F. (1985). *Regular and special educators' preference for school-based consultation models: A statewide study* (Report No.101). Austin, TX: The University of Texas, Research and Training Project on School Consultation.

West, J.F., & Brown, P.A. (1987). State departments of education policies on consultation in special education: The state of the states. *Remedial and Special Education, 8*(3), 45–51.

West, J.F., & Cannon, G.S. (1988). Essential collaborative consultation competencies for regular and special educators. *Journal of Learning Disabilities, 21,* 56–63.

West, J.F., & Idol, L. (1990). Collaborative consultation in the education of mildly handicapped and at-risk students. *Remedial and Special Education, 11*(1), 22–31.

West, J.F., & Idol, L. (1987). School consultation (Part i): An interdisciplinary perspective on theory, models, and research. *Journal of Learning Disabilities, 20*(7), 385–408.

West, J.F., Idol, L., & Cannon, G. (1987). *A curriculum for preservice and inservice preparation of classroom and special education teachers in collaborative consultation.* Austin, TX: The University of Texas at Austin, Research and Training Project on School Consultation.

Westby, Carol E., & Ford, V. (1993). The role of team culture in assessment and intervention. *Journal of Educational and Psychological Consultation, 4*(4), 319–341.

White, G.W., & Pryzwansky, W.B. (1982). Consultation outcome as a result of in-service resource teacher training. *Psychology in the Schools, 19,* 495–502.

Wiederholt, L.L. (1989). Restructuring special education services: The past, the present, the future. *Learning Disability Quarterly, 12,* 181–191.

Wiederholt, J., Hammill, D., & Brown, V. (1983). *The resource teacher.* Austin, TX: PRO-ED.

Wiedmeyer, D., and Lehman, J. (1991). The "house plan" approach to collaborative teaching and consultation. *Teaching Exceptional Children, 23*(3): 6–10.

Wikler, L., Wasow, M., & Hatfield, E. (1981). Chronic sorrow revisited: Parent vs. professional depiction of the adjustment of parents of mentally retarded children. *American Journal of Orthopsychiatry, 51,* 63–70.

Wildman, T.M., & Niles, J.A. Essentials of professional growth. *Educational Leadership, 44*(5), 4–10.

Will, M. (1986). Educating children with learning problems: A shared responsibility. *Exceptional Children, 52*(5), 411–415.

Will, M. (1984). Let us pause and reflect—but not too long. *Exceptional Children, 51,* 11–16.

William T. Grant Foundation Commission on Work, Family, and Citizenship. (1988). *The forgotten half: Pathways to success for America's youth and young families.* Washington, D.C.: Author.

Williams, D.L., & Chavkin, N.F. (1987). *Final Report of the Parent Involvement in Education Project.* Washington, D.C.: National Institute of Education.

Witt, J.C. (1990). Collaboration in school-based consultation: Myth in need of data. *Journal of Educational and Psychological Consultation, 1*(4), 367–370.

Witt, J.C., & Elliott, S.N. (1985). Acceptability of classroom intervention strategies. In T.R. Kratochwill (Ed.), *Advances in School Psychology* (Vol.4, pp. 251–288). Hillsdale, NJ: Lawrence Erlbaum.

Witt, J.C., Moe, G., Gutkin, T., & Andrews, L. (1984). The effect of saying the same thing in different ways: The problem of language and jargon in school-based consultation. *Journal of School Psychology, 22,* 361–367.

Wolery, M., Bailey, D., & Sugai, G. (1988). *Effective teaching: principles and procedures of applied behavior analysis with exceptional students.* Boston: Allyn & Bacon.

Wolf, D.P. (1989). Portfolio assessment: Sampling student work. *Educational Leadership. 46*(7), 35–40.

Wood, J.W., & Meiderhoff, J.W. (1989). Bridging the gap. *Teaching Exceptional Children, 21*(2), 66–68.

Ysseldyke, J.E. (1986). The use of assessment information to make decisions about students. In R.J. Morris and B. Blatt (Eds.)., *Special education: Research and trends.* New York: Pergamon.

Ysseldyke, J.E., & Christenson, S.I. (1987). Evaluating students' instructional environments. *Remedial and Special Education, 8*(3), 17–24.

Ysseldyke, J., Thurlow, M., Wotruba, J. & Nania, P. (1990). Instructional arrangements: Perceptions from general education. *Teaching Exceptional Children, 22*(4): 4–8.

Zabel, R.H., & Zabel, M.K. (1982). Factors in burnout among teachers of exceptional children. *Exceptional Children. 49*(3): 261–263.

Zigmond, N., Levin, E., and Laurie, T.E. (1985). Managing the mainstream: An analysis of teacher attitudes and student performance in mainstream high school programs. *Journal of Learning Disabilities, 18*(9):535–41.

Zimet, E. (1993). Grant-writing techniques for K–12 funding. *T.H.E.: Technological Horizons in Education,* November, 1993, 109–112.

Author Index

Subject Index